Arabic, Self and Identity

Arabic, Self and Identity

A Study in Conflict and Displacement

Yasir Suleiman

OXFORD
UNIVERSITY PRESS

Oxford University Press, Inc., publishes works that further
Oxford University's objective of excellence
in research, scholarship, and education.

Oxford New York
Auckland Cape Town Dar es Salaam Hong Kong Karachi
Kuala Lumpur Madrid Melbourne Mexico City Nairobi
New Delhi Shanghai Taipei Toronto

With offices in
Argentina Austria Brazil Chile Czech Republic France Greece
Guatemala Hungary Italy Japan Poland Portugal Singapore
South Korea Switzerland Thailand Turkey Ukraine Vietnam

Published by Oxford University Press, Inc.
198 Madison Avenue, New York, New York 10016

www.oup.com

Library of Congress Cataloging-in-Publication Data
Suleiman, Yasir.
Arabic, self and identity : a study in conflict and displacement / Yasir Suleiman.
p. cm.
Includes bibliographical references and index.
ISBN 978-0-19-974701-6; 978-0-19-974700-9 (pbk.)
1. Anthropological linguistics—Arab countries. 2. Sociolinguistics—Arab countries.
3. Language and culture—Arab countries. 4. Ethnicity—Arab countries. I. Title.
P35.5.A65S78 2010
306.440917'4927—dc22 2010014366

9 8 7 6 5 4 3 2 1

Printed in the United States of America
on acid-free paper

In Memoriam

Ibrahim, Aziza, Khalil and Nadia
Salih and Nabiha
and
Sabha and Jamila

'O soul at rest, return to thy Lord, thou well pleased with Him and He well pleased with thee. So be among My chosen servants and enter My garden.'
(Qur'an 69: 28–31)

Contents

Acknowledgements

I was supposed to write a different book, for which I still have a contract and which still awaits being written, but whenever I sat down to work on it, the present book injected itself between us. Initially, I resisted the intrusion. In the end, I gave in, because the intruder refused to go away. What follows is the result.

Many people helped me along the way, and I would like to thank them all for their contributions, kindness and various forms of support. Yonatan Mendel's help was crucial in many important ways. Not only did he secure a lot of archival and nonarchival materials for me in Hebrew, Arabic and English, but he also read the entire manuscript and made many valuable comments that have improved the accuracy of sections of the book and their overall balance. Manar Makhoul read the entire manuscript and made some perceptive comments. He also provided some of the data I have used in chapter 5 and was instrumental in introducing me to the works of Sayed Kashua. To Yonatan and Manar I owe a huge debt of gratitude.

I am grateful to Amy Rowe for reading the first full draft of the book and for commenting on the style and presentation. Allon Ulmann and Ashraf Abdelhayy read sections of the book and gave useful feedback. I am grateful to them. Alaa Elgibaali invited me to present parts of chapter 3 at Maryland University. I would like to thank him for the invitation and the discussions this generated. I later presented an updated version of the chapter at Georgetown University. I would like to thank Reem Bassiouney for this invitation and for her and her colleagues' and students' feedback. My sincerest thanks go to the Arabic-language teachers in Qatar who attended the training I led during years in Doha and who unwittingly supplied the data I have used in chapter 3. Said Faiq of the American University of Sharjah invited me to lecture on the linguistic landscape (chapter 5). I would like to thank him and the audience who attended the presentation for their questions and comments, which helped clarify my thinking on some issues. I would also like to thank the British Society of Middle Eastern Studies for inviting me to give the 2008 Annual Lecture in which I presented parts of this book. The Critical Middle East Workshop, organised by John Chalcraft and Toby Kelly on behalf of the Council of British Research in the Levant in March 2009, provided an opportunity to discuss chapter 2. I would like to thank John, Toby and the participants for their interest and comments. Needless to say, the responsibility for any errors remains completely mine.

I started this book at a very uncertain period in my career, a period of 'displacement.' I was in transition between two universities: Edinburgh, which I was reluctant to leave, and Cambridge, which I was looking forward to joining. Many friends sustained me through this period but none more so than Carole and Robert Hillenbrand, in Edinburgh, and Khaled Hroub and Abdulla Baabood, in Cambridge. I want to thank them all for their friendship. Khaled and Abdulla adopted me as a friend from the very first day I arrived in Cambridge. And during this period of uncertainty, this intruder-book became my refuge. I would turn to it when my doubts erupted. I would, therefore, like to thank this friend for standing by me and for easing the transition from North to South.

In writing this book and in coping with all of the stresses of the transition in my career, one person has been a tower of strength: my wife, Shahla, whose loving support, at a time of family bereavement for her, made all the difference. I owe her the greatest debt of gratitude. And I thank Tamir and Sinan for their interest in my work. I hope that they, and Shahla, will find a bit of them and a bit of me in what follows.

Finally, I would like to thank the reviewers for their comments, some of which I adopted and some of which I did not.

King's College, Cambridge
December 2009

Arabic, Self and Identity

Chapter 1

Introduction

This book builds on my earlier research on the link among the Arabic language, identity and conflict, which I explored at some length in *The Arabic Language and National Identity: A Study in Ideology* (2003), *A War of Words: Language and Conflict in the Middle East* (2004b) and a series of other publications, some of which are listed in the bibliography of this book. But it also provides a major new direction. The point of departure in my earlier research was the role of language as a marker of national identity and the possibilities this offers for language to become entangled in the social and political conflicts of the Middle East, both intranationally and transnationally. Although language use, representing the functional role of language, is a form of action, the role of language in group-identity marking and in national and transnational conflicts is mainly delivered through the symbolic construction of identity and the concomitant exercise of symbolic violence. Under normal circumstances, the symbolism of language blends into a banal or quotidian view of identity that is hardly noticed in everyday life. However, its potency comes to the fore in situations of strife or conflict when it becomes particularly urgent to mark the boundaries of the group or the Self as a form of (sometimes atavistic) self-defence. Social and political conflicts propel language-based identity beyond the realm of banality to one of high relevance to society. As Gramsci (1985: 183) writes, 'every time the question of language surfaces [in society], in one way or another, it means that a series of other problems are coming to the fore.' This facet of language-in-society underlies its ability to serve as a proxy for the expression of extralinguistic anxieties and simmering problems in social life. Observing language and tracking its potency in society are, therefore, a good barometer for accessing deeper anxieties and problems that might surface in the sociopolitical realm if triggered by social and political tensions.

The present study builds on my interest in these symbolic realms of signification. As in my earlier work, it approaches the Arabic language as a marker of identity and as a factor in sociopolitical conflict in society. However, it also departs from this perspective in some important ways. First, it shifts the focus of interest from group identity to personal or individual identity, the Self, although group identity continues to be of paramount importance in understanding language in society. It is, in fact, impossible to separate issues of personal and group identity from each other. Second, this shift, coupled with my interest in qualitative research, gives prominence to two types of material in this work: autobiography and self-reports, the latter in the form of autoethnographic self-explorations of particular types of language behaviour. This is a novel departure in the empirical study of Arabic-language-based identity. Third, this study uses data from the Internet to augment its analysis. The Internet is an increasingly important site for the expression of views and opinions by actors who, in the past, had little opportunity to participate in debates of public interest nationally and transnationally. The immediacy or rawness of data from this resource is often reflected in their chatty style, as well as in their incorporation of spelling and other language errors that indicate, among other things, scant self-monitoring. These data also show a strong disregard for the imperatives of political correctness. Fourth, this research uses literary production as part of its data. Literature is more deliberate than Internet material, but it is a good source for issues of personal and collective identity that cannot be accessed through quantitative research methodologies. This variety of materials reflects the multifaceted nature of language as a social phenomenon that straddles many areas of cultural production. By studying these forms of data, and by shifting the balance of interest in favour of the Self in large parts of this book, I hope in this work to expand the horizons of language study in the Arabic-speaking world.

To frame these features of the present research, chapter 2 provides a critique of some of the underlying foundations of the study of Arabic in the social world. While acknowledging the importance of correlationist-variationist and quantitative research in Arabic sociolinguistics, the chapter argues for a complementary engagement with qualitative research, of the kind offered in this work. Such research is not beholden to some of the restrictive evaluation measures that govern the conduct of quantitative enquiry. The chapter further argues for accommodating the nativist understanding of Arabic diglossia to capture the dualistic perceptions of the Arabic-language situation among ordinary Arabs. This folk-linguistic perspective on the Arabic-language situation is not dissimilar to the view articulated by Charles Ferguson (1959) in his seminal article on the topic. Although this nativist perception of Arabic has been shown to be empirically defective, it nevertheless is not without sociopsychological validity for Arabic speakers. This nativist perspective is embedded in a deeply rooted language ideology that most probably goes back to pre-Islamic times; this ideology plays a determining role in Arab reactions to discussions of the language situation that appear to challenge the duality of the language (Suleiman 2006b).

Studying Arabic in its social context places the language at the intersection of many disciplines, including linguistics, anthropology, politics, literary theory, political geography and history. This multiplicity of perspectives recognizes the liminality of Arabic as an object of study in the social world. While the present research cannot approach Arabic from all of these perspectives, it will nevertheless try to engage some of them to reach a polyvalent description of the language that points to the limitations of single-perspective studies. In conducting this type of research, ideological intrusion is an ever-present danger, whether in the use of politically induced terminologies or in the setting up of loaded descriptive taxonomies, examples of which will be discussed in this work. To help ameliorate the effects of ideological intrusion, the present study recognizes the importance of identifying and monitoring the positionality of the author. The more this is done publicly in the body of the research, the greater the ability to escape the subterranean effects of ideology. It is, however, important not to discount the ideological debates surrounding language but to keep them in the purview of a critically engaged sociolinguistics. What matters in this regard is avoiding the treatment of ideological debates ideologically.

This theme is pursued in chapter 3 through an autoethnographic case study involving two sites of the author's language behaviour: the use of *fuṣḥā* (standard) Arabic and the avoidance of code-switching between Arabic and English while conducting Arabic-language teacher training in Qatar between 2003 and 2008. Using self-reports, the chapter identifies a variety of meanings in these two sites to reveal the complexity of the language-Self link in the Arabic context. The Self in this investigation is shown to be driven by ideological, professional, instrumental and even therapeutic or reparative considerations. This Self is also shown to be wary of linguistic in-betweenness, social affectation and the imitation of the Other. This set of interpretations reveals the ability of autoethnographic research to dig below the surface of the banal and the quotidian, to reveal identity-bound meanings of great importance in guiding group interaction and in negotiating the set of identities that inform this interaction. Recognizing that the relationship between the public persona of the researcher and his persona as a scholar is not watertight, this chapter emphasises the importance of guarding against the ideological intrusion of the former into the latter, while acknowledging the ideological nature of language as a sociopolitical construct. But it also argues for using the researcher as an object of study to get at areas of symbolic meaning that may be difficult to access through more traditional research methods. The chapter argues that adopting this approach requires external validation whenever possible but that the absence of such validation should not block the conduct of autoethnographic research, which can yield many important insights into the language-Self link.

Chapter 4 continues this line of enquiry by considering at length two autobiographies that deal with language and how it relates to issues of personal and national identity. The first is Edward Said's *Out of Place* (1999). The chapter reveals that 'place' for Said is linguistically and, perhaps less problematically, geographically defined. Pursuing the linguistic dimension of the 'out of placeness' signalled in the title of this memoir, the chapter reveals the extent to which Said's personal and group identity were angled in relation to the two languages that dominated his life: Arabic and English. Living in Arabic and writing about this experience in English is the subject of many reflections in *Out of Place*. Although Said lived most of his intellectual and personal life in or through English, he refrains from calling English his 'native language' or his 'mother tongue,' two terms that he completely reserves to characterize his relationship with Arabic in its standard and colloquial forms, respectively. A posthumous article, 'Living in Arabic' (2004), sums up this relationship with the language well. Written towards the end of his life, the article reveals the intimate relationship Said had with the language as a marker of his identity and as a bridge that linked him and his family in New York with their ancestors back in Palestine and Lebanon.

Aspects of this relationship form part of his memoir, but this memoir also reveals how complex Said's relationship with Arabic and English had been in his early years. Arabic emerges as a source of pride and personal embarrassment, rebellion and resistance, as well as the location of moments of joy, playfulness, belonging, alienation and motherly intimacy. English emerges as the hegemonic language of the private educational system Said attended, as the language of the ex-colonizer and as the object of aspirational desires on the part of the social class to which he belonged. Moving between these two languages and the worlds they mediate, Said negotiated his complex identity in ways that expressed his never-ending displacement culturally, linguistically and geographically.

The second memoir dealt with in chapter 4 is Leila Ahmed's *A Border Passage* (2000). Sociopolitical displacement dominates the narrative in this memoir, just as, in fact, it does Said's. However, Ahmed articulates a different relationship with Arabic. She posits *fuṣḥā* Arabic as the location of state hegemony, false national consciousness in Egypt and the misogyny of an intellectual tradition that uses religion to oppress women with skewed, male-dominated readings and interpretations of the foundational texts of Islam. Ahmed refers to the *fuṣḥā* as an instrument of internal colonialism in Egypt. By contrast, she holds a more favourable view of the colloquial dialect, which she considers the defining vernacular of Egypt in identity terms, although her view of this variety of Arabic was less than complimentary in her early years in a family that seemed to put more emphasis on English than on the native language of Egypt. Thus, Ahmed's antagonistic relationship with *fuṣḥā* Arabic contrasts sharply with her positive relationship with English, which binds her to communities of affiliation that transcend the bonds of national identity. It is interesting to note here how the problem of Palestine is central to both memoirs in the language-identity domain but how this problem produced different reactions and trajectories for the two authors.

Language anxiety is a running theme in the two memoirs. This theme is picked up in two additional texts, one by Moustapha Safouan (2007, Arabic original 2001) and the other by Amin Maalouf (2000). The first study highlights the link among war, trauma and language, using the 1967 defeat of the Arabs at the hands of Israel as the cause of this trauma. Linking this defeat to the entrenched despotism in the Arab political order, the study forges another link with the *fuṣḥā*, treating it as a major cause of cultural ossification and backwardness in society in a way that, in some respects, is reminiscent of Salama Musa's trenchant criticisms of the language in the first half of the twentieth century (1947; and Suleiman 2003). In this respect, there is a close similarity between Safouan's and Ahmed's views of the *fuṣḥā*, although Safouan's position has a greater sociopolitical reach. This similarity further extends to Safouan's belief that the only option available to the Arabic-speaking peoples is to adopt the colloquial dialects as national vernaculars. This decision, he argues, would lead to demystifying the world of writing and to challenging the power of the political elite over it. These, the argument runs, are necessary steps to bring participatory democracy to the Arabic-speaking world.

Maalouf's study of identity links language anxiety to globalisation and the displacements produced by political conflict and socioeconomic diasporisation nationally and transnationally. Although most of Maalouf's comments about language anxiety relate to French, some of his views translate to the Arabic-language situation; in fact, some of these comments refer to Arabic directly, which is not surprising considering Maalouf's Lebanese background. For this purpose, the present study will consider some of the discussions of language anxiety and globalisation in the Arabic-speaking world by analyzing the terminologies used in a small set of writings on the topic. This lexical analysis reveals a strong view of globalisation as a form of symbolic violence against Arabic and Arab culture. The sexually charged connotations in some of these terminologies locate globalisation and its effects in a moral economy that is intended to generate strong cultural resistance against it.

Chapter 4 tackles issues of identity at both the personal and the group level. This perspective is continued into the last chapter. Personal names, place names and code names make up the main topic of chapter 5. The starting point of this chapter is the treatment of Arabic names as linguistic materials by virtue of their ability to signify through the meanings of the roots from which they are derived. Using this premise, this study links names to issues of identity, conflict and displacement at the personal and group levels. It is this link to the personal, the Self, framed against the background of collective identity, that justifies the inclusion of this study of names in this work. This link, in other words, shows how the Self and group identity come together to reveal the rich texture of the networks that frame the ascription, maintenance and subversion of identities in society. Name giving is further linked to issues of social modernisation and to the emergence of transnational diasporas that have retained links to their ancestral countries and cultures while developing new ones in their present settings. The use of place names in transnational conflicts is linked to the structures of power and hegemony in the international political order. In this regard, the linguistic landscape in urban spaces offers rich material through which to study the politics of place. Structures of power are heavily involved in the use of code names to signify wars and military operations in the Middle East. The inclusion of code names is another new departure in this research.

It is surprising that, considering the volatility of the Middle East and its many conflicts, code names have not been the subject of sociolinguistic study. While it will not be possible to plug this lacuna completely in the present research, I think it is important to bring it into the orbit of sociolinguistics in a way that creates links between language and other phenomena in the social world.

In discussing these issues, the chapter exploits Internet-posted materials and self-reports. The latter provide a retrospective glimpse of the naming process, which is further calibrated against data from the field of literary production. Through this, the naming process is shown to be complex and positional. Trends in names over time are linked to political changes in society. In all of these areas, names act as a barometer of the sociocultural mood of society. They enable us to access archaeologies of meaning, providing a glimpse of tense presents that are set against more harmonious pasts. With its characteristic rudimentary maps, the Palestinian genre of memorial books provides a poignant example of this phenomenon. The ascription of place names to persons inscribes the body with the memory of a place that no longer exists, as if to resist the ravages of time. Names of this type are signs of belonging rather than banal means of identification. They also serve as the carriers of moral imperatives that bind the name carrier to a fate that he must accept and honour through action that is intended to redeem the past.

A number of methodological and thematic strands run through this book, which I will summarize here. On the methodological front, the book applies a qualitative and noncorrelationist approach, *not* as an alternative to quantitative and correlationist-variationist research but as *complementary* perspectives that can add depth and insight to the study of Arabic in the social world. The book also focuses on the symbolic meanings of language, over its instrumental/communicative role, as objects of study and interpretation to yield further insights into issues that straddle many disciplinary divides. This expansion of disciplinary horizons is long overdue in the study of the Arabic language. This study is offered as a contribution in this direction rather than as a correction to the lack of research with such wider disciplinary horizons. Accommodating the nativist view of the duality of the Arabic-language situation is another important methodological perspective in this study. Although it is true that this perspective may not be supported by the findings of fine-tuned descriptive studies of the language—in fact, it may be challenged by them—the fact remains that this nativist tradition has its own social-psychological validity, at the levels of both the Self and group identity, which Arabic sociolinguists must not ignore. Finally, the present research is aware of the role of political ideology, whether overt or covert, in studying Arabic in the social world. Although it is important to guard against ideological interference in studying Arabic, it is also important to incorporate language ideology as a topic of investigation in studying the symbolic meanings that the language carries. It is, in my view, imperative to do this, because language ideology is an important factor in framing conceptions of the Self and the group, as well as in guiding interactions in group situations. Chapter 2 lays the foundation for these methodological considerations.

On the thematic front, the book is dominated by a number of overarching themes. These include the central notions of Self and group identity insofar as they are marked in and through language. Connected to this bundle of concepts are the notions of conflict, displacement, anxiety, trauma and diaspora, which I have tried to pursue through autobiography, autoethnography, reflective writing, limited self-reports, literary production, Internet postings, names (personal names, toponyms, ethnonyms and code names) and the linguistic landscape. The intention behind this mode of organizing the present work is to create unities that underpin the different types of data dealt with here. The data are relevant to the extent that they display these thematic unities and help us exemplify what it means to study Arabic from a qualitative and symbolic perspective.

Finally, I have adopted the following conventions in rendering the Arabic materials in the book. All of the items in the bibliography appear in full transliteration. In the text, only those items that I judged to warrant full transliteration appear in this form. The remaining materials appear in an English form that is nearest to their full transliteration. I have adopted this strategy to reduce the impression of foreignness in the book.

Chapter 2

Seven Fault Zones and Beyond

Some Methodological Considerations

The aim of this chapter is to provide a critique of some of the concepts, methods and approaches that are used in describing and explaining facets of the Arabic-language situation in the social world. The points chosen for discussion provide an overview of some of the major methodological and epistemological fault zones in Arabic sociolinguistics. These points paint a partial landscape against which my research into Arabic sociolinguistics has been conducted. I have chosen to call these points fault zones, rather than fault lines, to indicate their complexity and interrelatedness and to avoid the impression that each of the points constitutes a single and uncluttered fracture in the methodological and epistemological edifice of Arabic sociolinguistics.

In pursuing this task, the chapter prepares the ground for the discussion that follows in the remaining parts of this study. In particular, it argues the need for studying the Arabic-language situation from a qualitative, symbolic and interdisciplinary perspective. Studying the Arabic language situation from this combined perspective can yield insights whose value can extend beyond Arabic sociolinguistics to politics, anthropology and history, into what I call the politics of culture in the Middle East or the cultural politics of the Middle East.

A LANDSCAPE OF SEVEN FAULT ZONES

1.

The first fault zone concerns the dominance of a correlationist-variationist approach in the study of Arabic in its social contexts. The main focus of this approach, which characterised research into Arabic sociolinguistics in the last two decades of the twentieth century, has been the attempt to describe variation in the language behaviour of Arabic speakers by correlating salient linguistic variants in their repertoire with a set of social variables to establish the distribution of the former in society by reference to the latter as, it seems, their determinants. A canonical example of this correlationist-variationist approach concerns the distribution of the variants of the *fuṣḥā* (standard Arabic) '*qāf*'—typically, /q/, /g/, /k/ and the 'glottal stop'—in some parts of the Levant with such social or demographic variables as the gender, age profile, educational level, class, ecological environment, locality or religious background of the speakers.[1] The results of this type of research are typically expressed in the form of 'such and such a percentage of subjects with a particular social profile (specified by reference to social variables) use x or y variant of '*qāf*' in a particular speech style/context.'[2] This interest in the pattern congruities characterising the link between Arabic and the social world provided an important taxonomic description of language in society.

A good number of PhD theses on Arabic, written mainly in U.S. universities in the 1970s and 1980s, followed this approach (for example, Abd-el-Jawad 1981; Hussein 1980; al-Jehani 1985; Shorrab 1981).[3] These theses, and the research outputs they led to in the form of research papers in journals, conference proceedings and sometimes books,[4] followed in one way or another the insights of the paradigm developed by William Labov of the University of Pennsylvania in the 1960s and 1970s in his work on variation in English in New York (1966; 1972).[5] Driven in part by a desire to counter the Chomskyan dichotomy between competence and performance, as well as the allied competence-bound notions of 'a homogeneous speech community' and the 'ideal native-speaker hearer who knows his language perfectly'—which Chomsky posited as necessary abstractions to develop his theory of transformational/generative grammar—Labov was right to stress the variability of language and to use correlations of the above type to (a) describe this variability as a patterned phenomenon in language and (b) predict change in progress in language. In this respect, Labov 'argued convincingly that to accept the myth of the ideal speaker-hearer in the homogeneous speech community was not to screen out a few surface irregularities, but rather to miss a fundamental general property of language' (Cameron 1990: 81).

This Labovian paradigm of 'linguistic variants <—> social variables' linkages was important in countering the scientific and, to a much lesser extent, the institutional hegemony of transformational/generative grammar in the

1 Contextual factors such as topic, setting or level of formality are invoked in this research, but they do not concern us here, not least because, with the exception of level of formality, they tend to assume little importance in the research on Arabic sociolinguistics in the correlationist-variationist tradition.

2 For clear examples of this approach, the reader may refer to Amara (1995; 1999) and Amara, Spolsky and Tushyeh (1999), although not all of the social variables listed here—for example, 'class'—are invoked in this research.

3 See also al-Khatib (1988).

4 See, for example, Abd-el-Jawad (1987); Herbolich (1979); Hussein and El-Ali (1988); Haeri (1996).

5 The 1966 item is based on Labov's doctoral dissertation of 1964.

American academy.[6] At the hands of Labov and his close associates, the paradigm came with thick data descriptions and explanations that spoke to structural and historical linguists who refused to accept that the messiness of linguistic performance was a distraction from the real business of developing a theory of speaker-hearer competence in the Chomskyan paradigm. For these linguists, variation in performance was as much a feature of a speaker-hearer's linguistic repertoire as the rules that govern his linguistic competence. However, the mechanical application of this paradigm in Arabic sociolinguistics denuded it of its power, turning it into a poor parody of itself. Furthermore, these acts of parody led to a closure in the horizons of research into Arabic in the social world, as I will explain shortly. It must, however, be pointed out that notable exceptions exist to this incarnation of the Labovian paradigm in Arabic sociolinguistics, including Holes's (1987) study of the language situation in Bahrain.

One of my 'gripes' about the correlationist-variationist approach concerns the transfer of a model lock, stock and barrel to deal with different empirical terrains in Arabic without proper contextualization, a problem that is all too pervasive in the transfer of Western models and concepts to the Arabic-speaking world (see al-Banki 2005; Kush 2002). In some studies, the social variable 'class,' for example, was transferred to the Arabic context uncritically, treating it almost as a 'given' of the social world rather than as a construct that is in need of interrogation and deconstruction (see Haeri 1996: 73–82). More important—and this is my biggest gripe—is that the Labovian model in its Arabic guise failed to recognise that models in the social sciences carry in them genealogical traces of the empirical domains and the theoretical concerns in relation to which they were originally developed, no matter how strong their claims to universality. These traces may be located in what these models include in their theoretical and descriptive scopes. But they may also be inferred from what these models theoretically or descriptively either exclude or downplay. These problems, however, are not specific to sociolinguistics. They apply with equal force to the so-called theories of nationalism, particularly modernism, as I have tried to show in my book *The Arabic Language and National Identity: A Study in Ideology* (2003).

In this context, the Labovian model in its Arabic incarnation failed in two important ways. On the one hand, it failed to recognise and cater to the hugely political nature of language as a social phenomenon.[7] The exclusion of the political from the social may be understandable in the context of variation in New York English in the 1960 and 1970s, but it is bound to constitute a major lacuna when dealing with the major language (Arabic) of a Middle East that was, and still is, riddled with some of the most endemic

6 For a methodological critique of the Labovian paradigm, see Cameron (1990) and Romaine (1984).

7 See Joseph (2006) for a discussion of language and politics.

intra- and interstate conflicts of the modern world. The depoliticisation/apoliticisation of language in Arabic sociolinguistics may be the result of the strict compartmentalisation of disciplines, coupled with the belief that the political in and about language belongs to politics, not to linguistics or to any of its hyphenated disciplines, sociolinguistics being the prime candidate. The fact that political scientists of the Arabic-speaking world have not treated the politics of language as one of their research concerns, not even at the margins of their scholarly activities,[8] produced a vacuum into which the political aspects of language fell by default rather than by design. I have dealt with this issue at length in my book *A War of Words: Language and Conflict in the Middle East* (2004b). To this we may add that the political conditions in the Arabic-speaking world, being characterised by repression and censorship, including self-censorship, may have caused researchers to avoid the political in and about language.

Design, however, cannot be completely excluded. An example of this is the exclusion of the effects of the Middle East conflict in Spolsky and Cooper's (1991) study of the language situation in the Old City of Jerusalem in the 1980s from their research design, in spite of the fact that this conflict has pervaded the daily life of the city since its occupation by Israel in 1967. Although this study does not follow the correlationist-variationist approach, I cite it here to underscore the point that exclusion cannot be regarded as the result of accident in all cases. In Spolsky and Cooper's study, the main organising principle is that of a linguistic market that is dominated by tourism and the administrative imperatives of the city's Israeli authorities. In this sanitized linguistic market, questions of identity and conflict are downplayed to a point whereby, to the unsuspecting reader, they fail to register on the linguistic map of the city in a way that can puncture its constructed calm and normality.

On the other hand, the correlationist-variationist approach failed to consider as part of its research agenda the ideological debates about Arabic and their role in signposting the political competition in society over ethnic or national identities. With its theoretical and descriptive feet rooted in linguistic behaviour and variation, the correlationist-variationist approach considered these debates as second-order data about language rather than as linguistic data in themselves, in the descriptive sense of the term, that are worthy of study and analysis, as Woolard (1998) convincingly argues. As meta-discourse *about* language, these data are driven by ideology and politics,[9] a fact that, for linguists, renders them fit for description and analysis in politics, not linguistics or sociolinguistics. Here again, the issue may be one of discipline compartmentalisation/boundaries and the

8 Palonen (1993) makes this point in speaking about street signs in Helsinki.

9 In this study, ideology is understood as a 'system, or at least an amalgam, of ideas, strategies, tactics, and practical symbols for promoting, perpetuating, or changing a social and cultural order' (Friedrich 1989: 301).

concomitant division of theoretical and empirical labour that follows from it, but the fact that politics from its side evinced little interest in these second-order data meant that an important corpus/field of materials has been left to languish in a sphere of benign neglect between the realms of linguistics and politics, in spite of the fact that the study of this material would not only benefit the two disciplines empirically but could also help in building interdisciplinary bridgeheads between them at a more abstract, theoretical level.

Let me illustrate the fault zones I have been discussing by considering the broad outlines of language variation in Jordan in the last three decades of the twentieth century in relation to the salient *fuṣḥā* phoneme '*qāf*'. The standard treatment of this variation from the correlationist-variationist perspective associates the shift from /k/ and the 'glottal stop' variants to the /g/ variant of '*qāf*' in the colloquial varieties as a male-determined phenomenon, producing percentages of distribution by reference, principally, to the speakers' ecological backgrounds, educational levels and age profiles as determining or motivating social variables in language behaviour (see Suleiman 1993; 2004b). But there is another shift in Jordan that is female-dominated, this one from the variants /k/ and /g/ to the 'glottal stop' colloquial variant of the *fuṣḥā* phoneme '*qāf*'. This shift is similarly and principally correlated with the age profiles and the educational backgrounds of the speakers as determining or motivating social variables in language behaviour. In correlationist-variationist studies of the Arabic-language situation in Jordan, this is the end of the story. Once correlations have been established, tested and corroborated the research is concluded.

While these gender-based correlations are observationally valid, they fail to capture the political archaeology that pervades parts of this variation: the fact that the male shifts to /g/ were politically induced under the impact of a specific active conflict. While the female shift to the 'glottal stop' continued an earlier urbanizing process in the Levant, the male shifts to /g/ were sudden in terms of both onset and intensity. These male shifts seem to have occurred at a crucial moment in the country's history, in 1970–71, following the bloody clashes between the East Jordanian-dominated army supported by the state security apparatus and East Jordanian political forces, on the one hand, and the Palestinian-dominated guerrilla movements, on the other. These clashes resulted in a radical realignment of the political structures of the Jordanian state decisively in favour of the East Jordanians at the expense of the Palestinian Jordanians, in spite of the constitutional equality in citizenship rights and responsibilities that the two segments of the population theoretically enjoyed.

The correlationist-variationist approach could, of course, deal with the observational facts of the language situation in Jordan as sketched out above by including national/ethnic identity as a social variable that determines the gender-based linguistic variations in male behaviour I have just described. To that extent, the correlationist-variationist framework can succeed in describing the 'surface structures' of the language situation in Jordan. But such a success would provide only a truncated analysis of the data, with their rich political archaeology extending back to the conditions surrounding the creation of Jordan as a nation-state in the first half of the twentieth century (Abu-Odeh 1999; Massad 2001; Nanes 2008). Clearly, to appreciate the complexity and contextuality of the language situation in Jordan, a lot more than the 'language variants <—> social variables' linkages is needed. This means not that correlations of this kind are not important but that they only serve as second-order data upon which further operations of interpretation, historical contextualisation and regional or extraregional comparisons must be applied to yield what I consider to be thicker and deeper orders of analysis and interpretation (see Suleiman 2004b). Providing these orders of analysis is not only more insightful, but it also serves to emphasise the political nature of language in society; it can further help forge closer interdisciplinary links—which are woefully lacking—among sociolinguistics, politics and historical enquiry in the study of Arabic.

The closure of horizons referred to above as exemplified in the Jordanian context has impoverished the study of Arabic as a sociopolitical phenomenon. As a severe theoretical limitation on the part of the correlationist-variationist approach, this impoverishment is, in fact, related to the unsuitability of this approach in dealing with the complex and messy issues of identity and conflict in language in an insightful way. But there is a deeper problem at the centre of this limitation, this being the fact that the correlationist-variationist approach is methodologically wedded to a quantitative and positivist framework for understanding the facts of variation in language and society, as I shall discuss in the next section. It is this kind of intersection of factors that underpins my use of the term *fault zone* in preference to *fault line*.

2.

The second fault zone concerns the obsession with quantities, expressed as percentages of language use vis-à-vis populations of speakers, which the correlationist-variationist approach has generated as an expectation for research on Arabic in the social world. Research in this mould is often expressed in tables and bar charts with comments on standard deviations about the occurrence of this or that linguistic variant in the research population. There is no doubt that this kind of information is necessary and important in understanding the sociolinguistics of Arabic. But, as I have said above, this information is best treated as partly processed data that need further analysis, elaboration and interpretation to be fully understood, as, in fact, is suggested by Sankoff (1988), a prominent variationist sociolinguist. Correlationists, however, are wary of this turn in investigating the social world of Arabic, because it might take them into the realms of speculation. This is the only interpretation I can put on their reluctance to engage in this kind of work. How can we interpret this reluctance? Or what are the reasons behind their stance?

The only answer I can give for this is the belief on the part of the correlationists in a positivist view of science, which,[10] according to Hammersley (1995: 2), may be characterised by, among other things, the following principles: (1) 'quantitative measurement and experimental or statistical manipulation of variables are essential, or at least ideal, features of scientific research'; (2) 'research can and should be concerned with producing accounts which correspond to an independent reality'; and (3) 'research must be objective, with subjective biases being overcome through commitment to the principle of value neutrality.' The first principle, which replicates one of the benchmarks often in use in the exact sciences, applies to the correlationist-variationist approach as previously outlined. However, the second and third principles will need further exploration.

Arabic correlationist-variationist sociolinguists seem to adopt a realist, almost naïve realist or God's-truth, view of their objects of study to produce what Cameron calls in her critique of the variationist and quantitative paradigm the 'language reflects society' proposition (1990: 81). This is most evident in the attitudes of these Arabic sociolinguists towards the social variables they employ to explain variation in language. These social variables are treated as part of the 'givens' of correlationist-variationist research, as alluded to above in my comment on the notion of 'class' and as pointed out for this kind or research more generally by Cameron (1990) and Romaine (1984). Epistemologically, therefore, the relationship between the accounts produced by correlationist-variationist research and the sociolinguistic realities they map onto may, in fact, go beyond the 'correspondence to reality' view mentioned in point (2) above to one of 'capturing that reality' in a way whereby the account of the correlationist sociolinguist stands in a relationship of '*re*/presentation' to the reality that preexists it. Correlationist-variationist sociolinguists may disagree among themselves about which of their results better maps onto sociolinguistic reality, but this is not a disagreement over principle, about underlying epistemologies, but is one that relates directly to the truth-claims of specific pieces of research. The issue here is not whether correlationist-variationist studies can in principle be said to '*re*/present' reality but whether this or that piece of research gives a more accurate '*re*/presentation' of reality. The idea that these realities may be hocus-pocus constructions that happen to fit the 'facts' of the language situation is not one that correlationists entertain.

The commitment to a quantitative, positivist and realist research agenda in correlationist-variationist sociolinguistics may be regarded as a protective belt against (inter)subjective bias; hence the disregard of ideological discourse *about* language as an object of study, although data of this kind are

10 The following is a simplified view of positivism, which is adopted here to reach general conclusions about Arabic correlationist sociolinguistics. The fact that this mode of enquiry does not explicitly attend to its underlying methodological or epistemological foundations, but that these have to be inferred, makes it difficult to be specific about positivism in this context.

very important for investigating what it means for language to a be a political phenomenon in society. This commitment is further considered as a guarantee of the objectivity and value-neutrality of the findings of correlationist-variationist research, the enemy here being the injection of external or ideological research agendas that can skew the findings of correlationist-variationist work in a predetermined manner.[11] This is a laudable aim, but the pursuit of value-neutrality through quantification is not the only or best way of guarding against bias, nor is the commitment to quantification in itself a sure guarantee against bias. The effects of bias may, in fact, be ameliorated through open declarations of interest, individual self-monitoring or team surveillance of processes and results and/or cross-validation against similar research problems obtained in different settings.

However, my strongest objection to the commitment to 'quantification as a guarantee against bias' has to do with the 'closure of horizons' discussed above as one of its unintended impacts. If measurement and quantification are held as the 'gold standards' for research in Arabic sociolinguistics, as is the case in the correlationist-variationist approach, the result would be a severe restriction on the types of data that can be investigated in this area of enquiry, with a corresponding loss of information and insights whose significance would extend beyond sociolinguistics into the neighbouring disciplines of anthropology, politics and history. Although interdisciplinarity may have become an overused or, some might say, abused term in social science, I think that the restriction in scope produced by the quantitative and positivist emphases of the correlationist-variationist approach would, if given full rein, be harmful to the study of language as a sociopolitical phenomenon, precisely because this approach elides that in-between space of liminality that requires a multiplicity of perspectives to excavate it. Having positioned some of my work in this in-between-ness I, naturally, regard the *overzealous* commitment to quantification to be a dangerous position to take. My research into ethnolinguistic labels or ethnonyms, toponyms, place names, cartography as textuality and the linguistic landscape was intended to point to the productivity of this in-between space when investigated from a multiplicity of perspectives (see Suleiman 2004b: 137–230). These areas

11 Cameron et al. (1992: 5) comment on some of the features of 'quantitative sociolinguistics' as follows: In quantitative sociolinguistics, 'we have a paradigm in which researchers want to gather data on language use from which its general rules can be induced. Accordingly, they are preoccupied with the "observer's paradox," the idea that good quality data entail careful recording by an outside investigator, who none the less should ideally be absent from the scene in case she influences or interferes with the behaviour of the speakers being recorded. This implies that, ideally, researchers would produce wholly objective representations of reality. Of course sociolinguists recognize that they fall short of the ideal, but still they make efforts to distance themselves as far as possible from the researched and deliberately attempt to reduce or transcend interference.' The points made in this description of 'quantitative sociolinguistics'—for example, the question of objectivity, the relationship of the researcher to the researched and the issue of advocacy—will be dealt with in various places in this chapter.

will be investigated at length in chapter 5 to exemplify further the productivity of nonquantitative and nonpositivist approaches.

3.

The third fault zone is closely related to the second: it is the suspicion that surrounds qualitative research into the Arabic-language situation in correlationist/positivist sociolinguistics. In spite of the absence of a clear articulation of this suspicion in the literature, research of this type may be judged by correlationists to be subject to bias and ideological manipulation and therefore not to be value-free. Furthermore, research of this kind may be criticized for straddling disciplinary divides in a way that produces a hodgepodge of results that answer to a mélange of concepts and approaches that sit uncomfortably together. I have heard some linguists describe work of this kind dismissively as 'cultural studies' masquerading as linguistics; for people of this persuasion, the use of the term *liminality* above would be a cultural-studies red rag to an angry positivist linguistics bull.[12] This reaction reflects in part the success of the Labovian quantitative paradigm in pressing its 'claim to the central and dominant position in language and society studies' to the extent that 'for most people "sociolinguistics" does indeed [refer] primarily if not exclusively [to that paradigm]' (Cameron 1990: 82).

However, before proceeding further, it is important to provide a working definition of qualitative research. For this purpose, I will rely on Denzin and Lincoln's (2000: 8) characterization of this mode of research: 'The word *qualitative* implies an emphasis on the qualities of entities and on processes and meanings that are not experimentally examined or measured (if measured at all) in terms of quantity, amount, intensity, or frequency. Qualitative researchers stress the socially constructed nature of reality, the intimate relationship between the researcher and what is studied, and the situational constraints that shape enquiry. Such researchers emphasize the value-laden nature of enquiry. They seek answers to questions that stress *how* social experience is created and given meaning.'

I cannot pursue all of the strands in the above 'working definition' here, although my views about some of them, in particular the reference to measurement in terms of quantity, must be familiar by now, as I have tried to exemplify these in relation to linguistic variation in Jordan. Instead, I will mainly focus on the reference to the 'intimate relationship between the researcher and the researched' to highlight a few methodological issues in the study of Arabic in its sociopolitical settings from the qualitative perspective. This issue will be further pursued in chapter 3, in which I offer an autoethnography of aspects of my language behaviour in a well-defined setting.

12 I hasten to add that I am not presenting my work as one that falls within 'cultural studies.'

The acknowledgement of the above relationship and its activation in research, which may be referred to as the (ideological) positionality of the researcher in relation to the researched subject, is bound to raise the hackles of the positivist Arabic sociolinguist because of the dangers of personal reflection, bias and the strong possibilities of violating the principle of value-neutrality that it carries. I think this positivist concern is justified in some cases, as the unmonitored injection of the Self of the researcher and its ideological baggage into the conduct of research can lead to skewing the results of this research in predetermined ways to serve predetermined agendas. An example of this is the seemingly innocuous use of terminology in the social sciences in the Middle East to mask geopolitical realities or, even worse, to give currency to expansionist claims of ownership over land in situations of conflict; this is to be found in the almost complete avoidance in some research of the term *occupied* to refer to the Palestinian 'Occupied Territories,' preferring instead such terms as 'Administered Territories,' 'the territories captured by Israel in the Six Day War of 1967,' 'the territories,' the 'West Bank, Judea and Samaria' and 'Administered (Occupied) Territories' (Cohen and Kliot 1992). This is a blatant example of bias occurring in peer-reviewed journals in well-established fields of enquiry.

However, bias may occur in more subtle and, I am prepared to accept, in ideologically unconscious or less conscious ways. An example of this is the way the Old City of Jerusalem in the 1980s emerges as Hebrew-dominated in Bernard Spolsky and Robert Cooper's otherwise pioneering book *The Languages of Jerusalem* (1991), in spite of the fact that the majority population in the city are Arabic-speaking Palestinian Arabs, as the authors do acknowledge. This is marked in four ways. First, the limits of the Old City are described in relation to a Jewish-dominated archaeology that goes back to ancient times instead of the all-pervasive wall that visually marks the limits of the city. This archaeology constructs a picture of the city as Jewish-dominated. An alternative definition by reference to the wall of the Old City would have created a different nuance that is more favourable to Arabic. Second, instead of focusing on the Old City of Jerusalem in the 1980s, the declared period of research, more than half of the book is spent describing the language situation in the Old City before the 1980s, as these chapter titles reveal: Chapter 2, 'Jewish Multilingualism' (covering the sociolinguistic situation in Jerusalem two millennia ago); Chapter 3, 'The Socio-Linguistics of Old Jerusalem: Non-Jewish Languages in the Late Nineteenth Century'; Chapter 4, 'The Socio-Linguistics of Old Jerusalem: Jewish Languages in the Late Nineteenth Century'; Chapter 5, 'The Revitalization and Spread of Hebrew'; Chapter 10, 'The Spread of Hebrew among Arabic Speakers.' These chapter titles give the impression of a Hebrew-language dominance in the Old City. Third, this tilting of the scales in favour of Hebrew at the expense of Arabic is marked in the absence of the latter from the two paratexts at the start of the book (for 'paratext,' see Genette 1997). As the jacket copy of Genette's book explains, paratexts are those 'liminal devices and conventions, both within and outside the book, that form part of the complex mediation between book, author, publisher and reader: titles, forewords, epigraphs . . . are part of a book's private and public history.' One of the two paratexts in the book is from the Jerusalem Talmud (Tractate Sotah 7: 2,30a); it reads as follows: 'Rabbi Jonathan of Bet Gubrin said, Four languages are of value: Greek for song, Latin for war, Aramaic for dirges, and Hebrew for speaking.' This paratext links well with the underlying ideology of the book which does not allocate to Arabic in the Old City in the 1980s the primacy it commands demographically, giving this somehow to Hebrew. Fourth, as I have mentioned above, political conflict, though mentioned in the book, is not activated as a major theoretical perspective in describing the linguistic market of the Old City, with the result that the language situation in Jerusalem is made to differ in texture only from other situations for which linguistic-market studies have been conducted. As a result, the political significance of the language situation in the Old City is erased, depriving us of the context that makes this situation quite distinctive.

In Spolsky and Cooper's research, as in Cohen and Kliot's study, ideological frames of thinking—whether conscious or not—cannot be excluded as a factor (perhaps an overarching factor) in the way the objects of study, which the positivists would call 'reality,' are determined, described and analysed.[13] On the surface, however, these studies seem to conform to the routine stricture of separating the researcher from the researched, in that the relationship between the two is not regarded as an issue. Avowedly, these studies start from an assumption of value-neutrality and may, in fact, be accepted by some of their readers in the same spirit on the assumption that they have been subjected to peer review before they were selected for publication. This impression is underpinned by the fact that Spolsky and Cooper's study is based on extensive empirical research in the Old City (between 1983 and 1986) by a team of researchers that included two Arabic-speaking Palestinians (a male and a female), one of whom is now a published sociolinguist in his own right. The combination of these factors appears to offer a guarantee of neutrality or at least some protection against unguarded bias, but if my arguments are accepted, this does not seem to have happened effectively. If that is the case, what can we do to ameliorate the effects of ideological interference of the kind described here?

My answer revolves around the positionality of the researcher and the importance of making this positionality manifest.[14] Statements of positionality, like declarations of interest in public life, are important in two ways. On the one hand, they alert the audience to the possibility of bias, thus

13 This would, I am sure, apply to works on Hebrew from the Arab/ic perspective had these existed in any serious way. I say this because of the paucity of serious scholarship on Hebrew in the sociopolitical sphere in the Arab world.

14 This point is consistent with the view of Cameron et al. (1992: 5) on the social location of researchers in social science: 'researchers cannot help being socially located persons. We inevitably bring our biographies and our subjectivities to every stage of the research process, and this influences the questions we ask and the ways in which we try to find answers.'

making them more vigilant in tracking any bias or, at least, less prepared to take the value-neutrality of the research on trust. On the other hand, statements of positionality act as reminders to the researcher not to let his guard down against all forms of bias or 'subjective interference,' particularly those more subtle ones of the type I presume to have occurred in Spolsky and Cooper's study. By promoting self-monitoring in the conduct of research, statements of positionality can act as reminders to the researcher not to transgress into advocacy but that, if he chooses to do so, any such foray should be the result of theoretical calculation and overt planning rather than accident. These stipulations, however, are not sufficient to ensure neutrality, but they can go some way towards ameliorating the effect of bias, particularly ideological bias, in the conduct of social research in contexts where conflict and ideological contestation are salient features.

To this effect, I have in my earlier research started from the assumption that the separation between the private Self of the researcher as an individual in society and his academic or scholarly persona as the member of a community of scholars, who are bound by what may be called the 'code of practice' of their peer group or their academic 'regime of truth'—whatever that may be—is more tenuous than what we are prepared to admit (Suleiman 2006d). The interconnectedness of these two personas, the private and the scholarly, should not surprise us at all, for the academic Self is not so purely or hermetically academic after all; it is shaped and reshaped by experiences, feelings, opinions, ideologies, doctrinal beliefs, self-reflections, self-interpretations, intersubjective interactions, contexts and historical trajectories. The same is true of the private Self in its openness to the impact of its academic partner. The idea, therefore, that academic discourse carries in it the footprints of the Self should not be an anathema in social science; one does not have to be a poststructuralist to accept this.[15]

If we accept this, we must then accept that the relationship between the private and academic/scholarly Self is porous, with leakage running in both directions. Scholarly knowledge can shape the private Self in the same way that the personal and ideological dispositions constitutive of the private Self can shape the scholarly persona with which this Self is associated and with which it (subliminally) interacts. This double system of mutual influences is reminiscent of what Anthony Giddens has called the double hermeneutic to 'refer to the application of lay knowledge to the technical language of the social sciences, as well as the utility of social science findings to the reality of a person's day-to-day life' (Elliott 2001: 6). This double hermeneutic does,

15 This stance is in tune with the autoethnographic idea in qualitative research to the effect that 'If you couldn't eliminate the influence of the observer on the observed, then no theories or findings could ever be completely free of human values. The investigator could always be implicated in the product. So why not observe the observer, focus on turning our observations back on ourselves? And why not write directly, from the source of [one's] experience?' (Ellis and Bochner 2000: 747). However, I am not advocating this as an alternative to quantitative research, as qualitative researchers sometimes do or seem to advocate.

in fact, go deeper than imagined, as research on identity and professional academic writing strongly suggests (Ivanič 1997).

It is these methodological considerations that led me to alert the reader to my positionality as a researcher in *A War of Words: Language and Conflict in the Middle East* (2004b).[16] Telling the reader that I was of Palestinian origin was intended to achieve the above two objectives, not to parade a part of my identity for personal reasons (Suleiman 2004b: 1).[17] I also felt that my repeated declarations of this positionality in different parts of the book further allowed me to use my own experiences as a researcher in Israel, Jordan and Palestine as part of my data in an open and self-critical way. I was very aware that by reducing the distance between the researcher and the researched in places, I was treading on thin methodological ice and that I should, therefore, do so with sufficient caution and vigilant self-monitoring to avoid any accidental falls. In particular, I was careful not to use my experiences as the primary linguistic data but to employ them as either supportive evidence to other data, as in the case of Jordan (119–20), or as the basis for making theoretical points that have been articulated in other disciplines, such as my comments on the nature of power and how it applies to linguistic interaction in situations of conflict in particular (13–4). Although I was alert to all of these methodological stipulations and although I tried my best to live by them (as I think I have), I know I have not escaped the very criticisms I set out to avoid, a fact that signals the precariousness of social research. In a largely favourable review of *A War of Words*, which continues beyond the limits of the quotation below, Eliezer Ben-Rafael of Tel Aviv University wrote:

> The book is interesting and valuable for its attempt to elaborate a sociolinguistic approach to political and social conflicts. Yet the book is clearly intended to serve the Palestinian cause against the Israelis. Suleiman, it is true, is aware of the literature and of the historical and political contexts; moreover, he

16 Asimilar point has been raised in researching the role of language as a factor of disunity in Germany between 1945 and 2000. Commenting on this issue, Stevenson (2002: viii) writes: 'The position of the researcher in academic studies has come under increasing scrutiny in recent years . . . but in most publications on the east-west question [in Germany] the authors are surprisingly silent on their own origins and readers are left to infer this important aspect of the research from the way it is reported. . . . Yet this is particularly important in an area of research that deals with relations between two social groups [East and West Germans] which are conceived of in opposition to each other.' If this is relevant in the German context, it must be even more relevant in some contexts in the Middle East, particularly in the context of the Arab-Israeli conflict.

17 I felt that by openly acknowledging my group identity, I would be better able to check any 'contaminating' intrusions that my private Self might make into my public persona as a scholar, for example, by opting for neutral terms that do not skew a particularly sensitive topic in a predetermined direction. Such acknowledgements of the private Self in the conduct of research are not the norm in the literature, but they are not totally absent, either (Baugh 2000). In some cases, these acknowledgements of the private Self are assigned to the paratexts accompanying the main text (see Joseph 2004).

> shows a genuine competence in the discussion of relevant material, notwithstanding the fact that a large part of it has been produced by Israeli scholars, some of whom do not share his views. Nonetheless, his stance is far from 'objective.' As an example among many, he espouses a clearly overstated interpretation of the Ashkenazi-Mizrahi cleavage. (Ben-Rafael 2006: 206–7)

These comments may have given the impression that ideological positioning is restricted to situations of open conflict. This is not the case. Diglossia in Arabic has been considered by some linguists as a cause of the high illiteracy in some Arab societies or, through the high veneration and allegiance given to the *fuṣḥā*, as a reason for the inability of Arab societies to modernize effectively. The latter argument is advanced by Niloofar Haeri in her book *Sacred Language, Ordinary People: Dilemmas of Culture and Politics in Egypt*; she also alludes to the former without, however, declaring her hand unequivocally (Haeri 2003: 117).[18] Haeri believes that effective and sustainable modernization in a country such as Egypt (presumably, the argument would apply to all Arabic-speaking countries) cannot be achieved without vernacularisation, the adoption of Egyptian Arabic as the national language, thus dealing a body blow to diglossia immediately in symbolic terms and, in the long run, marginalizing it functionally.[19] Not a new argument, as I will suggest in chapter 4, this position is underpinned by the assumption that the Egyptians do not have authority over the *fuṣḥā* for two reasons: (1) it is not their mother tongue, and (2) it is a 'sacred' language—the author does not tell us what this, in fact, means—over which they exercise a right of custody that does not give them the authority to modify or modernize it.

18 Haeri says: 'The distance between the mother tongue of students [in Egypt, i.e., the *'āmiyya*] and the language of education is seen by some as one of the causes of persistently low literacy rates (53.7 percent for adults and 68.3 percent for youth)' (2003: 117).

19 Joshua Fishman, a leading sociolinguist, has expressed strong views on the nexus of ideas concerning diglossia, literacy and modernization, which reveal the ideological nature of some of the criticisms of diglossia. I have a great deal of intellectual sympathy with these views, which the following excerpt exemplifies:

> The . . . criticism that accuses diglossia arrangements of being unsympathetic to the economic mobility aspirations of the 'masses of urban poor,' or to economic factors in social change and in social control, are simply further evidence of a regrettable tendency to confuse one's own political-ideological rejection of a particular sociocultural convention with the responsibility for objective and parsimonious description of that convention. Economic factors and socioeconomic 'advancement' may or may not be the crucial factors or the crucial issues at any particular time or in any particular sociocultural context in which the language and ethnicity nexus is being investigated. To assign unquestioned priority to such factors is a type of vulgarization that social scientists should eschew, every bit as much as they eschew the vulgarization of their pet political principles. It is even stranger, however, to find economic determinants opposing diglossia, as if its abandonment per se could be an effective means of altering class-related economic facts, processes and potentials. (Fishman 1984: 40)

These views of diglossia and its presumed consequences in the Arabic-speaking countries are not supported by valid empirical data or incontrovertible intellectual arguments.[20] One can point out, with Fishman (1984), that arguments of this kind are, in the final analysis, ideological in nature. In some societies, such as in the Swiss German/High German case, high literacy exists side-by-side with diglossia. This suggests that on its own, diglossia cannot be held responsible for the high levels of illiteracy in so-called traditional societies. Furthermore, Fishman is right when he says that the 'price that society may need to pay for diglossia arrangements . . . may be worth every penny, relative to the price of 'simplified' equalization solutions [as those predicated on vernacularisation may be classified] that would destroy such arrangements but would bring with them a host of problems tantamount to cultural disruption as well' (1984: 40). Opposing diglossia and seeking, effectively, to dissolve it in favour of vernacularisation, as Haeri seems to advocate, is an ideological position as much as defending diglossia for political reasons, in fact, is. There is nothing wrong in principle with advocating either of these two positions, provided that one is clear about the nature of the epistemological claims one is making. Notwithstanding the fact that language ideologies are a worthy field of enquiry, presenting the ideological in either case as intellectual and empirical is, at best, a case of 'category hopping' or, at worst, an attempt at dressing up ideology as 'science.' I will return to diglossia later to outline another fault zone in researching the Arabic-language situation. I will also return to the mix of ideology and empiricism in discussing the sixth fault zone.

4.

The fourth fault zone concerns the neglect of the symbolic function of language in researching the role of Arabic in the social world. Linguists are interested in the instrumental function of language, its ability to convey meanings through the deployment of its system resources (phonology, morphology, syntax, lexicon, etc.) in what Sankoff (1988: 150) calls the 'form-function' relationship in language and the social world. They tend to be fairly uninterested in the symbolic role of language, what lies beneath and beyond its instrumental function. Belonging to a "hyphenated discipline," sociolinguistics ought to provide the framework for dealing with this symbolic function, which is displayed at its richest in the study of the nexus of identity—especially in the context of conflict between groups—and language. It is this nexus that makes language supremely political in society. The fact that Arabic sociolinguistics, in the correlationist mode, is traditionally not interested in questions of identity and conflict has led to the exclusion of the symbolic role of Arabic from its purview and, therefore,

20 Whether Arabic is a sacred language is a hotly debated issue in the Arabic intellectual tradition; this is an issue to which I hope to return in the future.

from much of the field as a whole, apart from a few exceptions, such as Haeri's (2003) study and some of the work done by this writer. As I argued above, this has resulted in the theoretical and empirical impoverishment of the discipline by removing from its scope data of some political significance. It has further weakened the possibility of linking language with other semiologies of banal nationalism in their capacity as signifiers of aspects of the quotidian experiences of most people that help mark them as members of the same nation.

In this respect, my earlier research was aimed at turning the researchers' gaze to Arabic as a semiology among other semiologies of identity representation and communication, including food, dress, music, art and the state apparatus of national imagining through artefacts such as flags, stamps, national anthems, national holidays and school curricula. By doing this, I hoped to show the rhizomatic[21] nature of identity as a phenomenon that pervades culture in all of its systems of representation, including language. Studying identity through language is, therefore, one entry point in a network of multiple entry points that can be accessed through politics, sociology, anthropology, literary expression, social psychology and critical analysis.

I am, of course, aware that it is not always easy to separate the instrumental from the symbolic in considering the role of language in society. These two functions often interact with each other, as I will discuss below; however, the symbolic function comes into its own when language acts as a marker of identity and as a site of belonging and emotional attachment, almost symbolizing identity as a motif in discourse. Acting in this way, language can be used as a boundary marker between groups of people, whether at ethnic and national levels or at supranational levels, as in the case of pan-Arabism. As a symbol, language continues to garner the allegiance of people who have little or no communicative facility in it, for example, as a heritage language. An example of this is provided by the 1975 findings of the Committee on Irish Language Attitudes Research, which concluded that 'strong sentimental attachments to Irish were not accompanied by language *use*, nor by desire to actively promote it, nor yet by optimism concerning its future, among the population at large' (Edwards 1988: 51). Language symbolism further extends to the script in which a language is recorded, although linguists do not regard the script of a language as part of that language as a cognitive system. This is why script changes are read more politically than linguistically by both their instigators/promoters and the audiences at which they are aimed. The replacement of Arabic by Roman script for Turkish in 1928 was primarily a sociopolitical act, rather than one of pure linguistic reform, although the

21 See Sermijn et al. (2008) for the idea of selfhood as a rhizomatic story; however, my use of the *rhizome* is different in that it does not espouse a poststructuralist/postmodernist interpretation of identity as being cut loose from any fixities.

official policy of the new Turkish state tended to promote the language-reform agenda as the front reason for embarking on the modernisation of the language at all levels.[22]

It is the symbolism of language as a motif for identity that makes it amenable for political deployment as a proxy in contestation and countercontestation, the idea being that wherever there is power in society, there is resistance. In situations where the political is tightly controlled or where it is embargoed in society by the coercive apparatus of the state, language, as an issue of entitlement, can be pressed into service to articulate the political. Correlationist-variationist sociolinguistics does not engage this aspect of language use. In the United States, the English-only movement is more about promoting a particular kind of anti-immigration politics and a particular vision of a racially white America than the declaration of English as the official language of the state (Schmid 2001). In Algeria and Morocco, discussions of Berber and the translation of the Qur'an into this language is code for intra- and interstate ethnic politics, although the substance of this talk concerns language as an issue of functional entitlement in society (Ennaji 2005). In Israel, claiming Arabic-language rights in certain spheres represents low-intensity political talk about autonomous Palestinian cultural rights, the claim for which can be hugely political in a state that is very protective of its exclusive Jewishness.

Elias Koussa, a Palestinian advocate who lived and practised law in Haifa before and after the establishment of Israel in 1948, was excellent at deploying language as a proxy to articulate political arguments. In 1943, he wrote to the high commissioner for Palestine to protest the inclusion of Arabic, below Hebrew, in a pamphlet announcing the screening of the film *Desert Victory*, dropped over Haifa by 'His Majesty's aeroplanes' (see figures 2.1 and 2.2). Koussa pressed the point that this ordering of the two languages constituted 'a flagrant violation of the provision of Article 22 of the Mandate,' which stipulated the order as English, Arabic and then Hebrew in vertical manifestations. Koussa, however, did not hide his real concern, for which the language issue served as the proxy for his national concerns about the larger political landscape in Palestine at the time. 'The Arabs,' he wrote, 'look upon the matter with serious apprehension lest this instance, and the many other cases in which the same order was adopted imply a settled policy of subordinating their rights and interests to those of the Jewish community.'[23]

Koussa continued this mode of arguing by proxy after Israel was established in 1948. In 1955, he wrote to the director general of the Postal and Telecommunications Department in Israel to protest the lack of bills of exchange (*kumbyālāt*) of the 50-*pruta* denomination in Arabic at the Central

22 See Aytürk (2004) and Lewis (1999) for a discussion of the Turkish language reforms.

23 I am grateful to Yonatan Mendel for making this document available to me.

ELIAS N. KOUSSA
ADVOCATE
TELEPHONE 341
P.O.B. 14

Haifa, 22nd May, 1943. (1)

Your Excellency,

I have the honour to enclose a copy of printed pamphlets with regard to the "Desert Victory Film" which were thrown over Haifa by one of His Majesty's aeroplanes from which it will be observed that Arabic is printed last instead of immediately after the English version, and that the Hebrew language has been given precedence over Arabic.

2. It is respectfully submittted that the order in which the three versions of the advertisement are printed constitute a flagrant violation of the provision of Article 22 of the Mandate. The Arabs look upon the matter with serious apprehension lest this instance, and the the many other cases in which the same order has adopted imply a settled policy of subordinating their rights and interests to those of the Jewish community.

3. It is prayed that Your Excellency will be kind enough to direct that the necessary measure be taken to ensure that such an offensive conduct shall not recur in future.

I have the honour to be,
Sir,
Your Excellency's Obedient Servant.

Elias N. Koussa.

His Excellency,
The High Commissioner for Palestine,
Jerusalem.

State
297/16 – 3
297/16 – N

Figure 2.1. Elias N. Koussa's letter of protest. (Israeli State Archive, File M 297/16.)

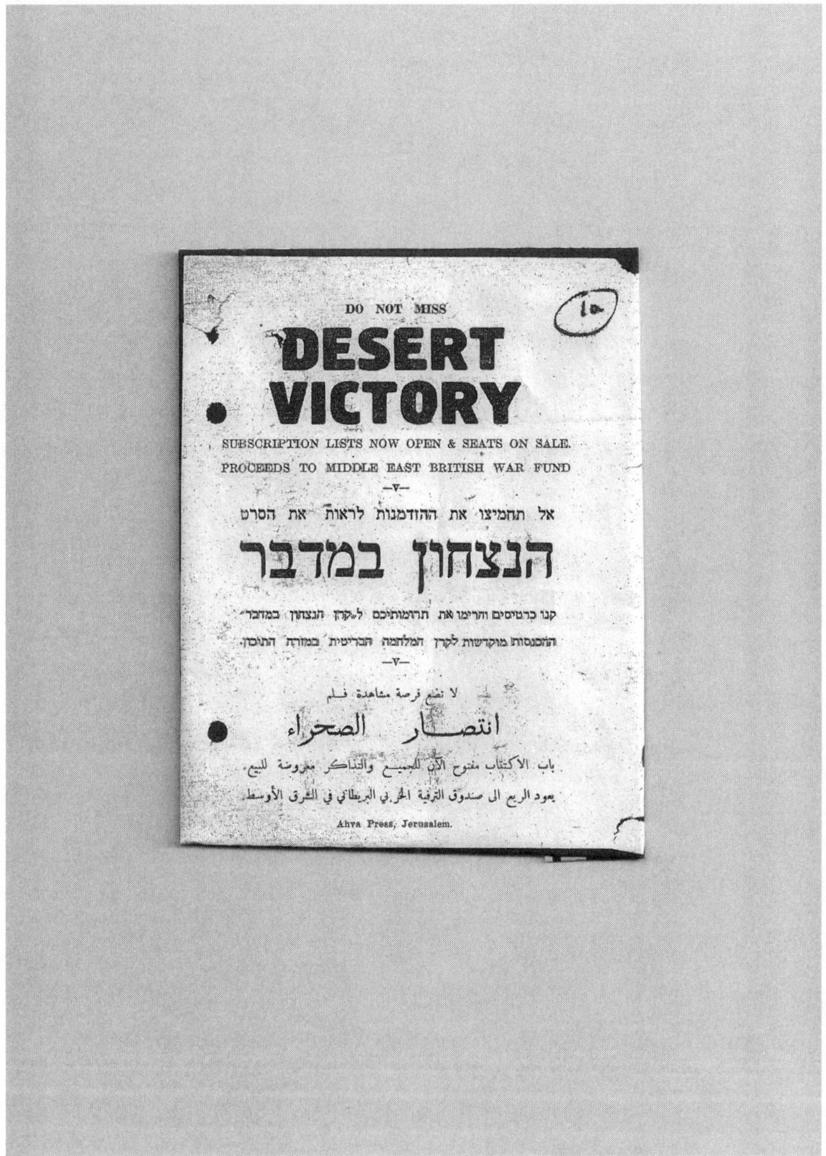

Figure 2.2. *Desert Victory* pamphlet.

Post Office in Haifa (see figure 2.3). Writing in Arabic, no doubt to emphasize his right to use the language (in addition, perhaps, to a lack of competence in Hebrew), Koussa complained that one of the office staff denied the existence of these or any other bills in Arabic but that his superior later admitted that they had some in response to Koussa's protestations but only

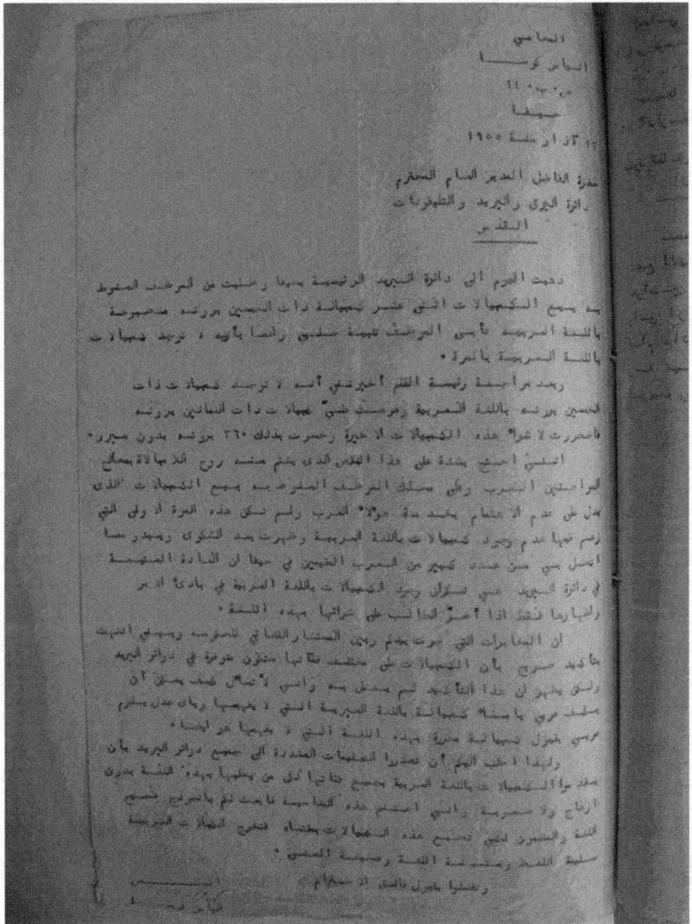

المحامي
الياس كوسا
ص.ب. ١١٠
حيفا
١١ آذار سنة ١٩٥٥

حضرة الفاضل المدير العام المحترم
دائرة البرق والبريد والتلفونات
القدس

Figure 2.3. A letter of complaint. (Israeli State Archive, File RG74/8002/20.)

in the 80-*pruta* denomination. Koussa told the director general that he had no choice but to buy those bills, thus spending more than he had originally budgeted (he wanted to buy ten bills of the 50-*pruta* denomination, but it seems he ended up buying ten bills of the 80-*pruta* denomination). He then complained that this kind of denial was routine at the Haifa Central Post Office and that the office staff admitted the existence of the bills only when an Arab insisted on having them in Arabic. Koussa ended his letter by demanding that the bills, in all denominations, be made available in Arabic, because the Arabs did not know Hebrew and needed to know what they were signing for when they obtained the bills in legally binding transactions. He also insisted that the Arabic on any future bills had to be 'correct in form, succinct in style and semantically well composed' (*salīmat al-lafẓ wa-matīnat al-uslūb wa-raṣīnat al-ma'nā*).[24] To help the director general in his task of providing the bills, Koussa included a specimen he must have devised for the purpose (*unmūdhaj*), embodying these requirements for the director general to follow in the design of the bills (unfortunately, I do not have a copy of this).

Koussa's letter was written with political intent: to argue that the Arab citizens of Israel had rights and that these rights must be upheld not just in theory—the fact that Arabic is an official language of Israel—but also in practice, including the procuring of services. Language is an entitlement issue for the Arabs in Israel, but there is no doubt that Koussa was using it to argue against the diminution or even the loss of Arab rights in the newly formed state of Israel. His mood was one of defiance; his use of the verb *aḥtajju* ('protest,' line 8), the emphatic particle *inna* (lines 8, 15), the adverb of intensity *bi-shidda* ('strongly,' line 8) and the accusatory tone in *rūḥ al-lāmubālā* ('couldn't-care-less attitude,' line 8) signalled this defiance. His offer of help through the bills of exchange that he sent to the director general as specimen signaled his distrust of the Israeli authorities who might produce the required bills in Arabic but do so carelessly. Hence his insistence that the language used in the bills must not only be fit for purpose but must also show respect to Arabic and, transitively, its Palestinian speakers in Israel. He signalled the latter by using stock Arabic phrases that are routinely used at secondary school to evaluate literary style in Arabic culture (*salīmat al-lafẓ wa-matīnat al-uslūb wa-raṣīnat al-ma'nā*), as if the bills belonged to this genre of writing. However, the serious tone of Koussa's letter was mixed with a mocking attitude, which he signaled by cancelling the respectful gesture conveyed by the term *aghtanim hādhihi al-munāsaba* ('I take this opportunity') through using the expression *unmūdhaj ṣaḥīḥ* ('correct specimen'), as if to define the relationship between himself and the director general as that of master and apprentice or teacher and pupil, respectively.

Koussa's letter exemplifies the coalescence of the two functions of language, the instrumental and the symbolic, in arguing the political in society.[25] In this case, the instrumental emerges as a meta-discourse about the symbolic, leading to a layering of messages and the doubling of discursive impact. The letter further reveals the intersection of the linguistic and the political, which correlationist-variationist sociolinguistics, by virtue of its insistence on quantities, cannot capture or leaves to languish 'in a sphere of benign neglect between the realms of linguistics and politics,' as I have

24 Koussa was an indefatigable defender of Arabic-language rights in Israel, no doubt as a proxy for the larger nationalist struggle, as series of documents from the Israeli State Archive reveal (ISA/GL/17009/16). I am grateful to Leena Dallasheh and to Yonatan Mendel for making these documents, including the one under analysis in this chapter, available to me.

25 See also Suleiman (2004b: 146–49) for a similar case involving a Palestinian Arab member of the Israeli Knesset.

pointed out earlier. Even if correlationist-variationist sociolinguistics can achieve greater precision through its insistence on measurements and quantities, as if language behaviour was viewed as a set of events rather than the actions of speakers with agency, the price for this may turn out to be a massive loss in the insights we can derive from the full richness of the data on the politics of language in society.

5.

The fifth fault zone relates to the rejection or marginalization of nativist dualism in discussions of diglossia in the literature in English, whether by Arab or non-Arab scholars. As the cornerstone of the Arabic-language situation, diglossia is the most extensively studied topic in Arabic sociolinguistics. In fact, well before the concept gained massive currency in Arabic (socio)linguistics in the West, following the publication of Ferguson's study (1959), the Arabs—who referred to it by the term *izdiwājiyya lughawiyya* ('linguistic duality') in the nineteenth-century debates over language in the Levant (Khuri 1991)—summed it up by reference to the two terms *fuṣḥā* ('standard Arabic') and *'āmiyya/dārija* ('colloquial Arabic'). I propose to use *fuṣḥā* and *'āmiyya* here in preference to any of their translations or equivalents in English.[26] Recent scholarship on diglossia has challenged the concept of duality implicit in the *di-* of *diglossia* in favour of a continuum of varieties between the polar ends of the *fuṣḥā* and the *'āmiyya*, although there is no agreement on the number of these intermediate forms of the language.

In spite of this, I have argued elsewhere for preserving the concept of duality in diglossia, because this concept accords well with how the Arabs generally conceptualize their language situation, which I have referred to as the insider perspective (Suleiman 2008). As Eid (2002a: 204) rightly observes, 'the perceived dichotomy between [*'āmiyya* and *fuṣḥā*] is deeply engrained in the collective consciousness of speakers/writers' in the Arabic-speaking world. In holding to this dichotomy, I am, therefore, following a nativist folk-linguistics tradition rather than any of the variations on diglossia that have been proposed in the literature of professional linguistics, most, if not all, variants of which agree on rejecting this duality.[27] This is a methodological

26 The term *dārija* tends to be used in the countries of North Africa (Algeria, Morocco and Tunisia). In the countries of the Middle East, *'āmiyya* is the dominant term.

27 Arabic correlationist-variationist sociolinguistics absorbed from descriptive linguistics a negative attitude towards folk linguistics in line with the thinking on the topic in the Labovian variationist paradigm. Cameron (1990: 92) comments on this thinking as follows: 'Metalinguistic activities and beliefs have received, at least in urban western societies, less attention than they merit. For it is surely a very significant fact about language in these societies that people hold professional beliefs about it; that it generates social and political conflicts; that practices and movements grow up around it both for and against the *status quo*. . . . With some honourable exceptions, though, [most researchers in the variationist-quantitative paradigm] tend to treat laypersons' views on usage as manifestations of ignorance to be dispelled, or crankishness and prejudice to be despised,' preventing 'sociolinguistics from [taking] folk-linguistics seriously.'

choice on my part, not an ideological one, driven by the view that giving credence to the folk-linguistics beliefs of a language community in our discourse about language has something to commend it intellectually, even though these folk beliefs may not be supported by empirical studies of the language situation of the community in question, as Parkinson (1991) illustrates in his study of the boundary between the *fuṣḥā* and the *'āmiyya*. The fact that Arabic (socio)linguists have been unable to agree on the number or the content of the varieties or levels, along the diglossic language continuum, in characterising the Arabic-language situation is indicative of the complexity of this situation and, therefore, of the importance of keeping in play as many perspectives on variation in the language as possible, including folk-linguistics dualist nativism. The ability of this nativist dualism to serve as a crossroad for a set of important sociopolitical debates about tradition versus modernisation, change versus authenticity, pan-Arab national identity versus territorial and nation-state identities argues for the intellectual efficacy of this nativist, folk-linguistics view of the Arabic-language situation. If that is the case, there is no absolutely compelling reason for privileging the linguistics-based perspective on diglossia over the nativist one, since each of these two perspectives is underpinned by different assumptions and serves different objectives. Both perspectives, the scientific linguistic one and its folk-linguistics counterpart (Niedzielski and Preston 2000), are needed if we are to deal with the complexities of and about the Arabic language.

Allied to the nonnativist tradition in the study of diglossia is what I call the 'mother tongue' quandary in Arabic scientific (socio)linguistics. This quandary goes as follows: If the *'āmiyya* is the mother tongue of an Arab and the *fuṣḥā* is not, what is *fuṣḥā* to an Arab? The usual answer is that it is the language of the Qur'an, the Arab intellectual tradition, high literature, schoolbooks and education more generally. While this is true, this characterisation of the difference between the two varieties does not capture some of the widely held 'anti-*'āmiyya*' views that coalesce around the *fuṣḥā*, views to which many Arabs may, in fact, subscribe. Study after study, including Haeri's, which argues for vernacularisation, have revealed how deeply rooted these *fuṣḥā*-centred anti-*'āmiyya* views can be in the Arabic-speaking world,[28] in spite of the fact that the *'āmiyyas* do command the loyalty of their mother-tongue speakers. Indeed, in spite of the fact that the Arabs may express equal loyalty to their *'āmiyyas* and to the *fuṣḥā*, they may, if asked to be critical of these two varieties, be less critical of the latter

28 Haeri comments on this attitude in Egyptian society (2003: 117): 'At state schools, as in schools within the Al-Azhar University system, Egyptian Arabic and other vernaculars are explicitly denigrated, associated with ignorance, illiteracy, backwardness and so on. This is the case despite the fact that in elementary school and in later stages, oral interaction such as lectures are mostly in that language.'

than of the former, although the *'āmiyya*s are the Arabs' mother tongues. This, in my view, calls for a reconceptualisation of the place of the *fuṣḥā* in the Arabic-speaking world far beyond the one I have given earlier in this paragraph.

For this purpose, a distinction needs to be drawn between *linguistic* communities and *speech* communities, where 'the former are groups professing adherence to the normatively constructed, ideologically articulated "standard" language . . . and the latter are groups characterized by the actual use of a specific speech form' (Blommaert 2006: 243, following Silverstein 1996; 1998). The distinction between linguistic communities and speech communities seems to me to be a useful one to make in the context of Arabic diglossia, whereby the *fuṣḥā* acts as a site of loyalty for Arabic speakers as a linguistic community, while the *'āmiyya*s derive their place in society from being the sites of loyalty for speech communities. This distinction points to the transnational nature of the *fuṣḥā*-centred linguistic community, while the *'āmiyya*s can operate within the boundaries of the nation-state, or at the regional level in intrastate situations, to mark the existence of multilayered speech communities that may be defined geographically or socially. Thus, instead of marking the distinction between the *'āmiyya*s and the *fuṣḥā* as a matter of natural versus socially constructed language acquisition, respectively, which indeed is the case psycholinguistically, we mark this distinction for our purposes in sociolinguistics as one that is structured around standard versus nonstandard varieties in a way that enables us to analyse the double and conflicting allegiances that Arabic speakers have towards the *fuṣḥā* and the *'āmiyya*s.

The above distinction provides a new way of thinking about diglossia from an insider, folk-linguistics and nativist perspective. As I have said above, this distinction is driven not by ideology but by the need to explain some of the facts of diglossia as perceived by the very people who have to lead their lives through it. These facts are facts *about* language rather than primarily facts *of* language as a system that exhibits variation on the phonological, morphological, syntactic and lexical levels. I am aware that the distinction I have drawn cannot stand the scrutiny of scientific-descriptive linguistics, but this is not a relevant consideration here. What matters for our purposes is providing a framework that can capture the perceptions that linguistic and speech communities—which may be demographically coterminous—have about their language situation; these may include views that modern linguistics rejects, such as the inequality of languages or the belief that nonstandard language varieties are 'an aberration or deviation from the standard' (Suleiman 2004b: 60), which the Arab grammarians have described as *laḥn* ('solecism'). Furthermore, by finding a theoretical niche for the *fuṣḥā-'āmiyya* duality in diglossia, Arabic sociolinguistics can track language-centred debates about modernisation, authenticity, identity and conflict in society from a nonideological position, although these debates are immersed in ideology. I will return to the question of diglossia in chapter 4.

6.

The sixth fault zone concerns the basis for establishing language varieties in Western-based Arabic linguistics that can be justified only on ethnolinguistic grounds, although these classificatory categories are overwhelmingly used and given taxonomic credence as categories of structure-based variations. Although the Arabic grammatical tradition in premodern times operates in terms of the *fuṣḥā* and deviations from it, which are categorized as *laḥn* ('solecism'), Western scholarship on Arabic posits far more categories, including Proto-Arabic, Old Arabic, Early Arabic, Classical Arabic, Early Middle Arabic, New Arabic, Middle Arabic, Muslim Middle Arabic, Christian Middle Arabic, Judaeo Arabic, Modern Standard Arabic and Educated Spoken Arabic, sometimes called *al-lugha al-wusṭā* ('the middle language') or *al-lugha al-thālitha* ('the third language'), as these two terms are consecrated in the title of a recent study of Arabic (al-Ma'tuq 2005). While the taxonomy of varieties in the Arabic grammatical tradition tends to concentrate on continuities and unities, no doubt for reasons that are ideological, Western scholarship tends to emphasise change and fragmentation, nevertheless without ignoring the continuity of the *fuṣḥā*. The Western taxonomy of labels that I have described above seems, however, to reflect three principles: (1) diachronic variation, which operates most clearly in the transition from Proto- to Modern Standard Arabic through Old Arabic, Early Arabic and Classical Arabic; (2) synchronic variation, for example, the distinction between Classical Arabic and Middle Arabic or Educated Spoken Arabic along the lines of standard and nonstandard varieties; and (3) ethnolinguistic variation as pertains to the three varieties of Arabic within Middle Arabic: Muslim, Christian and Jewish Arabic. The main point of discussion in this section is the last taxonomy because of its socio/ethnolinguistic significance.

In the *Encyclopedia of Arabic Language and Linguistics*, the most comprehensive work on Arabic to date, only Christian and Judaeo-Arabic are recognized by name as special classificatory categories within Middle Arabic (see Grand'Henry 2006 and Khan 2007, respectively). Middle Arabic is also listed but without qualification (Lentin 2008). Does this mean that this unqualified Middle Arabic is Muslim Middle Arabic by default? The *Encyclopedia* is silent on this, perhaps on the basis that since most of the Arabs were/are Muslim, then it goes without saying that the major manifestations of Middle Arabic were Muslim. Under this interpretation, labelling Middle Arabic as Muslim Middle Arabic would be redundant, since in setting up taxonomies, one tends to qualify the marked categories (Christian and Jewish Middle Arabic here) while leaving the unmarked one (Muslim Middle Arabic) unqualified. There is a principle of economy in this practice. But there is also an implication that Muslim Middle Arabic is the norm of all Middle Arabic varieties in terms of which Christian and Judaeo-Arabic are defined/referenced. However, Kees Versteegh, the general editor of the *Encyclopedia*, has, in my view, been more logically consistent in his own work (1997), when he recognized Muslim Middle Arabic as a distinct variety of Middle Arabic on a par theoretically with Christian and Jewish Middle Arabic. This means that for Versteegh, all of these ethnically inflected Middle Arabic varieties are equidistant from a parent/common Middle Arabic. If so, what are the criteria that make these varieties distinct from one another?

Versteegh seems to consider ethnicity as the basis of this triad of Middle Arabic varieties. Khan and Grand'Henry subscribe to this position in their definitions of Christian and Judaeo-Arabic, respectively, although Grand'Henry openly recognises that these two categories are ill defined: 'Current research on Middle Arabic has not gone into deep enough detail to allow a linguistic definition of different layers of Middle Arabic' (2006: 383). Versteegh recognizes the ill-defined nature of Middle Arabic: 'Middle Arabic is not a special variety of the language but the name for a category of texts with deviations from the classical standard language' (1997: 121). In spite of the competing terminology of 'variety' and 'text' here, Versteegh puts forward the view that 'since for Christians and Jews the model of the language of the Qur'an was not as powerful or authoritative as it was for Muslims, they felt much freer than Muslims did to use colloquial forms in their written language' (117).[29] He goes on to say, 'When Jews and Christians write in Arabic . . . it is legitimate to regard their language as a special variety, since their brand of written Arabic became a special in-group form of the language, a new norm' (121). This is a sweeping claim for which Versteegh offers no substantiation and which, in fact, he undermines when he says that Middle Arabic is 'the name of a category of texts' rather than a 'special variety of the language.' Why, we may ask, would something that is part of Middle Arabic, conceived of as a 'category of texts,' suddenly become a special variety of Arabic when its users are ethnically Jewish or Christian?

Considering the two criteria (ethnicity and deviation from the classical language), Versteegh offers as part of the basis for recognising Christian and Judaeo-Arabic as special varieties of Middle Arabic, what conclusions can we draw for the viability of Muslim Middle Arabic as a classificatory category in its own right? Since Muslims do not seem to have the same freedom to deviate from the language of the Qur'an as Christians and Jews do, according to Versteegh (a questionable assumption), and since we are not told that Muslims used their Middle Arabic variety 'as a special in-group form of the language,' what grounds do we have to talk about Muslim Middle Arabic as a classificatory category, as Versteegh does? The answer is very little.

Let us pursue this discussion on taxonomy further by focusing on Judaeo-Arabic, which has received the greatest attention in the literature. The existence of this variety is additionally justified by the fact that it was used by Jews, who used Hebrew letters to record its written texts for use by Jews.

29 This may be intuitively true, but we need hard evidence to support it. In fact, the evidence may show that the kinds and extent of deviations from the *fuṣḥā* shown by all of these varieties of Middle Arabic may not justify this widely held view.

These two criteria (of script and of authorship and reception) are not linguistic in the way modern linguists define their discipline but ethnolinguistic in nature. There is nothing wrong in defining Judaeo-Arabic in this way. However, a problem arises when most discussions of this variety proceed to establish what is structurally distinctive about it in a way that strongly suggests that the variety is defined structurally by these distinctive features, rather than by reference to ethnicity as an overarching principle.

A good summary of the properties of Judaeo-Arabic is given in Khan's article in the *Encyclopedia of Arabic Language and Linguistics* (2007). However, this summary makes clear that Judaeo-Arabic is characterised by great diversities synchronically and diachronically, making it a basket of features that are glued together by an ethnolinguistic criterion of authorship and consumption, the use of the Hebrew script and the inevitable (sometimes large) borrowings of lexical items from Hebrew into Judaeo-Arabic. The summary, however, leaves open a number of questions. Are some Judaeo-Arabic varieties structurally more similar to Muslim or Christian Middle Arabic than they are to some other varieties of Judaeo-Arabic? If the answer is yes, as it may well be in the context of some Karaite varieties of Arabic, at least, what justification do we have, apart from the principle of ethnolinguistic classification, for considering these varieties as structurally Judaeo-Arabic? Might it be the case that the differences between some Moroccan Judaeo-Arabic varieties and their Muslim Moroccan counterparts are structurally less pronounced than those that exist between these Muslim varieties and their counterparts in the countries of the Middle East (*Mashreq*)? If this can be shown to be the case, as it might, what justification do we have structurally to establish a sharper distinction between Judaeo- and Muslim Middle Arabic than between one Muslim and another Muslim Middle Arabic?

There are two problems with the Western classification of Judaeo-Arabic. First, the classification can be valid only if based on ethnolinguistic criteria. There is nothing wrong with this, as I have suggested above, provided that we are ready to accept that this is an ideological way of defining this type of Arabic and that this mode of defining it derives from its ability to act as a symbolic motif of loyalty and belonging for its community of users. But for us to accept this, we must have evidence that shows that Jews and Christians did indeed exhibit an awareness of the distinctiveness of their Middle Arabic varieties, that they had a sense of allegiance to them as varieties distinct from so-called Muslim Middle Arabic and that they did use them to differentiate themselves from their Muslim compatriots. This is important to avoid the charge that Christian and Judaeo-Middle Arabic are the result of reading an ideological present into a largely undifferentiated past on the (structural) linguistic front, something that may, in fact, apply to Blau's view of Judaeo-Arabic (1988). This evidence may exist, but I am not aware of it. Second, the pursuit of specifying a set of structural properties for Christian and Judaeo-Arabic, while important, must be clearly framed not as an attempt at defining these varieties structurally but as a way of enriching our understanding of these varieties as Middle Arabic varieties rather than as deviations from some well-defined norm that is specifically Muslim. Structural descriptions of Christian and Judaeo-Arabic in the literature seem to veer away ideologically from this stipulation.

To illustrate the confusion surrounding the sociolinguistic status of Judaeo-Arabic, let us examine very briefly Joshua Blau's views of this linguistic construct.[30] Joshua Blau has done more than most linguists to promote the notion of Judaeo-Arabic as a special category of the Arabic language.[31] In his essay 'Medieval-Judeo-Arabic,'[32] Blau refers to this construct as a 'Jewish language' (1988: 87),[33] which he later says does not 'in the main . . . differ from the Middle Arabic used by both Muslims and Christians' (88), except in 'two important features peculiar to Judaeo-Arabic texts which reveal their Jewish aspect: (1) the general use of Hebrew script in writing; and (2) the frequent occurrence of Hebrew (and Aramaic) words and phrases, interspersed in the Arabic text' (88).[34] Blau then tells us that 'whatever the ratio of Hebrew elements [in Arabic texts] they do not alter the basic structure of Judaeo-Arabic—with only a few exceptions the Hebrew words are absorbed to a surprising degree into the grammatical patterns of Arabic, thoroughly adapting themselves to its structure. Accordingly, even where the proportion of Hebrew words is high, texts in Judaeo-Arabic have to be always regarded as treatises written in the Arabic language containing Hebrew phrases, rather than vice versa' (90). Later in the same essay, Blau declares that Judaeo-Arabic texts can sometimes be so suffused with Hebrew linguistic elements that the 'language ceases to be intelligible to the non-Jewish Arabic-speaking population' (94). These texts seem to be the exception, not the rule, since this is the way Blau presents them in this essay against the output of Jewish writings in Judaeo-Arabic. Blau summarises his view of the status of Judaeo-Arabic as a 'special sociolect within Middle Arabic' (94) in spite of the fact that he more than once refers to this sociolect as a language.

Blau begins by describing Judaeo-Arabic as a Jewish language, but in the end he retreats, in the face of the evidence he himself amasses, to establishing it as a sociolect of Middle Arabic, having in the transition from language to sociolect described Judaeo-Arabic as a 'set of texts,' rather than as a language or sociolect. In an earlier essay, 'Judaeo-Arabic in its Linguistic Setting,'[35] Blau interprets the same evidence in favour of declaring that Judaeo-Arabic is a distinct language: 'We could contend that the Jewish

30 For a more nuanced but less canonical treatment of Judaeo-Arabic from a sociolinguistic perspective, the reader may refer to (Harry 1995, 2003).

31 Joshua Blau was born in 1919. He was professor of Arabic at the Hebrew University and served as president of the Hebrew Language Academy in Israel.

32 First published in 1987.

33 Blau (1988) is a collection of some of his essays on Middle and Judaeo-Arabic.

34 I will ignore the problem of defining what language means, as this is not a significant issue for the discussion here.

35 First published in 1968.

flavour of the topics dealt with, the almost universal presence of Hebrew elements, and the employment of the Hebrew script have left such an unmistakable imprint on the Middle Arabic of the Jews as to give us the right to speak of a separate Judaeo-Arabic language, clearly distinct from all other forms of Middle Arabic' (1988: 102). Blau seems to base his view of Judaeo-Arabic as a distinct language on the fact 'the writers of Judaeo-Arabic . . . had the feeling that they were writing in a separate language' (102).

In a still earlier essay, 'The Status of Arabic as Used by Jews in the Middle Ages: Do Jewish Middle Arabic Texts Reflect a Distinctive Language?'[36] Blau explains this criterion of 'feeling' by referring to Judaeo-Arabic writers who were proficient in Classical Arabic and had good formal knowledge of its grammar but chose to 'flout' (1988: 115) these rules in favour of writing in a 'markedly vulgar form of the language' (115–16). Blau adds: 'If Judaeo-Arabic was employed as a separate literary language by authors whose knowledge would equally have enabled them to write in Classical Arabic, the reason is that a clearly defined Jewish community made use of Judaeo-Arabic in connection with everything that had any bearing on it as a group' (116). Blau ends by stating: 'We come therefore to the conclusion that the status of a language in its own right has to be accorded to Judaeo-Arabic' (116).

Blau's argument and his conclusion in the above essays raise many questions. Why is the evidence he adduced in these essays, spanning almost thirty years, interpreted differently in different publications as pointing to the existence of a 'national language' in its own right or to a 'separate language' or to a 'sociolect' or to a 'group of texts'? If writing in Judaeo-Arabic on the part of Jewish writers is expressive of a 'feeling' of Jewish group identity, as we are told in the essays of 1959 and 1968, how would we interpret texts in Classical Arabic on Jewish topics written by Jewish writers who write exclusively in this medium in terms of the identity these texts express? Do these texts indicate that their writers do not regard themselves as part of a Jewish group identity? Or do these texts indicate that their writers aim to express a noncommunal group identity that transcends ethnic boundaries? The problem in invoking 'feeling' on the part of Blau is that he assumes the existence of a single Jewish group identity for which there is a restrictively distinct expression in the linguistic domain that is Judaeo-Arabic. This view causes Blau, in his essay of 1959 and, to a lesser extent, his essay of 1968, to consider texts that approximate the ideals of Classical Arabic to fall outside the norms of Jewish group identity. Put differently, this equation of a one-to-one relationship of a single group identity and language must imply that texts written in Judaeo-Arabic only are truly Jewish, branding those texts written in Classical Arabic or in codes approximating it as non-Jewish, even if these texts deal with distinctively Jewish material in grammar, exegesis or astronomy and are written by those who 'feel' and

36 First published in 1959.

consider themselves to be Jewish. Blau's argument is based on a concept of identity that is univalent rather than multiple and contingent.

The confusion surrounding the establishment of Judaeo-Arabic as a distinct Jewish language may, in fact, be no more than an ideologically rooted attempt, conscious or unconscious, at reading the present into the past. In arguing the point that Judaeo-Arabic is a distinct language of the Jews, Blau argues against another fellow Jewish linguist, Israel Friedländer, who concludes that 'Judaeo-Arabic is not to be distinguished from the Arabic of the Muslims, although . . . Jewish authors are generally a shade nearer to popular Arabic than their Muslim counterparts if they are compared, as writers, category for category' (Blau 1988: 110). In his 1959 essay, Blau says that he believes that this view on the part of Friedländer is formulated against the sociopolitical climate of postemancipation Europe in which Jews like himself thought of themselves as members of their wider society, rather than as members of a closed Jewish community as obtained in Muslim lands: 'not even such excellent scholars as Israel Friedländer can always avoid the influence of the mental climate of their period' (Blau 1988: 110). According to this mental climate, a Jew can choose to forge for himself a non-Jewish identity, but this same opportunity was not available to the Jews in the Middle Ages because of the communal organisation of Jewish life, which blocked the possibility of a free identity choice by Jews. In a strange extension of this argument, Blau declares that Friedländer's conclusion 'sounds almost as if it had been put forward by "Arab nationals of the Mosaic persuasion"'(111).

Here, I think, we have a clue. Declaring that Judaeo-Arabic is not a distinct language but a variety of Arabic in Blau's early discussions of the topic would have eaten away at the argument of a historically rooted Jewish identity that is distinct from Islamo-Arab identity. Is it possible that in the same way that Friedländer might not have been able to escape the 'mental climate' of his time, Blau himself was unable to escape the mental climate of his time? Blau, in fact, raises this same question of positionality when he says that 'the present writer [Blau] is too conscious of himself being exposed to his own contemporary *Zeitgeist* in precisely the same way [as Friedländer] to be able to take his immunity [from the influence of this *Zeitgeist*] for granted' (110–11). Having raised the issue, however, Blau does not tell us in his 1959 essay what *Zeitgeist* he has in mind and what influences this *Zeitgeist* might have had on him as a scholar of Judaeo-Arabic. Might this *Zeitgeist* be, and this is speculation on my part, the political Zionism that could have dominated his life as a scholar and later as a citizen of the newly established state of Israel?

This speculation is, in fact, a guess, but it is the best guess I can offer to explain Blau's early views on the status of Judaeo-Arabic. The rise of Zionism and the establishment of the state of Israel have operated in two ways vis-à-vis the Arabic language. On the one hand, Arabic in the early decades of the twentieth century served as a repertoire for the revival of Hebrew. On the other hand, Arabic was the language of the Other, even the enemy, who resisted the claims of the Zionist movement of ownership over historical Palestine. Part of this claim was the positing of a historical continuity of Jewish identity (and its link to Palestine) that sought to distinguish it from Arab identity. And since Arab identity in most of the twentieth century was based on a unity of language above everything else, as well as on a hypothesised rootedness of this language-based identity in the past, being in this regard a mirror image of Hebrew-based identity, it would be consistent for Zionism to want to deny that the Arabs and Jews could have shared an intercommunal language-based identity in the past through Arabic in its various manifestations. In times of active political conflict, difference, rather than sameness or commonality, tends to operate across group boundaries.[37] The establishment of Judaeo-Arabic as a distinct language of the Jews in the Middle Ages and up to the modern period in its various manifestations would seem to lend itself to this Zionist ideology of difference and distinctiveness (which Arab nationalists also practised). If this is true, Blau's views on the status of Judaeo-Arabic in his 1959 and 1968 essays may be considered as an expression of the not uncommon practice in cultural and political nationalism of reading the present into the past and of positing greater differentiation and exclusivity between groups in the past than may have existed.[38]

This 'invention of tradition' type of conclusion,[39] tentative though it may be, may constitute another example of the workings of ideology (see above), in this case political ideology, in the conduct of linguistic enquiry. Put differently, this conclusion may be interpreted as providing evidence of how the Self of the researcher may, in fact, be ideologically implicated in the conduct of supposedly neutral and objective enquiry. Blau hints at his positionality as a researcher in his 1959 essay, but he does not specify the nature of this positionality, nor does he tell us about the changes affecting this positionality between this essay and his 1987 essay, in which he seems to have changed his mind radically about the linguistic status of Judaeo-Arabic, reverting to a position closer to that of Friedländer, whom he criticized for succumbing in his work to the 'mental climate' of his time.

37 This strategy of differentiation may be illustrated by the sociolinguistic phenomenon in Israeli society in its early days of treating linguistic amnesia and the active loss of the Arabic language as a sign of an emerging Israeli identity (see Suleiman 2006c).

38 In a conference on the 'Jews of Arab Culture' held in Cambridge, U.K., in June 2009, I heard one of the participants call the Arabic used by Iraqi Jews in Baghdad, where she was born and lived her early years, *'arabī yahūdī* ('Jewish Arabic'). When I asked this participant whether this was a description or a name of the Arabic she spoke, she insisted that it was a name. An Egyptian Jew who was with us at the time said that she never heard Jews in Egypt refer to their spoken Arabic in the same way. I later asked ten Iraqi Jewish participants at the conference if their Arabic speech in Iraq was called *'arabī yahūdī* by name, but they all denied it. The Jewish Iraqi lady's position represents the layperson's equivalent of reading the present into the past, seeking to establish greater distinctiveness and separation in Arabic than might have, in fact, existed at the time.

39 For the notion of the 'invention of tradition' in nationalist movements, see Hobsbawm (1983).

7.

The seventh fault zone concerns the existence of an important gap in the study of the Arabic language. I have referred to this gap in several places in this chapter, linking it to the notion of 'liminality' in some cases: it concerns the existence of a *residual space* between sociolinguistics and the neighbouring disciplines of politics, history and, to a lesser extent, anthropology, where some facts of and about language are left to languish in neglect. I have ascribed the existence of this residual space to discipline compartmentalization, the narrowing of empirical horizons in disciplines, and to the existence of a critical, if not, in fact, dismissive, attitude towards interdisciplinarity in the social sciences. There may also be institutional reasons behind this neglect, most of which have to do with the way the academy structures itself into units of teaching and research, as well as how funding is disbursed by research bodies and what counts as core and peripheral activity in disciplines with respect to researchers' career choices and ambitions.[40]

The political dimension of the Arabic language has been a long-term occupant of this residual space. I was so struck by this situation that more than a decade ago, I decided to suspend my research on the Arabic grammatical tradition and Arabic applied linguistics in order to excavate aspects of this space. Having read widely around the topic of the rise and progress of Arab nationalism, I was struck by how many times scholars have pointed to the importance of the Arabic language in nation building; but I was struck even more by the absence of any sustained study that explains the ways in which Arabic was used in this respect. The same is true of the role of Arabic in articulating political and social conflict in society or of the role of Arabic literature, especially poetry, in the formation of national consciousness (see Suleiman and Muhawi 2006). Translation could be another productive area for pursuing issues of national consciousness formation and nation building from this residual space of liminality. Political scientists, students of nationalism and historians tend to avoid these areas of residual research, maybe because they tend to think of them as belonging to the linguist and the literary critic or perhaps because they consider them to be fickle or soft data that are unable to yield the kind of information the various disciplines would take seriously within their parameters. Whatever the cause of neglect, there is no doubt that leaving residual sociopolitical linguistic spaces unmined is detrimental to our understanding of social phenomena in their full complexity and variety. As Joshua Fishman rightly reminds sociolinguists (1984: 45), using 'a number of methods could contribute to the

40 Sankoff (1988: 142) mentions the following factors that affect research paradigms in linguistics, including variationist sociolinguistics: 'disciplinary vogues and dogma, careers and ambitions, and thematic and strategic programmes of universities, foundations, and government agencies, as well as the less obvious processes determining the role of knowledge production and distribution in society.'

illumination of a common problem such that the sum total of contributions, from a variety of perspectives, was greater than that from any one alone, no matter how good that one might be or how attuned it might be to the preferences of individual researchers and to the traditions of particular disciplines.' Correlationist-variationist sociolinguistics has made important contributions to the study of Arabic in society, but its inward-looking ethos has not enabled it to interact with neighbouring disciplines in ways that can enrich our understanding of the multifaceted nature of language as a social phenomenon.

BEYOND THE FAULT ZONES

The seven fault zones described above have been framed against a set of binaries: correlationist versus noncorrelationist research, quantitative versus qualitative research, positivist versus nonpositivist methodology, realist versus nonrealist epistemology, symbolic versus instrumental function, folk-linguistics versus professional linguistics, ethnolinguistic versus structural taxonomies and disciplinary versus interdisciplinary enquiry. It would, however, be wrong to think of the terms in each of these binaries as standing in an either/or relationship, as the 'versus' in their formulation suggests, in the study of the Arabic-language situation; hence my avoidance of the term *fault line*, preferring instead *fault zone* to signal a sense of methodological and epistemological in-between-ness. Having been trained as a doctoral student years ago in the absolute value of ideological and methodological monism for reasons of consistency and because of the fear of eclecticism and having followed this path in some of my research, I am of the view that the residual place of liminality in the study of the Arabic language in the social world calls for a multiplicity of perspectives on which the above approaches converge with their methods, interpretations and epistemologies as partners and equals rather than as mutually exclusive trends. In offering this perspective, I am in complete agreement with Joshua Fishman when he points out: 'Methodological monism will get us nowhere . . . with respect to epistemological and substantive issues [in the study of language in the social world], just as it has gotten us nowhere in the past. There are various levels of analysis, various types of data, various approaches to proof, and they must each be appreciated for their contributions . . . as they must each be criticised for their limitations and blind spots . . . and, above all, they must be used together, in tandem, to reinforce and clarify each other, for the sake of the common enterprise' (1984: 41).

However, in pursuing a nonmonist approach to the study of the Arabic language in the social world, we must ensure that the ideological is recognised for what it is, that it should not be made to replace the intellectual or empirical in our frameworks of argumentation, but we should not ignore it, either. Each has its own place in the social sciences. However, the two may combine, as they do in critical methodologies, but this admixture must be the result of theoretical design and overt calculation, not accident or the pursuit of hidden agendas. An activist sociolinguistics is acceptable but only if it is built on secure nonideological foundations as far as possible, in which the positionality of the researcher is publicly declared and signposted whenever it comes into play. Labov (1982) provides an example of how this activist sociolinguistics may be pursued, although his positivist stance is thought to be too restrictive by more activist scholars.[41]

Following on from the above, this study will continue along the trail of the previous work I have done on Arabic, identity and conflict (Suleiman 2003; 2004b), in terms of subject matter and by applying a qualitative, symbolist and interdisciplinary framework for dealing with the issues it raises. As a study in cultural politics, the following chapters will reveal the multiple ways in which Arabic is networked into the structures of meaning in society. Chapter 3 will offer an application of the qualitative approach I have highlighted above to the study of Arabic and identity, in relation to the symbolic, rather than the instrumental, function of language, calling for the institution of a 'symbolic turn' in studying Arabic in the social world. The chapter will perform this task through an autoethnography of two sites of my language behaviour in the course of my work as an Arabic-language trainer of teachers in the Arabian Gulf region between 2004 and 2008. Linking Arabic to Self, I will reveal the situatededness or contextuality of identity at the individual level, the ideological nature of this identity and its instrumentality as a resource with which to do things for defined purposes, this being an aspect of identity that is not sufficiently stressed in the literature. The chapter will further investigate some of the methodological problems associated with autoethnographic research, including the implications for subjective bias of the precarious relationship between the Self of the researcher as researched subject.

Chapter 4 continues exploring the above interest in language and Self by investigating how the link between the two is constructed in autobiography. Linking this nexus of Self and language to displacement as an outcome of war or the reorganisation of the political and economic structures in society, the chapter will reveal the ubiquitous nature of language as a political phenomenon, both as a resource and as a proxy for articulating larger concerns in society. On the level of Self, language is linked with both fracture and reconciliation. The chapter further discusses the link between language and trauma in the context of war and the possibility of recovery at the societal level

41 See Cameron et al. (1992: 15–17) for a critique of Labov's views on activism in sociolinguistics. In this context, Cameron et al. (13–26) draw a distinction between ethics, advocacy and empowerment in sociolinguistic research. They describe the first as 'research *on* subjects,' the second as 'research *on* and *for* subjects' and the third as 'research *on*, *for* and *with* subjects.' Research on linguistic rights (Skutnabb-Kangas and Bucak 1994) and language ecology (Mühlhäusler 1996) provides examples of advocacy and some empowerment in language research. For empowering sociolinguistic research, see Cameron (1992); Frazer (1992); Harvey (1992); Rampton (1992).

through vernacularisation in Arabic. This perspective on vernacularisation as a path to recuperation reveals the extent to which Arabic diglossia is considered by some as a source of stagnation and underdevelopment in Arab society. However, this view on diglossia belongs to the realm of ideology, rather than intellectual argument, for the reasons I have suggested in the preceding section and as I will argue in due course.

Chapter 4 will further deal with the link among globalisation, language and anxiety in society. For this purpose, the chapter reveals that language-linked anxieties, as reflexes of the English-language-dominated globalisation of recent times, are not an Arab-specific phenomenon. It is important to note this to counter any conclusion that can feed into the Othering perspective in some Western discourse, which produces what is called Arab 'exceptionalism' or 'particularism' (see Halliday 2001). However, whether we are dealing with political or social displacement, anxiety or trauma, and whether the link between language and any of these is imagined or real, the ubiquity of language imposes itself on us as a space where interdisciplinary interest can be brought to bear on what I have called 'the residual space of liminality.'

Chapter 5 moves the discussion forward by considering the phenomenon of names in society against the background of Self, group identity, the diaspora as a form of displacement from an original point of departure and sociopolitical conflict. In Arabic sociolinguistics and anthropological linguistics, names have been studied primarily in terms of frequency patterns to discern the forces of continuity and change of social values in society. Social and cultural modernisation versus tradition is the main organising principle in framing the results of studies from this perspective. Arabic names lend themselves readily to this kind of study, because most of them are semantically transparent. The study of names in chapter 5 exploits this semantic transparency to get at the changes in the politics of meaning in Arab society.

While most previous sociolinguistic studies of names in the Arab milieu have focussed on personal names, chapter 5 expands this domain to include toponyms, ethnonyms and code names to show how naming is embroiled in conflict in the Middle East at the levels of Self and identity. This expansion creates strong links, through the power of symbolism, among language, history, anthropology and politics, which add to those forged with the study of personal names in these disciplines. The historical contexts for names of these types help situate them in frames of reference that can decipher their involvement in structures of power between nations and ethnic groups in conflict. Names of these types can also reveal in a clear way how language can be manipulated to achieve defined ends through acts of hegemony and resistance. The linguistic landscape in some parts of the Middle East, such as the Old City of Jerusalem, provides a palimpsest of the archaeology of power and control in this fragile urban space during the past eight decades. The city of Haifa provides another example of the intense politics of street names under both British and Israeli control.

Ideology is present at every turn in this book. This is what makes language quintessentially political, enabling it to be used as a campaigning tool and as a target against campaigning. The politics of language ideology may in some cases be well pronounced, either directly or through its deployment as a proxy for other tensions in society; this typically occurs in situations of active or heightened conflict such as exist in many parts of the Middle East. In other cases, language ideology may have low visibility or may, in fact, be invisible, but the dimmed lights of ideology should never be read as diminution in its ability to reignite, igniting language with it.

Chapter 3

Arabic, Self and Autoethnography

The aim of this chapter is to investigate the language-and-Self link in the study of Arabic in the social world. For this purpose, the chapter will investigate two sites in the authors' own linguistic behaviour as a teacher trainer in the Arabian Gulf region for the symbolic meanings they can yield in line with chapter 2. Central to this investigation is the concept of identity as a continuum that is bounded on one side by fixity and on the other by variability. The Self here is treated as a repertoire of roles, resources and attributes that are context-dependent.

The material in this chapter is presented as an autoethnography. It is written in a first-person voice to reflect on the experiences of the researcher as researched subject, using memory, introspection, self-reports and personal interpretation to retrieve the data and explain them. I am aware that autoethnography is controversial in social research and that its employment here is a novel practise in Arabic sociolinguistics; for these reasons, the chapter ends with a critique of the application of this mode of enquiry in this case.

FROM COLLECTIVE IDENTITY TO THE SELF

During the past decade, the main focus of my research has been the intersection of language, identity and conflict in the Middle East. Initially, my main interest was in collective identity in its national and ethnic manifestations, which I approached by examining how these forms of identification (the ethnic and the national) are articulated ideologically for task orientation in the cultural and, most important, political domains. This research led me to examine how languages in the Middle East are involved in social and political conflicts over cultural representation, school curricula, political and legal rights, nation building, state formation, memory and territory. In conducting this research, I was mainly interested in the macroanalysis of language as a cultural formation, or in its role as sociopolitical location for investigating the complex ways in which the group expresses its identity and pursues its interests in situations of conflict. In this connection, collective identity is sometimes treated as an essentialist construct or as a prediscursive phenomenon that points to an objective reality 'out there,' especially in ideologically driven discourse. In this sense, collective identity is viewed as a 'natural' or essentialist category of identification that is characterised by fixity and continuity over time and that is constrained by social structures that minimize or neutralize the role of human agency in shaping and reshaping identity. This, clearly, is an exaggerated and naïve view of identity.

But equally exaggerated are poststructuralist and postmodernist views that insist on the fracture, fragmentation, incoherence, amorphousness, decentring or incessant flexibility of identity.[1] Identities are not given, but they do not undergo radical transformation all the time. They are expressed through lifestyles, but they are not in themselves lifestyles. This is particularly true of individual identity, which I call Self here to distinguish it from collective identity.[2] While the Self cannot be completely fixed and homogeneous, the postmodern idea that it has 'no stable core but is . . . discontinuous and fragmented' cannot be true, either, as an alternative paradigm (Sermijn et al. 2008: 634). The emphasis on the rampant variability and mercurial temporariness of the Self in postmodernism is categorically the same, in spite of the difference in content, as the emphasis on the fixity and coherence of the Self in naïve-realist or realist-positivist modes of thinking. As two ends of the spectrum, these two views agree on eliminating the middle ground, denying that identity exists on a continuum that is bounded by fixity on one end and by variability on the other.

For this reason, I steer a middle course between these two views in this study, although it is hard to establish where fixity ends and variability begins. This is a weakness in my position that I cannot eliminate, but in the competing rhetorics of the Self between the total coherence of the realist-positivist paradigm and the incoherence of its postmodernist alternative, the middle ground is bound to have some intuitive appeal that accords with how people experience their identity (or aspects of it). Embodying stability with change, continuity with discontinuity, homogeneity with heterogeneity and unity with fragmentation, these currents in the making and marking of the Self and collective identity are to be conceived not as separate or unrelated binaries but as forces in a buzzing beehive of order and diversity. In thinking about the Self, I take a view that considers the individual as a 'basket [or, better still, 'repertoire,' to avoid the notion of accumulation conveyed by 'basket'] of selves which come to the surface at different social moments as appropriate' (Cohen 1994: 11). This view will be expounded in the linguistic autoethnography that follows.

I have dealt with issues of identity and conflict in the Middle East insofar as these relate to language in two book-length studies (Suleiman 2003; 2004b). The main focus of these two studies was group identity and

1 This postmodern concept of identity is linked to globalisation, multiculturalism and the emphasis on consumption and political struggles in modern society (see Widdicombe 1998: 204–6).

2 In this work, *identity* is used as a cover term for both *collective identity* and *Self*.

intergroup conflict at the supranational, national, subnational and ethnic levels. These studies were driven by a quantitative and symbolist framework, with the aim of mining the political meanings in what I have described in chapter 2 as 'residual spaces of liminality.' This book continues this interest in the nexus of language, identity and conflict in the Middle East from the twin perspectives of qualitative and symbolist research, as I have discussed these in chapter 2. But it also injects a new direction. It focuses on many parts on the Self (individual identity) and language, a topic I introduced into play in my study of language and conflict in Israel and Jordan (Suleiman 2004b).

In this context, my main interest in this chapter will be aspects of my own linguistic behaviour as an Arabic-language trainer in the Arabian Gulf, with the aim of showing that issues of identity are complex and positional and that they crop up in ordinary contexts to serve a variety of extralinguistic purposes. In particular, I am interested in a set of sites of identity, as these are displayed in my language production, while training the Arabic-language teachers in Doha on the use of the *Curriculum Standards for the State of Qatar: Arabic Grades K to 12,* which I authored with Alaa Elgibali of the University of Maryland (2004). In analysing these linguistic sites of identity, I will reflect on what I think informs them, whether it is my ideological views, public self-image, instrumental purposes, the immediate contexts of situation, the role of the audience as a constraining factor, private fears, or any historically situated social or political frames of reference pertaining to these sites.

I am aware that this kind of exploration is fraught with methodological problems, not least the fact that I am acting as informant and analyst or as researcher and researched subject at the same time and that my data are delayed[3] or retrospective self-reports[4] that I, as a researcher, have retrieved from memory (long) after the event. This is why I am offering the following accounts of identity in the form of an exploratory linguistic autoethnography, as a self-reflexive set of observations and analyses which, I hope, may receive cross-subjective validation in future research. Such validation would induce confidence in this line of enquiry and ascertain the reliability of the conclusions I draw. However, I am also aware that others may disagree with my views, as will become clear in chapter 4 in my discussion of the place of the *fuṣḥā* in Arab culture. I will deal with these and other methodological issues later in this chapter.

Some contextual information about my work as Arabic-language teacher trainer in the Gulf region is necessary here before I begin this autoethnographic exploration. In 2002, Qatar initiated a wide-ranging and, in the Arab

3 For an interesting application of 'delayed data,' see Köroğlu (2007).

4 See McDonough (1978) and Suleiman (1992) for the use of self-reports in language learning.

context, pioneering educational reform, which led to the writing of the *Curriculum Standards for the State of Qatar* in 2004 (Suleiman and Elgibali 2004), along with standards for English, mathematics and science (biology, chemistry and physics). The production of these standards coincided with the establishment in September 2004 of what have been called the Independent Schools in Qatar (*madāris mustaqilla*), which roughly equate to the Charter Schools in the United States (Brewer et al. 2007). In 2005, I was additionally asked to produce a set of *Arabic Schemes of Work for the State of Qatar* (Suleiman et al. 2006) to help teachers implement the standards. Starting in September 2004, I was asked to conduct standards-based teacher training, which continued until the spring of 2008. In 2007, most of the training took place in the basement of the Education Institute in Doha. The building has four training halls in the basement. Sometimes the training for all four subjects (Arabic, English, mathematics and science) took place at the same time, mostly in the evenings. During prayer times and coffee breaks, teachers congregated in an open space in the basement to socialize. The training for all subjects was mixed; it was attended by male and female teachers from a variety of Arab backgrounds (mainly Egyptians, Iraqis, Jordanians, Palestinians, Syrians and female Qatari teachers). For most of the training, I was the principal trainer, but I had help from cotrainers who also acted as observers for feedback purposes.[5]

USING THE *FUṢḤĀ*, MARKING THE SELF

In the context of my teacher-training work in Qatar (and elsewhere), *fuṣḥā* refers to a continuum of styles or levels of language that are perceived to be noncolloquial by the teachers participating in the training. *Fuṣḥā* here is a matter of perception and degree, rather than a precisely defined category of inclusion and exclusion. Furthermore, as used in this chapter, the term *fuṣḥā* does not completely describe the materials used in the training, a very limited portion of which was, in fact, in the colloquial, but refers to the variety of Arabic I used to conduct the training. This *fuṣḥā* aimed at eliminating the following: (1) salient phonological and morphological features of the principal trainer's colloquial dialect, for example, the use of the glottal stop instead of [q] of the *fuṣḥā*; (2) lexical items and classroom-management expressions that are identifiably colloquial, for example, *kwayyis* instead of

5 Between 2003 and 2008, my training was observed by a number of experts: Amal Ayoubi (School of Oriental and African Studies), Alaa Elgibali (University of Maryland), Hanna Haidar (City University of New York), Ronak Husni (American University of Sharjah, UAE), Gada Khalil (UNRWA, Jordan), Muna al-Kuwwari (Education Institute, Qatar), Abir Najjar (Jordan University), Ibtisam Naji (Education Institute, Qatar), Saleh Nusseirat (University of Maryland), Abdul Gabbar al-Sharafi (Sultan Qaboos University) and Iman Aziz Soliman (American University in Cairo). To the best of my knowledge, all institutional associations are current ones.

aḥsanta/i ('well done!') in *fuṣḥā* Arabic; (3) prosodic features, mainly tones of voice, that are characteristic of speech in the colloquial dialect; and (4) rare words and expressions that characterise the high end of the *fuṣḥā*. This *fuṣḥā* further aimed at using as much word-final vowelling (*i'rāb*) as possible, especially when I was certain of its correctness. In cases of doubt, I did not vowel the endings of words, using what is called the principle of *taskīn* in Arabic, in conformity with the linguistically sanctioned maxim *sakkin taslam* ('when unsure, suppress word-final vowels to be on the safe side'). This operational definition of *fuṣḥā* corresponds to what Badawi (1973) calls *fuṣḥā al-muthaqqafīn* ('educated *fuṣḥā*') in his study of the Arabic-language situation in Egypt.

In what follows, I will provide a set of reflections on my use of the *fuṣḥā* in the Qatar training insofar as this relates to questions of the Self and identity. The immediate aim of these reflections is to provide autoethnographic explanations of why I opted for the *fuṣḥā* in conducting this training, although I know I make mistakes in it, instead of using a form of Arabic that is heavily inclined towards my own dialect to minimize error making on my part. I knew this was a risky choice; some of the teachers were very proficient in the use of the *fuṣḥā*, and some among them felt very strongly about using it correctly. The fact that these teachers made their displeasure clear when their colleagues committed errors made my choice even more risky: I could become the target of their criticisms.[6] So, what were the factors that drove me to use the *fuṣḥā* at such a high intensity in my training when, in fact, I could have been exposing myself to damaging criticism and some loss of face professionally through this choice?

The most obvious answer may relate to a desire on my part to respond to the expectations of the audience in a particular professional setting: as Arabic-language teachers, they would expect me to use the *fuṣḥā*. This expectation on the part of the teachers may be justified but only up to a point. I say this because my experience in teacher training in Qatar and other Arab countries suggests that Arabic teachers may, in fact, prefer to use an elevated form of their colloquial dialect in professional settings, either out of habit or, most probably, because they want to avoid making mistakes in the *fuṣḥā* in front of their peers.[7] However, this fear of making mistakes,

6 Teachers in this group think of themselves as guardians and defenders of the language. In a recent intervention, the head of the Department of Arabic at King Saud University in Riyadh, Saudi Arabia, has dubbed these guardians the 'neo-cons' of Arabic grammar. Pursuing this analogy further, he calls the extremists among them *al-Luyīsiyyūn*, after Bernard Lewis, who is reputed to take a strong pro-Zionist line in his advice to the neo-cons on matters related to Islam, the War on Terror and the Arab-Israeli conflict. See *Al-Watan* (2008).

7 This, in my experience, is particularly true of female teachers and, also, most Egyptian teachers regardless of gender. Prestige as a factor in the speech habits of Arabic speakers operates differentially across the sexes, with women favouring prestige dialectal forms and men preferring *fuṣḥā* forms (see Ibrahim 1986). This may explain why members of the awkward squad were mainly men.

bordering on some kind of linguistic anxiety,[8] may be counterbalanced by the fact that teachers who may dare to criticise their colleagues—the 'awkward squad,' as I privately would call them in my Qatar training—often end up criticising each other the harshest, driven in this regard by their having an axe to grind or by the desire to author acts of one-upmanship for social and professional display, or for public ratification of their expertise and group affirmation of their self-worth.[9] In spite of this, the consistent use of the *fuṣḥā* in professional settings, even among Arabic-language teachers, is not a norm in my experience. This implies that my choice of the *fuṣḥā* was not a foregone conclusion, since I could have safely opted for an elevated form of my colloquial dialect or, alternatively, what is sometimes called Educated Spoken Arabic (Mitchell 1978; Mitchell 1986; Sallam 1979; Sallam 1980). Owing to this, my use of the *fuṣḥā* must have been motivated by additional factors.

Before dealing with these factors, it may be worth considering the extent of personal and professional risk to which I exposed myself through my choice of the *fuṣḥā* as the medium for the training. For a start, I knew that my exposure to risk could be serious but that it was, nevertheless, quite manageable. It was obvious to me that any critical behaviour by members of the awkward squad would most probably lead to antagonising their colleagues, the majority in the training, who would feel personally threatened by them. These teachers would most probably reason to themselves that if members of the awkward squad could get away with criticising me, they would definitely feel emboldened to criticise them. Defending me would, therefore, be their first line of self-defence. Second, I knew that members of the awkward squad would be inclined to think twice before daring to criticise me; they were bound to calculate that such an act on their part might not come without a cost. Criticising me in this situation would be tantamount to criticising a person in a position of professional authority in relation to them who, in retaliation, might do them harm by writing negative training reports about them or by criticising their performance on his visits to observe their teaching in the schools where they worked.

Clearly, I was in a position of institutional power in relation to the teachers attending the training, including members of the awkward squad.

8 A telling example of this linguistic anxiety occurred at the time of the Egyptian Revolution in 1952. Gamal Abdul-Nasir instructed Brigadier Jamal Hammad to write the First Declaration of the Revolution. Hammad related (in *Akhir sa'a*, an Egyptian weekly magazine, 22 July 2009, p. 32) that in composing this declaration, his first priority was to write it in a 'well-knit [*raṣīn*] style that is free of any linguistic mistakes lest people inside or outside Egypt do not take us seriously.' This anxiety seems to be deep-rooted in Arab culture. The Umayyad Caliph 'Abd al-Malik Ibn Marwan (d. AH 86/AD 705), an accomplished user of the language, is reported to have said that his diligence in avoiding mistakes in his Friday sermons 'turned his hair white prematurely' (Suleiman 2003: 53–54).

9 Most teachers in this category were male and university-educated, with degrees (ranging from BA to PhD) in Arabic.

This power was further bolstered by the fact that I had a doctorate, which, in Arab society, still endows its holder with status and prestige, particularly if it was gained from a Western university, as mine was. I could add to this, as another source of power, the fact that I am male, while most of the teachers in the training were female, and that I was older than most of the teachers, two prestige factors that in Arab society could cushion me against blatant criticism, provided that I was not hopelessly bad at my job. Not only would criticising me be seen as a risky matter because of my power as the (principal) trainer, but it would additionally constitute an infringement of some of the norms in Arab society that bind members of the majority in the training to one another, maybe causing them to stand up to members of the awkward squad.

I was fully aware of all of these considerations, including the need to co-opt members of the awkward squad socially in the coffee breaks to minimise any desire on their part to criticise me if I made mistakes in the *fuṣḥā*. My decision to opt for the *fuṣḥā* in my training did not, therefore, seem to be all that risky. Furthermore, I knew that even if I made mistakes, I could always try to have them 'forgiven' by invoking the maxim that it would be better to try to use the *fuṣḥā* though I make mistakes in it than not to use it at all, exploiting as background to this defence strategy the Prophetic Hadith according to which those who strive to provide sound judgement/opinion (*ijtihād*)—in my case, correct *fuṣḥā* Arabic—but fail will receive in the hereafter double the reward given to those who try to offer such opinion and succeed. I did, in fact, use this strategy to compliment teachers who made mistakes in the *fuṣḥā* when I felt that they might come under attack from members of the awkward squad. The point behind this defence strategy is simple common sense that is also socially and religiously sanctioned: making mistakes in the *fuṣḥā* is better than avoiding it. This may be considered as an overextension of the scope of the Hadith, but it is justified by the connection between Islam and the *fuṣḥā*.

Clearly, my decision to use the *fuṣḥā* was not such a big risk after all. It was a rational decision that I made by reference to a number of calculations. First, using the *fuṣḥā* enabled me to project the professional image of a trainer who valued this highly regarded variety of Arabic and was not afraid of making mistakes when using it. Using the *fuṣḥā* in the training, therefore, signalled cultural belonging and professional self-confidence on my part, two important attributes in constructing a healthy relationship with the teachers. The appeal to the Prophetic Hadith to justify or explain away mistakes in the *fuṣḥā* was clearly intended to take the high moral ground against the awkward squad by appealing to the commonsense notion that it was better to try and fail than not to try at all. The reference to the Prophetic Hadith also depicted me as a trainer rooted in his culture, a fact that I knew would enhance my standing among the teachers, the majority of whom displayed outward signs of religiosity (veils, beards, rosary beads, Islamic modes of greeting and praying in the coffee breaks). Using this strategy was ultimately aimed, should the need arise, at turning the tables on members of the awkward squad by depicting them as mean-spirited and untrue to the spirit of tolerance inherent in their cultural and religious traditions. Finally, I knew that in the context of the training, the cards were stacked in my favour. I had authority and power by virtue of my position as the principal trainer; this was supported by my status as the holder of a doctorate from a Western university and by my being older than most of the teachers in the training.

My decision to use the *fuṣḥā*, therefore, showed me to be a good risk taker. However, I knew that this would only work if (1) I did not make too many mistakes or big 'howlers,' such as putting a singular subject (*fā'il*) in the genitive; and (2) I was able to maintain good rapport with the teachers, including members of the awkward squad, to keep them on my side and even to learn from them (which would appeal to their vanity or self-esteem). The point, however, in all of this is the centrality of issues of personal identity as a site of language behaviour that, on the surface, might have been considered banal and mundane. By digging deeper into this site, the language-Self link is revealed to be complex, positional and subject to the machinations of human agency.

But there were other reasons behind my use of the *fuṣḥā*. One relates to my view of myself as an Arab first *before* being a Palestinian or perhaps as an Arab first because I am a Palestinian. Notwithstanding the difficulty of defining what being an Arab means, I am so content to be one that when people (especially Arabs) ask me where I come from, I sometimes answer that I am an Arab. I did this particularly in my training in Qatar. This response confused my interlocutors, causing them to answer, 'I am an Arab, too, but I am from Egypt [or Syria or Jordan], so which country are you from?' Sometimes they tried to get the same answer by asking me where I was born, but when I refused to tell them, they would walk away in frustration. On these occasions, some of my interlocutors felt socially rudderless and confused, because I had deprived them of a compass direction in relation to which they could start the work of locating me in their social world, to read into me all of the preexisting sociopolitical meanings they might have associated with my 'submerged' nationality. For these teachers, I constructed myself as a semi-open/semi-closed book or as a nameless map in deciphering of which they would need to look for alternative clues, for example, any vernacular inflection in my *fuṣḥā* speech. My use of the *fuṣḥā* was, therefore, intended to obstruct any attempt to this effect on their part, as I will discuss below.

The teachers' insistence on establishing my country-linked identity shows the extent to which nation-state identities have become entrenched in the Arabic-speaking world. The teachers were not satisfied with the broadest definition I gave them, that of being Arab, as a specification of my identity. They felt that this did not identify me with sufficient precision. They wanted an identity label with a higher degree of specification. I did not blame them for feeling that way, not least because Arabic speakers tend to use nation-state identities in mixed national settings, such as those in the Gulf region, as passwords to unlock a set of predetermined indices of interpretation that help them orient themselves in interacting with one another. Being Egyptian, Syrian, Lebanese, Saudi or Palestinian carries with it stereotypical and other constructed meanings which interlocutors use in interacting with one another. With these indices, Arabic speakers can determine the degree of intimacy or distance they may wish to contract with one another in social interaction, or they may use these indices to open or close further spaces for finer readings of their interlocutors, for example, by asking in which village, city or part of a city an interlocutor was born to apply to them more refined schemas of interpretation. For example, among Palestinians, the main schema of identification consists of whether a person is *Madani* ('city person') or *Fellahi* ('country person') and if *Madani*, which city in Palestine he came from or even in which part or quarter of that city he originated. For the teachers, these categories acted as though they were cartographic conventions on a map that could help them navigate through their interlocutor (the principal trainer, in this case) as if he were a topographic text. These subcategories of identification could then be used in an economy of social values to determine the kind of status or prestige a person might be allocated, or they might be used to tell an interlocutor that they themselves came from the same city or village or that they had a friend in common who came from the same city or village, thus creating bonds between these interlocutors directly or indirectly.

By telling the teachers that I was an Arab, I tried to foreclose these avenues of interpretation and social-value allocation that would box me into a preconceived category of group-related meanings. This move on my part afforded me more freedom to construct who I wanted to be, while at the same time expressing my Arab signs of belonging as indices of my identity. Furthermore, by saying that I was an Arab and by using the *fuṣḥā* as the medium of my speech—this is the important point here—I tried to thwart any attempt on the part of any group of teachers to claim me as their own on nation-state grounds. To be an Arab and to use the *fuṣḥā* as a motif for this Arabness meant belonging to all of the national groups represented in the training, rather than to one exclusive *fuṣḥā*-based state-national identity. This more inclusive identity was important for my professional persona: I wanted to be perceived as equidistant from (or equally near to) all of the teachers, knowing that if I was not, I might be accused of favouritism. It was important to avoid this charge, not least because accusations of favouritism could affect my chances of being invited back to conduct more training in future years. The loss of such an opportunity would not only have a financial cost but would deprive me of (1) a golden opportunity to play a role in a flagship project of reforming Arabic-language teaching, which, as an Arab, I considered to be a great privilege; (2) the opportunity to collect more data on this reform, which I wanted to use in my research, as I am doing here; and (3) the opportunity to practice self-therapy by exorcising some of the demons of the past as represented in the excesses of the grammar-based teaching I had to endure and suffer as a student in Palestine.[10] Clearly, my saying that I was an Arab and my speaking in the *fuṣḥā* in the training were interconnected and multilayered practises through which I intended to (1) express my views of who I was in nationality terms, rather than nation-state or citizenship terms; (2) bolster my professional persona as a teacher trainer; (3) protect my interests as a researcher who needed to have access to data; (4) protect an income stream through renewed opportunities for consultancy work; and (5) in a form of DIY therapy, cleanse the Self of the pedagogic demons of the past, of the excesses of 'grammar abuse' I had suffered as a student.[11] Speaking in the *fuṣḥā* was a choice laden with a variety of symbolic meanings for me: national, professional, economic and personal.

To ensure that I stood a good chance of achieving the above objectives, I knew I must use the *fuṣḥā* and do so without country-specific inflections as much as I could, which I think I did successfully. Arabic speakers use these inflections to guess the nation-state identity or region of a *fuṣḥā* speaker. I am attuned to these inflections myself and use them for exactly this purpose, for example, when I am watching the news on Arab satellite TV.

The following example from the training illustrates how teachers resort to these country/region inflections to guess the national identity of a speaker. In January 2008, the Education Institute in Qatar asked the trainers of the first four core subjects in the educational reforms (Arabic, English, mathematics and science) to exchange experiences by training the teachers in the other subjects on aspects of their (the trainers') work. As part of this programme, I trained the mathematics teachers on the Arabic standards. As was my usual practise, I spoke in the *fuṣḥā*. I was, however, surprised that instead of following the training, the mathematics teachers wanted to know my country of origin. I gave them my usual answer that I was an Arab, but this did not satisfy them. At several points in the training, the teachers interrupted me to guess my country of origin, using my spoken *fuṣḥā* as their main clue. Some thought I was Syrian or Lebanese, others were sure that I was Tunisian or Libyan, while others, a minority, believed that I was Jordanian. Now, I am a Jordanian citizen, but I do not speak with stereotypical (male) Jordanian inflection in the *fuṣḥā*, for example, a throaty *'ayn* or a hard *jīm* (as in 'jam,' instead of the soft *jīm* as in 'pleasure,' which I tend to use). Not a single teacher, however, thought I was Palestinian (my nationality), although all agreed that I could not be Egyptian, which indicates the high

10 Instead of proposing a grammar-based set of standards, we opted for standards that were text-type-driven. Not only did this make the grammar teaching function-based, but it also reduced the excessive reliance on grammatical forms as the organising principle pedagogically. The teaching of grammar in Arabic schools is the most challenging part of the Arabic curriculum, which most students tend to dread, as I did.

11 See Niazi (2008) and Khalifa (2008) for discussions of the teaching of Arabic grammar and, therefore, the *fuṣḥā* in Arabic schools. Khalifa provides a reading of an amusing poem by the Saudi poet and diplomat Ghazi al-Qusaybi on the topic.

recognisability factor of this variety of Arabic. The attempt to guess my identity went on for the duration of the training session, reflecting social curiosity and anxiety at the same time.[12]

This intense interest in my identity on the teachers' part indicates the importance in mixed Arab settings of establishing the nationality of interlocutors as a way of navigating social and professional interactions. It also reveals how language provides important clues in establishing these identities. The fact that the colloquial dialects are the norm in these, as in most, interactions provides speakers with rich clues to perform this task of 'identity spotting.' However, these clues become impoverished when speakers use the *fuṣḥā*. On these occasions, speakers look for country/region-bound inflections in the way the *fuṣḥā* is used, mainly through phonological and lexical clues. Some of these clues are easily recognised, for example the pronunciation of [j] as [g] or [dh] as [z] in Egyptian Arabic, but most of the clues the speakers use are inchoate. This makes the task of identifying a person from the dialectal inflection in his spoken *fuṣḥā* an impressionistic judgement. This impressionism increases when a speaker uses the *fuṣḥā* in a country/region-neutral way, as do, for example, most of the news readers on Al Jazeera.

In this respect, my use of country-neutral *fuṣḥā* was intended to underpin my claim of being an Arab, which, in my mind, is not linked to a particular Arab country. But it was this that the teachers could not accept at face value. For them, Arabness was not enough to identify an Arab when nation-state identities are the norm in the identity parade.[13] My refusal to identify myself in country terms and the absence of country-linked clues in my spoken *fuṣḥā* were, therefore, disconcerting 'postures' to the teachers. Instead of being read as I intended them, these 'postures' were viewed as attempts at dissembling, at withholding some relevant information to which the teachers felt they were entitled. In fact, some teachers felt that I was hiding something from them. Some also felt that I might be doing this because I was ashamed of my background, the typical expression being 'Are you ashamed of your origins?' (*inta/e khajlān min aṣlak?*). Others thought that I did not 'play ball fairly' in the identity game: they were entitled to know where I came from, since they told me where they came from. At times, teachers would walk away displeased with me, or they might come back again to interrogate me, having spoken to a cotrainer.

12 This session was attended by my cotrainer, Amal Ayoubi of the School of Oriental and African Studies in London.

13 Arabness and Palestinianness are constructed categories. This implies that they are imagined differently by different people, while at the same time showing some overlap or a 'common core.' Both the overlaps and the differences enable these categories to be used as resources in identity negotiation in society. In this research, these two categories represent long-term subject positions in comparison with my negative attitudes towards affectation and display in speech, which will be discussed later.

This intense activity in class and in the coffee breaks signals the importance of identity in mixed Arab settings and how closely linked this identity is to language as a marker of nationality. In fact, I never anticipated that my use of the *fuṣḥā* would arouse such intense interest or that it would be so strongly and intimately linked with issues of identity. The curious thing is that this marking of identity worked in reverse as a kind of unmarking of identity in relation to the dominant nation-state identities. Speaking a country/region-neutral *fuṣḥā* marks the speaker with a weak form of identity, which challenges the nation-state norms of reference that are heavily inscribed in Arab social life.

I said above that my view of my own identity as an Arab is strongly linked to my being Palestinian.[14] In view of this, the question may arise about why my *fuṣḥā* speech was not marked with a strong Palestinian vernacular inflection in the training. Was it because I was ashamed to acknowledge publicly that I was Palestinian?[15] Or was it, indeed, because I genuinely felt as an Arab first and a Palestinian second or equally as a Palestinian and an Arab? In response, I can say that I am not ashamed of being Palestinian and that I do genuinely feel as an Arab first and as a Palestinian second or, at least, equally Arab and Palestinian. I can go further and say that this play of identities is directly linked to my use of the *fuṣḥā* without country/region inflection in the training. Let me explain.

I happen to believe that the problem of Palestine is not a purely Palestinian problem but an Arab one. My identity in this respect is the product of many influences, including the school curricula under which I was educated in Jerusalem in the 1960s. I also happen to believe that the Palestinians do need Arab help and support, at the official and popular levels, to achieve their independence and secure their national rights. Because of this, I think it is important that I, a Palestinian, do what I can to maintain and service all existing links and channels of communication with all Arabs, regardless of their nationality, ethnic affiliation, religious background or gender. Claiming that I am an Arab and, more important, using the *fuṣḥā* on those occasions where I can do so in public fora are considered by me, delusionally perhaps, as important steps in this direction. This allows me to claim symbolically that—at some sociocultural and even political level—I am Syrian, Lebanese, Qatari, Omani, Tunisian, and so on.

14 I am, of course, aware that my identity is more complex. Having spent most of my life in Scotland and England, I also feel a strong sense of belonging to Scottish and British identities. And having moved to Cambridge in 2007, I know I have started to develop additional layers of belonging to my identity repertoire.

15 I was very surprised when the minister of religious endowments of a Gulf country, on a visit to Cambridge in November 2009, responded in this way when, having told him that I was an Arab, I added to a further question about my identity that I was Palestinian. To my surprise, he said that there was no need for me to be ashamed of being Palestinian. This was the first time that I was met by this response (this incident took place almost a year after I had finished writing this chapter).

Owing to this, my identity as an Arab must be a mixture of personal conviction and national interest. But as the discussion above has revealed, it is also a matter of principle and instrumentality, conviction and convenience, the personal and the collective, in addition to being context-bound. It is a complex identity, plural, not singular. It is a repertoire rather than a single theme. It involves roles and is used as a resource. And it is intimately linked to my positive attitudes towards the *fuṣḥā* and my using it without country/region-linked inflections in my training to achieve as many objectives as possible. The *fuṣḥā* may, therefore, be considered a motif for aspects of my identity repertoire. Using it may further be considered a form of self-deployment in public fora for image projection, as well as for instrumental purposes.

But there is more to this *fuṣḥā*-linked identity than the points I have made in the preceding discussion. I strongly feel that the state of being Palestinian is one of being an underdog in the Middle East. In these days of the hegemonic and coercive nation-state in the Arabic-speaking world, pan-Arabism is another manifestation of the underdog in the political life of the Middle East. And so is the *fuṣḥā*, which is being challenged from different directions and for different reasons by the colloquial dialects and by English and French, as will be discussed in chapter 4. And as a motif of aspects of my identity, the *fuṣḥā* symbolises my deeply felt personal marginality. As a Palestinian in exile, I have always thought of myself as a marginal (though not necessarily marginalised) person, even when in my professional life, I was close to the centre of some important institutional or national developments or events. Speaking in the *fuṣḥā* on my part was, therefore, a way of standing up for a number of underdogs in the political and cultural life of the Arabic-speaking world. It was also a way of dealing with my personal marginality.

Standing up for the *fuṣḥā*, for this is how I conceptualised my use of it in the training to what was a captive audience, was a proxy for matters of great concern to me at the personal and national levels. It was a way of asserting an identity that encompassed my exilic/diasporic and preexilic/diasporic life. It was a mode of cultural and psychological resistance against marginality in my personal life and hegemony in the public sphere. And it was a way of symbolically resolving some of my deep-seated anxieties, albeit momentarily. The *fuṣḥā* was not just a motif of aspects of the Self; it was also a form of therapy for this Self.

The teachers at the training knew that I was educated in Britain, that I worked in Britain, and that I had lived most of my life in Britain. I could have used these facts to opt for an elevated form of my colloquial dialect or for Educated Spoken Arabic, instead of using the *fuṣḥā* in the training, on the grounds that my Arabic had gotten rusty over the years. The fact that I did not avail myself of this option but insisted on using the *fuṣḥā* helped me project an image to the teachers of an Arab who had remained true to his roots and cultural heritage. The teachers appreciated this and reciprocated by trying to use the *fuṣḥā* as much as possible. Some transferred this interest

(روائع التعبير)

أي ياسر أتحفتنا بروائع　　أزهارها من لمعة التنوير
اليسر في حسن الكلام دلالة　　للرشد بل للعلم والتفكير
هذي طرائق درسنا في دورة　　قدمتها بوسائل التغيير
أبدعت إذ فصلت كل صغيرة　　والنحو يخدم من عرى التصوير
والبيك يبكي بعد عز قد مضى　　استبدل الأوطان بالتهجير
تعطي عطاء لا يحاكى مثله　　في الوصف في الإقناع في التفسير
لافض فوك جمعت كل كريمة　　حسنا يقال لكل لفظ حرير
لله درك كم جمعت محاسنا　　في البحث عن معنى بلا تقصير
أسعدتنا بطريقة أسلوبها　　سهل منيع دائم التدوير
وختمتها ببطاقة لهوية　　قسمتها بحرائر التعبير
بقصيدة حبكت نسيج خيوطها　　أنا عربي من ثورة التحرير
إنا نقدم شكرنا لك خاصة　　ولكل من يسعى إلى التطوير

إهداء للأستاذ الدكتور : ياسر
منسق اللغة العربية : عبد العزيز الحرباوي
مدرسة محمد بن عبد الوهاب الثانوية المستقلة .
١٨/ ١ /٢٠٠٧ م

Figure 3.1. Exquisite expression (l. 5, reference to Mikhail Na'imeh's short story '*Sa'adat al-beik*'; l. 10, Darwish's poem '*Bitaqat huwiyyah*').

to the schools and insisted on using the *fuṣḥā* in their teaching, even at grade one.[16] Students picked up the language and started to use it spontaneously and without affectation or embarrassment, as I was able to observe on my school visits. By giving the teachers pride in the language and confidence in their ability to use it, I wanted to bring about a change in the image of the *fuṣḥā* in the schools. I wanted it to be seen as a vibrant and living language, instead of a boring and frozen one, as it is often perceived in schools throughout the Arabic-speaking world. I felt that I was on a crusade/*jihad* to achieve a number of pedagogic and national goals, each of which was expressive of aspects of my identity.

16 Some schools, in fact, added to this by conducting extended workshops on speaking *fuṣḥā* for their teachers. Most schools employed Abdulla al-Dannan for this purpose. A renowned proponent of the *fuṣḥā*, al-Dannan was responsible for scripting the popular children's programme *Iftaḥ yā simsim* ('Sesame Street' in Arabic) in a simplified form of the language. See Abu-Absi (1990); Abu-Absi (1991); Alosh (1984); Palmer (1979).

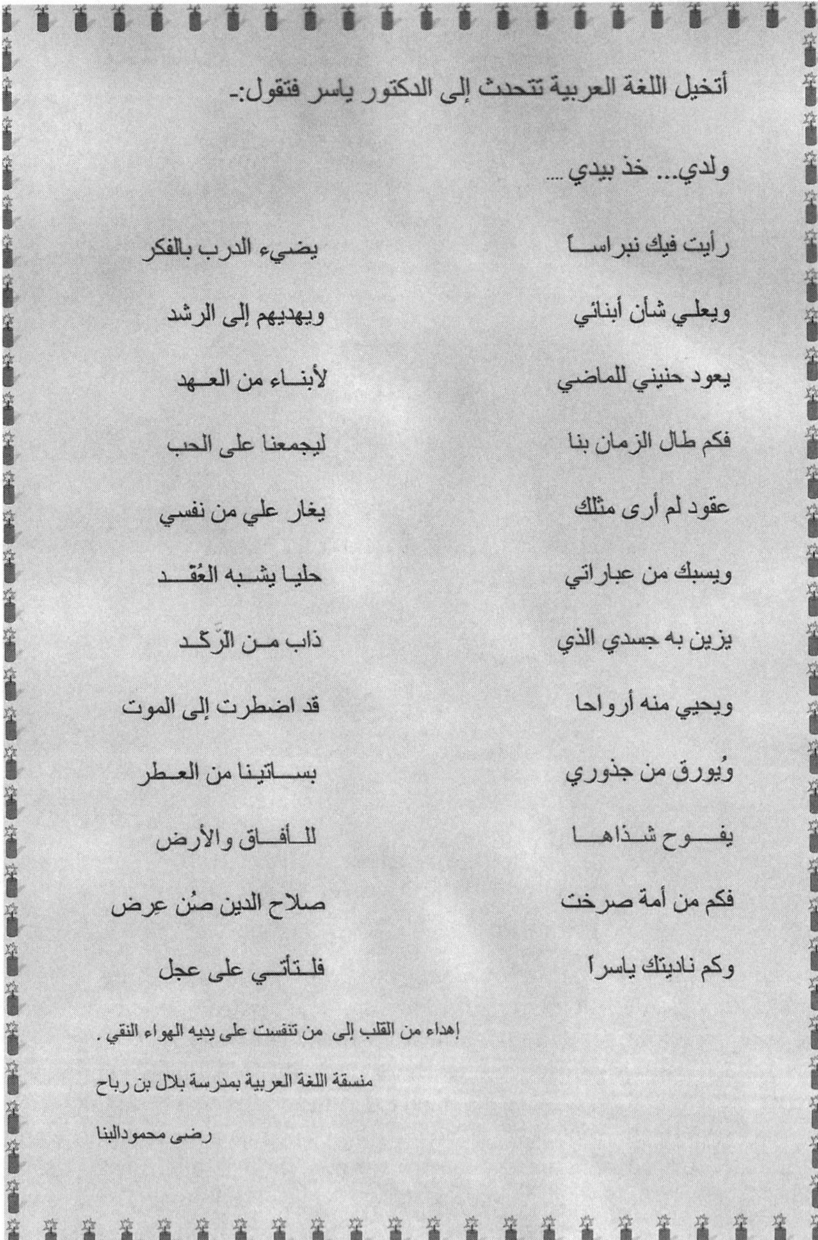

أتخيل اللغة العربية تتحدث إلى الدكتور ياسر فتقول:-

ولدي... خذ بيدي ....

رأيت فيك نبراسـاً   يضيء الدرب بالفكر

ويعلـي شأن أبنائي   ويهديهم إلى الرشد

يعود حنيني للماضي   لأبنـاء من العـهد

فكم طال الزمان بنا   ليجمعنا على الحب

عقود لم أرى مثلك   يغار علي من نفسي

ويسبك من عباراتي   حليا يشـبه العُقـد

يزين به جسدي الذي   ذاب مـن الرَّكـد

ويحيي منه أرواحا   قد اضطرت إلى الموت

وُيورق من جذوري   بسـاتينا من العـطر

يفـوح شـذاهـا   للـأفـاق والأرض

فكم من أمة صرخت   صلاح الدين صُن عِرض

وكم ناديتك ياسراً   فلـتأتـي على عجل

إهداء من القلب إلى من تنفست على يديه الهواء النقي .

منسقة اللغة العربية بمدرسة بلال بن رباح

رضى محمودالبنا

Figure 3.2. The Arabic language addresses Dr. Yasir.

Standing for a host of symbolic meanings, the *fuṣḥā* acted as a bridge between my exilic and preexilic selves. The *fuṣḥā* also acted as a link among my professional identity as a trainer, my collective identity as an Arab and a Palestinian in exile and my personal identity as a risk taker with deep-seated

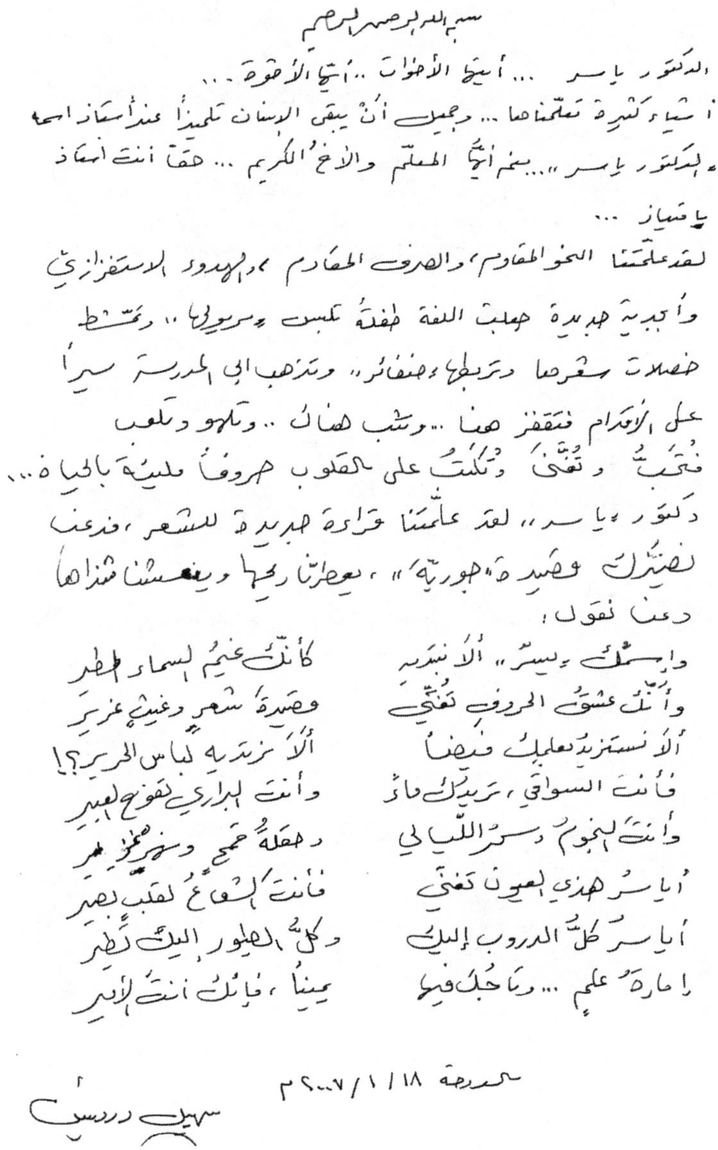

بسم الله الرحمن الرحيم

- الدكتور ياسر ... أيها الأخوات .. أيها الأخوة ...

أشياء كثيرة تعلمناها ... وجميل أن يبقى الإنسان تلميذاً عند أستاذ اسمه الدكتور ياسر ... نعم أيها المعلم والأخ الكريم ... حقاً أنت أستاذ بامتياز ...

لقد علمتنا النحو المقاوم، والصرف المقادم، والهدوء الاستفزازي وأبجدية جديدة جعلت اللغة طفلة تلبس بسربولها .. وتمشط خصلات شعرها وتربطها بضفائر، وتذهب إلى المدرسة سيراً على الأقدام فتقفز هنا .. وتثب هناك .. وتلهو وتلعب فتحب وتغني وتكتب على القلوب حروفاً مليئة بالحياة ...

دكتور ياسر، لقد علمتنا قراءة جديدة للشعر، فدعنا نضيف لك قصيدة "جورية" تعطرنا ريحها وينعشنا شذاها ودعنا نقول:

واسمك يسر، ألا نبتدر / كأنك غيم لسماء المطر
وأنك عشق الحروف تغني / وقصيدة شعر وغيث غزير
ألا نستزيد تعليك فيضاً / ألا نزيده لباس الحرير؟!
فأنت السواقي، تريدك ماءً / وأنت البراري نفوح العبير
وأنت النجوم وسر الليالي / وحقلة قمح وسر الزهور
أياسر هذي العيون تغني / فأنت الشعاع لقلب بصير
أياسر كل الدروب إليك / وكل الطيور إليك تطير
إمارة علم ... وتاجك فيها / يميناً، فإنك أنت الأمير

المدرسة ١٨/١/٢٠٠٧م

سهيل دريس

Figure 3.3. Your name is *yusr* ('ease').

anxieties. Using the *fuṣḥā* enabled me to engage in personal therapy to get relief from my fear of it as a schoolboy and, to some extent, from my exilic marginality. The teachers' positive feedback, some of it expressed in poetry and prose writing (see figures 3.1–3.4), validated my choice of the *fuṣḥā* and the image I wanted to project of myself. The more the teachers approved of my use of the *fuṣḥā*, the more determined I became to use it. Audience

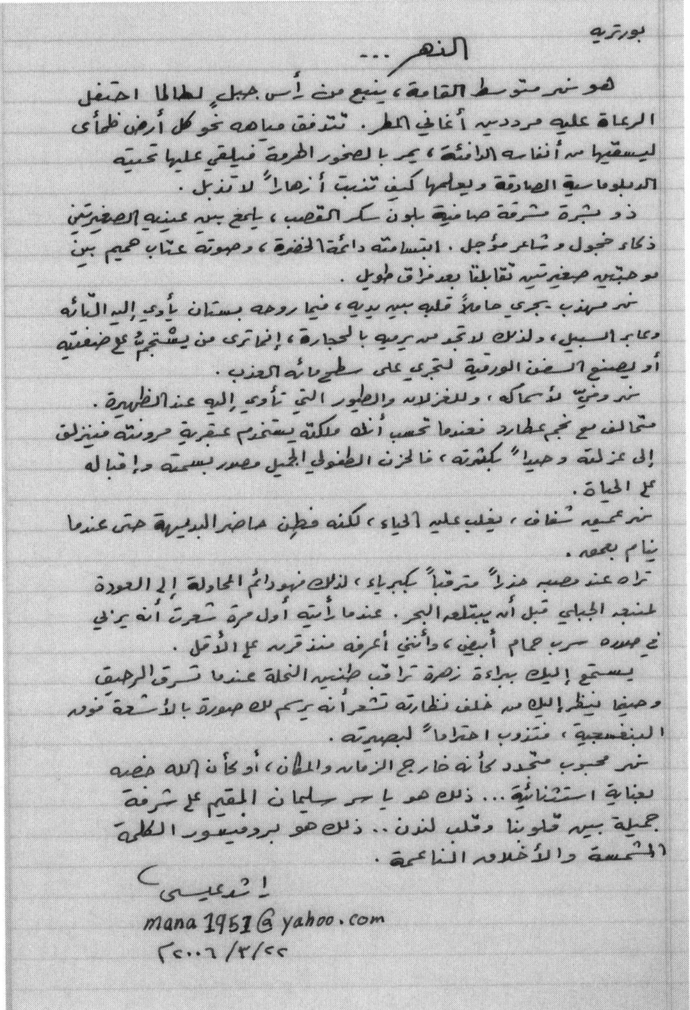

بورتريه

النهر ...

هو نهر متوسط القامة، ينبع من أس جبل لطالما احتفل
الرعاة عليه مرددين أغاني المطر. تتدفق مياهه نحو كل أرض ظمأى
ليسقيها من أنفاسه الدافئة، يمر بالصخور الحرونة فيلقي عليها تحية
الدبلوماسية الصادقة ويعلمها كيف تنبت أزهاراً لا تذبل.
ذو بشرة مشرقة صافية بلون سكر القصب، يلمع بين عينيه الصغيرتين
ذكاء خجول وشاعر مؤجل. ابتسامته دائمة الخضرة، وصوته عتاب حميم بين
موجتين صغيرتين تقابلتا بعد فراق طويل.
نهر مهذب يجري حاملاً قلبه بين يديه، فيما روحه بستان يأوي إليه التائه
وعابر السبيل، ولذلك لا تجد من يرميه بالحجارة، إنما ترى من يستحم في ضفته
أو يصنع السفن الورقية لتجري على سطح مائه العذب.
نهر وفي لأسماكه، وللغزلان والطيور التي تأوي إليه عند الظهيرة.
متحالف مع نجم عطارد فعندما تحسب أنك ملكته يستخدم عبقرية مرونته فينزلق
إلى عزلته وحيداً بكبرته، فالحزن الطفولي الجميل مصدر بسمته وإقباله
على الحياة.
نهر عميق شفاف، يغلب عليه الحياء، لكنه فطن حاضر البديهة حتى عندما
ينام بعمق.
تراه عند مصبه هادئاً مترقباً بكبرياء، لذلك فهو دائم المحاولة إلى العودة
لمنبعه الجبلي قبل أن يبتلعه البحر. عندما أتيته أول مرة شعرت أنه يربي
في صدره سرب حمام أبيض، وأنني أعرفه منذ قرن على الأقل.
يستمع إليك ببراءة زهرة تراقب طنين النحلة عندما تسرق الرحيق
وحينما ينظر إليك من خلف نظارته تشعر أنه يرسم لك صورة بالأشعة فوق
البنفسجية، فتذوب احتراماً لبصيرته.
نهر محبوب متجدد كأنه خارج الزمان والمكان، أو كأن الله خصه
بعناية استثنائية... ذلك هو ياسر سليمان المقيم على شرفة
جميلة بين قلوبنا وقلب لندن.. ذلك هو بروفيسور الكلمة
المشمسة والأخلاق الناعمة.

راشد عيسى
mana 1951@yahoo.com
٢٢/٣/٢٠٠٦

Figure 3.4. A river portrait.

approval was, clearly, an important element in my self-construction;[17] this fact points to the dialogic nature of the Self. However, I am not claiming that my positive attitude towards the *fuṣḥā* is shared by all Arabic speakers. As chapter 4 will show, some share this attitude but with a different inflection, and others oppose it, replacing it with a very negative assessment of the *fuṣḥā* on the personal and group levels.

17 This is why I have included the pieces written by the teachers as figures here, at the risk of appearing vain.

BANNING CODE-SWITCHING, MARKING THE SELF

In this chapter, *code-switching* refers to the mixing of Arabic with, mainly, English in spoken discourse. This phenomenon has been the subject of study in the literature,[18] comment in Arabic newspapers[19] and a TV discussion documentary, *Arabizi* (a blend of *'arabī* [Arabic] and *inglīzī* [English]), aired on the Alarabiyya Satellite TV several times in 2006–08 and in which I have taken part. This scholarly and popular interest signals the increasing popularity of code-switching among young, educated speakers with a good level of competence in English, particularly women. The mixing of English and Arabic is a recent phenomenon in the Middle East in comparison with the much more established phenomenon of Arabic-French code-switching in North Africa and Lebanon. This phenomenon is called *'aransiyya* in North Africa, a blend of portions of the two words *'arabiyya* ('the Arabic language') and *faransiyya* ('the French language'). Code-switching, whether with English or French, involves the colloquial dialects or the *fuṣḥā*, although its occurrence with the former is far more widespread than with the latter.[20] For those who use it, code-switching is a style of speaking with strong symbolic meanings, most of which are related to notions of modernity and prestige.

It is, however, important to distinguish between code-switching and the use of borrowed words and frozen expressions from English into Arabic (for example, 'missed call'). Borrowing does not carry the same loadings in symbolic terms as code-switching does. For example, the use of English computer-related and mobile-telephone terminologies in Arabic is most probably a case of borrowing. Some of these terms have actually become productive in Arabic. For example, spoken Arabic has the verb *sayyiv* (from the English 'save'), which occurs in a productive conjugation paradigm: for example, *anā sayyavt* ('I saved'), *inta sayyavt* ('you [masc.] saved'), *inti sayyavti* ('you [fem.] saved'), *hū sayyav* ('he saved'), *hī sayyavat* ('she saved'), *hum sayyavū* ('they [masc./fem.] saved'). Borrowed terms do not elicit the same reactions of prestige and modernity as code-switching does, nor do they generate negative reactions or ridicule, as code-switching sometimes does. This is why the reactions of the teachers in the training to the poem about 'Computer Love' (see figure 3.5) were different from their reactions to the poem 'Hi, Arabs!' (see figure 3.6). In the former case, the teachers thought the lover was clever and funny in the way he used computer terminology, whereas they thought that the speaker in 'Hi, Arabs!' was affected and ridiculous. All of the English words in 'Computer Love' are borrowed terms; the same is not true of 'Hi, Arabs!' which is built around code-switching. The test for

18 For code switching with Arabic, see Bader and Mahadin (1996); Bentahila (1983); al-Dhuwadi (1981); al-Dhuwadi (1983); al-Dhuwadi (1986); al-Dhuwadi (1988); al-Dhuwadi (1996); Kamhawi (2000).

19 See al-Abtah (2001).

20 Among Israeli Palestinians, the code switching is with Hebrew, not English.

عشق كومبيوتري

هذه قصيدة طريفة عثرت عليها في أحد مواقع الإنترنت ثم قيل لي أنها للشاعر علي السبعان (على مسؤولية.. نايف الرشيدي)، وفيها يستخدم حبيبنا الغارق حتى أذنيه في عوالم الكومبيوتر والإنترنت خلاصة خبراته للتعبير عن مكنونات صدره، فيقول:

في (ديسك توبّ).. القلب: سوّيت.. (فايل)
.. باسمك،.. وخزّنته.. بوسط (الديكومنت)
و(بيجك).. على (الفيفورت).. ما له بدايل
في (الميموري.. والهستوري).. قد تدوّنت
و(ايميل) قلبي صار لك حيل.. مايل
يكشف لك (الباسوورد).. من وين ما كنت
مبرمجه: (ديليت).. كلّ الرسايل
و(بلوك سندر) للمخاليق... إلاّ.. انت
سوّيت (شت داون.. وريستارت).. احايل
أثرك على (السيرفر) بحاله.. تمكّنت
جرّبت (داون لود).. باصعب وسايل
عيّا.. يتحمّل غيرك، وتالي اذعنت
لو سوّت (الماوس) بقلبي هوايل
سوّيت له (ريفرش)، وبحبّك اعلنت
يا (ويب ماستر) خاطري.. بالقبايل
ما لي (سبايت) غيرك،.. ولا بعد.. أنت
نذرت لك.. (كيبورد) قلبي، وشايل
لك في (فلوبّي) القلب.. صورة، ولا خنت
(دَبل كليكّ) اضغط.. على كلّ فايل
في القلب.. ما تلقى من الناس... إلاّ.. انت

المختلف، ع ١٥٩ ، أكتوبر ٢٠٠٤م.

• • •

Figure 3.5. 'Computer Love' (al-Khalidi 2007: 100).

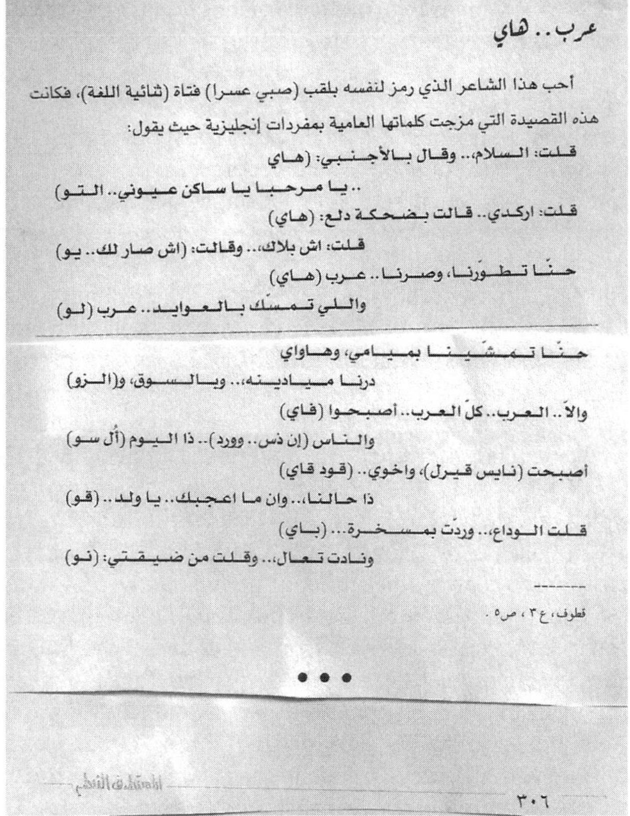

عرب.. هاي

أحب هذا الشاعر الذي رمز لنفسه بلقب (صبي عسرا) فتاة (ثنائية اللغة)، فكانت هذه القصيدة التي مزجت كلماتها العامية بمفردات إنجليزية حيث يقول:

قلت: السلام،.. وقال بالأجنبي: (هاي
.. يا مرحبا يا ساكن عيوني.. التو)
قلت: اركدي.. قالت بضحكة دلع: (هاي)
قلت: اش بلاك،.. وقالت: (اش صار لك.. يو)
حنّا تطوّرنا، وصرنا.. عرب (هاي)
واللي تمسّك بالعوايد.. عرب (لو)

حنّا تمشّينا بميامي، وهاواي
درنا ميادينه،.. وبالسوق، و(الزو)
والآ.. العرب.. كلّ العرب.. أصبحوا (فاي)
والناس (إن ذس.. وورد).. ذا اليوم (أُل سو)
أصبحت (نايس قيرل)، واخوي.. (قود قاي)
ذا حالنا،.. وان ما اعجبك.. يا ولد.. (قو)
قلت الوداع،.. وردّت بمسخرة... (باي)
ونادت تعال،.. وقلت من ضيقتي: (نو)

قطوف، ع٣، ص٥.

• • •

٣٠٦

Figure 3.6. 'Hi, Arabs!' (al-Khalidi 2007: 305–6).

this was the fact that the Arabic teachers knew all of the borrowed terms in 'Computer Love,' but the English material in 'Hi, Arabs!' had to be explained to them. The degree to which code-switching has become a style of speaking among Arabs has found expression in a parody of this phenomenon by the Syrian comedian Yasir al-Azma, well known for his comedy sketches *Marāyā* ('Mirrors,' in the sense of holding a mirror to Arab society).[21]

A few factors stand behind Arabic-English code-switching. First, there is the massive spread of English through education, the media and new technologies in the Middle East in the last few decades. However, while the spread of English is a necessary condition for Arabic-English code-switching, it is not a sufficient one. What makes English available for code-switching is the perception of prestige and modernity it evokes by virtue of its connection with power and globalisation (see chapter 4). Another necessary

21 See http://www.youtube.com/watch?v=W0Se4D4DQRE (accessed 4 January 2010).

condition is the view of Arabic, particularly the *fuṣḥā*, as a traditional and, for some code-switchers, boring language that is unable to keep pace with the massive developments in modern society. For these code-switchers, the *fuṣḥā* is frozen in time and lacks the vitality associated with English and the colloquial dialects. To this may be added peer pressure facilitated by the fact that code-switching has, for some young people, become a style of speaking. Code-switching is a badge of belonging among code-switchers. Through it, they identify (with) one another as members of a social elite or as outsiders aspiring to join this elite.

These factors are part of the cultural landscape at work in code-switching in Qatar. However, for the Arabic-language teachers in the Independent Schools, there were three additional institutional factors that seemed to encourage code-switching. The first was the massive transformation in the school environments where they worked. Qatar took the decision to teach mathematics and science through the medium of English in the Independent Schools. This added massively to the prestige of the language in these schools, which, naturally, started to recruit teachers and administrators with competence in the language. Arabic mixed with English, or vice versa, started to be used more widely by the students, not just in their learning but also in communicating with their teachers and with one another inside and, I am sure, outside the classroom. This mixing of languages was inevitable, since neither the mathematics and science teachers nor the students were very proficient in English. In this newly emerging situation, the Arabic-language teachers began to feel marginalized; some started to learn English not just to move with the social trends in the new school environments but also to enhance their employment opportunities, since knowing English, or mixing it with Arabic, became symbolic of the Independent Schools culture.

The second factor is related to the first. To build schoolwide capacity on the administrative side and to support the introduction of English as the medium of instruction for mathematics and science in the Independent Schools, the Education Institute established what were called School Support Organisations (SSOs), the contracts for which were awarded to American, Australian, British and New Zealand education consultants.[22] These organisations were embedded directly in the schools. Most of their staff members spoke English as their first language, and only a very limited number knew or learnt Arabic. Their presence in the schools enhanced the position and prestige of English even further, motivating some Arabic-language teachers to learn English in order to communicate with them, instead of relying on school-based interpreters. This factor contributed to the spread of code-switching among the Arabic teachers, the idea being that the more access these teachers had to English, the greater their propensity to code-switch in the new school environments. I was able to track this

22 There was one German SSO, but its staff all spoke English, some as their native language.

myself on my visits to the schools. Thus, some Arabic teachers who at the beginning of the school year spoke Arabic only would start to code-switch as their English began to improve, whether through formal study or informally through contact in the school.

Finally, these two factors had a negative impact on the image of the Arabic teachers of themselves and of their subject. Some felt that Arabic started to lose ground to English and that this trend, if not checked, might be unstoppable. This was also a frequent subject of discussion in the press. In fact, some Arabic teachers in the Ministry of Education schools, which continued to teach mathematics and science in Arabic, started to send their children to the Independent Schools precisely because they taught these subjects in English. This was ironic, because these teachers often criticised the Independent Schools for what they perceived to be their poor standards in Arabic. As I said above, for code-switching to occur, the native language, in this case, Arabic, has to lose some or much of its prestige and standing in relation to its partner in code-switching. The *fuṣḥā* was that loser in symbolic terms, if not, in fact, in domain terms, in spite of serious attempts on the part of many Independent Schools to counter this trend. The use of code-switching by some Arabic-language teachers was part and parcel of the brave new world in the Independent Schools. Teachers who code-switched wanted to buy into the new culture in their schools. Code-switching was the symbolic capital they tendered to gain entry into, acceptance in or membership in this new culture.

In response to this trend, I banned all code-switching between Arabic and English in the training. One reason behind the ban had to do with the operational definition of the *fuṣḥā* as it has been outlined in the preceding section. Since this definition sought to exclude the colloquial dialects, it would be inconsistent for it to include code-switching. Code-switching involves a foreign language, and it often occurs with the colloquial dialects. Excluding it from the training hits two birds with one stone. The other reason had to do with raising the teachers' morale by giving them pride in the *fuṣḥā*.[23] I thought I was well placed to do this, because the teachers were aware that I knew English well. They often heard me use it in the training and on my visits to talk to the English-speaking staff in the Education Institute and to the staff in the (school-based) SSOs. They also knew that I live

23 In 2007–08, I used to call the Arabic teachers back from coffee breaks by referring to them as *ahl lughat al-qur'an* ('the people of the language of the Qur'an'). The mathematics, science and English teachers who would be talking to one another in English or in a mixture of Arabic and English used to object to this, saying that the language of the Qur'an belonged to them, too. Not only did the Arabic teachers find this amusing, but they also derived a lot of pleasure from being summoned back into the training with this morale-boosting call. However, on those occasions when a cotrainer or an observer was Christian, I did not use this call. I thought this might be insensitive because it excluded that person. Also, the omission of this reference is, in fact, closer to my own view of Arabic as the language of all Arabic-speaking people, regardless of their religion, ethnic background or state nationality.

and work in the United Kingdom in an environment completely dominated by English. In fact, English, more than Arabic, dominates my life in professional terms. I could have used this, as some Arab expatriates in a similar position sometimes do, to justify code-switching on my part, but I never did. Avoiding code-switching was not, therefore, triggered by lack of facility in English on my part but was the result of conscious choice. The teachers were very aware of this and often complimented me for acting in this way. This positive feedback convinced me that I was right to insist on a total ban on code-switching.

As important as the above considerations were, they do not directly touch on the language-Self link that is the main focus of this chapter. From the perspective of this study, there is a more important question to answer: How was the ban on code-switching related to my conception of my identity as I have described it above? First, the ban served to bolster my image among the teachers as a person who had remained loyal to the *fuṣḥā* and its associated culture, in spite of the allure of other internationally more prestigious cultures and languages in my life. This was more than a matter of image; it was a statement of fact, which the teachers knew to be true. Banning code-switching in the training was, therefore, not a cosmetic or (just) instrumentally driven matter but an expression full of identity-linked meanings. It was a symbolic act through which I asserted my Arabness. The teachers, however, knew that I was not against learning and mastering foreign languages, including English, but that I objected to their mixing them with Arabic in (and outside) the training. I did so because I think of code-switching as expressive of a relationship between Arabic and English in which Arabic, whether the *fuṣḥā* or the colloquial dialects, is treated as the less prestigious partner, a language characterised by cultural and, for the individual using it, psychological deficit. More important, my objection to code-switching is not because it mixes two languages but is owing to the connotations of superiority and inferiority between cultures that I believe it signifies. Code-switching, thus read, is expressive of defeatism. It is this attitude that I was trying to fight in instituting the ban on code-switching. This ban may be no more than a hopelessly romantic gesture against the unstoppable forces of globalisation, but I felt that in cultural politics, symbolic gestures similar to mine may not be completely futile. By giving the teachers confidence in the *fuṣḥā*, I thought they might be able to impart them (confidence and the *fuṣḥā*) to their students. The fact that the teachers were using the *fuṣḥā* in their teaching, as I explained above, gave me the confidence that the ban on code-switching was making a difference.

There is another identity-linked reason for the ban on code-switching. I think of this phenomenon as an affected style of speaking through which code-switchers seek to project a contrived image of modernity or high class. According to this, code-switching is a matter of display, which extends to espousing Western-oriented lifestyles in food and music, among other things, that, in their native settings, may, in fact, signify the opposite of high class. For a long time in Jordan, eating at McDonald's in Amman was, curiously, considered an expression of a McDonald's-ised modernity and high class among young Jordanians, no doubt because only the well-off could afford the price.[24] McDonald's in Amman was a place where code-switchers could be seen in abundance. Because of these subliminal connections, code-switching was linked in my mind to an espousal of a modernity that, in my exilic life, is marked as low-class, not high-class. The modernity of the code-switchers was not the kind of modernity with which I felt any affinity; in fact, it was an alienating modernity for me when compared with the modernity that dominates my exilic life. It represented in its Arab context an act of misappropriation of something I thought I belonged to and hoped would find a genuine expression in Arab life through the arts, music and culture in its widest meanings. Code-switching, therefore, represented for me a motif of one culture mimicking another, rather than positively interacting with it. It was, furthermore, an expression of cultural defeat, an act of jumping the cultural ship before it sinks into oblivion. I find these meanings alienating and threatening, because they seem to indicate that there is no place for cultural resistance and rejuvenation and that being Arab is somehow being moribund and doomed to failure politically and culturally.

These meanings challenge my image of myself, my identity. But is it possible that this challenge has other dimensions? In particular, could this challenge have an age-related force owing to the fact that code-switching tends to be associated with young speakers? In other words, does code-switching appear threatening because it reminds me that I am no longer a young person and that I am hopelessly out of touch? I do not think so, for two reasons. On the one hand, I know I disapproved of code-switching when I was a student precisely because I thought it pointed to a frame of mind that signalled affectation, cultural defeatism and psychological deficit on the part of the code-switchers. My position in the Qatar training in 2004–08 was, therefore, not new. On the other hand, I tend to disapprove of code-switching even more when it is practised by older speakers, not least because I think that these speakers should know better. In fact, I tend to view code-switching among these speakers as a case of arrested development, the implication being that code-switching is an age-related phenomenon that people 'grow out of' as they get older and more mature.

Another reason behind my negative attitude towards code-switching is my view of it as representing a state of in-between-ness, of characterising people who are neither one thing nor another in cultural terms but (most probably) a superficial mixture of aspects of two cultures and two languages, none of which seems to be properly understood or mastered (although there are bound to be exceptions). But why should in-between-ness elicit a negative reaction from me? Is this not a case of the much-vaunted 'hybridity' that

24 The first branch of McDonald's in Jordan opened in the late 1980s or early 1990s in al-Suwayfiyya, one of the most expensive parts of Amman.

is said to characterise the postmodernity of our times? And aren't I in some sense a hybrid person, having been born in the Middle East but having lived most of my adult life in the West? If I disapprove of the hybridity of others, should I not also disapprove of my own hybridity if I am to avoid the accusation of having double standards?

These are difficult questions to answer, but I think that my negative reaction to the in-between-ness of code-switching has to do with the fact that I conceive of code-switchers as people who want to hedge their bets in terms of cultural belonging. They want to be in and out at the same time. They are masters of hyphenation and of sitting on the fence. In short, they are the sort of people who cannot be relied on if the cultural chips on the Arabic side were really down. These may not be rational reactions, but they sum up some of the feelings I have about this phenomenon as a (private) individual. As a researcher, I am, of course, aware that code-switching can be read in a variety of ways and that some of these may be totally different from mine.

To probe a little deeper into my reactions to the in-between-ness of code-switching, I will compare this mode of speaking with the use of English by Arabic speakers. As a supporter of Arabic, I should find code-switching more acceptable than the wholesale use of English by Arabic speakers. After all, code-switching is still rooted in Arabic on one side of the language amalgam. The use of English exclusively makes little or no reference to Arabic. However, my reaction is the opposite. I find the use of English, particularly if it is free of major errors, to be more acceptable than code-switching precisely because it does not signal in-between-ness. I am struggling to understand the basis of this reaction, but in doing so, I find Mary Douglas's comments on Sartre's ideas on stickiness to be helpful: 'The viscous is a state half-way between solid and liquid. It is like a cross-section in a process of change. It is unstable, but it does not flow. It is soft, yielding and compressible. There is no gliding on its surface. Its stickiness is a trap, it clings like a leech; it attacks the boundary between me and it. . . . Plunging into water gives a different impression. I remain a solid, but to touch stickiness is to risk diluting myself into viscosity' (Douglas 2002 [1967]: 47).

Code-switching is like stickiness for me. It is halfway between Arabic and English. It is a 'cross-section in a process of change,' the end point of which is not known. And most important of all, it 'attacks the boundary' between me and the Other, thereby challenging my identity. Speaking English is like water: coming into contact with it, I remain who I am. English, unlike code-switching, preserves the principle of alterity that is so important to the definition of one aspect of my identity curiously against one of its partners. Code-switching challenges this alterity by injecting ambiguity into it. Code-switching blurs the boundary between me and the Other, thus threatening my sense of Arab Self, whereas the use of English exclusively does not.

But does this mean that I do not code-switch at all? I know I do, but I also know that I do so mainly with Arabic-speaking interlocutors who, I think, have no linguistic or cultural chips on their shoulders. These people tend to be friends whom I know to have a deep-rooted allegiance to Arab culture and the Arabic language. In fact, the moment I know that a person is using code-switching with me for display purposes, I find I either move completely towards English, if he or she speaks English well, or towards Arabic. In some cases, I would even exaggerate by using the *fuṣḥā* instead of my colloquial dialect, as if to put sufficient distance between me and him or her. My use of code-switching is, therefore, very positional; it depends on whom I am talking to and on my assessment of where my interlocutors locate themselves in identity terms. Furthermore, these interlocutors tend to speak English very well. This level of competence in the language is important for my assessment of code-switching, because it signals that the person could use English fluently if he or she wanted to; this, in turn, acts as a guarantee that the person concerned cannot be code-switching for display purposes.

Banning code-switching in the Qatar training was driven by operational (the definition of the *fuṣḥā*), instrumental (raising the teachers' morale and their confidence in the *fuṣḥā*) and, most important of all, identity-centred reasons. This ban is closely linked to my identity as an Arab who rejects cultural defeatism, dislikes affectation in speech, disapproves of the public display of affected prestige in language behaviour and feels uncomfortable with banal cultural in-between-ness and the ambiguity of identity that it signals. The ban on code-switching was not directed against English but against the attitudes towards this language that trade on the view of Arabic as a traditional, boring or frozen language.

CONCLUSION: ARABIC, SELF AND AUTOETHNOGRAPHY

The reflections in this chapter have dealt with two aspects of my linguistic behaviour: my use of the *fuṣḥā* and the ban on code-switching in the training of Arabic-language teachers at the Independent Schools in Qatar in 2004–08. Analysing these aspects of my language behaviour as sites of identity exploration, I have tried to show how by focussing on the symbolic meanings of language use, on what is beneath and beyond language, we can tap into rich layers of signification that can help us decipher the complexity of the Self and identity. At no point in this exploration did I refer to what I actually said in the *fuṣḥā* in the training. My reflections were restricted to readings of the symbolic meanings of the *fuṣḥā* as form, rather than analysing its content or semantic import, and to the ban on code-switching, rather than investigating stretches of discourse in which code-switching is embedded. I am not denying the importance of instrumentality (as opposed to symbolism) here or of analysing how identities are enacted in discourse,[25] but my aim has been to show how symbolic meaning is important for

25 For the study of identity in discourse, see Benwell and Stokoe (2006); De Fina et al. (2006); Wodak et al. (1999).

studying language in society, which I have called *symbolic sociolinguistics* in earlier research (Suleiman 1999b). I am aware that the term *turn* has been bandied about a lot in the last few decades in the humanities and social sciences (*cultural turn, narrative turn*, etc.), but at the risk of adding to this expansion in the terminology of 'turns,' my research into Arabic sociolinguistics has been aimed at encouraging researchers to inject a 'symbolic turn' into their work. This symbolic turn is necessary if the study of Arabic in the social world is to be made relevant to other areas of enquiry, such as politics and history. However, for this interdisciplinary cross-fertilization to occur, neighbouring disciplines must be prepared to widen their scope to be able to take advantage of the interest in language symbolism.[26]

Another aim of the exploration above has been to show the richness of meanings that can be generated by adopting a qualitative approach to studying sites of language production or nonproduction.[27] While quantitative studies will always be important in studying language in the social world, by revealing correlations and causal links between linguistic variants and social variables, qualitative explorations can yield a very rich catch of insights and interpretations that may not be captured using frequency counts or similar statistically based methods. In this chapter, the link between language and Self was explored through personal experience, memory recall, introspection and life story or self-reports to reach deep into the factors that motivate aspects of the language behaviour of the researcher as researched subject. The immediate aim here is not to arrive at generalisations that apply beyond the life story being studied but to offer subject-specific details and interpretations that may or may not resonate with other Selves. My use of the *fuṣḥā* may not convey the same set of symbolic meanings as those of other subjects; the same is true of my symbolic reading of code-switching. However, regardless of the specific meanings these two phenomena may convey, identity, as a constructed entity, is always invoked in the interpretation and analysis of these data.

The combination of the symbolic and qualitative orientations above creates a powerful instrument for exploring sites of identity in, through, beneath and beyond language use, as I will discuss in the next two chapters. They turn what may seem mundane and banal into a productive field of enquiry. They have the effect of problematising or unfamiliarising the familiar, the use of the *fuṣḥā* and code-switching in this case, thus turning it into

26 See Myers-Scotton (1993) for a discussion of the social, including symbolic, meanings of code-switching. Poplack's (1988) study of the symbolic meanings of code-switching in identity terms in the context of Brussels and Catalonia may also be of interest.

27 Qualitative research uses a variety of empirical materials, including 'case study; personal experience; introspection; life story; interview; artefacts; cultural texts and productions; observational, historical, interactional and visual texts—that describe routine and problematic moments and meanings in individuals' lives' (Denzin and Lincoln 2000: 2). In this chapter, 'personal experience, introspection and life story' are the most relevant. Other chapters in this work use other types of material.

a social location for multilayered analysis through which archived aspects of the Self are revealed. This approach to investigating language in society helps reveal the Self as a multifaceted construct that is fashioned by considerations of collective affiliation, the moral economies of society, professional interests, personal therapy and economic self-interest. As it emerges from this mode of reflexive investigation, the Self is not an accumulation of attributes but a construct that stands at the intersection of many forces in social life; hence the reference to it as a 'buzzing beehive' at the beginning of this chapter. It is not just a set of roles that people perform; it is also an important resource that people deploy to achieve a variety of objectives.

In addition, the exploration above powerfully affirms the situatedness of language use and, thus, the positionality of identity as discussed in chapter 2. As Elliott writes, 'social practices, cultural conventions and political relations are a constitutive and powerful backdrop for the staging of human experience and the drawing of self-identity' (2001: 6). In discussing my use of the *fuṣḥā* and my attitude towards code-switching, I have taken full advantage of the point Elliott makes. I have thus related these aspects of my linguistic behaviour to my being an Arab, a Palestinian, an exile, a researcher, an educational consultant driven by considerations of instrumentality, a calculating or shrewd risk taker, a wounded subject driven by the need for some performance therapy and a person who does not like affectation and veneerlike display in language behaviour. I have also related this behaviour to a set of observations I made about the teachers attending the training, including their interest in nation-state identities, their responses to social and school trends in language behaviour, the solidarities that might exist among them, the fault lines that might divide them and their morale in their work environments. The Self that emerges through this exploration in language use is a constructed one over which I, as author, exercise some agency. It is not a prediscursive or a given Self but one that is forged in, through, beneath and beyond discourse in relation to a community of practise (the teachers) whose members have shared conventions and norms.

In this respect, identity is a 'project of the Self,' to use a popular formulation in recent studies of identity in discourse (Benwell and Stokoe 2006). But it is also an intersubjective project based on an assumption of *alterity*, 'the fact that it is not possible to posit identity without speaking of difference, of otherness' (Suleiman 2006d: 51). Identity, therefore, is as significantly about inclusion as it is about exclusion. My pan-Arab identity has meaning only when considered against, among other things, nation-state identities with which it is contrasted. My use of the *fuṣḥā* acquires meaning in identity construction only because it is contrasted with the use of the colloquial dialects or other linguistic forms in speech, for example, Educated Spoken Arabic. The same is true of code-switching; this type of linguistic behaviour acquires meaning only because it contrasts with other ways of speaking. Otherness or difference helps structure the Self and enables symbolic meanings to emerge.

And yet identity is an ill-defined concept. For some, it is a matter of being (a noun); for others, it is a matter of becoming and doing (a verb). For some, identities stand for roles that people internalise and enact in their lives; for others, they are social categories that, through internalisation and differentiation, acquire a psychological reality that is relatively stable. Do these and other differences mean that we should do away with identity as an analyst's tool?[28] Opinions differ on this. My own take on it is driven by utilitarianism: until we can develop a more precise understanding of identity or a different one altogether that replaces it, we have little choice but to continue to work with the concept, in spite of all of the vagueness and ambiguities it carries (Hall 2000; Suleiman 1997). Doing away with the concept of identity because it is vague will not cause it to disappear. Nor will it make those phenomena with which we deal under this concept disappear. They would still be there, and they would need to be dealt with using something like the present concept of identity or a variant of it.

I have referred to the above set of reflections as autoethnographic and to the text of this chapter as an autoethnography.[29] This classification will need some explanation because of the different understandings of autoethnography in qualitative research; I will use as background Ellis and Bochner's discussion of autoethnography (2000). As an autobiographical form of writing, autoethnography is usually written in the first-person voice and aims through a collage of personal experience, memory, introspection and reflection to produce texts that link the Self to culture contextually through description and interpretation. Using a variety of formats—for example, short stories, novels, poems, memoirs, fragmented essays or social-science research reports—autoethnography is a form of personal narrative or a narrative of the Self in which the author turns his scholarly gaze on his own personal life, feelings, thoughts, ideological positions and emotions, with the aim of producing a multilayered text that is evocative and full of contextual details. Challenging the strict separation of researcher and researched subject (or gazer and gazed) in quantitative and positivist modes of practice, which I discussed in chapter 2, autoethnography 'often focuses on a single case and thus breaches the traditional concerns of research from generalization across cases to generalization within a single case' (Ellis and Bochner 2000: 744). In autoethnography, the authoring 'I' does not stand outside the text but is embedded in it at different levels: 'the subject and object of research collapse into the body/thoughts/feelings of the (auto) ethnographer located in his or her particular space and time' (Gannon 2006: 475).

28 For the difference between identity as an analyst's and participant's resource, see Widdicombe (1998).

29 See the following for examples of autoethnography: Brogden (2008); Ellis (2004); Evans (2007); Gatson (2003); Kaufman (2005); Kirova (2007); LaRaviere (2008); Magnet (2006); Pelias (2003); Waymer (2008).

Furthermore, autoethnographic texts blur the boundaries among different genres of writing, producing what are sometimes called 'messy texts' that 'move back and forth between description [and] interpretation,' 'erase the dividing line between observer and observed,' 'produce local, situated knowledge' and 'recreate a social world as a site at which identities and local cultures are negotiated and given meaning' (Denzin 1997: 225). Autoethnographic texts are often written in evocative language that invites the reader to interact with the text on a personal level to generate deep intersubjective understanding. The Self in an autoethnography is vulnerable because the 'I' of the emerging text may appear in a 'less than flattering' light because of doubt, the fear of self-revelation, anxiety about 'not being able to take back what [has been written] or of [not] having any control of how readers interpret it' (Ellis and Bochner 2000: 738). There is, therefore, double jeopardy in the critiques of autoethnography: the target of these critiques may include the researcher and, more dangerously for the individual, the researched subject.[30] Denzin's demand that writers 'strip away the veneer of self-protection that comes with a professional title and position . . . to make themselves accountable and vulnerable to the public' (2003: 137) may, because of this double jeopardy, prove to be difficult to apply fully in autoethnography. While using metaphors is said to be part of the attempt to be vivid and evocative in autoethnographic writing, there is no doubt that metaphors are sometimes used to avoid peeling away at the protective layers of the Self; they are used for their suggestive power rather than concreteness. Finally, autoethnography may serve a therapeutic function for its author and, through the act of sharing personal experience, for the reader with whom this experience resonates. Autoethnographic writing is not motivated by therapy, but the opportunity to face some of the 'demons' of one's past may make the gazer a better researcher. That is so because the more aware we become of our own likes and dislikes, the more able we are as researchers to monitor them and to ameliorate their excessive influence on our research.

To what extent does the text of this chapter conform to the preceding outline of autoethnography? The use of the first-person voice, the reliance on personal experience and reflection and the utilization of both description and interpretation to link language to Self in society are autoethnographic features of the text in hand. As a self-narrative, the present text breaches the traditional positivist separation of the researcher and the researched subject. It concentrates on a single site of personal experience in the professional life of the researcher, reads it for the sociocultural meanings it can convey and stops short of claiming that these meanings are generalisable in

30 Davies et al. (2004: 383) comment on this aspect of autoethnography: 'Reflexive writing can be passionate and emotional. It can be writing in which the mind, heart, and body are all engaged. Yet once those words are out there in the world, objects themselves for reflection by others as well as ourselves, they can become weapons to turn against us.' Their comments summarise the point well.

the way they have been formulated to other subjects (without, however, denying that it may resonate with them). Therapy is not an aim of this autoethnographic text, but it emerges as a factor in it, in that the researcher's use of the *fuṣḥā* offers him an opportunity to overcome some of the pedagogic demons of the past.

In spite of these factors, the present text is best described as a 'tame' autoethnography. Compared with other autoethnographies I have read, it is not as evocative, vivid, full of detail, rhizomatic or messy. The language is still restrained, fairly abstract and reluctant to let go of a traditional form of rationality whereby logically calculated moves are made from one argument or interpretation to another. The Self that emerges is multiple, but it is still fairly coherent, rather than amorphous or fractured. Because of this, the present autoethnography is weak on vulnerability. This may be the result of self-surveillance on my part or the fear of criticism from fellow Arabic sociolinguists who will read this work from a predominantly variationist, correlationist and nonsymbolic perspective. For example, I was aware in writing this autoethnography that readers from these horizons of expectation may think of its author and the Self it portrays as self-absorbed, self-indulgent, narcissistic, culturally blinkered, instrumentally driven and nationality-obsessed. However, even if these were the conclusions that readers might draw from this linguistic autoethnography, the fact that it may be construed to convey these meanings would suggest that autoethnographic reflection is a useful mode of investigating the language-Self/identity interface in Arabic sociolinguistics.

In offering this self-reflexive text, I am aware that autoethnography, along with other forms of qualitative research, has been the subject of methodological criticism. Most of these criticisms are aimed at the lack of evaluation measures that correspond to validity and reliability in quantitative research. Being based on memory, introspection and self-reports in which the dividing line between the researcher and the researched subject is breached, autoethnography is said to be subject to data contamination, subjective bias and other kinds of distortion that render its results problematic in methodological terms. Offering self-reported data, interpretations and constructions of the Self, autoethnography acts as judge and jury in its own court of scientific evaluation. The question facing autoethnography, therefore, is what measures can be used to assess the quality in this type of qualitative research. If truth, generalisability/applicability, consistency and neutrality—as the 'gold standards' in quantitative research—cannot be used to interrogate autoethnography methodologically, what other criteria can be used for this purpose?

There is not an agreed-upon set of criteria for performing this task in the literature, not least because autoethnography itself is ill defined.[31] However,

31 See Seale (1999) for a useful discussion of measuring quality in qualitative research. Seale deals not with autoethnography specifically but with qualitative research as a category.

the following may be used here (Seale 1999). First is transferability, which means that the results of autoethnographic research, its interpretations through symbolic connotation, can be found to apply in comparable situations with similar meanings or values. Thus, the link between my positive attitude towards the *fuṣḥā* and my identity as Arab or as Palestinian may be found to apply to other subjects in similar or different contexts. However, not all of the results in an autoethnography may be transferable intersubjectively, the reason being the highly personal nature and context boundaries of some of these results. For example, my view of the *fuṣḥā* as an underdog may not be shared with other subjects who think of their identity in Arab and/or Palestinian terms and who, in fact, may be well disposed towards this variety of the language. The same applies to code-switching: while some Arabic speakers may share my attitude to this style of speaking, others may read this phenomenon very differently, endowing it with positive connotations of modernity and liberalism.

Second is confirmability; this is basically about confirming the dependability of an autoethnography. Auditing is one procedure for doing this. In the present autoethnography, I have listed the names and current institutional associations of all those who monitored my work as a teacher trainer or who worked as cotrainers with me,[32] the idea being that these individuals can provide eye-witness accounts that can confirm some of the data. However, confirmability operates vis-à-vis events and situations, for example, what happened in the training or my descriptions of the language situation in the schools, but it does not apply to the interpretations given to these events and situations.[33] To use an old-fashioned formula, confirmability here is a matter of surface structure, not deep structure. As an extra measure, I have also kept some field notes on what happened in the training and what I thought about events, situations and characters at the time of the training. These field notes are not records of events or situations but representations of those events and situations. The use of these field notes offers some protection against the wear and tear of memory over time.

Autoethnography as a technology of self-representation that stresses unfettered constructivism, (infinite) open-endedness and variability is not a view to which I subscribe in the study of the language-Self link.[34] I believe

32 See notes 5 and 12 above.

33 This also applies to quantitative and positivist research. In this connection, Cameron et al. (1992: 12) provide the following comment: 'You cannot validate a particular observation by repeating it. However many questionnaires you give out or interviews you conduct, it is impossible to be sure that all respondents who gave the "same" answer meant the same thing by it, and that their responses are a direct representation of the truth.'

34 See Cameron et al. (1992: 11) for a similar position with respect to ethnomethodology: 'People are not completely free to do what they want to do, be what they want to be. . . . On the contrary, social actors are schooled and corrected, they come under pressure to take up certain roles and occupations, they are born into relations of class, race, gender, generation, they occupy specific cultural positions, negotiate particular value systems, conceptual frameworks and social institutions, have more or less wealth and opportunity . . . and so on, *ad infinitum*.'

that there must be limits to construction if, as Seale rightly warns (1999: 470), constructivism is to avoid descending into nihilism; hence my insistence on the importance of quantitative, correlationist and functionalist research in Arabic sociolinguistics, alongside research that is driven by qualitative and symbolic agendas such as this one. Like Seale, I subscribe to a middle way between the naïve realist and the instrumentalist or hocus-pocus views of reality.[35] Following the Popperian paradigm,[36] it is not logically possible to observe a preexisting reality without a point of view; observation is, therefore, always mediated by 'pre-existing ideas and values' (Seale 1999: 470); in other words, observation, or gazing, as the autoethnographers call it, takes place not in a vacuum but in relation to something else that guides it, helps structure it and makes it cohere. It is this middle position that, in fact, explains the deviations from standard autoethnography that I have identified above. Rather than being accidental, these deviations are intended. They are meant as a counterposition to what I consider to be the excesses of constructivism and postmodernity in the study of identity.[37]

35 For naïve realism and instrumentalism in science, see Chalmers (1978); Householder (1952); Nagel (1974).

36 See Popper (1969; 1975; 1976).

37 It is these excesses that have given rise to what is known as the Sokal affair or hoax in the literature, wherein Allan Sokal, a physicist, submitted a hoax article to the journal *Social Text* to expose the sloppy and bogus attitude towards evidence and 'objective reality' that characterises postmodern scholarship (see Dimitriadis 2008: 6–8).

Chapter 4

Arabic, Self and Displacement

This chapter investigates the language-Self link by examining a corpus of four texts authored by writers of 'Arab' origin who spent most of their lives in exile or in the diaspora: Edward Said, Leila Ahmed, Moustapha Safouan and Amin Maalouf. Attention is given to the interplay between language and Self, on the one hand, and the notions of displacement, trauma and globalisation, on the other. Akey thesis here is that language is as relevant a marker of individual identity, the Self, as it is of group or collective identity. It is, however, important not to draw a sharp distinction between the Self and collective identity; the two feed into each other.

The discussion of the texts chosen for study will proceed as follows. First, I will provide a fine-grained analysis of each text separately, focusing on how it conceptualises the language-Self link. This analysis will highlight those conceptualisations that are of direct link to displacement, trauma and globalisation. Second, a long conclusion will be devoted to comparing these texts against the background of the three operative notions of displacement, trauma and globalisation.

Through these discussions and in line with chapter 2, language is treated as a symbolic resource that can enhance our understanding of how individuals conceive of themselves and their communities. Its function here is to mark identity at the macro level. To achieve a richer understanding of the language-Self link, however, we would need to adopt a micro-level perspective that moves investigations of this link from identity marking to identity inscription. This can be achieved by tracking how the Self is expressed through discourse features in stretches of text. As important as this perspective is, I will not pursue it here but hope to return to it in future research.

OUT OF PLACE, BETWEEN LANGUAGES

The title of Edward Said's (1935–2003) memoir *Out of Place* (1999) hovers tantalisingly over a rich field of signification that is very difficult to pin down. The most obvious interpretation of the title relates to a geography-decentred world, the fact that Said lived through many displacements which had a defining impact on him as a person and on his work as an intellectual, a leading scholar and a public figure. These displacements were, paradoxically, both alienating and enticing, combining in them strong centrifugal and centripetal forces, emanating from liminal sites of self-reference, which had kept Said in perpetual motion, both physically and intellectually (until his death). 'To me,' he writes in *Out of Place*, 'nothing more painful and paradoxically sought after characterises my life than the many displacements from countries, cities, abodes, languages, [and] environments that have kept me in motion all these years' (Said 1999: 217). In the preface to his memoir, Said prefigures this comment by telling us how 'displaced forms of departures, arrivals, farewells, exile,[1] nostalgia, homesickness, belonging, and travel itself' were at the 'core' of his memories, linking them to his abiding feeling of being 'out of place' for all of his life (xiv). Said's use of the term *displaced forms* to characterise the list that follows in this quotation helps us understand the layered way in which he experienced his being 'out of place': it suggests that these forms of displacement are themselves 'displaced' in what is a complex web of entangled and never-ending displacements. It is, however, revealing that this geography-decentred interpretation of being 'out of place' comes, in the preface, after another sense of displacement for Said, that of being linguistically 'out of place.' In fact, for Said, this linguistic displacement is no less foundational than the physical displacements he lived through to his understanding of who he is as a person or, more accurately, perhaps, to some of the confusions he experienced about who 'Edward' was, as he incisively inscribes this in his memoir (xiii–xiv): 'Everyone lives life in a given language; everyone's experiences therefore are had, absorbed, and recalled in that language. The *basic split* in my life was the one between Arabic, my native language, and English, the language of my education and subsequent expression as a scholar and teacher, and so trying to produce a narrative of one in the language of the other—to say nothing of the numerous ways in which the languages were mixed up for me and crossed over from one realm to the other—has been a complicating task' (emphasis added).

Out of Place contains a set of fascinating reflections on language and its impact, directly or indirectly, on Said's conception of himself as a person[2] and as the member of the network of groups to which he belonged, whether that of family or those of being Arab, American, Arab-American, Palestinian, Christian, Palestinian Christian or any combination of these and other

1 Said prefers the term *exile* to *diaspora*. A critical difference between the two terms is that the former signals imposition (by an external power), while the latter implies choice.

2 Said explains the importance of language to him in his 2004 posthumously published article 'Living in Arabic' as follows: 'Having left behind locales that have either been ruined by war or for other reasons no longer exist, and having very little by way of property and objects from my earlier life, I seem to have made out of these two languages [Arabic and English] at play, as experiences, an environment that I can carry about within me, complete with timbre, pitch, and accent specific to the time, the place and the person. I remember and still listen to what people say, how they say it, what words carry the stress and exactly how.' (Said 2004).

markers of the Self. This interest in language on Edward Said's part is, therefore, a topic worthy of exploration, not just because of what it tells us about one of the most brilliant intellectuals of the twentieth century but also because of what it says more generally about the intersectionality of language, identity, displacement, exile, diaspora, trauma and globalisation, which will be explored from different vantage points in this chapter.[3] I am, however, surprised that, considering how extensively Said's work has been studied, this topic has received scant attention in the literature. The fact that Said based some of his arguments in *Orientalism* (1978)—his groundbreaking book on how language was used to essentialise and stereotype the Oriental subject, his culture and 'mind' as the attributes of the Other in Western thought and discourse—adds to the importance of delving into his reflections on language. Yet this continuity between *Orientalism* and *Out of Place* is not the primary reason for my interest in the topic. The main reason is that Arabic has been the subject of reflections from exile and the diaspora in recent years and that some of these reflections are at odds in very important ways with Said's views on the topic, reflecting different experiences, histories and trajectories, as will become clear when dealing with Leila Ahmed in the next section. On a personal level, I am interested in this topic because of the way some of Said's experiences and views resonate with me as an Arab who has lived most of his adult life exilically in the West (United Kingdom); I will draw on this point of comparison later. The topic further interests me because my views on it, as set out in chapter 3, differ drastically from those espoused by Ahmed. In all of these cases, as in others that will be dealt with in this work, conceptions of the Self at the individual and national level will prove to be fundamental to our understanding of the link between language and identity as this link is forged under conditions of personal and national trauma.

In the quotation above, Said characterises the play of languages that he experienced since his early childhood as the 'basic split' in his life, which the writing of his memoir brought into sharp relief because it forced him to inscribe the life he had in one language (Arabic) through the lens provided by another (English).[4] Language must, therefore, be regarded as a primary

3 The term *diaspora* is problematic in dealing with the Palestinians outside their national homeland. See Peteet (2007) for a discussion of this and related terms. Evidence suggests that Said would prefer to describe his condition as one of exile, not strictly diaspora. In this connection, it would be useful to set out some of the ways in which Said characterised exile: '[Exile] is the unbearable rift forced between a human being and a native place, between the self and the true home' (Said 2000: 173); 'Exile is predicated on existence of, love for, and bond with, one's native place'; and 'For an exile, habits of life, expression and activity in the new environment inevitably occur against the memory of these things in another environment' (186). These excerpts are taken from a book containing forty-six essays, one of which is called 'Reflections of Exile.' The fact that Said used the title of this essay as the main title of the book suggests that exile was of central importance to him.

4 Witness the fact that the narrative in *Out of Place* sticks to Said's preuniversity years at Harvard, in which Arabic played an important role in his life.

location for deciphering what being 'out of place' actually means for him. However, Said hints elsewhere that this split was not a dichotomy, a matter of 'either/or' relationship, but, it may be suggested, a series of Janus-like 'both . . . and' locations on an experiential continuum where the two languages, Arabic and English, interacted with each other in variable and complex ways. At times, the two languages worked in tandem, but they also *Othered* each other in a shifting myriad of experiences and forms of being and becoming. Living *in* and *between* two languages, Said must have felt that a part of him was lost in translation, through the semantic leakage that the transfer of feelings and meanings from one language to another inevitably produces; his references to translation in *Out of Place* (for example, 1999: pp. xiv, 4 and 69) suggest this strongly, as does a comment he made about bilingualism in an article that was published posthumously. In this context, it is not surprising that as a young boy, Said was confused about which language was his 'beyond any doubt' (1999: 4). His mother used both English and Arabic with him in what seem like fairly well-defined domains and, whether intentionally or not, for particular effects: 'Her English deployed a rhetoric of statement and norms that has never left me. Once my mother left Arabic and spoke English there was a more objective and serious tone that mostly banished the forgiving and musical intimacy of *her* first language, Arabic' (4).

This contrast between the 'objective' and what may be called the 'subjective' deployment of English and Arabic, respectively, created some strong linguistic-domain associations for the young Said. Arabic was a 'first' mother language for him, but in a very important sense, it was also his mother/mother's tongue: the language of the hearth, with its strong umbilical associations of motherly warmth, private feelings, 'musical intimacy,' 'forgiving' attitude and 'infinitely maternal atmosphere,' as he says.[5] It is clearly in this language that Said, as a young boy, felt most secure and most 'at home,' in the psychological sense of the term, in spite of the fact that English also *seemed* to him an equal partner-language to Arabic in his early years. The fact that Said addresses the language issue on the second page of his memoir is an indication of how important language was in his early memories and of the way he located himself in his social world at this stage in his life. His reflections on this matter are compelling:

> I have never known what language I spoke first, Arabic or English, or which one was really mine beyond any doubt. What I do know, however, is that the two have always been together in my life, one resonating in the other, sometimes ironically, sometimes nostalgically, most often each correcting, and commenting on, the other. Each *can* [original emphasis] seem like my absolutely first language, but neither is. I trace this *primal instability* [emphasis added] back to my mother, whom I remember speaking to me in both English and Arabic, although she always wrote to me in English—once a week all her

5 For the distinction between 'mother tongue' and 'native language,' see Suleiman (2008).

> life, as did I, all of hers. Certain spoken phrases of hers like *tislamli* ['May the Lord preserve you for me!'] or *mish 'arfa shu biddi a'mal?* ['I don't know what to do']. Or *rouhha* ['My soul/my very being']—dozens of them—were Arabic, and I was never conscious of having to translate them or, even in cases like *tislamli*, knowing exactly what they meant. They were a part of her infinitely maternal atmosphere, which in moments of great stress I found myself yearning for in the softly uttered phrase *'ya mama'* ['Mummy!'], an atmosphere dreamily seductive then suddenly snatched away, promising something in the end never given. (Said 1999: 4)

We must, however, draw a distinction between Said's concept of mother/mother's tongue and what he refers to in his memoir as 'first' language. For Said, one's mother/mother's tongue is not necessarily the same as one's first language. Being a mother/mother's tongue, a language must carry with it, as I have suggested above, those feelings of intimacy and warmth that are associated with the figures of the 'mother' and 'home,' as these are intimately inscribed in some deeply personal expressions and forms of language use that act as mnemonic and archival sites of belonging and return. Being a first language is a matter of competence in the various registers and domains of the language, without, however, the need to have complete equality across all registers and functional domains between the first language and the mother/mother's tongue. This is an important distinction in *Out of Place*, a matter that Said regards as the source of 'primal instability' in his life (1999: 4). For although Said declares that neither Arabic nor English was his first language par excellence, we can nevertheless detect a nuanced distinction in his early years between the two, allocating Arabic to the subjective domains of 'home' and 'orality' and English to the objective domains of deliberate social transactions and textuality. This distinction is reflected in Said's references to Arabic in his memoir as his 'mother tongue' and 'native language,' descriptions he never uses to characterise English, the language in which he wrote his memoir and that of his breathtaking intellectual output. For Said, the epithets 'mother' and 'native' when prefixed to 'language' always refer to Arabic, never to English.

So if neither English nor Arabic was Said's first language par excellence, does this mean that he had no first language at all? The answer is no, in spite of the fact that he tells us that neither was. I would like to suggest that Said had two first languages, Arabic and English *together* and *separately*, with emphasis simultaneously on this togetherness and separateness. Each was an equal partner of the other, and each was a first in relation to the other, since neither could fulfil all of his life's needs and each had its own domain associations.[6] Neither had precedent over the other, except that in Said's

6 In 'Living in Arabic' (2004), Said offers the following interesting reflections about his Arabic-English bilingualism, in which he makes the distinction between the bilingualism of 'knowing' two languages and that of 'living in' two languages. While the former kind of bilingualism is possible for Said, the latter is not:

early childhood, Arabic was very much the language of 'home,' not just in the physical, domestic sense of 'home' but in the sense of belonging, of defining symbolically where some of one's most important roots are, a point to which Said returns towards the end of his life, as I will suggest later.

Contrasting his family's linguistic behaviour in Cairo, where English dominated his life, with its linguistic behaviour in Jerusalem, where Arabic was the dominant language—in spite of the fact that Egypt and Palestine were both under British control in one form or another at the time—Said associates Arabic with 'home' in what may be called the community or national sense of the term: '[In Jerusalem,] our daily conversation in school and home was uniformly in Arabic; unlike in Cairo, where English was encouraged, our family in Jerusalem "*belonged*" and our *native* language prevailed everywhere [emphasis added], even when talking about Hollywood films: Tarzan became "Tarazan" and Laurel and Hardy "*al-Buns wal rafi*"'(Fatso and the Thin Man)' (1999: 108). At home, English transmutes into Arabic, thus 'Tarzan' becomes 'Tarazan' (with emphatic /t/), and Laurel and Hardy lose their English names, becoming epithets of themselves in Arabic. And commenting on his school days at St. George's from this period in Jerusalem in 1947, Said writes: 'Very quickly I felt totally at home [in Jerusalem]; for the first and last time in my school life I was among boys who were like me' (1999: 108). Here Said refers to Arabic as his 'native language,' an appellation he never uses to refer to English or French—a language he also mastered well. The association of Arabic with this meaning of 'home' reveals in an uncontested way where the original site of departure for Said is: it is both in Jerusalem and in Arabic, not in Cairo or English, in spite of his enduring love for Cairo and his enormous competence in English.

This strong association of language and home underlies the double meaning of displacement I have associated with what it means to be 'out of place' for Said. When he is not in Jerusalem, Said is *out of place*, both linguistically and geographically. In Jerusalem, he is at home, and thus *in place*,

---

> 'Because Arabic and English are such different languages in the way they operate, and also because the ideal of eloquence in one language is not the same as in the other, a perfect bilingualism of the kind I often dream about, and sometimes boldly think that I have almost achieved, is not really possible. There is a massive technical literature on bilingualism, but what I've seen of it simply cannot deal with the aspect of actually *living in* [emphasis added], as opposed to knowing, two languages from two different worlds and two different linguistic families. This isn't to say that one can't be somehow brilliant, as the Polish native Conrad was, in English, but the strangeness stays forever. Besides, what does it mean to be perfectly, in a completely equal way, bilingual? Has anyone studied the ways in which each language creates barriers against other languages, just in case one might slip over into new territory?' (Said 2004)

The last sentence recognises the role of languages as boundary setters at the personal level. Furthermore, the distinction between 'living in' and 'knowing' a language for Said must correlate with Arabic and English, respectively; hence the use of 'living in' in the title of the article to signal that 'Arabic is home.'

both linguistically and in terms of human geography. In Jerusalem, Arabic emerges as Said's *first* 'first language,' relegating English to the status of *second* 'first language,' unlike in Cairo, where the two languages had to live side-by-side as 'first' languages with some domain specialisation for each, with English as the primary language for the objective domain and Arabic as its primary counterpart in the subjective domain. In Jerusalem, therefore, Said seems more at home with himself than in Cairo, both linguistically and geographically. It is a matter of great interest to me how this association of home and language in Jerusalem coincides with my own experience when I visited the city in the 1990s after approximately thirty years of absence, an experience I analysed at some length in my book *A War of Words: Language and Conflict in the Middle East* (2004b: 8–13). This coincidence suggests very strongly that conceptions of home are for some exiles or diasporics inseparable from where they position themselves linguistically in relation to their original point of belonging and departure.

Even if Arabic were not the dominant language of home in Cairo, its relative invisibility compared with English must have been symbolically marked as a deviation from what Said seems to have tacitly conceptualised as a norm according to which the language ought to be dominant. This explains to some extent Said's critical comments on his father's 'linguistic clumsiness' in Arabic (1999: 168), his 'quixotic mixture of Egyptian and Palestinian dialects' on his visits to Lebanon (167) and how *Shami* (Levantine) family friends in Cairo made gentle mockery of his 'unrelenting use of English' (220) and other American habits as publicly displayed badges of his American citizenship, which he was very keen to impress on his only son as the privileged compass of belonging and loyalty to a country thousands of miles away. By contrast, Said praises his mother for her 'excellent command of classical Arabic as well as the demotic' (vernacular/*'āmiyya*) variety of the language (5). He also praises her for challenging the trend in Cairo of using French in preference to Arabic to display class or status in society, although she was very fluent in French. One of Said's comments on this aspect of his mother's linguistic behaviour is worth reproducing in full: 'Our families shopped for food at Groppi's, talking with the plainly Greek and Egyptian employees who staffed the elegant tearoom's delicatessen in jaw-shattering French, when it was perfectly clear that we all could have done better in Arabic. I was *proud* of my mother for conversing in Arabic, since she alone of the entire social group to which we belonged knew the language well, was literate in it, and *seemed to feel no social disadvantage about using it*, even though the prevailing atmosphere was such that using French gave one a higher (perhaps the highest) status' (emphasis added).

Clearly, Said has little regard for members of his parents' 'social group,' the Egyptians and the *Shamis*, because of their sociolinguistic affectation and for preferring to speak in 'jaw-shattering French' to 'plainly Greek and Egyptian employees' rather than Arabic, the language in which, by implication, we suspect both parties—the clientele and the employees—could speak at a higher linguistic level. The issue here is not one of linguistic competence or mundane communicative functionality but one of linguistic symbolism, of the second-order signification of language that, in very subtle ways, is as impregnated with meaning as the ordinary use of language is, albeit a different kind of meaning. Being typical of the linguistic behaviour of members of 'native' satellite groups in (ex-) colonial settings, the use of broken French in preference to good/perfect Arabic is a form of language display by Egyptians or *Shamis* that, while intended to proclaim status, is deployed to mask social inferiority towards colonial culture, a case of 'internalised colonialism,' as Leila Ahmed describes this behaviour in her memoir, *A Border Passage* (2000). Said's pride in his mother derives from her refusal to succumb to peer pressure in spite of the fact that she could have spoken French, we are told, with greater facility than her peers had she wanted to.

Said was also proud of his mother because, by speaking Arabic, not French, she refused to validate one of the sociolinguistic norms of her social group, whose linguistic behaviour conformed to (ex-) colonial models of regulating the interaction with the 'natives,' wherein the (ex-) colonial languages rule supreme. Said's mother understood the symbolic meanings of language use and the significance of linguistic 'border crossing,' no matter how momentary this crossing might be; in particular, she seems to have understood how linguistic choice socially refers to both the language that is used in a particular setting and those discursive possibilities, though available to a speaker, that are deliberately discounted by him or her in those settings out of institutionalised social practise or because of deliberate choice. Her linguistic behaviour shows her to be not just strong-willed and independent-minded but someone who is also capable of displaying what I will call 'reverse or inverted linguistic snobbery,' of using the marginalised language of the 'native,' the voice of subalternity, so to speak, to communicate both distance (from her social group) and proximity to the norms of a lower status out-group. Flouting or even resisting the dominant sociolinguistic norms of one's in-group as an act of border crossing is often a calculated strategy of commenting on those norms by signalling to members of that group that one's membership in it is not hermetically sealed. In the colonially dominated culture of the time, such acts of border crossing and resistance have great symbolic value: they are acts of subversion and negative social comment that puncture the relationship of the subject to her environment.

Out of Place contains more pointed reflections on the marginalisation of Arabic in the Cairo of Said's early years in the 1940s and early 1950s. Most of these reflections concern the place of Arabic in the curricula of the foreign schools he attended. Being English-medium institutions, the curricula of these schools were devoted to English and its associated cultures (mainly British or American), with little or no regard for Arabic, as well as Egyptian or Arab culture. Although these schools were undoubtedly all in the colonial mould in this regard, the point I am making is not, strictly speaking, intended as a criticism of these schools. It is the parents who make choices for their young children, and Said's parents could have chosen to send him to schools where Arabic and its associated culture(s) were sufficiently embedded in the curricula and in the educational philosophy of those schools, instead of presenting the language tokenistically—as the foreign-language-medium schools did—as a sop to the local culture in an early form of intercultural political correctness. What is important for us, however, is to explore the way Said describes and responds to this aspect of his schooling.

At the Gezira Preparatory School (GPS), Said was taught by British teachers whose children attended the same school. Commenting on the curriculum at this school, Said juxtaposes his world with that of his schoolmates who are native English speakers: 'Our lessons and books were mystifyingly English: we read about meadows, castles, and kings John, Alfred and Canute with the reverence that our teachers kept reminding us they deserved. Their world made little sense to me, *except that I admired their creation of the language they used,* which I, a *little Arab boy,* was learning something about' (1999: 39; emphasis added).[7] He later tells us that at GPS, '"All things are bright and beautiful" had meant bright and beautiful England, the distant lodestar of good for all of us' (82). As I pointed out earlier, orienting the school system around the (ex-) colonial culture and its language is a prominent feature of the education of the aspiring classes in countries under (ex-) colonial domination or influence. Further, this is an enactment of a principle enunciated by the Arab sociologist Ibn Khaldun in the fourteenth century, which states that the defeated party tends to imitate the victorious one in its practises and social mores. In these satellite environments, the (ex-) colonial culture becomes the norm that marginalises the local culture and inscribes it with inferiority. Here again, we have a sense of what it means for Said to be 'out of place' when language and geography, as the stuff from which our socialised worlds are made, come to the fore. Instead of being exposed to a curriculum that relates to the native culture in some meaningful way, Said had to submit to the culture of the politically dominant power in Egypt, almost exclusively. In this sense, Said is not just 'out of place' but also 'out of body': he is corporeally in Egypt but intellectually in England. He may not accept the England he is fed, but he, a 'little Arab boy,' in both senses of 'young' and 'insignificant,' cannot help but admire the language that the English have, God-like, created and made available to him for moral, social and educational self-elevation.

The Americans seem to have adopted a somewhat different educational policy in Egypt from the British in their attitude towards the vernacular. At Said's second school, Cairo School for American Children (CSAC), Arabic was a school subject but only at the margins of the school curriculum and presented to pupils condescendingly in the form of 'kitchen Arabic.' It was taught to all schoolchildren, regardless of national or ethnic background,

7 See Pennycook (1998) for the relationship between the English language and colonialism.

but perhaps through no fault of the school, Said ended up being taught his 'mother tongue' (1999: 82) as a foreign language. The effect of this experience on this Palestinian Arab boy with American citizenship must have been one of sheer boredom and, at the psychological level, must have represented a case of foreignisation, estrangement, infantalisation and patronisation through education, an enactment of the presumptuous stupidity of teaching one's grandmother how to suck eggs. He describes this in his memoir as follows: 'Somehow I had to conceal my perfect command of what was my mother tongue in order to fit in better with the inane formulas given out to American youngsters for what passed for spoken (but really was kitchen) Arabic. I never volunteered, rarely spoke, often crouched near the back of the room' (1999: 82). Opting for a strategy of invisibility among his peers on his own linguistic turf (hence the crouching at the back of the classroom), where, in fact, he should have had a clear advantage, Said acted in a way that must have given the impression that he either was ashamed of his language or was not a good language learner. Either way, Said was justified in feeling that he and the language he calls his mother/mother's tongue were condescendingly marginalised, as, in fact, were the teachers who taught the language to them (142–43).

Arabic must have felt like a social scar, a source of embarrassment and even shame to the Edward Said of CSAC. This is consistent with the following reflection from the same period in *Out of Place*: 'The overall sensation I had was of my *troublesome identity* as an American inside whom *lurked* another Arab identity from which I derived no strength, only embarrassment and discomfort' (199: 90; emphasis added). Instead of being proud of his native language in Egypt as an Arabic-speaking country, Said felt that he had to run away from the language, to feign foreignness in it to avoid the discomfort its educational marginality and low social status created for him and in him, as though this status was an indelible linguistic pigment that he could not hide. By doing this, Said must have felt that he was being untrue to himself, but he had little choice as a young boy, who was unsure of himself, but to camouflage his linguistic competence in Arabic as if it was a social handicap that at some future point may strike back as the term 'lurked' in the above quotation suggests.

There is an important point to consider in all of this. When (language) inclusion becomes a matter of tokenism and lip service and when it is driven more by good intentions or considerations of political correctness than real and equitable engagement in the curriculum and the social world, inclusion is strongly perceived and experienced as a form of social hypocrisy, even exclusion. Said's engagement with Arabic at CSAC exemplifies this phenomenon. This feeling on his part, the fact that language was a handicap and a barrier in the liminal world in which he existed, characterised his relationship with Padre Fedden, whose help his parents enlisted with some private religious tuition. Said liked Padre Fedden, who he thought was a lot 'more approachable and human' (1999: 144) than other English-speaking teachers in his environment, but he could not relate to him unproblematically:

'I always felt the *rift* [emphasis added] between white man and Arab as separating us in the end, maybe because he was in a position of authority and [English] was *his* language not mine' (144). Although Said does not link authority (and power) to language directly here, there is little doubt that the two are interlinked, at least at the psychological level: English is part and parcel of Padre Fedden's authority and racial superiority as a 'white man.' Without it, he might not have been hired to teach Said. It is partly because of his knowledge of his subject *through* English that Fedden acquires authority and the educational capital that enables him to engage in gainful private tuition. Furthermore, by describing English as '[Fedden's] language not mine,' Said divests himself of any ownership he might have had over the language through claiming that it was his 'first' language in his memoir. The use of the marked word 'rift' in the preceding quotation indicates the intensity of the difference Said felt with what Padre Fedden symbolised in both their social worlds.

Arabic was the source of many painful rebuffs for Said. At Mount Hermon School in New England, where his father sent him to finish his secondary education in 1951, Said was reminded of the estrangement associated with Arabic in his life when he went to meet Edmund Alexander, the tennis coach and English teacher, for whom, we are told, Arabic was a 'native language' (1999: 228). Having been received frostily, Said switched to Arabic, 'thinking that his [Alexander's] and my native language might open up a more generous avenue of interaction,' but he was stopped in 'midsentence' by Alexander, who gave him short shrift, saying in a rebuffing tone of voice: 'No brother . . . no Arabic here. I left that behind. Here we are Americans . . . and we should talk and act like Americans' (228). Trying to create bonds through language, Said falls flat on his face but not before he mocks Alexander's English, which, we are told, is impregnated with Arabic discursive practises. Commenting on Alexander's 'No brother,' Said says it was 'a very Arab locution, I thought, even though uttered in English' (228). Similarly, commenting on 'Here we are Americans,' Said calls it 'another Arabic turn of phrase, instead of "We're in America now"' (228). Said's comments are intended to show how the inner recesses of Alexander's English archived an Arabic voice that somehow mocks his treatment of English as a new badge of identity for him. Even when exorcised, Arabic refuses to disappear from Alexander's discourse; it still hangs there archaeologically, refusing to depart completely. Although resentful of the way Alexander treated him, Said could still see in his acts of denial an affirmation of that which continued to bind them together, those subterranean habits of speaking that override the surface structures of disparate languages and expose deeper archaeologies of embargoed bonds.

But there was another side to Said's engagement with Arabic in his school days. At Victoria College—often described as the Eton of Egypt and the Arab world—which he attended between 1949 and 1951, Rule 1 in the *School Handbook* stated: 'English is the language of the school. Anyone caught speaking other languages will be severely punished' (Said 1999: 184).

Language bans usually have the effect of turning the languages that are subjected to them into symbols and instruments of subversion and resistance to the dominant social and political order. This is precisely what happened at Victoria College. For Said and some of his Arabic-speaking peers, Arabic served symbolically as an instrument of undermining the authority of the school administration at all levels. Instead of hiding Arabic, Said and his friends started to deploy it, often, it seems, in prankish and imprecatory behaviour, to unsettle their foreign teachers, who had no clue about what was being said inside or outside class. At Victoria College, Arabic became a tool of counterhegemony (although with what conviction we do not know), of fighting against English as the symbol of the dominant culture of the school and the 'hated British' (1999: 198). Said's description of this is worth quoting in full because of the language of conflict he uses to describe the oppressive moral economy of the school:

> [Because of Rule 1] Arabic became our *haven*, a *criminalised discourse* where we *took refuge* from the world of *masters* and *complicit* prefects and *anglicised* older boys who *lorded it over* us as *enforcers* of the *hierarchy* and its *rules*. Because of Rule 1 we spoke more, rather than less, Arabic, as an *act of defiance* against what seemed then, and seems even more so now, an *arbitrary, ludicrously gratuitous symbol of their power*. What I had formerly hidden at CSAC became a *proud insurrectionary gesture*, the *power* to speak Arabic and not be caught, or, more riskily, the use of Arabic words in class as a way of answering an academic question and *attacking* the teacher at the same time. (1999: 184; emphasis added)

Arabic at Victoria College has emerged as a 'haven' and 'refuge' and as a source of 'defiance,' 'power' and 'pride' for an Edward Said engaged in a language war with the school authorities and their agents, consisting of the 'masters' and a retinue of co-opted local informers and others who, we are told, considered 'being and speaking Arabic . . . delinquent activities' (: 188) to be forgone in favour of acquiring the superior language and culture of the British as the dominant power in Egypt. This lowly status of Arabic in the Victoria College culture had an impact on the treatment of the Egyptian teachers of Arabic in the school as 'plainly second-class citizens,' who, because of this, were 'held in contempt' by the students (: 185). The fact that these teachers stuck to the mechanical drilling of grammar and to offering a literature curriculum of 'dreadful patriotic encomia to King Farouk' did not endear them to their students, whose resentment of them was compounded by perceptions of servility and greed connected with their work as private home tutors. Reflecting on the three languages in his repertoire from this period—Arabic, French and English—Said tells us: 'The three languages became a pointedly sensitive issue for me at the age of about fourteen. Arabic was forbidden and 'wog'; French was always 'theirs,' not mine; English was authorised, but unacceptable as the language of the hated British' (198). The fact that it took Said half a century to overcome his handicap in, and alienation from, Arabic—the 'wog' language of his early years—is indicative of the deep estrangement that had existed between them. He declares in *Out of Place*, 'Only now [towards the end of my life] can I overcome my alienation from Arabic caused by education and exile and take pleasure in it' (198).

But which variety of Arabic does Said have in mind when he talks about the language in *Out of Place*? Does he mean *fuṣḥā* Arabic, the standard language of writing and books, or the colloquial dialects in his repertoire? The answer is both. There is no doubt that the primary location of the feelings of intimacy and belonging he expresses about the language relates to its colloquial form. The examples he quotes, some of which have been mentioned above, make this clear. It is this form of Arabic that he treats as his mother/mother's language, the one in which he had his early quotidian experiences. It is also certain that it was this form of Arabic that Said and his friends used to taunt and torment the school authorities at Victoria College, to subvert the 'English only rule' and to challenge the authorised use of the *fuṣḥā* in the Arabic classes. Thus, it is almost certain that when Said talks about alienation from Arabic, he is, in fact, talking about *fuṣḥā* Arabic, the language of education and culture with which he had an uneasy relationship as a schoolboy. It is, however, revealing that when he uses the term *native language*, he seems to refer to both the *fuṣḥā* and the colloquial dialect, his mother/mother's tongue. It is also revealing that he never uses the term *native language* to refer to English—a point made earlier but worth repeating here—which he describes in his memoir as one of his two 'first' languages.

This analysis of the relationship between the *fuṣḥā* and the colloquial dialects is supported by Said's posthumously published article 'Living in Arabic' (2004), which appeared in the Egyptian English-language publication *Al-Ahram Weekly*. In this article, Said makes a pitch for the eloquence of the *fuṣḥā*, from which he was alienated as a schoolboy but to which he returned later, a return occasioned by the crushing and humiliating defeat of the Arabs at the hands of the Israelis in the 1967 War. The fact that only the trauma caused by a national disaster of the extent of the Six Day War could jolt Said back into a real and sustained engagement with standard Arabic is another indication of the deep rift that had previously existed between the man and his newly reclaimed language. This cataclysmic event of national defeat and deep trauma marked the engagement of Said publicly with Arab issues, the Palestine question in particular. This return to his 'roots,' to an identity that for a long time remained dormant, exposed Said afresh to the written language and to its stilted and lifeless manifestations in much of the Marxist-dominated Arabic discourse of the time, which Arab intellectuals produced and reproduced as a revolutionary mantra that signalled the way to national salvation. This negative encounter with the language did not, however, dent Said's enthusiasm for the *fuṣḥā*, from which he was alienated in the past for a variety of reasons.

One reason relates to the mind-numbing experiences of being taught Arabic grammar in a rote-learning format that made the subject boring and even repellent, very much as it does today for millions of students in the

Arabic-speaking world.[8] However, when Said made the decision to reengage with his native Arabic culture and to '*re*commit [himself] to a *re*-education in Arabic philology and grammar'[9] (Said 2004; emphasis added), he turned to the well-known Lebanese linguist and onetime professor of Semitic languages at the American University of Beirut, Anis Frayha, for tuition.[10] Frayha, famous for his attempts to simplify Arabic grammar for pedagogical purposes, succeeded in introducing Said to the workings of the language in a way that resonated with his intellectual interests.[11] One such interest must have been Said's fascination with the work on eloquence of the eighteenth-century Italian scholar Giambattista Vico, a subject (i.e., eloquence [*faṣāḥa*]) of seminal importance in the Arabic linguistic tradition,[12] in spite of the differences between this and the European tradition on the topic.

Another reason for Said's early antipathy to the *fuṣḥā* had to do with the symbolic meanings it had acquired for him as an instrument of parental and societal authority and control across the fields of education, religion, politics and professional interest. His lack of commitment to learning the language was, therefore, constructed by him as a means of resisting these sources of authority and control, which manifested themselves on social occasions that the young Said found extremely dull and excruciatingly boring because of their didactic tone, pompous displays of bogus expertise and

8 Said comments on grammar learning in Arabic as follows: 'Arabic grammar is so sophisticated and logically appealing, I think, that it is perhaps best studied by an older pupil who can appreciate the niceties of its reasoning' (2004). My experience working on Arabic-language pedagogical reforms during the past few years suggests that a delay of the kind suggested by Said cannot make Arabic grammar palatable to students. What is needed is a real simplification of pedagogic grammar that attends to the meanings and functions of the language instead of the centuries-long obsession with the theory of regents, governance and detailed grammatical parsing.

9 Notice the use of the prefix *re-*, which indicates that Said had contact with these disciplines before.

10 See Al-Batal (1994) for Anis Frayha's contribution to the reform of pedagogic Arabic grammar.

11 This is how Said describes this experience:

> I was fortunate in having an old friend of my father's, retired Professor of Semitic Languages Anis Frayha at the American University of Beirut, as my tutor and who, like me, was an early riser; for almost a year between the morning hours of seven and ten he took me on daily explorations through the language without a text-book, but with hundreds of passages from the Qur'an, which at bottom is the foundation of Arabic usage, classical authors like Al-Ghazzali, Ibn Khaldun and Al-Mas'udi, and modern writers, from Ahmed Shawki to Mahfouz. An amazingly effective teacher, his tutorials disclosed the workings of the language for me in a way that suited my professional interests and philological training in Western comparative literature. . . . Thanks to Frayha I was introduced to, and later introduced into my own teaching and writing Arab grammarians and speculators, including Al-Khalil bin Ahmed [*sic*], Sebawayh [*sic*], and Ibn Hazm, whose work antedated my European figures [of academic interest] by seven centuries. (Said 2004)

12 See al-Kawwaz (2006) for a good survey of the concept of eloquence (*faṣāḥa*) in Arabic scholarship.

hypocritical moral posturing.[13] Although Said does not comment on this, the *fuṣḥā* must have afforded him a soft target for resistance and rebellion, a kind of proxy considering the fact that the language was not as highly valued as it might have been at home, particularly, it seems, by his father or in the social circles in which he moved in Cairo. Said's comments on this are interesting:

> During my early years the classical language [the *fuṣḥā*] was symbolic of parentally and institutionally enforced, not to say imprisoning, circumstances, where I would have to sit in church regaled by interminable sermons, or in all sorts of secular assemblies preached at by orators proclaiming a king's or a minister's or a doctor's or a student's virtue, and where as a form of resistance to the occasion I would tune out the droning and gradually come to gain a sort of dumb incomprehension. In practise, I knew passages from the hymnal, the *Book of Common Prayer* (including the Lord's Prayer) and such similar devotional material by heart, and even some (to me at the time) intolerably smarmy and usually patriotic odes in classical poetry, but it was only years later that I realised how the atmosphere of rote-learning, lamentably ungifted and repressive teachers and clergymen, and a sort of enforced 'it's good for you' attitude against which I was in perpetual rebellion undermined the project [of learning the *fuṣḥā*] altogether. . . . So alienated was I from the layers of repressive authority blanketing my person as a child and teenager that rebellion took the form of keeping to the language of the streets, reserving the respectable classical language [the *fuṣḥā*] solely for use as all-purpose mockery, savage imitations of tedious pomposity, and imprecations against church, state and school. (Said 2004)

Later in life, Said was able to distinguish between the *fuṣḥā* and the way it was taught and put to use by speakers in a canny realization on his part of Ibn Jinni's (d. 1002) dictum that speech, and therefore all linguistic production, is an act of the speaker. Translated into modern terminology, this dictum implies that styles and modes of expression are not language-made but user-made. The faults of excess and ossification according to this view, therefore, lay not with the language but with those who used it with affectation and lack of sincerity or thought: 'Recalling my childhood attitudes to [the *fuṣḥā*] I soon felt that, as presented at rallies or meetings, political analyses were made to sound more profound than they were, or that much of what was said in these rather-too-pedantic approximations of formal speech were based on models of eloquence that had been rote-learned as emulations of seriousness, rather than the thing itself' (Said 2004).[14]

But having effected a rapprochement with the *fuṣḥā*, Said came to be a great admirer and champion of the language because of its eloquence and the elegance of its grammar; hence his criticism of Leila Ahmed's (2000)

13 This is another example of the associations that the *fuṣḥā* may have to speakers; compare this with its meanings for this author in chapter 3.

14 For a discussion of this topic, see Suleiman (1999c).

call for adopting the colloquial as the means of writing in Egypt, a topic I will explore in the next section. Said writes disparagingly about Ahmed's views saying that she 'waxes eloquent on the virtues of spoken Egyptian while admitting that she really doesn't know the *fuṣḥā* . . . at all,' the point being that for a comparison of this kind to be characterised with intellectual honesty, it ought, according to Said, to be based on competence in both forms of the language, something that Ahmed admits she does not possess on the *fuṣḥā* side; he admonishes her further, pointing out that this lack of knowledge of the *fuṣḥā* 'doesn't seem to have impeded her teaching of Islam at Harvard [where she is a professor] even though it scarcely needs repeating that Arabic is Islam and Islam is Arabic at some very profound level' (Said 2004). Said comes close to accusing Ahmed of 'professional hypocrisy' for accepting a professorial appointment at Harvard that requires extensive and intimate knowledge of the *fuṣḥā* while publicly professing a lack of deep knowledge of it.

Said's reconciliation with the *fuṣḥā* was, in fact, so deep and long-lasting that he set out in his later years on a quest to try to master it for professional purposes, including public speaking. He describes his performance in this endeavour as one that still mixes the *fuṣḥā* and the colloquial for pragmatic purposes, and he says that his aim in the way he uses Arabic is to adopt a voice that avoids 'circumlocution and ornamental preciosity' (2004). But he admits that his attempts at doing so have not always impressed, declaring that they may, in fact, be an 'excuse [he uses] to cover [his] sense of still *loitering* on the fringes of the language rather than standing confidently at its centre' (2004; emphasis added).

When one reads these words, one does not detect the slightest note of indignation or self-pity on Said's part at the fact that he has not fully made the grade in his use of the *fuṣḥā*; on the contrary, one feels a sense of pleasure in a man who has discovered what to him could have been an almost lost heritage but who now lovingly, caringly and self-mockingly is trying to reclaim it as his through the *fuṣḥā*. The word 'loitering' above gives the game away, as do the loving details of his family's relationship with Arabic, which he chooses as the substance of a most delicate closure to the aptly titled 'Living in Arabic.' In this exquisitely beautiful finale, in which Said affords us a rare glimpse of his life as husband and father, English recedes out of sight, giving way to Arabic to enact closure but not before affirming that the Saids in New York lived in Arabic in some important, symbolic and diachronically bonding and bounding sense:

> I think of my earliest years . . . in terms of both striking images that seem as vivid to me now as they did then, and of states of languages and English that always begin in the intimacy of the family: my mother's strangely accented English, acquired in mission schools and a cultivated Palestinian milieu early in the [twentieth] century, her wonderfully expressive Arabic, vacillating charmingly between the demotic of her native Nazareth and Beirut, and that of her long residence in Cairo, my father's eccentric Anglo-American dialect, his poor Jerusalem and Cairo melange, the sense he gave me both

> of admonishment and an often unsuccessful search for the right word in English as well as in Arabic. And, then, more recently, my wife Mariam's Arabic, a language learned naturally in national school without the disturbance of English or French at first, although both were acquired a little later. Hence her ease in moving back and forth between [the *fuṣḥā*] and [the] colloquial, which I could never do as she does or feel as competently at home in as she does. And my son's amazing knowledge of the Arabic language as a magnificent, somehow self-conscious structure which he painstakingly got on his own at university and then through long residence in Cairo, Palestine, Jordan, Syria, Lebanon, noting down every new expression: legal, Qur'anic, dialectal that he learned until he, a New York city kid now a lawyer whose obvious first language was English, has in effect become a learned user of his great-great-grandfather's (Mariam's grandfather) 'matter,' the Arabic language which he taught as a university professor in Beirut before World War One [*sic*]; or my daughter's perfect ear as accomplished actress and as a precociously early literary talent who, while she didn't do what her older brother did and go out and make herself master the strange quirks of our original *Muttersprache*, can mime the sounds exactly right, and has been called on (especially now) to play parts in commercial films, TV serials, and plays, roles that are of the 'generic' Middle Eastern woman, and which has slowly led her to her interest in learning the common family language for the first time in her young life. (2004)

In one of those very rare moments of proud self-indulgence, Said chooses Arabic as the occasion and fitting finale to talk about his family life. He marvels at his wife's facility in the language, acquired naturally, as he says, 'in national school without the disturbance of English or French'. There is no doubt that Said's use of 'national school' and 'disturbance' is meant as an oblique comment on his own educational and language-learning experience, where English must have acted as a source of disturbance for Arabic. This is very true these days, when studying and knowing English or French in most of the Middle East and North Africa have become a badge of sophistication and modernity and when feigning, or asserting, weakness or lack of facility in Arabic is sometimes paraded as a sign of status, class and, perversely, even education through a mélange of code-switching practises, as I have set out in chapter 3 (see also Suleiman 2004b). Mariam's ability to move between the different forms of Arabic is of a different order from his; it thus emerges as a subject of loving and admiring envy on Said's part: she does what he cannot do but wished he could do, and she does so with the ease and spontaneity that only a person who is confident and assured of her linguistic ability can have.

Said's pride in his son Wadie's Arabic linguistic accomplishment is no less heartfelt.[15] The proud father describes his son's painstaking achievement

15 Said came to lecture at Edinburgh University a few times in the 1990s, where I was working at the time. On one occasion, I think it was in the late 1990s, I entered the lecture hall to find him sitting on the edge of his seat before moving to the platform to deliver his public lecture. As I walked in and headed towards him to greet him (I had just finished giving a lecture), we exchanged the traditional Arab kisses on the cheek in front of a packed hall. He then

in the 'magnificent' Arabic language as 'amazing' for a New York 'city kid' who travelled for long periods to Cairo, Palestine, Jordan, Syria and Lebanon in search of the language not just of his father but also of his maternal 'great-great-grandfather,' who taught it in Beirut at the beginning of the twentieth century. This linguistic journey back in time is further celebrated by the proud father when he lovingly talks about his daughter Nejla's attempts to learn 'our original *Muttersprache*' and 'the common family language,' not just as a way of furthering her career but also to connect with her linguistic roots and the culture these roots sustain. Said's choice of 'original' in the above quotation to refer to Arabic is not accidental; it is a deliberate employment of expression in one language, English, to comment on another, Arabic. And there is no doubt that the kind of Arabic Said is talking about is not the colloquial but the *fuṣḥā*, which Leila Ahmed would like to see replaced by the colloquial as a medium of writing. There is no doubt, of course, that English is far more Wadie's and Nejla's mother tongue and common language than Arabic is in instrumental terms, but this is not the only side to language in which Said is interested when he talks about Arabic. He is at least as interested in the symbolic meanings of language as he is in its instrumental loadings as a means of day-to-day communication.

In the Said household, Arabic thus emerges on the instrumental and, even more so, the symbolic plane as (1) an important bonding factor that binds father to son and daughter in feelings of intimacy and belonging synchronically, as it did bind Said to his mother; (2) an element of pride and loving envy that binds husband to wife in life and death, as the posthumous publication of 'Living in Arabic' suggests; and (3) a means of vertical journeys back in time to bind grandson to great-great-grandfather diachronically across distant physical spaces. Language, the Arabic language, is the element that binds and bounds the Saids together as a family unit, which, in spite of years of life in exile, still angles itself to an original point of remotely archived departure with all of the cultural associations and political meanings this point has. Answering to the three-generation rule in studies of immigration to America as—so the official rhetoric goes—a melting pot, Wadie the grandson reclaims for himself what Wadie the grandfather had wanted his son Edward to relinquish: the link with a language, a culture and a past heritage that the grandfather was prepared to forgo. The same seems to be true of Nejla.

Said had a complex relationship with the two languages *in* and *between* which he lived: Arabic and English. In his elegy to Said, Palestinian poet

---

said to me, 'Yasir, I have great news for you! Wadie has spent the last year studying Arabic intensively and he now speaks it like a *bulbul* [nightingale],' the comparison with the nightingale in Arabic being the traditional way of commenting on a person's fluency in a language, particularly a foreign language. Edward 'broke the news' to me with a big smile and with evident fatherly pride in Wadie's achievement. This story set me thinking about Said's link to Arabic, the result of which is the discussion in this chapter.

Mahmoud Darwish–who passed away as I was working on this chapter in August 2008—captures this relationship perceptively and movingly:

> He [Edward Said] says: I am from there, I am from here,
> But I am neither there nor here.
> I have two names which meet and part . . .
> I have two languages, but I have long forgotten
> which is the language of my dreams.
> I have an English language, for writing,
> with yielding phrase,
> and a language in which Heaven and
> Jerusalem converse, with a silver cadence,
> But it does not yield to my imagination. (Darwish 2004)

These lines make it clear that Arabic and English existed side-by-side as two complementary languages for Said. English was, as Darwish says, the language of writing, of intellectual production, with phrases that yield to Said's pen and his fertile imagination. Arabic, on the other hand, was the language of celestial communion that transcends all time, of belonging wherein Jerusalem becomes a metaphor for an earth that is linked to heaven in an invocation that recalls the Lord, a Palestinian Jesus. English and Arabic are first languages for Said in which he sought refuge to overcome his spatially decentred world. He lived out of place, but he lived in these two languages and between them. However, of these two linguistic abodes, Arabic was 'home,' 'native' and 'original,' as he describes it in his memoir. English was 'crafted' and in the most technical sense 'concocted.' Geographically, Arabic is connected with 'there': English is connected with 'here.' Psychologically, Arabic is connected with 'here,' English with 'there.' But 'there' and 'here' are not just spatiotemporal counterpoints; they are also coexisting psychological states of an undifferentiated 'now' and 'then'; or, better still, they are the two engines of a dynamic that is in perpetual motion, thrusting forwards and backwards in search of meaning and of an identity that defies closure and finality.

IDENTITY AND GENDER: LANGUAGE, SELF AND DISPLACEMENT

Language is an important element in another memoir, Leila Ahmed's *A Border Passage* (2000 [1999]), which was published in the same year as Edward Said's *Out of Place*. These two memoirs overlap historically, the main difference between them being Ahmed's treatment of Nasser's era in Egypt (1954–67), which postdates Said's travel to the United States in 1951 to continue his education at Mount Hermon School in New England. As we shall see below, this difference is important to how Ahmed conceptualises her identity and her relationship with the *fuṣḥā* and English, the two languages that instrumentally and, in the case of the *fuṣḥā*, symbolically dominated Said's life.

While Said blurs the difference between the *fuṣḥā* and colloquial Arabic, as many Arabic speakers do, believing them to be part of a totality (Suleiman 2006a), and while he seems to have considered the *fuṣḥā* as an important site of identity location, especially towards the end of his life, Ahmed draws a sharp distinction between the *fuṣḥā* and colloquial Arabic, considering the latter as the only legitimate site of identity location in her case. This, in part, explains the critical remarks Said (2004) directed at Ahmed, whose extremely negative attitude towards the *fuṣḥā* he deplored. For Ahmed, the main contender for her identity as an Egyptian is colloquial (Egyptian) Arabic. The *fuṣḥā* was the Other language, the language of textuality, hegemonic masculinity and intrusive Arab nationalism/Arabism, as we shall see later. Thus, while Said may be considered a pan-Arab cultural subject, even nationalist, for that matter,[16] Ahmed is an Egyptian nationalist for whom Arab nationalism has little or no resonance; in fact, it is a form of identity that she deeply resents. This attitude on Ahmed's part is bound up with her educational and family background, as well as with her reaction to Nasser's rule and pan-Arab ideology.

First, let us deal with Ahmed's attitude towards English, comparing it with Said's. Both studied at foreign, English-medium schools in Cairo, but it seems that this experience marked them in somewhat different ways. Ahmed poses the question of why her father 'who loved the Qur'an, as he clearly did, had somehow neglected to see to it that his children would have as sure a command of its language—written Arabic—as he had' (2000: 23). Although Ahmed does not give a definitive answer to this question, it is clear that class and social status are at the heart of this attitude. Knowledge of European languages was seen as a sign of social standing and as a badge of modernity, advancement and enlightenment in Egyptian society in the first half of the twentieth century, as it still is to this day in the Arabic-speaking world. Thus, we are told that among 'the intellectual, professional and governing classes of Egypt . . . it was entirely ordinary to grow up speaking English or French or both, and quite ordinary to attend an English or French school' (6–7). While in Said's case, the negative effects of this practise and orientation on the *fuṣḥā* did not seem to have been lasting, the opposite is true of Ahmed. Reflecting on her early childhood experiences, she tells us that English must have been marked 'as innately . . . "superior"' to the *fuṣḥā* throughout her school years (23).

The fact that Arabic was banned in the foreign schools Ahmed attended seems to have marked it as the language of the native Other, an acquiescent

16 I am aware that Said was critical of nationalism, but this seems to have been restricted to extreme, jingoistic and strident forms of nationalism that annihilate the Other (see Said 2000: 172–86). It is interesting to note in this connection that Ahmed read Said's *Orientalism* (1978) as echoing Arab nationalist discourse: 'And yet the burden of my own history layered my experience of [*Orientalism*] with a degree of unease. Most difficult of all probably was *Orientalism*'s profound resonance to my ears with the perspectives and rhetoric of Arab nationalism' (Ahmed 2000: 240).

and consenting Other that is willing and ready, by virtue of its social norms and instrumental aspirations, to Other itself not just against the dominant European culture, which was held in high regard, but, more significantly, against its own indigenous culture and native language, which this Other held in low esteem. English, not Arabic, was the prestige language whose purveyors, in the form of British teachers, represented the models the young Egyptians of Ahmed's generational background looked up to and sought to emulate. Representing a self-conscious community of practise and aspirations, young Egyptians of this background adopted English (or French) as a badge of modern cultural identity, which they took into the home with, it seems, the acquiescence and, perhaps, tacit encouragement of their parents, who, as one witnesses in upwardly mobile Arab families these days, value their children's facility in the foreign language over their competence in Arabic. Sometimes these children would use the language with their parents when the parents were able to speak it, but when they could not, the children found the language useful as an instrument of subversion, of 'circumventing and baffling the adults around us and of communicating around them' (23). Whether intentionally or unintentionally, the juxtaposition of 'us' and 'them' here signifies the difference that existed between the young, foreign-educated Egyptians and their parents in the social milieu in which Ahmed circulated.[17]

This 'inferiority of Arabic' attitude extended beyond language to other cultural products, in particular film and music in the native language. Ahmed tells us how young children of similar social and educational background preferred to watch English films because 'the glamorous worlds in which they were set' conjured up the 'imaginary worlds' of their British teachers, who were constructed in their minds as their role models (23). The same was true of their musical tastes, which considered Arabic music as 'lesser' than and 'inferior to' English music (24). Ahmed openly states in her memoir that 'this show . . . of looking down on Arabic music [was common] among English Schoolers. Arabic music was the music of the streets, the music one heard blaring from radios in the *baladi*, the unsophisticated folk regions of town' (24). This childhood feeling of derision towards *baladi* (native) music is at odds with the positive attitude Ahmed evinces later in her memoir towards oral language and culture, in their capacity as the opposite of the written language, the *fuṣḥā*, and the textual culture she abhorred and considered to be a source of stagnation in society. The

17 Bishr (1995: 145) describes the foreign schools in Egypt in the first half of the twentieth century as a complex phenomenon. This phenomenon is associated with the feelings of superiority imparted by these schools to their students, which made the upper classes believe that attendance at these schools empowered their children to benefit from the socioeconomic advantages that are associated with the superior Westerners. However, more often than not, attendance at these schools led students to look down upon their native languages and cultures or to distance themselves from them, exactly as happened with Ahmed.

supposed inferiority of the Arabic language, music and film was part and parcel of the inferiority of the subjects who purveyed them in whatever form, including Ahmed's mother: 'The fact that mother loved Arabic music and sang in Arabic, and even the fact that we nearly always spoke to her in Arabic, undoubtedly marked her, too, in some way silently, in my child's mind, as inferior' (24–25). It is quite ironic that by trying to make their children European-like through education, these very same parents end up being nativised, in the colonial sense of the term, and considered inferior by their children.[18] In fact, this same process is depicted by Ahmed as having lost these parents their children in a tangible, real and sad way: 'For my mother, these were some of the hidden, uncounted costs of colonialism: her children's growing up speaking a language she did not understand and going off in their teens to college in a faraway land and a culture that would eventually steal them away. Among other things, there were hard, practical consequences. The children would not be there in the way that children traditionally (and according to the Bible and the Qur'an) were supposed to be there when parents grew old and frail' (111–12).

Ahmed's attitude towards Arabic and its culture is completely absent from Said's *Out of Place*. There were occasions when Said resented the *fuṣḥā* or was even ashamed of it and of the status assigned to its teachers in the schools he attended, but this feeling never coloured his attitude towards his mother, Arabic film or Arabic music. In fact, if anything, he seemed to be embarrassed by his father's insistence on using English and displaying American habits in public, including, one can infer, American speech habits. There is also Said's pride in his mother's use of Arabic with the local staff at Groppi's tearoom, which I described earlier as an act of subversion, inverted snobbery and border crossing. In addition, Said used Arabic as an instrument of subversion and resistance at Victoria College, where the language was banned from use in the school. This contrasts with Ahmed's acquiescence to the Arabic-language ban at her school and her extreme annoyance at being taught the *fuṣḥā* in her Senior School after the 1952 Egyptian revolution, when Nasser's government made the language compulsory in all foreign schools in Egypt. This positive attitude towards Arabic as the national language in Nasser's Egypt was accompanied by a hostile attitude towards the European languages in the new Egypt, which must have challenged Ahmed's value system and turned what she had up to this period considered as an advantage, a privilege and a sign of European-oriented modernity into a sociopolitical liability: 'But for a time in the Nasser era, when Arab nationalism and socialism were the

18 Fanon's remarks about the influence of cultural production on the colonial subject apply here: 'There is a constellation of postulates, a series of propositions that slowly but subtly—with the help of books, newspapers, schools, and their texts, advertisements, films, radio—work their way into one's mind and shape one's view of the world of the group to which one belongs' (Fanon 1986: 152).

going dogmas, fluency in European languages and Western education became discredited, things that one tried to hide, markers of belonging to the wrong class, the class of the once affluent, privileged, unjust oppressors of "the masses." In those days of unceasing nationalist rhetoric, a rhetoric of denunciatory rage as well as of nationalism, it became quite acceptable to discriminate against, and be openly hostile toward, people who betrayed (by their fluency in a European language, say) that they belonged to these classes' (152).

Reflecting on her deep-rooted and contrasting attitudes towards English and Arabic as a young student, Ahmed considers these attitudes as an expression of the 'internalised colonialism' that the intellectual, professional and governing classes in Egypt practised, without being aware that admiring and coming under the spell of European institutions, cultural products and languages would carry with them a diminution in the value of native cultural products and physical spaces in their eyes, of branding these products and spaces as defective and inferior: 'We lived in our heads and in the books we lost ourselves in, in a world peopled with children called Tom and Jane and Tim and Ann, and where there were moles and hedgehogs and grey skies and caves on the shore and tides that come in and out. And where houses had red roofs. Red roofs that seemed far better and more interesting and intriguing to me than roofs that were like, say, the terraced roof of our house in Alexandria. We grew up believing that some world over there was better, more interesting, more civilised than this world here [in Egypt]' (154).[19]

Language is the bridge through which acts of cultural subordination, and mental and psychological displacement are injected, sometimes self-injected, into the (ex-) colonised culture. In this culture, Ahmed assumes an English-sounding name, Lily, to mark her as a putative member of the (ex-) colonising culture—or, at least, to mark her as an 'intermediary' (152) between the superior European culture and the inferior Egyptian culture—while, at the same time, distancing her from her native culture. However, her accepting attitude towards this name differs vastly from Said's attitude towards his first name, which is the subject of critical comment in *Out of Place*, as will be explained in chapter 5, and which Mahmoud Darwish captures well in his elegy to Said when he says: 'I have two names which meet and part' (see above). Furthermore, English was the means through which members of Ahmed's social background were internally colonised by making them more knowledgeable about the history,

19 Asimilar situation existed in India: 'English literary education in India . . . was a way of imparting hidden quasi-Christian religious values to Indians. . . . It championed the ideal Englishman and was concomitantly a means through which Indians could become estranged from their own culture. Through the educational process they would readily accept British culture and domination.' (Talib 2002: 11). In fact, Ahmed tells us that she 'came close, really quite close to converting' to Christianity when she was at Cambridge (2000: 233).

geography, literature and flora and fauna of the British Isles than about those of their native country. Existing in a relationship of asymmetrical power allocation, the (ex-) colonised subject is prone to come under the influence of the dominant (ex-) colonial culture and, in the process, to regard himself as being a cut above those compatriots of his who had no access to this culture.

In this paradigm, language and knowledge are not neutral, but they carry in them structures of power and forces of co-option which the (ex-) colonial subject finds difficult to resist and, once they are imbibed, finds even more difficult to dislodge psychologically. Fanon comments on this in *Black Skin, White Masks*. His words aptly sum up what Ahmed means by 'internalised colonialism,' setting out the role that language plays in expressing that colonialism and in creating a class of native 'interpreters' or 'intermediaries,' as Ahmed calls them, between the (ex-) colonizing and (ex-) colonized cultures: 'Every colonised people finds itself face to face with the language of the civilising [colonising] nation; that is, with the culture of the mother country. The colonised is elevated above his jungle status in proportion to his adoption of the mother country's cultural standards. . . . In the French colonial army . . . the black officers serve first of all as interpreters. They are used to convey the master's orders to their fellows, and they too enjoy a certain position of honour' (Fanon 1986: 18).

It seems that Ahmed's extremely negative attitude towards the *fuṣḥā* is deeply coloured by some traumatic personal experiences.[20] One experience involved a private tutor her parents had hired to teach her the language. Ahmed tells us that she had learnt very little from this teacher, who, in fact, put her off learning the language, because during the lessons, she was occupied 'with figuring out how to stay beyond reach of his wandering hands groping at [her] under the table as [she] clinched [her] chair away from him' (Ahmed 2000: 26). This must have been an extremely distressing experience for a young Egyptian schoolgirl who, because of social custom, may not have been able to bring it to the attention of her parents for fear of being accused of having invited the tutor's advances. However, considering Ahmed's view of the *fuṣḥā* as a male's language, a matter with which I will deal below, it is not unreasonable to assume that this incident is somehow lodged in her mind as an expression of this maleness, of the linguistic maleness of the language personified.

Another traumatic experience involved Ahmed's Arabic-language teacher at Senior School, a Palestinian refugee by the name of Miss Nabih.[21] Because Ahmed was not showing keen interest in Arabic at Senior

20 Ahmed does not raise the question of different prestige norms for the *fuṣḥā* (male) and local dialects (female) in line with the argument made by Ibrahim (1986).

21 The combination of 'Palestinian' with 'refugee' seems to carry strong negative connotations for Ahmed, explaining her strong feelings towards Miss Nabih.

School—which was taught through endless memorisation, tedious repetition and the study of 'alien and unimaginative' prose—Miss Nabih slapped her across the face.[22] This traumatic incident seems to have played an extremely negative role in Ahmed's life and attitude towards the *fuṣḥā*. She recalls Miss Nabih with palpable anger and bitterness, returning to the incident and the psychological scars it etched in her memory in a few places in her memoir. As far as Ahmed is concerned, Miss Nabih did not punish her for her 'insouciant attitude toward Arabic' but because she considered her a representative of the 'corrupt [and] irresponsible Egyptian upper classes' who had shown lack of responsibility towards the Palestinians (148). Using this traumatic incident as a site from which to reflect on

22 Ahmed describes this incident as follows:

> The teacher called on me to read. I started haltingly. She began interrupting me, correcting me, quietly at first but gradually, as I stumbled on, with more and more irritation, leaving her desk now to stand over me and pounce on every mistake I made. She was an irascible woman, and I had not prepared my homework.
>
> 'You're an Arab!' she finally screamed at me. 'An Arab! And you don't know your own language!'
>
> 'I am not an Arab!' I said, suddenly furious myself. 'I am Egyptian! And anyway we don't speak like this!' And I banged my book shut.
>
> 'Read!'
>
> I sat on stonily, arms folded.
>
> 'Read!'
>
> I didn't move.
>
> She struck me across the face. The moment afterward seemed to go on forever, like something in slow motion.
>
> I was twelve and I'd never been hit before by a teacher and never slapped across the face by anyone. *Miss Nabih, the teacher, was a Palestinian. A refugee* [emphasis added].
>
> The year was 1952, the year of the revolution. What Miss Nabih was doing to me in class the government was doing to us through the media. I remember how I hated that incessant rhetoric. *Al-qawmiyya al-Arabiyya*! *Al-Uraba* [*sic*]! *Nahnu al-Arab*! Arab Nationalism! Arabness! We the Arabs! Even now, just remembering those words, I feel again a *surge* of mingled irritation and resentment [emphasis added]. (2000: 243–44)

This extract links language with national identity, whether in the affirmative or not. Miss Nabih links the *fuṣḥā* with being Arab. Ahmed rejects this link, asserting her Egyptian identity, which overrides Arabism as constructed around the *fuṣḥā*. The fact that this incident is seen as a replication of government policy and is associated with Arab nationalism and Arabism signals the intensity of the connection, in Ahmed's mind, between language and identity. The last two sentences—'Miss Nabih, the teacher, was a Palestinian. A refugee'—express very powerfully the strength of feeling Ahmed had about Miss Nabih and, presumably, what she stood for: the Palestine question, the Palestinian refugees, Arab nationalism and the *fuṣḥā*. Looking at Arab and Egyptian identity through the prism of Palestine, Ahmed later describes the dialectic between these two identity constructs, in which the *fuṣḥā* is implicated, as follows: 'For Egyptians to debate or question their Arabness ("search" for their identity) is usually code . . . for debating the extent of our responsibility toward the Palestinians. And it is accordingly read by Arabs and by Egyptians as a covert way of advocating either support for or abandonment of the Palestinians' (256).

her identity, Ahmed links it with the change in her family's fortunes after the Egyptian Revolution in 1952, which not only led to changing the name of her school from the English School to al-Nasr School (witness the play on the name 'Nasser') but also made Arabic a compulsory subject in all foreign schools and, as was mentioned earlier, considered the public display of European languages a sign of loyalty to the old corrupt power structures in Egyptian society.

Ahmed further links this incident to the Palestinian problem, which she seems to have resented because it was the trigger that led to the Egyptian Revolution and, consequently, the socialist policies of land expropriation and wealth distribution to the poor that Nasser's government instituted against people of her socioeconomic background. In Ahmed's thinking, Miss Nabih, the Palestinian problem, the Egyptian Revolution, Nasser's rule and his ideology of pan-Arab nationalism have created deep and lasting displacements in her life. The trauma generated by these events and the ideological formations they gave rise to coalesced around the *fuṣḥā*—by virtue of the fact that the language represents a challenge to, even a negation of, her identity as first and foremost an Egyptian—as a convenient site through which Ahmed could vent her anger. The *fuṣḥā* has somehow become a token of or a motif for all of the ills in Ahmed's personal and family life and for all of the excesses of Nasser's rule towards the Egyptians of her social background. The following quote sets out how Ahmed reasoned this in her life: 'I have always thought that those moments between me and Miss Nabih were in large part responsible for the feelings of confusion, anger and guilt that I've felt all my life in connection with issues of Arabness, identity, the Arabic language and the like. In reality, though, these incidents were the only tangible things I could fasten onto in the enormous turbulence and upheaval we were then living through. My relations with Miss Nabih were only a symptom of the times: of the battering and reshaping of our identities that the politics of the day were subjecting us to' (148).

One of the basic distinctions in Ahmed's thinking about language, culture and identity is between literacy and orality. The former is associated with the *fuṣḥā* and official culture as these are articulated through school textbooks and the various avenues of formal education. The latter is treated as the living and authentic culture of groups of communities throughout the Arabic-speaking world who use the colloquial dialects, which she refers to as languages, to articulate it. The culture of literacy is said to be stilted and frozen in time,[23] using as its medium of expression a language that is no

23 Ahmed comments on this as follows: 'I have yet to hear or read any piece of Arabic poetry or prose by a modern writer that, however gorgeous and delicate and poetic and moving, is not also stilted and artificial. There is a very high price to pay for having a written language [the *fuṣḥā*] that is only a language of literature and that has only a distant, attenuated connection to the living language' (283).

one's mother tongue.[24] The *fuṣḥā* may be revered by the cultural elite, its producers and guardians, and no doubt has a sanctioned cultural and religious place as the language of the Qur'an, but, she argues, it is also the language of the Arab literary heritage, with which she has little aesthetic sympathy,[25] as well as that of the medieval Islamic culture, which were 'produced over the centuries by men and, by and large, by middle class men who lived in deeply misogynist societies' (281).

Ahmed is very critical of the *fuṣḥā*-based culture because it is frozen or fixed in time, exclusionary towards women and hegemonic—even coercive—in its attitude towards the living culture of orality with all of its diversity, vitality and richness, in spite of the fact that this culture was the subject of dismissive comment by her, as we have seen above. Ahmed considers the *fuṣḥā*, through its association with school, textbook and other forms of cultural production, as the greatest threat to this oral culture and its languages, the mother tongues of the ordinary people who use them in the Arabic-speaking countries without artificiality as they go about their daily lives. Because of its association with literacy, masculinity and class structure (as she sees it), Ahmed considers the spread of the *fuṣḥā* as a case of 'linguistic, cultural and . . . class imperialism that is being conducted in the name of education and of Arab unity and of the oneness of the Arab nation' (282).[26] She also denies that the *fuṣḥā* or even the different forms of colloquial Arabic can form a bond of identity among Arabic speakers: 'Was I . . . really likely to feel more kin, more at home, with someone from Saudi Arabia than with someone, say, from Istanbul? I doubted it' (254–55). Then, as an

24 Ahmed bases her definition of *mother tongue* on that of the Kenyan writer Ngugu wa Thiong'o, who 'describes his mother tongue as the language that people used as they worked in the fields, the language that they used to tell stories in the evening around the fireside. . . . Our appreciation of the suggestive magical power of language was reinforced by the games we played with words through riddles, proverbs, transpositions of syllables, or through nonsensical but magically arranged words' (280–81).

25 Ahmed describes her reaction to an event at Cambridge, where, in the course of a guest lecture, the Lebanese writer Hanan al-Shaykh quoted poetry and prose in the *fuṣḥā*: 'I loved the lines [Hanan al-Shaykh] was quoting—but I appreciated them, I realized, only the way I might the poetry of a foreign tongue that I only somewhat knew. They did not have for me the resonances of lines learned long ago. Nor of course, since they were written in [the *fuṣḥā*], did they have the charge and redolence and burdened evocativeness of a language spoken in childhood and youth and in love and anger and just in the ordinary moments of living' (253–54).

26 Ahmed describes the impact of the *fuṣḥā*-based Arabic on oral, colloquial-based culture as follows: 'Steadily throughout the Arab world, as this Arab culture of literacy marches inexorably onward, local cultures continue to be erased and their linguistic and cultural creativity condemned to permanent, unwritten silence. And we are supposed to applaud this, not to protest it as we would if it were any other form of imperialism or political domination. This variety of domination goes by the name of "nationalism," and we are supposed to support it' (282). In fact, if anything, local cultures and local dialects have been flourishing in the Arabic-speaking world in (among other things) advertisements, TV shows, TV and radio drama, and poetry in the local dialects (*nabaṭī* poetry).

afterthought, she adds, '(Saudis speak Arabic, Turks don't)' to drive the point home that the *fuṣḥā* does not create bonds of affiliation, let alone act as a marker or ingredient of identity for her.

Having asserted that the *fuṣḥā* is implicated in structures of linguistic, cultural and class imperialism, Ahmed argues that the only way to break out of these structures is to commit the colloquial dialects, the mother tongues of the ordinary Arabic-speaking nations, to writing to turn them into official languages for use in all purposes of the state. It is not surprising that in arguing for committing Egyptian Arabic to writing as a measure of modernizing in her book *Sacred Language, Ordinary People* (2003), Niloofar Haeri refers several times to Ahmed's memoir as supporting evidence. Writing the mother tongues will, in Ahmed's view, preserve the local cultures against the threat posed by the *fuṣḥā* and the alien culture with which this overpowering language is bound. 'For me,' Ahmed writes '*this language of standard Arabic* [i.e., the *fuṣḥā*] was not my mother tongue and the values purveyed by the Arabic texts that we read were not those of my mother culture' (2000: 282; emphasis added). Writing the colloquial dialects will also elevate these mother tongues to the status of languages. In this, Ahmed is right, because in the canons of nation building, writing is not just a matter of recording the spoken languages, but, more important is that it serves the function of marking them as signs of identity and high culture. In Ahmed's own scheme of things, English, in fact, feels 'somehow closer and more kin' to Egyptian Arabic than the *fuṣḥā*: 'both are living languages and both have that quickness and pliancy and vitality that living spoken languages have and that the [*fuṣḥā*] of our day does not' (283). However, when talking about colonialism in Egypt, Ahmed treats the *fuṣḥā* and English as equal partners: both represent a case of colonialism and domination vis-à-vis the mother tongue and the mother culture of the Egyptians.[27] This is an unbalanced equation, since, as we have learnt earlier, she seems to have a more benevolent view of English than she does of the *fuṣḥā*, which, for her, is a rank outsider.

Another plank in Ahmed's critique of the *fuṣḥā* relates to its being the medium of the extensive Islamic medieval heritage, the corpus of writings on Islamic *sharia* that has spawned an official Islamic theology/ideology, which is said to keep Islam frozen in time, thus encouraging fundamentalism and, consequently, some of its most detested consequences. Ahmed describes this kind of Islam as a set of almost invariant readings or interpretations that have been produced by and passed on to the literate classes

27 Ahmed writes: 'Whatever school my parents sent me to, Arabic or English, I would have found myself imbibing a culture and studying a language and learning attitudes that were different from those of the world in which I lived in Cairo and Alexandria. The choice either way entailed alienation from my home culture and home language and from the language and oral culture of other Cairenes. In short the choice was always between colonialism and colonialism, or at any rate between domination and domination' (283).

down the centuries by a minority of self-serving men who have excluded women from the processes of production and transmission, although it is assumed that 'there are differences between women's and men's ways of knowing' in all societies, but especially in the 'segregated societies of the Middle East' (123).[28] Not only do these processes of production and transmission skew the reading of the foundational texts of Islam, notably the Qur'an, in a male-oriented, even misogynistic direction, but, it is further argued, they also act to suppress the living Islam of the mother culture and the mother language,[29] an Islam that is vibrant, ever evolving and ready to accommodate the newly emergent needs of the community of believers.

But how does Ahmed make the connection between the *fuṣḥā* and the above reading of the Islamic medieval heritage? Her starting point is the orality-aurality of Arabic, even in its scripted form, which she assumes to be one of its defining characteristics. She contends that (unvocalised) written words in Arabic, in their capacity as sets of consonants, have 'no particular meaning' and 'only acquire final, specific [and] fixed meaning when given vocalised or silent utterance' (127). Until this stage in language production, Ahmed continues, 'they are not words but only potential words, a *chaotic babble* and possibility of meanings' (127–28; emphasis added). In other words, what makes real words out of potential words on the page is oral production and aural reception. It is this orality and aurality that breathe life into the *fuṣḥā* words. But since the oral and the aural are of the 'here and now,' it follows that textuality or literacy, by aiming at fixity, undermines this often contingent spatiality and the temporality of language, as well as the living heritage, religious and cultural, that the language of the 'here and now' articulates. Ahmed raises this analysis to the level of a metaphysical principle when she says: 'Meaning always only here and now, in this body, in this person. Truth only here and now, for this body, this person. Not something transcendent, overarching, large, bigger, more important than life—but here and now and in this body and in this small ordinary life.' If we were to accept this principle without any qualification, we would have to exorcise any old meanings that ancient texts may have been given in the past that are not sanctioned as valid by the principle of the 'truth [exists] only here and now, for this body, this person.'

Ahmed's critique of the *fuṣḥā* is part and parcel of this critical attitude towards the closure enacted by male-generated readings, which have acted in a discriminatory way against emergent female-generated interpretations of the foundational texts of Islam, those of the 'here and now, for this body, this person.' Challenging the dominance of literacy, textuality and

28 Ahmed describes official or textual Islam as follows: 'The Islam of the texts is quite a different, quite other Islam: it is the Islam of the arcane, mostly medieval written heritage in which sheikhs are trained, and it is a "men's" Islam' (125).

29 According to Ahmed, 'literacy has played a baneful part both in spreading a particular form of Islam and in working to erase oral and living forms of the religion' (128).

the *fuṣḥā* is, therefore, a necessary step towards opening up a space for, gender-wise, a more inclusive reading of the Islamic heritage, a reading that can challenge the sway of fundamentalism and its autocratic world-views. By conceptualising the challenge in this way, Ahmed endows it with a liberationist perspective that sets up the *fuṣḥā* as an active accomplice in cultural domination, which she referred to elsewhere as a form of 'internal colonialism.'

Ahmed builds her views about the *fuṣḥā* by invoking two basic notions. The first revolves around the concept of the 'mother tongue,' which enables her to argue that because the *fuṣḥā* is no one's mother tongue, the language can be described as a superimposed variety that lacks mother-culture validation. In addition, she describes the *fuṣḥā* as a hegemonic code and, consequently, as a language of cultural domination and colonialism in relation to the mother tongue, being in this respect on par with English in Egypt in the first half of the twentieth century. While Ahmed is right in describing the *fuṣḥā* as no one's mother tongue in Egypt, her conclusions are counterintuitive, to say the least. To begin with, most Egyptians would object to calling the *fuṣḥā* a colonialist language and would certainly strongly disagree that the *fuṣḥā* is on par with English in relation to Egypt and its culture. No matter how distant from the mother tongue and no matter how artificially learnt, the *fuṣḥā* is, it is still a lot closer to the mother tongue phonologically, morphologically, syntactically, lexically and semantically than English could ever be.

The view of the *fuṣḥā* as a foreign language was the exception even during the heyday of Egyptian nationalism in the first two decades of the twentieth century (Suleiman 2003; Suleiman 2008). Egyptian nationalists used a number of strategies to argue for a language-identity link that either excluded the *fuṣḥā* in favour of the mother tongue as the mainstay of this link or included it but on the basis that Egypt's *fuṣḥā* was environmentally determined and, therefore, was different from other *fuṣḥā*s in the Arabic-speaking world, with the Nile basin playing this environmentally determining factor in Egyptian Arabic. Ahmed's view must, therefore, be seen as a minority position even within radical forms of Egyptian nationalism. The notion that the *fuṣḥā* in Egypt is a colonialist language would be strongly opposed by the majority of the Egyptians—including Egyptian nationalists who have little sympathy with pan-Arab nationalism—not least because of the standing of this variety as the language of the Qur'an. If anything, some Egyptians may be inclined to consider the *fuṣḥā* as a sacred language because of its link with the Qur'an, even though this is far from being a straightforward view of the language (see Suleiman 2004a).

Ahmed seems to have been driven to her conclusions because she considered the language situation in Egypt through the single prism of the mother tongue. Had she widened the scope of her perspective by incorporating the notion of 'native language' in thinking about the language situation in Egypt—along the lines I have set out in chapter 2—she might have been able to reach a more nuanced understanding of this situation. I have argued elsewhere (Suleiman 2008) that in the context of the Arabic-speaking countries, a distinction between the mother tongue and the native language is necessary to capture the insider perspective of the language situation in these countries, which I have called the folk-linguistic perspective in earlier research (Suleiman 2004a). Adopting this distinction would enable us to assign significance to both the mother tongue, which is referred to as *'āmiyya* ('colloquial') in Egypt, and the native language as represented by the *fuṣḥā* and, additionally, to take account of the difference in status between these two varieties of Arabic sociolinguistically. This distinction is not devoid of sociolinguistic and sociopsychological validity, because it does resonate with how most Egyptians think about their language situation. If we accept this, as I think we should, we can then proceed to draw a distinction for Egypt between *speech* and *linguistic* community, linking the former with the colloquial dialects as the mother tongues and the latter with the *fuṣḥā* as the native language. One of the characteristics of linguistic communities is that they coalesce around a 'normatively constructed [and] ideologically articulated "standard" language' (Blommaert 2006: 243, following Silverstein 1996 and Silverstein 1998), as is the case in Egypt. Had Ahmed proceeded in this way, she would have been able to recognise the duality in the language situation in Egypt as it revolves around both forms of Arabic.[30] This, in turn, might have stopped her from constructing *fuṣḥā* Arabic as a colonialist language in Egypt.

The second operative notion in Ahmed's deconstruction of the *fuṣḥā* is the concept of literacy. It is, however, not clear why the fact that the *fuṣḥā* is a written language should necessarily lead to fixity and to the closure of meaning in respect of the medieval Islamic heritage. Are fixity and the closure of meaning characteristic of, or unique to, Arabic because of its characteristically unvocalised written forms, as Ahmed seems to suggest, or can they apply to other languages? In other words, are fixity and closure a feature of all literacies (written languages), or are they characteristic of Arabic and, perhaps, other Semitic languages only, which Ahmed believes to be the case? If that indeed is the case, is it ever possible to challenge the fixity and the closure of meaning in written Arabic (and other Semitic) texts? Or are fixity and meaning closure a result of reception and the gradual canonisation of a certain body of written texts that has taken place over a long period of time? Are fixity and closure culturally, rather than linguistically, produced? And does Arabic literacy have to be marked by a male ethos that

30 I have characterised this language situation in the following terms: 'The use of "mother tongue" to link [the colloquial] to speech community captures the nature of this form of Arabic as a spoken variety that is informally acquired and as a site of cultural intimacy. The use of "native language" to link the *fuṣḥā* to linguistic community is intended to express the ideological meanings of "nativeness," the fact that although the *fuṣḥā* is not a mother tongue to the Egyptians (due to being acquired formally through instruction in school), it still is a site of belonging and intimacy to them in socio-psychological terms' (Suleiman 2008: 30).

marks the *fuṣḥā* as a male-gendered language system, as Ahmed states?[31] And is it true that Arabic words on the page are a 'chaotic babble' (Ahmed 2000: 128) until they are uttered or silently vocalised? If so, does this not argue for latitude in the interpretation of texts? These are extremely important questions, which need answering before we can accept Ahmed's deterministic views of the *fuṣḥā*.

However, it is very clear that Ahmed's views on the *fuṣḥā* and the mother tongue are shaped by the social, economic and political trauma she and her family went through during Nasser's regime and in response to the Palestine conflict, leading to the loss of privilege and opportunity in society. Nasser's efforts to reconfigure Egyptian identity as primarily Arab are subject to strong criticism in *A Border Passage*, because it set out to eliminate or replace the idea that Egypt was Egyptian, not Arab: 'To question our Arabness and all that our Arabness implied became unthinkable. Only despicable, unprincipled traitors would do such a thing. And it is with this sense of complicated legacy that my own sense of identity as Egyptian and as Arab is entangled' (246).

Within the autobiography genre, Ahmed is, of course, free to set her views in any way she likes without having to justify them, even when these are internally inconsistent, as, in fact, is the case with her attitude towards oral culture, including music and song. Had she, therefore, adhered to this autobiographical convention, there would have been no attempt here to interrogate what she had to tell us in *A Border Passage*. But the fact that she considers it necessary to argue for her views makes it imperative that the basis of these views is subjected to critical analysis. In this respect, Ahmed's memoir crosses the boundary between autobiography and discursive writing.

LANGUAGE, WAR AND TRAUMA: FROM DESPOTISM TO FREEDOM

Leila Ahmed's support for using the colloquial dialect, vernacular language or mother tongue—terms that I use here interchangeably—in writing is motivated by three considerations: (1) challenging closed, male-gendered and, according to her, misogynistic readings of the foundational texts of Islam to promote religious and cultural modernisation; (2) protecting mother-tongue cultures from the onslaught of the *fuṣḥā*-centred literacy as a measure of preserving an authentic and ever-changing tradition of knowledge production; and (3) providing the Egyptians with a vernacular language that can serve as an authentic marker of an Egyptian national identity that is different from other language-based identities in the Arabic-speaking world.

31 See Muqaddam (2010) for a feminist critique of the male orientation of Arabic grammar, which she sums up under the notion of *al-ḥarīm al-lughawī* ('linguistic *harim*').

This interest in using the colloquial in writing is not a new phenomenon in modern Egypt. In the history of modern Egyptian culture, one of the most 'reviled' interventions in promoting the colloquial dates back to 1893, when Sir William Willcocks,[32] a British agricultural engineer working in Egypt at the time, published a paper in the monthly magazine *Al-Azhar* under the title '*Lima lam tūjad quwwat al-ikhtirā' ladā al-miṣriyyīn al-ān?*' ('Why are the Egyptians deprived of the power of invention now?'). In this article, Willcocks uses a language with some colloquial features to argue that the *fuṣḥā* acts as a veil that prevents the Egyptians from seeing clearly, thus stunting their ability to be creative and standing as a barrier between them and achieving the necessary reformation that can lead to political freedom. Willcocks argues that Egyptian Arabic is a 'living and vibrant' language (Suleiman 2004b: 67). In contrast, the *fuṣḥā* is said to be a dead language, thus 'consigning everything inscribed in it to certain death.' The solution for the Egyptians, therefore, is obvious: it lies in adopting the colloquial as the medium of writing and communication.

Amodern and modernising Egypt can exist and flourish only if it adopts this solution. To help the Egyptians take this leap from the *fuṣḥā* to the colloquial dialect, Willcocks argues with great emotional enthusiasm that the varieties of Arabic spoken in Syria, Egypt and North Africa—which practically means all of the countries outside the Arabian Peninsula and Iraq—are examples of Punic, Phoenician or Canaanitish language. In elaborating this claim, for which he provides no credible substantiation, Willcocks mounts a vicious attack on the *fuṣḥā*, or literary Arabic, which he clearly despises, preferring instead the spoken vernacular of Egypt,[33] as the following quotes make clear: 'As a Punic language, Egyptian is full to the brim of sharp words and short, effective expressions. All these words and expressions literary Arabic avoids as though they were poison; to the infinite loss of all business qualifications in the Egyptian nation. Egypt pays dearly for thus squandering its national wealth at the bidding of dreamy pedants and professors of one language for its own sake. As a language of business and commerce and quick grasp of one's work, Egyptian is as quick as English' (Willcocks 1926: 13).

And:

> The soporific effect of listening to sonorous words not one of which is understood is very easy to see [in Egypt]. Acourse of such listening kills all originality of thought in those who cannot read, just as effectively as lessons in artificial literary Arabic, which reaches the head but never reaches the heart, kills all originality in every so-called learned man in this country. I have been

32 See Sa'id (1964) for a discussion of this intervention.

33 Willcocks's enthusiasm for the Egyptian colloquial may, in fact, be linked with his work as an evangelist who believed in taking his message to the people in the vernacular to counter the link between the *fuṣḥā* and the Qur'an. This may help explain why Willcocks spent quite a bit of his energy and his personal resources to translate the Bible into Egyptian Arabic.

> in Egypt for forty years and I have never met an original Egyptian. Their mental energies are consumed in eternally translating to themselves what they read in literary Arabic into familiar Egyptian, realising what they have read, and then translating it back to into literary Arabic before they can put their thoughts on paper. It is a kind of mental *corvée* which can only be compared to the physical *corvée* which cleared slush out of a canal [in Egypt, where Willcocks worked as agricultural engineer] at a cost of 100 piasters per cubic metre when dredges could have done it for 5 piasters. (14)

Following in the footsteps of Leila Ahmed, while sidestepping Willcocks's views, Niloofar Haeri (2003)[34] argues in favour of adopting Egyptian Arabic in writing. Basing herself on the dubious claim that Egyptians are custodians rather than owners of the *fuṣḥā*,[35] owing to the presumed sacredness of the language,[36] Haeri states that the language cannot be subjected to change or modernisation. Not even the alphabet/script can be modernised, because of the link to the Qur'an and Islam, as any such move would generate stiff resistance from a variety of radical and nonradical forces in society.[37] To sidestep this cultural and political dilemma in Egypt—which Haeri expresses by juxtaposing 'sacred language' and 'ordinary people' in the title of her book—she strongly advocates turning to the vernacular as the solution that can aid the cause of modernisation in Egypt. In comparison with the *fuṣḥā*, the Egyptian vernacular is relatively free from any doctrinal and ideological associations with Islam and its cultural heritage (a very dubious claim) and, therefore, can be modified without any social upheaval or political opposition. Egyptian Arabic is the mother tongue of the Egyptians, which they know without having to undergo the extensive schooling associated with the *fuṣḥā* acquisition. These facts give the Egyptians ownership over the language and, therefore, the entitlement to modify it as they see fit, without having to counter the hegemony of the conservative forces in society.

For obvious reasons, Haeri is very careful not to associate herself with Willcocks's call on the Egyptians to turn to the colloquial for self-expression in the scientific and other fields; in fact, she makes no reference whatsoever to him in her book, owing, we suggest, to the negative connotations that his

34 Niloofar Haeri is at the time of this writing a professor at Johns Hopkins University.

35 While the term *custodian* may suggest that the Egyptians have no authority to change their language, this term is unsatisfactory, because it fails to account for the diachronic changes that have taken place in the language, which, in Western scholarship on Arabic, have led to coining the term *Modern Standard Arabic* to refer to the *fuṣḥā* in its modern form. In their comprehensive grammar of modern written Arabic, Badawi et al. (2004) provide ample data on the changes that have affected Arabic in modern times.

36 See Suleiman (2004a) on this issue.

37 Haeri is right in asserting that the modernisation of the alphabet would be met with stiff resistance in Arab societies. However, it would be wrong to think that this resistance would be exclusively linked to the use of the alphabet in the text of the Qur'an. Many secularists and others would, I am sure, be inclined to reject script modernisation for cultural and national, not religious, reasons. Speaking as an Arab, the present writer would be one.

name still evokes in Egyptian and Arab cultural life. But, like Willcocks, Haeri is driven by what she regards as one of the most fundamental imperatives of modernisation: the need to have a language that is not fettered by the limitations of the past or, particularly in her case, the constraints of a heavenly order, a native language that the Egyptians can be proud of and can call their own. Haeri sums up Egypt's dilemma as follows, although, it must be added, most Egyptians may not accept her diagnosis, as what she says, in fact, suggests:

> An uneasy relation to the Self is not the same as an identity crisis. Egyptians in fact have a very strong sense of their national identity and of their difference with other Arabs. But the obligation to disown a central defining aspect of their identity—their mother tongue—when it comes to writing, to creating and evaluating what or what is not knowledge, mediates and intervenes in their relations to themselves and to the world. The censure of Egyptian Arabic from official and national culture, seem to prevent Egypt from tapping its many potentials. Egypt's constitution makes no mention of the existence of Egyptian Arabic, educational institutions do not teach it, in textbooks no historical characters seem to have spoken in this language, and in cultural production involving print, it is shunned. For these and other similar reasons . . . Egypt has a fraught and uncertain relationship with its own contemporaneity. (Haeri 2003: 150)

Calls to use the colloquial in writing have been traditionally promoted to serve the twin aims of nation creation or state building and socioeconomic modernisation. The contributions by Ahmed, Willcocks and Haeri have been used here as illustrative examples to show the historical depth of these calls and the different backgrounds of the authors contributing to the *fuṣḥā*-versus-colloquial debate. However, in a new departure, the promotion of the colloquial has been linked directly to the cause of freedom and democracy in society. This is the subject of a recent book by the Egyptian psychoanalyst Moustapha Safouan:[38] *Why Are the Arabs Not Free?—The Politics of Writing* (2007).[39] We are told that this book, whose genesis goes back to the Arab defeat at the hands of Israel in 1967, was written in two parts: one in the Egyptian vernacular, which the author sometimes refers to as the 'Egyptian demotic' and other times as the 'mother tongue,' and the other in the *fuṣḥā*. This mode of writing seems to be germane to the argument of the book, as

38 Safouan has lived in Paris since 1947. While this book is not a memoir, it is a set of reflections rather than a tightly argued scholarly treatment of the topic of the *fuṣḥā* versus vernacular.

39 The book appeared in Arabic under the title *Al-Kitāba wa-l-sulṭa* (Ṣafwan 2001). The following parts of the book are written in Egyptian Arabic: introduction, pp. 5–14; *Al-Shu'ūb wa-l-kitāba* ('Peoples/Nations and Writing'), pp. 101–13; *Dawr al-lugha fī takwīn al-ḥaḍārāt* ('The Role of Language in Constructing Civilisations'), pp. 115–31; *Al-Ḥukm wa-l-siyāsa wa-l-dawla* ('Government, Politics and the State'), pp. 137–41; and *Al-Kitāba wa-l-sulṭa* ('Writing and Authority'), pp 143–73. The remaining parts, making up almost two thirds of the book, are written in *fuṣḥā*.

we shall see below. The author tells us that the subject matter of the book was judged to be politically sensitive, so, to circumvent the Egyptian censor, the book had to be published as a work on clinical psychology.[40] The author mentions these facts to impress upon the reader that in a 'new world order' that is obsessed with the lack of democracy in the Arab world, language is a central issue, which must be tackled with urgency as a corrective to some of the most corrosive ills of society: despotism, theocracy and dictatorship.[41] The topicality of this platform, insofar as it relates to the American-driven democracy agenda for the Middle East (i.e., the Arabic-speaking world) under the George W. Bush administration (2000–2008), has no doubt been a determining factor in choosing the book for review in the weekly British magazine *New Statesman* (22 October 2007), although as the reviewer Samir el-Youssef points out, Safouan's book is not a systematic treatise on the topic but a 'collection of reflections on writing and political power.'

One of the starting points for Safouan is the view that the *fuṣḥā* is a dead language, in the sense that it is not a spoken tongue but a language that has to be learnt through a schooling experience that is designed to provide those who undertake it with knowledge *about* the language rather than knowledge *of* the language itself or, as he expresses it, basing himself on the famous fourteenth-century sociologist Ibn Khaldun, 'knowledge of the [language] faculty but not the faculty itself' (Safouan 2007: 47). However, it is this language that dominates the privileged world of writing, blocking the mother tongue from being used in this important domain. In addition, Safouan states that the gulf between the *fuṣḥā* and the colloquial dialects is bigger than that between French or Italian and Latin as their mother language. This makes the colloquial dialects, he argues, (1) separate languages from the *fuṣḥā*, rather than varieties of the same language as the *fuṣḥā*, and (2) more different from each other than, for example, Spanish and Italian are.

There is little that is new in the above. However, the twist comes through the claim that writing and despotism in Third World countries are closely linked, especially for those countries whose written languages are claimed to be sacred, as in the case of Arabic, a view with which I disagree, as I hope to set out in a future publication. Speaking as a psychoanalyst, Safouan refers to what he calls the 'hypnotic power' (2007: 1) of the written word, dating this back to ancient Egypt and Mesopotamia, the cradles of Middle Eastern civilisations to which Arabic culture ultimately relates. In these regions, the state maintained a distinction between the written language of the administration, religion, science and high culture, on the one hand, and

40 This fact should not obscure the intention of the author, a psychiatrist, to offer his book as a diagnosis and a remedy to an Egyptian (and, by extension, Arab) condition, that of democracy deficit. Publishing the book as a work on clinical psychology makes sense, even without the ruse of wanting to avoid the watchful eye of the censor, if we approach the material of the book from this perspective.

41 See Suleiman (2006a) for a discussion of recent studies of the language from the reform perspective.

the spoken language of everyday life, on the other, ascribing to the former a sacred character as a divinely crafted phenomenon or allocating to it a high and unattainable pedigree as the heir of a distant and revered past.

The mother tongue, by contrast, was downgraded in social prestige and 'scorned as a plebeian idiom' that is unfit for science, religion and high culture (2007: 9). In modern terms, this attitude towards the mother tongue is said to represent a form of (internal) colonialism. Using a language that is similar to some of the ideas put forward by Leila Ahmed about internal colonialism, Safouan writes: 'The coloniser, as soon as he conquers a foreign country, begins by despising the language of the natives so that the natives may despise and refrain from thinking about a freedom that they don't deserve and that doesn't suit them' (9), but at no point does he tell us how this applied to ancient Egypt or Mesopotamia. In a manner that is further reminiscent of Ahmed, Sofouan argues that a language policy based on this set of ideas (i.e., sacredness and pedigree) leads to banning the mother tongue from the schools and instils a reverence for the written language that separates its speakers from the rich cultural reservoirs of their mother tongues, as has obtained for Egypt. Acting in this way, members of the political class and the cultural elite accrued to themselves great powers, which enabled them to sanction self-serving and hegemonic readings of texts that, in turn, entrenched their privileges in society. By restricting knowledge of writing to a small class, the ancient rulers of Egypt and Mesopotamia endowed it with dignity, a sacred aura and the trappings of the esoteric: 'The creation of writing, just like the creation of the world itself, was always attributed to one of the gods,' to the extent that the ancient Egyptians called writing 'God's word' (75). Safouan adds: 'This applies especially to hieroglyphics since, perhaps more than any other writing, they make you feel the presence of hidden significations behind the visible images, as if they were seeing you without you seeing them. Even today if you meet a Coptic monk in a desert convent in Egypt, and if he notices that you do not believe completely in the stories of the miracles of his convent's saint, he will tell you: "This is history, it is *written*"' (75).

Safouan argues that in spite of the spread of literacy and writing in the Middle East, the view of writing as a form of power and as a 'means of exploitation' (75) still applies today in the Arabic-speaking world as it did in ancient times. By the same token, the negative view of the mother tongue is a feature of the modern linguistic, cultural and sociopolitical landscape of the Arabic-speaking countries. Within this framework, the codified and historically sanctioned association of writing with the *fuṣḥā* and the absence of a similar link with the mother tongue have a determining effect on the structure of power in society and on how the political and cultural elite exploit writing to maintain their authority and protect their privileges. The elite do this through servicing the age-old distinction between the *fuṣḥā* and the mother tongue by (1) continuing to ban the latter from the educational field, (2) usurping for themselves the right to legislate which forms of the language can be used in the official business of the state and which ones are proscribed from this domain and (3) acting as the guardians for the received and approved interpretations of the foundational texts and encouraging, in this regard, the forces of univalency and conformity over those of polyvalency or diversity. The ruling and cultural elite are said to do this under the pretence of wanting to protect the language and culture from contamination, to promote political unity in the body politic and to preserve the sacred, for to 'read or write [the *fuṣḥā* is] to enter a solemn world, full of glory, the glory of the past with all its history, a history full of pride of affiliation' (58). This is, Safouan tells us, why the ruling elite would sanction translating the amendments to the American Constitution—in spite of its emphasis on liberty and freedom—into the *fuṣḥā*, although the political values they carry are inimical to the interests of the ruling elite, but would strongly oppose the study, in schools, of the grammar of the vernacular or some of the 'admirable texts' written in it because of the revolutionary force such a move would inject into the sociopolitical sphere (10–11). Thus, rather than providing avenues for challenging despotism in the Middle East, the *fuṣḥā* is said to be an *instrument of despotism*. It is used to maintain the status quo, in which power is allocated to the ruling elite, who, in acts of self-interest, use it to exploit the ordinary people for whom the mother tongue is the medium of communication.

To break the hold of the ruling elite on power, start the move towards ending despotic rule and provide a platform and an impetus for the introduction of freedom and, ultimately, democracy in the Arabic-speaking world, Safouan proposes the elevation of the mother tongues to the status of languages and using them in writing as the media of education, cultural production and state administration.[42] Safouan is aware that these are radical measures, but he considers them to be necessary to counter the entrenched despotic political order in the Arabic-speaking world. Thus, he advocates translating the Qur'an into these newly crafted 'mother tongue' languages (63), not just to ensure that its message will reach the mass of mother-tongue speakers in an idiom they will understand and without mediation but also, and seemingly more important, to break the biggest taboo in Arab Muslim culture: the myth, as he sees it, that the *fuṣḥā* and the vernaculars are varieties of the same language, rather than different languages that relate to each other genealogically as 'mother to daughters' constructs. Safouan believes that a move of this kind would create a Reformation-style revolution in Arab culture, allowing God, as he sees it, to talk directly to his people through their own mother tongues and in a way that makes them all equidistant from him. Translation into spoken Arabic, whether of the Qur'an or of texts from other cultures, 'not only contributes to enlightenment of the common people, but it also contributes to the liberation of our

42 Safouan's translation of Shakespeare's *Othello* into Egyptian Arabic in 1998 is an example of cultural production in the *'āmiyya* whose intention is to challenge the practise of producing tragedies in the *fuṣḥā* in the Arabic-speaking world (see Hanna 2009).

thinking processes' (65), which is why a 'theocratic state will never accept that texts used to assert its legitimacy can be translated into the vernacular' (81). It is only when placed against this context that the unleashing of the awesome power of translating the Qur'an into the vernacular can be appreciated. However, Safouan argues that until this step is taken, efforts must be made to use the mother tongues in writing as a preparatory taboo-busting step that validates the vernacular culturally. This would serve to show that the mother tongues are capable of expressing high culture, as well as revealing their naturalness when compared with the artificial *fuṣḥā*, as Safouan tried to show through his translation of *Othello* into the Egyptian vernacular.[43]

Safouan's reflections on the Arabic-language situation in Egypt introduce a new and radical element in discussing the *fuṣḥā*-versus-colloquial controversy: promoting the latter in writing, education and the other functions of the state (1) to fight despotism, theocracy and dictatorship and (2) to nurture the growth of freedom, enlightenment and, ultimately, democracy. These are radical views, because they place language at the centre of social and political transformation in society in ways that have not been allocated to language before, at least in such a bold and uncompromising way. Whether such a transformation could lead to genuine reform or catastrophic social upheaval is uncertain. However, it is unlikely that this solution would be espoused in Egypt or other Arab countries at the scale of or for the purposes espoused by Safouan. This applies equally to the calls to adopt the vernacular issued by Willcocks, Ahmed and Haeri, in spite of the fact that their aims and motivations may be different from those of Safouan.

Two factors, at least, militate against the acceptance of Safouan's solution in the Arab contexts. First, the *fuṣḥā*-Qur'an link is highly charged in the Arab milieu at all levels: doctrinally, ideologically, culturally and politically. Translating the Qur'an into the vernaculars is, therefore, bound to be met with huge resistance and even bloodshed, because it will be interpreted as a major attack on one of the most fundamental principles of the Islamic faith: the fact that the Qur'an is believed to have been revealed in Arabic verbatim and that God has undertaken himself to preserve it as it has been revealed to Muhammad, the Seal of all Prophets. This principle blocks any comparison between translating the Qur'an into Persian or Turkish, for example, and its translation into an Arabic vernacular, which comparison Safouan makes. Whereas the former would be justified because the majority of Persians and Turks are non-Arabic-speaking Muslims who have a genuine need to understand the content of the revelation, the majority of mother-tongue speakers in the Arab world are Arabic-speaking. In other words, while translations into Persian and Turkish will be regarded as *inter*lingual translations, translations into the Arabic mother-tongue vernaculars would be considered as *intra*lingual translations that carry with them the implication that

43 See Hanna (2009) for an identity-based discussion of the vernacular translation.

the Arabic Qur'an, God's revealed word, is foreign to Arabic speakers. However, at a different level, translating the Qur'an into the Arabic vernaculars would be tantamount to saying that the vernaculars and the *fuṣḥā* are different languages and that what has been referred to above as *intra*lingual translations should be considered as *inter*lingual ones. Not only would this be counterintuitive to most Arabic speakers, but it would also imply that the Muslim Arabs are as distant from the text of the Qur'an as the non-Arab Muslims are, in spite of the fact that the Qur'an constructs this relationship differently in favour of a closer connection between the Arabs and the text of the Qur'an.[44]

Second, the comparison between the translation of the Bible into the European vernaculars and the translation of the Qur'an into the Arabic mother tongues falls foul of the belief among Muslims that the Qur'an is not just some record of what a number of disciples had thought Muhammad, their master, to have said but is, in fact, believed to be God's word verbatim. In this respect, the Qur'an is thought by Muslims to be different from the Bible.[45] Had it been the same as the Bible for Muslims, the situation would have been different: one could easily imagine the appearance of translations of such a Qur'an into the vernaculars. Using the vernaculars to record doctrinally unmarked texts would, therefore, be considered an attempt that at some deeper level constitutes a challenge to the *fuṣḥā*-Qur'an link. The use of writing for the vernaculars and their deployment in education and other functions of the state would, therefore, be read as the thin edge of a wedge that will, if it is not removed, undermine the sanctity of the *fuṣḥā*-Qur'an link. It is, in fact, the rank-and-file Muslims in the Arabic-speaking world who police this link, rather than the ruling elite. And if it appears that the ruling elites are preserving this linguistic status quo in their societies, for what Safouan says are self-serving purposes, they are most probably doing so not out of despotism, although they are or may be despots, but because of their keen awareness that challenging this status quo would lead to social and political upheaval, rather than to religious enlightenment, political freedom and democracy. Even if a ruler was so minded, he would know that the price of acting as Safouan suggests would most definitely cost them their rule and lead to bloodshed in society.

Safouan's arguments on the place of writing and its meanings in society are highly suspect. While they may be true of ancient Egypt and Mesopotamia, where the rates of literacy were very low, these arguments lose much of their force in the modern Arab world, with its relatively high literacy rates. To begin with, it is not true that writing in modern literate societies is imbued with the connotations of the esoteric and the sacred that existed in the past, even the recent past. Writing is an everyday occurrence and a

44 See Suleiman (2001) for a discussion of this point.

45 I am, of course, aware that this view may be contested by Jewish scholars. What matters here, however, is Muslim belief regarding the status of the Qur'an.

cultural commodity that is abundantly available on the market of cultural products in the Arabic-speaking world. It, therefore, no longer commands the value it used to have a few decades ago, let alone in ancient Egypt and Mesopotamia. Safouan's views on the sociopolitical meanings of writing in modern times must, therefore, be viewed as the result of telescoping history, of the rear-view reading of the past into the present and, it seems, the future. This is the opposite of reading the present into the past, a point I raised in chapter 2.

In addition, Safouan's analysis wrongly assumes that writing in the *fuṣḥā* cannot but be conformist and supportive of the existing power structures in society. Not only is this assumption counterintuitive, but it also blatantly overlooks the many nonconformist texts in the *fuṣḥā* that deliberately set out to undermine or challenge the existing sociopolitical orders, causing their authors to pay a heavy price, including loss of employment, social ostracisation, exile or imprisonment. Also, the notion that writers in the mother tongue will be more likely than not to be politically nonconformist is unwarranted. Arabic newspapers in the Gulf region and elsewhere are full of *nabaṭī* (folk poetry) in the vernacular, but most of this poetry is conformist, stereotypical and supportive of some of the moribund social structures and despotic political establishments that Safouan would like to wipe off the face of the Arab political scene. As the *New Statesman* reviewer of Safouan's book remarks, Safouan 'claims standard Arabic is a dead language—so how do we explain the fact that poets such as the Syrian Nizar Qabbani and the Palestinian Mahmoud Darwish, both elegant writers of standard Arabic, have been read and recited by millions of people across the Arab world? His claim that Arab rulers prevent the use of dialects is also absurd: many poets of the vernacular were and have been pampered by Arab regimes.'

The injection of freedom and democracy into Arab political life, therefore, can be premised not on whether or not the vernaculars are raised to the sociopolitical status of fully fledged languages but on the results of the tug of war among many sociopolitical factors, one of which may be print language as both a medium and a symbol. Writing in the vernacular may indeed bring culture close to the people, but this is bound to be a temporary achievement, because the newly established languages will inevitably start to drift from their originary source, to develop styles, registers and peculiarities that can distance them from their ordinary speakers, the nonelite in society, as happened with Turkish in the Republican era. If language is indeed a resource in society, it is, therefore, inevitable that some speakers—the elite—would want to claim more of this resource for themselves or their own group than they are prepared to concede to others. The majority of speakers may, in fact, end up being disillusioned with their new languages, because they will have metamorphosed into an old-style hegemonic system, thus replacing one master code with another.

Also, since knowledge of the *fuṣḥā* will have to be maintained for doctrinal and legal reasons, the creation of new languages out of the vernaculars will, in fact, concentrate more of the powers of interpretation and legislation into the hands of the few members of the religious establishment who are prepared to invest the time and effort needed to master what will be increasingly viewed as a foreign *fuṣḥā* language. This point applies with equal force against Leila Ahmed's call for vernacularisation. Rather than being socially and politically liberatory, the creation of the new languages and the attendant neglect of the *fuṣḥā* may, in fact, lead to even greater closure of meaning—a new kind of esoteric despotism centred around an older form of writing—induced by those who can access what, as time goes on, will become more and more abstruse sources of knowledge. In other words, rather than opening up the foundational texts of Islam for new interpretations, the new language situation will lead to the narrowing down of the horizons of interpretation even further.

It could be argued that the increasing isolation of the class of *fuṣḥā* interpreters will, with time, lead to their marginalization and the consequent secularisation of Arab societies. Within a generation or two of the development of the new languages, the argument might go, the *fuṣḥā*-encoded materials will start to lose their hold on society, thus allowing people to move in new directions in seeking social and political progress, instead of continuing to look back to existing forms of knowledge. The official past will recede more and more into the past, into a very distant memory that will wither and die. And the same will become true of the idea that the *fuṣḥā* is constitutive of an Arab identity that cuts across nation-state identities. In this new linguistic order, being an Arab because one uses *fuṣḥā* Arabic becomes redundant, a cultural marker that is 'surplus to requirement.'

On the technical front, the creation of standard languages out of the vernaculars would open up many thorny questions. Issues of status planning and corpus planning would have to be engaged head on (see Cooper 1989; Suleiman 1999a). In status-planning terms,[46] a choice would have to be made for each Arabic-speaking country about which dialectal variety should be chosen to serve as the new standard language for the country in question. In some countries, this may prove more divisive than the proponents of vernacular standardisation might be prepared to admit. Egyptian Arabic sounds like a coherent construct when judged against the *fuṣḥā*. This would most probably be true for all country-linked vernaculars; however, once the discussion about standardisation is launched, this coherence may sound more illusory than real. Dialectal differences that may at present be held at bay because of the diglossic opposition of the colloquial to the *fuṣḥā* may, in fact, get accentuated in a new and divisive, at least initially, substate linguistic politics. Accusations of hegemony and marginalisation along regional, gender or educational background may lead to resistance, accusations of

46 Cooper defines status planning as 'the allocation of language or languages to given functions, e.g. medium of education, official language, vehicle of mass communication, etc.' (1989: 32).

disenfranchisement or bias. In Jordan, for example, where there are two prestige spoken standards, one for men and the other for women,[47] which one would a Jordanian vernaculariser choose? The one, the other or a mixture (what mixture?) of both? Clearly, unitary countrywide linguistic identities may turn out to be more fragile and illusory than is currently assumed to be the case. Linguistic devolution will, therefore, not be risk-free. It will have its winners and its losers. Instead of all mother-tongue speakers in any one country being equidistant from the *fuṣḥā*, as they are now, some will be more distant from the new standard vernacular than others in the new linguistic regime. Some in this regime will be empowered; others will be disempowered. The sociopolitical consequences of the rearrangement of the linguistic capital in society will produce new power asymmetries, which may be contested and recontested in the way that might challenge the social and political fabric of society.

While in the present situation, the 'Other' for the vernacularisers is the *fuṣḥā*, this 'Other' in the new linguistic order will be replaced by another 'Other' for those whose dialects will not end up as a significant contributor to the new standard or in fact emerge as the backbone of that new standard. The vernacularisers may argue that to make a new and badly needed linguistic omelette, one cannot help but break some dialectal eggs, but this act of dialectal egg breaking has to be set against whether the new linguistic omelette will, in fact, be worth the price paid for it in sociopolitical upheaval, at least in the short to medium term, which often dominates decision-making horizons in political circles in most countries, including liberal democracies, which the Arab countries certainly are not. The vernacularisers may retort by arguing that as a massive and long-overdue project in social and cultural engineering, their position is driven by medium- to long-term strategic considerations for which they are prepared to pay whatever price in the short to medium term. But this is unlikely to cut ice with political decision makers, who tend to be risk-averse—especially when the gains may be deferred/delayed or considered to be intangible by those for whom they are intended—or with society at large, which may evaluate the discussion about a new standard as a side show or a red herring that diverts the attention of the population away from the more pressing problems of economic and social development, fighting foreign occupation and/or achieving genuine political participation in the workings of the state. Thus, what the vernacularisers may imagine as a Utopian dream may, in fact, be conjured up in the minds of a sizeable and cynical majority in the Arabic-speaking world as an externally induced nightmare and, most probably, as one big conspiracy that a Satanic power has unleashed against an Arab order that has assumed the status of the 'sick man' of the Middle East, if not the whole world.

47 See Ibrahim (1986).

On the corpus-planning front,[48] vernacular standardisation will consume enormous economic resources, which society may not be prepared to earmark for it, even if it was well disposed towards this standardisation. The questions will be: Who will foot the bill? And is the bill worth footing? New grammars will have to be crafted for the new standards, as well as new lexica, manuals and teaching resources. This would be a gigantic task by any standards, which some may relish but a lot more may abhor. But the most divisive of all corpus-planning measures may prove to be the adoption or development of new alphabets and orthographic conventions for the new standards, since orthography is the most visible sign of a written language and also functions as the aspect of a language that is most value-laden in the political and cultural spheres. Will the new scripts be based on the present Arabic alphabet? Or will Roman-based alphabets be developed? It is, of course, possible that different Arabic-speaking countries will adopt different solutions; this, in fact, could be one of the (un)intended consequences of vernacular standardisation, in so much as this may serve the development of unequivocally country-linked national identities that are free from the pull of larger suprastate national identities, especially pan-Arabism. The term *Arabic-speaking countries* would gradually drift out of use because of the disintegration of the empirical world it designates. The concept of an Arab world would in time disappear under the onslaught of the new linguistic regimes. Works published in Morocco or Iraq would gradually become less accessible outside their country or region, depending upon their depth of vernacularisation. The present print economies would fracture and shrink along newly constructed national lines. It is, therefore, unlikely that the publishing industry in the Arab world, weak though it is in comparison with other demographically comparable linguistic regions in terms of size and literacy levels, would espouse vernacularisation without a fight, waged not on the basis of a nebulous balance sheet of cultural gains and losses or the desirability of pan-Arab or state nationalisms but on the rational and hard-nosed basis of a balance sheet of bankable earnings, of real gains and losses.

The above discussion may help to explain why calls to replace the *fuṣḥā* with the vernaculars as standard languages—and there have been many of these in the last century—have not met with success.[49] This may further explain why those who would prefer to move away from the *fuṣḥā* have adopted two strategies that have significantly diverged from the bold espousal of the vernaculars. The first, exemplified by Ahmed Lutfi al-Sayyid of Egypt, calls for creating a rapprochement between the *fuṣḥā* and the

48 Cooper uses the term *corpus planning* to refer to 'activities such as coining new terms, reforming spelling and adopting a new script. It refers, in short, to the creation of new forms, the modifications of old ones, or the selection from alternative forms in a spoken or written code' (1989: 31).

49 See Suleiman (2003) for a discussion of some of these calls.

vernacular by levelling down on the side of the former and levelling up on the side of the latter to reach a common meeting point.[50] The other consists of sticking to the *fuṣḥā* but arguing that this *fuṣḥā* is imbued with the spirit and character of its nation-state speakers, thus making it different from the *fuṣḥās* in other Arabic-speaking nation-states. One of the best examples of this strategy is provided by the Tunisian al-Bashir Bin Salama (1974), who calls the *fuṣḥā* in Tunisia the 'Tunisian Language,' without an intervening 'Arabic' between 'Tunisian' and 'Language.' Whereas in Egypt and most Arab countries, using the national epithet before 'Arabic' generally refers to the dominant vernacular, commonly associated with the capital city, for Bin Salama, the term *Tunisian Arabic* refers to the *fuṣḥā*, not to the dialect of the capital city Tunis or any other variety of Tunisian Arabic.

LANGUAGE, SELF AND GLOBALISATION

An interesting work on identity from the Arab perspectives is Amin Maalouf's book *Les Identités meurtriéres* (*On Identity*, English translation, Maalouf 2000), which, to the best of my knowledge, was translated from the French into Arabic twice (1999 and 2004). This book does not pretend to be an academic treatise on the subject[51] but, like Safouan's book, is a set of reflections by a Lebanese-French writer who is better known in the Western world for his novels, especially the best-selling *Leo the African* (1998). Maalouf left Lebanon for France in 1976 to escape the ravages of the Lebanese civil war, which raged, officially, at least, until 1992. Maalouf adopts a view of the Self that emphasises its plurality, positionality, alterity and uniqueness. Identity for him is a unitary construct in spite of its complexity. It is context-dependent, rather than fixed and invariant. It is a project of the Self in which the existence of an 'Other' is necessary for definitional purposes and in which this 'Other,' through acts of ascription, partakes in authoring the Self. And finally, it is singularly different from all other selves.

Maalouf's concept of identity raises the issue of how collective identities are formed and reformed. According to Maalouf, this is done by people coming together under a commanding principle of classification—which may be colour, religion, language, class, genealogy, and so on—in situations of external threat to protect themselves against palpable danger. In such circumstances, collective identities can become very accentuated and highly charged, leading to excessive forms of action or reaction against those who are believed to belong to a threatening Other. When this happens, personal identities submerge themselves into collective identities that can act with mortal force, hence the title of Maalouf's book in French: *Les identités meurtriéres*. Clearly, Maalouf is reacting to the devastating and traumatic

50 See Suleiman (2003: 171–74).

51 This feature is one of the strengths of the book, making it accessible to a wide readership.

consequences of identity politics as he had experienced it during the first years of the Lebanese civil war.[52] This explains his insistence on the openness of the Self in its individual setting to counter the homogenising and totalising effects of collective identities. Maalouf's concept of identity may, however, be used to justify what may be called escapist politics, expressed as a desire or a tendency to withdraw from active politics by refusing to counter the hegemonic practises of an aggressive Other. However, this issue will not detain us here.

One of the main issues for Maalouf is the effect of globalisation on language and identity, hence my interest in him and how his concerns echo some of the anxieties about Arabic in the Arabic-speaking world. Maalouf takes an ambivalent view of globalisation as a modern phenomenon, arguing that it has its positive and negative effects. His most scathing remarks about it, however, relate to those cases where globalisation becomes synonymous with Americanisation,[53] arguing that, in this form, globalisation is often translated into a hegemonic form of homogenisation that acts against what may be called ecolinguistic diversity. The rise of English as the international language par excellence in the modern world is an aspect of this globalisation that challenges this ecolinguistic diversity, sweeping in front of it linguistic landscapes that are expressive of cultures and experiences that are of the essence of the rich mosaic that makes up humanity. Commenting on this from a diasporic perspective that is more related to his adopted home than to his original homeland, Maalouf considers the intense challenge that English poses to French to be implicated in many of the anxieties that France had been experiencing towards the close of the second millennium, when he was writing his book. This may sound exaggerated if interpreted literally, but its force can be appreciated, though not necessarily accepted as true, if we take it to represent the pressure that English puts on the symbolic order in which French has traditionally and historically operated. Starting from the premise that 'identity is in the first place a matter of symbols' (Maalouf 2000: 100) and that language is as important as—if not, in fact, more important than[54]—religion in marking the Self, Maalouf comments on this

52 Maalouf sounds this cautionary note about identity: Identity 'is not to be dealt with by either persecution or indulgence. It needs to be observed, studied calmly, understood, and then conquered and tamed if we don't want the world to become a jungle, or the future to resemble the worst images of the past, or our sons to have to look helplessly in 50 years' time as we do now at massacres, expulsions and other "cleansings"' (2000: 118).

53 Maalouf describes the challenge of globalisation as Americanisation as follows: 'If you want to avoid seeing [globalisation] unleash in millions upon millions of our fellow human beings a reaction of furious, suicidal, systematic rejection, it is essential that the global civilisation which globalisation in general is creating should not be seen to be exclusively American. Everyone must be able to recognise himself in it, to identify with it a little' (2000: 99).

54 In spite of the fact that Maalouf tries to establish a degree of parity between language and religion as markers of identity, he seems to accord the latter greater significance: 'While it would not be difficult to prove that a man can live without a religion, clearly he cannot live without a language. . . . It is equally self-evident . . . that whereas religion tends to be exclusive,

peculiarly French anxiety[55] in the following terms: 'In France, when I detect anxieties in some people about the way the world is going, or reservations about technological innovation, or some intellectual, verbal, musical or nutritional fashion; or when I see signs of over-sensitivity, excessive nostalgia or even extreme attachment to the past—I realise that such reactions are often linked in one way or another to the resentment people feel about the continual advance of English and its present status as the predominant international language' (112).

For Maalouf, the power of English as the international language par excellence represents the excesses of globalisation as a 'one size fits all' kind of phenomenon that works for a templated uniformity across cultures. It is, however, significant that Maalouf links his concerns about linguistic ecodiversity to the threat facing French, rather than Arabic, although the latter could be said to be his native language. This concern signals where he locates himself in identity terms. This does not mean that he is not concerned about the pressures facing Arabic in an increasingly globalised world but that he is more interested in French because he considers it to be a more significant badge of his identity. It may, however, be the case that by choosing French, not Arabic, to set out his case—in spite of the fact that there is a great deal of anxiety about the threat of globalisation to Arabic in Arab culture—Maalouf wants to emphasise the threat that globalisation poses to linguistic ecology, for if a language as strong as French proves unable to withstand the globalising pressure of English, then what chance do other languages, including Arabic, have to resist that pressure?

According to Maalouf, resisting the popularity and spread of English as a global language is a struggle doomed to failure. If so, the answer, therefore, resides not in rejecting English but in (1) taming the language, which he symbolises as a 'panther,' by using it within a circumscribed range of instrumental settings or purposes for nonnative speakers of the language; (2) 'maintaining and developing the national language' (113), which is easier

---

language does not. A man can speak Hebrew, Arabic, Italian and Swedish, all at once, but he cannot be simultaneously a Jew, a Muslim, a Catholic and a Protestant. Even if someone regards himself as an adherent of two religions at once, such a position is not acceptable to other people' (2000: 109). This comparison may, however, be taken to favour religion as a more marked marker of identity than language, but this is not how Maalouf intends it.

55 In a recent book on language anxiety with respect to change and variation in the history of English, Machan explores 'how anxiety over change and variation has transhistorically motivated and underwritten sociopolitical behaviour, ideological formation and mythological construction—how it has largely been a constant in the Anglophone world. . . . As a constant . . . this anxiety has served to displace and channel other kinds of social concerns, whether of economics, race, ethnicity, sex or class. Put more directly . . . anxiety over language change has euphemistically displaced anxiety about other issues and that so long as the anxiety remains centred on language, the other issues can never be fully addressed' (2009: 22). This linking of sociopolitical anxiety to English may come as a surprise to some readers, owing to the view of it as the hegemonic language of globalisation.

said than done in some cases; and (3) developing a language policy that gives space for a third language of personal choice, which Maalouf describes poetically as 'the language of the heart, the adopted language, the language you have married, the language you love' (116). Although Maalouf does not define a fixed range for the third language, there is no doubt that he hopes that French, in particular, will emerge as the leading contender in this range: 'Nowadays everybody obviously needs three languages. The first is his language of identity; the third is English. Between the two we have to promote a third language, freely chosen, which will often but not always be another European language' (115–16). If adopted, this measure could alleviate the pressure on French, but it could also allay some of the anxieties that Maalouf may have about the dominance of English.

Unlike Edward Said, Leila Ahmed or Moustapha Safouan, Maalouf seems to be more concerned about the language of the diaspora (although he may not accept that he is a diasporic individual) than about his native language, which, in a *volte-face* or just a slip of the pen, he calls the language of identity. This concern with French and its destiny as an international language may indicate a high degree of integration in the host society on the part of Maalouf. It may further indicate a personal anxiety on the part of an author who sees his adopted language, the one he loves and in which he lives his intellectual life, being internationally sidelined by a stronger and more aggressive language. Maalouf is no disinterested observer of language who is free of anxiety in this cultural arena; his is a linguistic anxiety that he shares with other French people. He speaks as a Frenchman with all of the anxieties he says the French have about their language, which, if we accept his diagnosis above, have struck deep into the French psyche. However, what Maalouf says about the effect of globalisation on language ecology, in particular the threat that English poses to other languages, is of great interest in the Arab public sphere, as will be outlined in the next section. In this sphere, rather than being a victim of globalisation, French is regarded as a predator language that exercises its influence through direct external support from metropolitan France and, even more vigorously, through Arabic-speaking francophone countries, particularly in North Africa, Lebanon and, to a lesser extent, Egypt.

LANGUAGE AND SELF: DISPLACEMENT, TRAUMA AND GLOBALISATION

The above exploration of how the Self is marked by language at the individual and collective level shows the complexity, positionality and context-dependent nature of this marking. To take one example, while both Leila Ahmed and Moustapha Safouan express interest in making the vernacular the written and national language of Egypt, they do so from different perspectives, with different emphases and from different historical and personal backgrounds and experiences. Whereas Ahmed is mainly interested in using the vernacular as the site of an exclusively Egyptian (non-Arab) national identity and as an instrument of social modernisation to counter the dominance of closed and 'misogynist' readings of the Qur'an and other satellite texts of exegesis and *sharia* legislation, Safouan is interested in the vernacular to counter despotism and dictatorship in public life in Egypt and to promote as an antidote the cause of political freedom and democracy in the country. Politics is at the heart of both projects, but the political aims of the latter are more pronounced and are treated with greater urgency than those coded in the former. These differences of perspective and emphasis are no doubt connected to the different histories and intellectual backgrounds of the two authors. Ahmed's views were shaped by the political upheavals in her life, mainly the Egyptian Revolution of 1952, and by her critical evaluation of the position of women under Islam. Safouan's ideas are shaped by the consequences of the 1967 Arab defeat at the hands of Israel, as he himself points out, and by more recent post-9/11 events, it seems, wherein the democratisation of the Arab world emerged as an important policy objective in the 'War on Terror' for American and European policy makers. Safouan's interest in psychology as a diagnostic tool for identifying problems and solutions at the individual and collective levels guides his exploration of the democracy deficit in Egypt and other Arabic-speaking countries. Language is placed at the heart of this diagnosis.

The texts that make up the corpus for this chapter differ in a variety of ways. Edward Said's and Leila Ahmed's are autobiographical works. They speak in first-person narratives about first-person experiences. Amin Maalouf's book combines first-person reflections with a broader perspective on issues of identity at the personal and collective levels; it focuses on the roles of religious belief and language in exploring these issues. Moustapha Safouan's work is not autobiographical; it is mainly a set of personal reflections on language and society. None of these works provides a systematic treatment of the subject of language, the Self and collective identity. The fact that these works are reflective in nature underlies the decision to treat them as parts of a corpus in this book, in spite of the differences among them in genre and tone. In addition, these works are similar in two important ways. On the one hand, they are all written from exile and the diaspora, whether they are anglophone (Said and Ahmed) or francophone (Safouan and Maalouf) in provenance. On the other hand, all four texts are connected to traumatic events in the lives of their authors, in which wars and revolution had a deep and lasting impact. For Said, the 1948 and 1967 wars over Palestine loom large on the personal and intellectual level. For Ahmed, the 1948 war over Palestine and, more decisively, the Egyptian Revolution of 1952 are of the greatest significance to her social and physical displacement; the former is important because it was the key factor in bringing about the latter. In Safouan's case, the 1967 War and 9/11 play a determining role in his diagnosis of and solution for the ills facing Arab society. Maalouf's views on identity are shaped by the civil war in Lebanon (1975–92) and the effects of globalization through American political and cultural hegemony on the international scene. Each of these texts is written under the impact of some national crisis whose aftereffects have marked the author's life in a deep and lasting way.

Let us explore some of these issues further to connect language as a site of the Self and collective identity inscription or marking with the aftereffects of war by way of displacement and traumas. Starting with Said, *Out of Place* describes language as a 'basic split' (1999: xiv) in the life of its author, connecting it with what he describes as 'displaced forms of departures, arrivals, farewells, exile, nostalgia [and] homesickness' (xiv), which cannot be divorced from the bloody history of Palestine and the impact this had on the Said family, as the book amply explains. Said further considers this 'basic split' in his life to be part and parcel of his 'primal instability' (4), which he traces back to his mother's interaction with him in his childhood, using Arabic and English for different domain purposes that assign homely intimacy to the former and transactionality to the latter, what I have called the subjective and objective functions of the language, respectively. This 'basic split' and 'primal instability' are no doubt further connected to what Said calls his 'troublesome identity' (90), the fact that inside the boy with the American citizenship he had inherited from his father, there 'lurked [an Arab] identity from which [he] derived no strength, only embarrassment and discomfort' (90). Language is also connected to what Said calls 'the rift between white man and Arab' (144) and to the painful rebuffs he had to endure on the rare occasion when he invoked Arabic as a common bond with individuals in the diaspora who disclaimed competence in the language and displayed rejection of what it symbolically represents on the identity front. Said's descriptions of his alienation from Arabic in the Cairo schools he attended flesh out this picture of 'split,' 'instability,' 'rift,' 'embarrassment,' 'discomfort' and 'troublesome identity.' While these are not the symptoms of trauma in the classical sense of the term, they are, however, indicative of acute psychological stress that perhaps borders on the traumatic. The fact that the narrative in *Out of Place* links language directly to this stress reveals the importance of language to the well-being of the Self.

Language for Said is, therefore, placed at the crossroad of many of his formative experiences, most of which were negative and painful. However, on those occasions when Said presents the use of Arabic in a positive light, the overwhelming mood is one of 'striking back' at the social and colonial order, as in his delight at his mother's use of Arabic at Groppi or his retaliatory deployment of Arabic to undermine the established order at Victoria College which banned the use of the language in the school outside the prescribed teaching. Said's description of the latter event as a 'proud insurrectionary gesture' and as an 'act of defiance' (1999: 184) against the English-only policy of the school not only highlights the ability of the language to act in a reparative or recuperative capacity at the psychological level, albeit tokenistically at this stage in his life, but it also prefigures his return to the language for formal study, under the tutelage of Anis Freyha, following the trauma of the 1967 War, which, in fact, ushered in on the intellectual scene the Said we publicly know. Furthermore, these acts of linguistic tokenism foreshadow Said's joy and pride in his children's competence in the language and his full reconciliation with it towards the end of his life, in a way that eliminates many of the demons of the past: his father's ambivalent attitude towards it and its being the source of identity alienation, 'embarrassment and discomfort' in the schools he attended in Cairo (90). The title of Said's posthumous article (2004) is 'Living in Arabic,' which I described as a fitting finale to his search for identity.

In light of the above analysis, an equally valid title for Said's essay might have been 'Arabic Strikes Back!' The source of alienation, embarrassment and discomfort has emerged as the source of loyalty, pride and joy, signalling the recuperation of an embargoed Self achieved through so many personal trials and public traumas in which the shock waves generated by war played a determining effect. Furthermore, the fact that language seems to have been a chronic and vexing issue for Said all his life perhaps justifies describing it as a kind of wound or, more accurately, the result of wounds that refuse to totally go away. 'Trauma,' says Caruth (1996: 4), 'seems to be much more than a pathology, or the simple illness of a wounded psyche: it is always the story of a wound that cries out, that addresses us in an attempt to tell us of a reality or truth that is not otherwise available.'

Let us now turn to Leila Ahmed's exploration of language, Self and displacement. *A Border Passage* makes clear that the 1952 Egyptian Revolution that ended the monarchy and brought to power Nasser's republican rule is the single, most important event in Ahmed's life and in her search for identity. She links this event to the 1948 Palestinian disaster (*nakba*), which she considers the most decisive event in the historical trajectory that led to the collapse of her world under Nasser's regime. Ahmed belonged to a family that had enjoyed many privileges under the Egyptian monarchy. Nasser's socialist policies ended these privileges of land ownership, class elitism and access to special educational provision through foreign private schools. In a number of vignettes strewn across different parts of her autobiography, Ahmed signals the ways in which the 1952 revolution turned her life and that of her family upside down. She explains how a demographically all-inclusive Egypt that was first and foremost conscious of its Egyptianness and secure in the quest of its privileged classes for European-centred modernity was quickly and coercively steered towards an imposed Arab identity through propaganda, bogus rhetoric and various forms of state intervention that scarred her for life. To make this point, I will cite a few quotations from *A Border Passage* to convey the tone and emotional charge carried by Ahmed's reflections on identity:

1.

> I obviously was not born but became black when I went to England [to study at Cambridge]. I was not born but became a woman of colour when I went

> to America [to teach at the University of Massachusetts at Amherst]. Whereas these are political identities that carry, for me, a positive charge, revealing and affirming connection and commonality, my identity as an Arab, no less a political construction, is an identity that, in contrast, I experience as deeply and perhaps irretrievably fraught with angst and confusion. (2000: 237–38)

2.

> I certainly felt no loyalty toward or solidarity with Nasser, with his empty, fraudulent rantings about *al-Uruba*—Arabness—and all that awful, badgering nonsense that I read about in the papers. (239)

3.

> [Egyptian] Jews and Copts were not, to me, abstractions. They were people my parents knew and saw and talked about, and they were my brothers' friends and my sisters' and my own, including my best friend, Joyce. I am sure I sensed [the regime's] insidious, subterranean shifts and rearrangements of our feelings that this new bludgeoning propaganda was effecting, or trying to effect in us. And I am sure that this, as well as the sheer hatefulness of being endlessly subjected to propaganda, was part of the reason I so much disliked and resisted the idea I was an Arab. (245)

4.

> To question our Arabness and all that our Arabness implied became unthinkable. Only despicable, unprincipled traitors would do such a thing. And it is with this complicated legacy that my own sense of identity as an Egyptian and as an Arab is entangled. (246)

When linked to identity formation, expressions such as 'irretrievably fraught with angst and confusion,' 'empty, fraudulent rantings about . . . Arabness,' 'awful, badgering nonsense,' 'insidious, subterranean shifts and rearrangements of our feelings,' 'bludgeoning propaganda,' 'sheer hatefulness of being endlessly subjected to propaganda,' and 'so much disliked and resisted the idea I was an Arab' indicate the strength of feelings Ahmed had against Arabness. Against this background, Ahmed's troubled and 'troublesome identity,' to use a term employed by Edward Said, orbits around language as one of the most important markers of the Self and of group identification. As explained above, Ahmed locates her identity on the linguistic front in the Egyptian vernacular, at both the personal and the national level. She argues in favour of using the vernacular in writing and as the medium of learning and cultural expression. Her attitude towards the *fuṣḥā* is very negative, as she describes it as an instrument of internal colonialism in Egypt.

This vituperative attitude is linked to the following sociopolitical associations of the language for Ahmed: (1) under Nasser, the *fuṣḥā* became one of the most potent symbols of pan-Arab nationalism, the *'urūba* that Ahmed found so repugnant and so baneful; (2) the *fuṣḥā* was the language of the 'empty,' 'fraudulent' and coercive propaganda that Nasser's regime used in an 'insidious' and badgering way to produce 'subterranean shifts and rearrangements' in people's false conceptions of the Egyptian national identity as something Arab not Egyptian; (3) for Ahmed, the new links of identity that the *fuṣḥā* was designed to produce were fabricated and bogus, lacking the 'connection and commonality,' that is, naturalness and spontaneity, which the ties of colour and gender could 'reveal' and 'affirm' for her in England (where she studied for her doctorate at Cambridge) and in America (where she has been working for two decades); (4) with great official zeal, the *fuṣḥā* was forced on Ahmed's generation (which had attended foreign private schools), replacing English as the language of science, high culture, civilisation and social privilege and marking English as the language of the enemy and an internal fifth column that wished to continue the old class structure; and (5) through Miss Nabih, the Palestinian refugee teacher who slapped Ahmed for refusing to read in the *fuṣḥā*, the language acted as a site of painful personal and group memories that linked it to Palestine and the Palestinians,[56] to the fall of the Egyptian monarchy, to the occurrence of the Egyptian Revolution and, finally, to the coming of Nasser's regime. These painful associations of the language explain why Ahmed strongly rejects it as a site of identity construction, preferring, instead, the vernacular. Striking out against the *fuṣḥā* in this way is, therefore, important in ridding Ahmed of some of the demons of her troubled and traumatic past under Nasser's regime.

But, as we have seen earlier in this chapter, there is another dimension to Ahmed's position vis-à-vis the *fuṣḥā* that makes the language more repugnant. The language is purveyed by lascivious men, as the story of her private Arabic tutor suggests. The language is further depicted as an instrument of coercion that misogynistically acts on behalf of men against women in the religious domain. According to this reading of the language, received gendered readings of medieval texts are deeply entrenched in Muslim societies, leaving little scope for new, more enlightened readings that are in tune with modernity. This is a central theme in *A Border Passage*. Ahmed advocates the use of the vernacular to dislodge the grip that the *fuṣḥā*, as a male language, has on interpreting the Qur'an. In other words, Ahmed believes that the vernacular is more able than the *fuṣḥā* to generate readings of the Qur'an

56 For Ahmed, Arabness and the question of Palestine are interlinked in discussions of identity in Egypt: 'For Egyptians to debate or question their Arabness ('search' for their identity) is usually code . . . for debating the extent of our responsibility toward the Palestinians. And it is accordingly read by Arabs and by Egyptians as a covert way of advocating either support for or abandonment of the Palestinians' (2000: 256).

that can exhibit greater gender balance and equality. Evaluated from this perspective, the vernacular emerges as an instrument of social liberation, in exactly the same way it was projected earlier as a tool of political liberation from the grip of (pan-)Arab nationalist ideologies. Through her support for the vernacular, Ahmed marks her identity as that of a liberal intellectual for whom social and political dogmas are anathema.

This concept of the Self animates Ahmed's charged views about the *fuṣḥā*. But it is a Self that is suffering from multiple wounds that refuse to heal totally. I have highlighted above some of the vituperative expressions concerning Arab identity that Ahmed uses. Reflecting on this identity further, she says: 'I remember how I hated that incessant rhetoric [by Nasser and his regime]. *Al-qawmiyya al-Arabiyya! Al-Uraba (sic), Nahnu al-Arab!* Arab nationalism! Arabness! We the Arabs! Even now, just remembering those words, *I feel again a surge of mingled irritation and resentment*' (2000: 244; emphasis added). The words 'again' and 'surge' here indicate the strength and continuity of Ahmed's feelings. The words 'irritation' and 'resentment' play down the true nature of those feelings. But this decrease in emotional intensity is compensated for by the expression 'how I hated that incessant rhetoric.' *A Border Passage* is full of such expressions about the *fuṣḥā*-identity link, such as the dismissive expression 'this language of standard Arabic' (282); these expressions reveal a state of acute and chronic psychological stress, which, while they might not constitute a case of trauma in the classical sense of the term, do border on the traumatic.

In various places in this chapter, I have referred to the defeat of the Arabs at the hands of Israel in the 1967 War as one of the most traumatic events in Arab political life in the modern period. Ahmed refers to this war and deals with the impact it had on her evaluation of her identity as being Egyptian rather than Arab-bound and by affirming her commitment to the vernacular as a marker of this identity. I have also pointed out that the 1967 War was a crucial factor in Edward Said's active and direct engagement in Arab political life, leading in subterranean ways to his path-breaking book *Orientalism* and many more subsequent publications in which Palestine was the primary focus. Moustapha Safouan's book on language, political freedom and democracy, although written forty years after the event, is directly related to this war as the author himself confirms: 'I began this book almost forty years ago and at that time I had no idea whatever about the relation between writing and power. I started writing in the aftermath of the Six Day War defeat, in June 1967, which I understood as part of a much more general and comprehensive defeat of the Third World, apart from India' (2007: 1). I have described this event as a trauma above. The fact that Safouan thought of the 1967 defeat of the Arabs as a 'comprehensive defeat of the Third World,' not just of Egypt, Syria and Jordan, which were, with Israel, the main combatants in this war, shows the depth of this trauma for one Egyptian writer and its deferred aftereffects in searching for a diagnosis and an antidote for this defeat. This assessment of the 1967 War thus provides a good example of how the link between language and trauma might be further amplified.

But in what sense was the defeat of 1967 a trauma in modern Arab life? One of the best treatments of the subject is offered by the Syrian writer George Tarabishi in his book *Al-Maraḍ bi-al-gharb: Al-taḥlīl al-nafsī li-'uṣāb jamā'ī 'arabī* (*Westernitis: A Psycho-analytic Study of a Common Arab Condition*, 2005). The psychoanalytic perspective of this book accords well with Safouan's use of psychology as a tool of analysis in his book. In the first chapter of *Westernitis*, *"Min al-ṣadma ilā al-raḍḍa"* ("From Shock to Trauma," 15–35), Tarabishi outlines four reasons for his view that the 1967 defeat was a colossal trauma in Arab life at all levels. First, there is the completely unexpected nature of this defeat, adding that it is in the nature of trauma to be unexpected and to follow a feeling of hyper-self-confidence and invincibility. In 1967, very few Arabs expected to be defeated; the majority of the Arabs considered victory as a 'given' outcome. Second, the defeat suffered by the Arabs could not be explained away as the victory of a massive military power or a coalition of combatants over a numerically smaller and weaker one.[57] In the Arab media, Israel was always belittled as the 'Zionist entity' (*al-kiyān al-ṣuhyūnī*) and as an artificial state that lacked the geographic, demographic and economic strengths necessary for long-term survival. The defeat of 1967 was therefore not just a military defeat (*hazīma 'askariyya*) but a comprehensive one that laid bare the backwardness of Arab society 'politically, economically, technologically and culturally' (Tarabishi 2005: 29). Third, the 1967 defeat heralded a series of Arab defeats to this day without any reprieve, conforming in a way to the notion that 'the experience of trauma repeats itself, exactly and unremittingly, through the unknowing acts of the survivor and against his very will' (Caruth 1996: 2). The limited Arab victory against Israel in the 1973 War did not buck this trend or heal the wounds of the 1967 defeat; on the contrary, it led to a peace treaty between Egypt and Israel on Israeli terms that confirmed the regional ascendancy of the latter power on all fronts. Finally, in a continuation of the post-1948 rhetoric, the Arab political discourse represented the occupation of Arab land in 1967 in sexual terms, describing it as an act of rape (*ightiṣāb*). This rape was all the more devastating to the victim because it was perpetrated by what was regarded as the weaker party in the conflict, against the stronger and numerically most dominant one regionally, which, since then, has suffered chronic political and military impotence. This act of rape penetrated deep into the Arab psyche, because in carrying it out, the perpetrator used the latest Western technology, which the Arabs had so much desired but were constantly denied.

57 See Schivelbusch (2004) for an excellent discussion of the culture of war defeat. Using the concepts of 'trauma,' 'mourning' and 'recovery,' Schivelbusch provides many insights that do apply to the experience of Arab defeats in the 1948 and 1967 wars with Israel.

Regardless of whether one agrees with Safouan's views on the role of Arabic in blocking (through the *fuṣḥā*) or opening (through the vernacular) the paths to freedom and democracy in Arab society, his analysis is interesting because of the clear link it posits between language and trauma. The 1967 defeat is an uncontested case of pan-Arab trauma whose aftereffects are still with the Arabs to this day. As is characteristic of trauma, it is an open wound that refuses to heal. Safouan's book is a case of delayed response, which, ironically, invites the reader to relive that defeat and, implicitly, to situate the occupation of Iraq in 2003 as the final chapter in a long chain of defeats. However, the point of interest for us is the injection of language into this chain, both as the root cause of all Arab defeats and as the solution to them. If the illness according to Safouan is dictatorship and if the solution is democracy, the fact that the former is linked to the *fuṣḥā* and the latter to the vernacular does put language at the centre of Arab political life. Alas, I could hear many an Arab say, 'How we wish that was true!'

For the Lebanese, the Civil War of 1975–92 is a massive traumatic chapter in the history of a country with a fragile sectarian political mosaic. This war was fought on all sides with terrifying ferocity and brutality. It would, therefore, be strange if it had left no marks on how the Lebanese, whether they remained in Lebanon during the war or left it to the safety of other countries, think about language (see Suleiman 2006c). Amin Maalouf's reflections touch on the language-identity link from this perspective, which, among other things, gives prominence to globalisation as a disruptive force economically, politically, socially and in terms of language ecology.

Zygmunt Bauman writes that 'a battlefield is identity's natural home' (2004: 77). He further adds: 'identity comes to life only in the tumult of battle; it falls asleep and silent the moment the noise of the battle dies down' (77). Maalouf's reflections on identity are written against this understanding of it coming to life in the 'tumult of battle' but not completely, as I will suggest below. Referring to the year 1976, the first sentence of *On Identity* makes an oblique reference to the civil war in Lebanon (which forced him to move to France) and returns to it in several places in the book. In addition, the book is full of references to situations and events, such as Bosnia and the Muslim world, where violent expressions of national identity and sectarian strife dominated the 1980s and 1990s. Maalouf recognises the devastating effects of identity politics, which finds its 'natural home,' as Bauman says, in the 'battlefield.' To counter this politics, Maalouf advocates what may be called portmanteau identities that can accommodate differences of allegiance,[58] as the following quotation illustrates:

> How many times since I left Lebanon in 1976 to live in France have people asked me, with the best intention in the world, whether I felt 'more French' or 'more Lebanese'? And I always give the same answer: 'Both!'

58 The title of the first part of *On Identity* is 'My identity, my allegiances,' signalling, therefore, the close connection between 'identity' and multiple 'allegiances' for Maalouf.

> To those who ask the question, I patiently explain that I was born in Lebanon and lived there until I was 27; that Arabic is my mother tongue; and that it was in Arabic translation that I first read Dumas and Dickens and *Gulliver's Travels*; and that in my native village, the village of my ancestors, I experienced the pleasures of childhood and heard some of the stories that were later to inspire my novels. How could I forget all that? How could I cast it aside? On the other hand, I have lived for 22 years on the soil of France; I drink her water and wine; every day my hands touch her ancient stones; I write my books in her language; never again will she be a foreign country to me.
>
> So am I half French and half Lebanese? Of course not. Identity can't be compartmentalised. You can't divide it up into halves or thirds or any other separate segments. I haven't got several identities: I have just got one, made up of many components combined in a mixture that is unique to every individual. (2000: 3)

Commenting on these reflections on identity, Suleiman writes:

> Maalouf is primarily interested in personal identity, but he is aware that this identity is at the crossroads of many of life's currents and social categories of self-definition. Personal identities, according to Maalouf, are both complex and unique. They are not 'single malts' but 'blends' for which there is no single recipe. Identities also engage an assumption of alterity, the fact that it is not possible to posit identity without speaking of difference, of otherness. Personal identities, as Maalouf also tells us later in his book, are both stable and changeable. Maalouf emphasises the potential for mutation, the fact that identity is always in a state of becoming, and he links it to different configurations in the 'hierarchy' of the elements making up an identity. Maalouf's use of the term 'hierarchy' in this context is not helpful. I personally prefer to talk in terms of the poly-centricity of identity instead. Finally, Maalouf recognises that the components of an identity may clash with each other under certain conditions. Yet these same components can exist in harmony under other, less inciting conditions. This is one of the paradoxes of identity: its capacity to combine the forces of relative harmony and fragmentation, of fusion and fission, into a single unit that manifests itself in different ways under different conditions. Owing to this, some scholars prefer to speak of an identity repertoire, rather than just 'identity' on its own. (2006d: 51)

Language, as the above quotation from *On Identity* reveals, is an important marker of identity; it comes second after 'place of birth' in this regard, signalling its salience in self-definition. Towards the end of the book, where he proposes the development of a linguistic triad of national language, a language of international communication and an in-between language of choice to counter the devastating effect of globalisation in the linguistic arena, mainly based on English, Maalouf refers to the national language as the 'language of identity' (2000: 115). According to this, we would be justified to call Arabic the language of identity for him, but he would counter that Arabic is just one of his languages and that since identity is not divisible, it cannot be uniquely or exclusively associated with any one of the languages that a person or even a community has in its repertoire. If this is the case, we might ask why Maalouf and, for that matter, Said and Ahmed are obsessed with identity. One could give many answers, but one of the best I could think of is eloquently expressed by Zygmunt Bauman as follows:

> Longing for identity comes from the desire for security, itself an ambiguous feeling. However exhilarating it may be in the short run, however full of promises and vague premonitions of an as yet untried experience, floating without support in a poorly defined space, in a stubbornly, vexingly 'betwixt-and-between' location, becomes in the long run an unnerving and anxiety-prone condition. On the other hand, a fixed condition amidst the infinity of possibilities is not an attractive prospect either. In our liquid modern times, when the free-floating, unencumbered individual is the popular hero, 'being fixed'—being 'identified' inflexibly and without retreat—gets an increasingly bad press. (2004: 29)

Bauman's view that identity 'falls asleep and silent the moment the noise of the battle dies down' (2004: 77) requires some modification in light of what Maalouf says about language and globalisation. Maalouf warns against the negative impact of globalisation on the world's linguistic ecology, directing most of his comments, as has been explained above, to the threat that English poses to French as a language of international culture and wider communication.[59] Maalouf links this threat to a network of public anxieties in France, which, ultimately, relate to the status of the country as a declining international power, with French acting as proxy. Although Maalouf does not raise the issue of identity directly in this context, identity is nevertheless involved in a subtle way in this threat, since any diminution in the status of France and its language will inevitably lead to a diminution in the status of French identity in the eyes of the non-French and, consequently, in the eyes of the French themselves. Furthermore, although globalisation is not a state of conflict in the sense described by Bauman, it nevertheless can generate symptoms that are not dissimilar to those associated with low-level conflicts, including status anxiety, oversensitivity, excessive nostalgia or attachment to the past and resentment towards others in possession of cultural commodities of greater value than one's own (Maalouf 2000: 112). These conditions in no way compare to those induced by trauma in the classic sense of the term or to the conditions associated with active and intense conflicts, but they represent a case of group stress that must be accommodated into discussions of language, the Self and identity. Rather than 'fall[ing] asleep and silent the moment the noise of the battle dies down' (Bauman 2004: 77), a better description might be that identity catnaps or

59 Being aware of this asymmetrical power between English and French, I am guilty of exploiting it, when the need arises, on my visits to North Africa. This generally happens when a person insists on using French instead of Arabic with me. On these occasions, I turn to English. This generally forces my interlocutor, especially if he or she does not speak English or speaks it poorly, to use Arabic with me. I intentionally use English in these situations as a language of power in relation to French, as a kind of 'deterrence' to reach a linguistic détente that brings Arabic back into the frame.

that it goes off the boil but continues to simmer gently until a time when it can return to the boil with some venom.

Maalouf claims that the group stress he describes 'seems in some ways peculiar to France,' owing to the global ambitions of France for its language and culture. He continues: 'For countries that had no such [ambitions], or had them no longer, the problem of relations with the dominant language [i.e., English] doesn't arise in the same way. But it does arise' (2000: 112). I would like to add that whenever the language is linked to conceptualisations of identity, threats to the language, whether imagined or real, will elicit a defensive cultural response, the intensity of which will depend on how strong the threats are and on how deeply embedded the language-identity link is in its culture. This threat-response relationship applies to French. But it also applies to Arabic, as I shall explain below by examining aspects of the discourse on globalisation and language in the Arab public sphere.

Discussions of globalisation and language in the Arab public sphere fall within the range of views one finds in standard works on globalisation as a phenomenon of the postmodern world.[60] I will highlight some of these views here to contextualise the discussion that will follow:[61] (1) globalisation is not just an economic phenomenon of finance and commodity flows transnationally but one that is intimately linked with culture; (2) globalisation is considered an extension, under a different guise, of old-style colonial and Western imperialist hegemony, with the ascendancy in this new phase being captured by American culture; (3) by changing the relationship between time and space and by operating through images and symbols that act semiotically, in subterranean ways, globalisation has an enormous reach culturally through the ever-expanding spread of modern communication technologies; (4) globalisation aims at transnational homogeneity through the commodification of culture, using as some of its agents pop music, the cinema, satellite TV, video games, the Internet, architectural design, education and tourism; (5) the homogenisation and cultural consumerism produced by globalisation are a threat to cultural diversity and authenticity; (6) the deterritorialisation of culture under globalisation threatens the core myths and symbols of a nation or ethnic group, replacing them with lifestyles and other forms of belonging that lack the same emotional pull in identity and memory work; and (7) as one of the most salient features of any culture, language is heavily implicated in globalisation either as a predator, a role that is mostly ascribed to English, or as a victim or potential victim. In the Arab discourse on globalisation, French is treated as another predator language but only as a minor partner to English and one that is more active in North Africa than in the Middle East. The fact that French is considered a victim language (in relation to English) by Maalouf reveals the complexity, contextuality and multilayered nature of globalisation.

60 See Beynon and Dunkerley (2000).

61 Like most pronouncements on globalisation, these views are contested in the literature.

Discussions of the link between globalisation and language in the Arab public sphere set up this link in antagonistic terms,[62] with English, as the dominant language of globalisation, acting as the main threat to Arabic in the media, education, the linguistic landscape (mainly shop signs), the new communication technologies and, therefore, prestige (see ʻAbd al-Salam 2001; Batahir 2001; Bishr 1995; al-Dubayb 2001).[63] Being dominated by the image industries, globalisation is further projected as a natural ally of vernacularisation because of the currency of the colloquial dialects as the preferred code for communication in the new media (Belqziz 2002; al-Dubayb 2001), including music, television, the cinema, the Internet, mobile telephone texting and advertising. Some scholars link the spread of code-switching to globalisation (al-Dhaouadi 2002). To give the reader a flavour of the antagonistic relationship between globalisation and Arabic, I will cite some of the ways in which this relationship is described in the Arabic discourse on the topic.

Globalisation is said to be a form of 'penetration' (*ikhtirāq*; al-Dubayb 2001: 7) that aims at 'cultural hegemony' (*haymana thaqāfiyya*; 13) using the 'long globalising arms' (*adhriʻat al-ʻawlama al-ṭawīla*; 13) of multinational companies (*al-sharikāt al-mutaʻaddidat al-jinsiyyāt*; 13).[64] Cultural globalisation

62 Although there are voices that support globalisation in the Arab public sphere, the majority do not, with some adopting an ambivalent position (see Abed 2007).

63 For a more nuanced view of globalisation in Arabic, see Ghalyun and Amin (2002). See also Ehteshami (2007), particularly chapter 3, 149-64. Ehteshami quotes the following comments from Arab writers on the impact of globalisation on Arabic: '[One] commentator has blamed American popular culture for the increasing use of English as the language of choice by urban youths: "some young people look down on [the] Arabic language. They think that it is old and that English represents life and desire." "If the trend continues," notes Haitham Sarhan (a linguist at Jordan University), "Arabic could be in danger. [For] young people think Arabic is boring."'

64 Abed gives the following set of attitudinal terms (with their meanings) used in Arabic discourse to describe globalisation. Group I: *inghilāq* (being closed-minded), *inghilāqiyya* (capable of being closed-minded), *taʻaṣṣub* (fanaticism), *inkimāsh* (withdrawal within one's self; becoming self-absorbed), *inkifāʼ* (retreat, withdrawal, remoteness), *tasharnuq* (hibernation, cocooning), *taqawquʻ* (withdrawing within oneself), *tahāwin* (to break down, to collapse) *tahmīsh* (marginalising). Group II: *ṭams* (obliterating, erasing), *amraka* (Americanisation), *gharbana* (Westernisation), *dhawabān* (melting away, dissolving), *indithār* (to be wiped out, to be forgotten), *inṣihār* (melting away, fusing, vanishing, breaking down [internally], assimilitaing), *inbiṭāḥ* (being prostrated, being laid down [implying 'surrender' and 'submission']), *talāshin* (to be suppressed, crushed, destroyed), *ghazw thaqāfī* (cultural invasions), *ta'ākul* (to be eaten away, to be consumed), *iqtilāʻ* (uprooting). Group III: *tafattuḥ* (to be open-minded), *ḥadātha* (modernity), *tanwīr* (enlightenment), *ḥiwār* (dialogue), *ḥiwāriyya* (subject to dialogue). The first group of terms describes the attitude of those who are critical of both globalisation and those who completely reject it. The second group describes the attitude of those who reject globalisation. The third group describes the attitude of those who welcome globalisation. The fact that the last group of terms is the smallest and that the second group is the largest indicates the strength of the antiglobalisation discourse in the Arabic-speaking world.

through the dominance of English in education,[65] commerce, the labour market, the media and the new technologies[66] is described as a form of 'cultural invasion' (*ghazw thaqāfī*; 33) whose aim is to 'sweep away the [national] culture' (*iktisāḥ thaqāfī*; 33), 'obliterate the Arab national character' (*ṭams al-shakhṣiyya al-'arabiyya*; 33), make the Arabs 'migrate mentally and linguistically to the West' (*nuhājir bi-'uqūlinā wa-alsinatinā ilā al-gharb*; 36) and turn them into 'disfigured/deformed midgets of their Western masters' (*numsakh khawājāt*; 37).[67] The lure of English under globalisation has made Arabs neglect the *fuṣḥā*, thus leading to a 'cultural blindness' (*'amā ḥaḍārī*; 172) that lost them their way among other nations. Through English, globalisation has 'laid many traps' for Arabic (*naṣaba lahā al-fikhākh*; 72), 'put many snares in its way' (*ḥāka fī ṭarīq ḥarakatihā al-shirāk*; 72) and 'concocted many conspiratorial plans' against it (*waḍa' al-khuṭaṭ*; 72) to prevent it from playing its role in Arab life as the 'first line of defending Arab identity' (*khaṭṭ al-difā' al-awwal 'an al-huwiyya*; 174).[68] As a form of 'cultural usurpation' (*istilāb thaqāfī*; 77), globalisation constitutes a 'ferocious attack' (*hujūm sharis*; 77) on the *fuṣḥā*, leading to 'linguistic corruption' (*fasād lughawī*; 70) and 'linguistic suicide' (*intiḥār lughawī*; 180) if not resisted. The spread of English in the labour market under the influence of globalisation is described as a 'cancer that eats away at our [Arab] identity, mocks our very existence [as Arabs], and turns us into disfigured midgets and ghosts of ourselves that orbit in a sphere that is very distant from our [indigenous] culture, from our original roots and from our distinctive character' (61).

Belqziz describes cultural globalisation as an act of 'cultural rape and symbolic aggression' (*ightiṣāb thaqāfī wa-'udwān ramzī*; 2002: 68). He further characterises it as a form of 'cultural violence' (*'unf thaqāfī*; 68) that treats subordinate cultures in a way that inscribes a relationship of superiority (*isti'lā'*; 68) and inferiority (*dūniyya*; 69) between them and eliminates the right of the inferior culture to differ (*ḥaq al-ikhtilāf*; 68). The lure of globalisation derives from its use of the image industries to provide its consumers with 'tinned . . . and easily digestible cultural products' (*mu'allabāt thaqāfiyya . . . jāhiza li-al-istihlāk*; 63)[69] that are difficult to resist because of the impotence

65 Abu Zayd (1416 AH) launches a stinging attack on the impact of globalisation on academic titles in the Arab and Muslim worlds. The rhetoric of this attack is worthy of analysis, but considerations of space do not allow this here.

66 See Larousi (2003) and 'Ali and Hijazi (2005: 303–90) for a discussion of some of the challenges that these new technologies pose for Arabic.

67 Al-Dubayb uses the term *maskh/miskh* (with the meaning of deformity and disfiguring with a diminution in size) in a few places in his book.

68 Although the quotes in this paragraph are sometimes taken from different parts of the book, their concatenation here accurately reflects the author's position.

69 Witness, for example, the huge popularity of such programmes on Arabic satellite TV, which borrow their formats directly from Western (British) TV: *Man sa-yarbaḥ al-malyūn* ("Who Wants to Be a Millionaire?"), *Al-Ḥalaqa al-aḍ'af* ("The Weakest Link") and *Stār akādimi* ("The X-Factor").

and the inane nature of the indigenous image industries (*'ajz wa-tafāhat al-mu'assasa al-thaqāfiyya*; 82), the result of which is a rise in the 'cultural cholesterol' levels (*ḥālat kulistrūl thaqāfiyya*; 88) in the 'awestruck' (*inbihāri*; 81) and 'spectating' (*furjawī*; 81) recipient. This attack against the indigenous culture weakens the ability of the recipient to resist and creates inside it an 'indigenous cultural colony/diaspora' (*jāliya thaqāfiyya ajnabiyya*; 91), a kind of cultural fifth column, which suffers from cultural foreignisation (*ightirāb thaqāfi*; 91) in its own native land. The occurrence of this phenomenon represents 'surrender' (*istislām*; 122), a case that is as corrosive in cultural politics (*al-thaqafa kā'in muḥārib*; 120) as cultural 'self-insulation' (*tasharnuq 'alā al-dhāt*; 125) and the 'retreat towards traditionalism' (*inkifā' turāthawī*; 92), which, in 'cultural resistance' (*mumāna'a thaqāfiyya*; 124), constitute a case of 'negative defensive behaviour' (*sulūk difā'ī salbī*; 125) and 'cultural suicide' (*intiḥār thaqāfi*, 125).

Kamal Muhammad Bishr, a well-known professor of Arabic in Egypt, describes the inroads made by foreign languages into the Arab world as a case of 'linguistic and cultural Western foreignisation' (*taghrīb fi al-lugha wa-l-thaqāfa*; Bishr 1995: 141).[70] Bishr says that this *taghrīb* is an epidemic (*'adwā*; 167) that has infected the body of the nation, leading to 'confusion and anxiety' (*balbala wa ḥayra*; 169), toadyism (*tabi'iyya*; 164), the acceptance of the superiority of the imported language (*fawqiyyat al-ajnabī al-mustawrad*; 166) and the inferiority of the national heritage (*dūniyyat al-qawmī al-mawrūth*; 166). He further describes its use on shop and other public signs as a 'deluge' (*ṭūfān*; 171) and as a case of the cutting off of the linguistic power of Arabic (*iẓlām lughawī*; 171).[71] English in the Arab sphere is akin to 'artificial flowers' (*zuhūr ṣinā'iyya*; 163), which lack scent and the acquisition of which is characterised by 'superficiality' (*saṭḥiyya*; 163). The injection of English into Arab life has disfigured Arabic in the media, in education, in the linguistic landscape of Arab cities and by creating a linguistic hybrid in which code-switching with English or French is the norm. As a result, Arabic has become a disfigured midget (*maskh*; 175).[72]

The above examples provide sufficient data to argue that globalisation is conceived in Arabic discourse as a case of war against the Arabic language and Arab culture by nonmilitary means. Globalisation is described as 'invasion,' 'attack,' 'aggression,' 'violence,' 'hegemony,' 'subordination,' 'colonialism,' 'deluge,' 'penetration,' 'rape,' 'conspiracy,' 'epidemic' and 'disfigurement'

70 The use of 'Western foreignisation' captures the sense of the 'foreign' and the 'Western,' which the Arabic word *taghrīb* carries, as well as the contrast with Arabisation (*ta'rib*), since *taghrīb* and *ta'rīb* in Arabic writing are separated by a dot in *gh*, the letter *ghayn*.

71 See chapter 5 for a discussion, with examples from Cairo, of this phenomenon.

72 'Abd al-Salam (2001) describes globalisation in the linguistic-cum-cultural Arab sphere as cultural invasion, cultural hegemony, cultural colonialism, leading to the disfiguring (*maskh*; 128) of Arab culture and the surrender to Western culture (*istislām li-al-thaqāfa al-gharbiyya*; 135).

that, if left unchecked, can lead to linguistic and cultural 'surrender,' 'internal colonialism,' 'superficiality,' 'corruption,' 'confusion,' 'anxiety,' 'illness,' 'loss of national character and distinctiveness' and 'suicide.' I would like to suggest that, at least on the symbolic level, globalisation is treated as a case of intense culture stress that shares some symptoms with those induced by acute psychological stress in individuals. Arab fears of globalisation might be characterised as a case of 'cultural phobia' involving the West as the menacing and threatening Other. Globalisation uses symbolic and material means of coercion, which, as Amin Maalouf says, induce status anxiety, oversensitivity, excessive nostalgia or attachment to the past and resentment towards others in possession of cultural commodities of greater value than one's own (2000: 112). Discussions of language and globalisation in the Arab discourse refer to the glories of the past and do exaggerate the dangers facing Arabic. In all of this, the *fuṣḥā* is at the heart of a nexus of conflicting forces and cultural stresses that paint a pretty gloomy picture of its future if the necessary protection is not accorded to it. In recent years, this protection has taken the form of laws (in Iraq under Saddam and in Syria in 2007) that aim, among other things, at banning the use of foreign languages (mainly English) in the linguistic landscape in Arab cities, although this phenomenon is a symptom of the malaise facing Arabic rather than its cause. In 2008, two societies for the protection of Arabic were established in Egypt and Morocco; these are the most recent, and they build on the work done by the language academies. An older society has been in existence since 1999 in Sharjah, United Arabic Emirates. The use of the word *ḥimāyat* ("protection") in Arabic in the name of these societies implies that the *fuṣḥā* is in danger and that this danger has reached a critical level that warrants direct intervention from the state or civil-society actors.

It might, of course, be argued that the above fears are exaggerated.[73] Arabic is still one of the world's major languages. The problem resides not in globalisation but in how Arab culture reacts to it. Instead of bemoaning the fate of Arabic, Arabs must allow it to breathe by reforming it and permitting it to borrow from other languages freely. The popularity of English in Arab society must be seen from a balanced perspective. For some Arabs, it is a source of strength in socioeconomic development and a necessary means of accessing international cultures. If so, not everyone reads the place of English in Arab life in the same alarmist way as what I have called the Arabic language guardians/defenders elsewhere (Suleiman 2004b). Some users of English might, in fact, argue that rather than being passive recipients of the language, they are active agents who mould it to suit their own communicative needs. The problem, however, is that one hardly reads these kinds

73 There is a basis for this fear, though. Warschauer et al. (2002) suggest that as a result of the widespread use of the Internet, the *fuṣḥā* Arabic in Egypt might, in fact, be squeezed from above by English and from below by Egyptian Arabic, which is used extensively in a romanised script with some adaptations in informal communications and in chat.

of responses fully and strongly articulated in the Arab public sphere. The language guardians dominate the discourse on language and globalisation in this sphere, which, I think, conveys the general mood of Arabs, some of whom jokingly refer to Arabic as the 'mother language' (*al-lugha al-umm*) and to English as the new 'father language' (*al-lugha al-abb*), which, in a male-dominated society, confirms that in symbolic terms, English has the upper hand.

This discussion provides a set of readings of the link between language and the Self in the Arab context by invoking displacement, trauma and globalisation as related operative notions. Displacement as one of the consequences of war, either in the form of exile or in the form of diaspora, is a chief cause of the acute psychological stresses and traumalike symptoms that affect the language-Self link. This symbiotic relationship has been shown to be most pertinent in Edward Said's case. It is also relevant to the way Amin Maalouf conceptualises this link and extends it to collectivities. However, displacement does not have to be exclusively tied to war as a cause and to exile or diaspora as its outcome. Displacement can also be linked to political and social upheavals that cause people, through systematic state policy, to lose their place in society and all of the privileges that come with their socioeconomic location in society. Displacement in this sense is most pertinent to Leila Ahmed's case. Her views about the language-Self link are directly related to the disastrous impact of the 1952 Revolution and Nasser's rule on her family's fortunes in Egypt. War is also relevant to the way Moustapha Safouan thinks about Arabic and its role in bringing about freedom and democracy to put an end to despotism and dictatorship in the Arabic-speaking world. The idea that language is an instrument of social and political oppression or liberation is shared by Ahmed, but she applies it to gender in Islam rather than to politics in the classic sense of the term. In all of these cases, language is associated with acute and chronic personal stresses, traumalike experiences or, in fact, the trauma associated with colossal defeat such as the 1967 War between the Arabs and Israel.

In tying these notions together, globalisation was also invoked as a warlike force that pursues its aims of displacing weaker cultures and languages through nonviolent and nonmilitary means. As a form of cultural cannibalism, globalisation gives rise in collectivities to feelings of psychological stress that are not dissimilar to those generated by wars and sociopolitical upheavals, though of a lower intensity. In the Arab world, globalisation is read as the pursuing of colonial hegemony through consumerism and the image industries, which favour spoken language and, therefore, the colloquial dialects over the *fuṣḥā*. If we accept this analysis, then globalisation is doubly dangerous. It attacks from the outside through English and from the inside through the vernaculars. It enlists external forces and internal fifth columns. And it does its work through hegemony, not coercion.

The data in this chapter show the complexity of the language-Self link in the Arabic-speaking world. They also show the Arab 'obsession' with language as a cultural product and as a symbol of belonging and alienation, of closed and open meanings, of despotism and freedom and of dictatorship and democracy. Arabic is not just a means of communication in the functional sense of the term but also a window through which we can look at how the individual and the group feel about themselves and their status. It is like a barometer: it registers the state of the nation and those who belong to it, whether at home, in exile or in the diaspora.

Chapter 5

Names, Identity and Conflict

This chapter studies the link between names and three notions in the social world: Self, identity and conflict. Dealing with three categories of names: personal names, toponyms or place names and code names, this study starts from the assumption that it is the symbolic meanings of names, rather than their indexicality, that make them suitable to investigate from a sociolinguistic perspective. In identifying and analysing these meanings, the study will use a variety of data, including name pools, Web-based materials, self-reported data and literary compositions.

In terms of scope, the chapter will be restricted to the Arab Middle East. North Africa presents its own problems because of the Arab-Berber/Amazigh mix in Algeria and Morocco in particular. However, the chapter will make reference to Israel, Turkey and, to a lesser extent, Iran for comparative purposes. In addition, reference will be made to Arabic names in exile/diaspora. The move from home to the diaspora will bring displacement and conflict sharply into focus in the study of names in a way that complements the discussion in chapter 4.

Two modes of analysis will be applied in this chapter. Macro-level analyses will be provided to outline the major themes in names and naming from the twin perspectives of identity and conflict. These analyses will be augmented with the micro-level deconstruction of selected data to show the multilayered nature of these perspectives.

WHAT'S IN A NAME?

As cultural products and social practise, names and naming are suffused with sociopolitical meanings—treated as symbolic meanings here—that operate at the level of the individual (Self) and the group identity in society.[1] It is this symbolic function of names and naming, perhaps more than their mundane utility of indexing or individuation—of distinguishing one

1 On the question of whether proper names, as opposed to common names, have meanings or not, see Bean (1980) and Carroll (1983). This question need not concern us here, because the main interest is in the symbolic signification of names, rather than their capacity to 'signify' by virtue of some defining property or properties of the objects to which they refer.

member of a group, unit or class from another—that renders the process (naming) and its outcome (names) a topic of great interest to ethnologists, folklorists, anthropologists, creative writers, literary theorists, historians, political scientists, advertisers and product designers, geographers, semioticians, security specialists and linguists and sociolinguists. Thinking of personal names as an exemplar of the category of proper names, it is difficult to conceive of any society that does not use names to distinguish its members from one another. For this reason, personal names have been declared a cultural universal (Alford 1987; Bean 1980). But this universal is subject to a grammar of cultural variability that accounts for the different practises of personal-name bestowals at work in society. Who gives the names, how they are given, when they are given, why certain names and not others are chosen for acts of bestowal, the circumstances under which names are given, how names are used in social interaction, whether or not names are subject to formal (official) or informal change, why certain names fall out of fashion and what sociocultural[2] and political meanings are attached to names are some of the parameters that come into play in constructing and accessing this onomastic grammar of cultural variability. Serving as headings in this grammar, these parameters situate names and naming at the intersection of phenomena that bind a language intimately to its society,[3] thus providing a window onto issues that relate to how the Self and group identity are signalled, maintained, transformed or contested in society. In times of peace and relative stability, personal names and naming practises undergo long-term evolutionary changes that are not easy to detect. In times of heightened conflict, when the political stability and social cohesion of a society are threatened, names and naming practises can signal high-voltage shifts in how individuals and groups conceptualise themselves, as well as in how they relate to those in their environment, particularly those to whom they stand in antagonistic relation.

As with personal names, toponyms—whether they are the street names that constitute a locality text, the names of places on a map in its capacity as a cartographic text or commercial and public signs as elements in the linguistic landscape of a locality—exhibit the twin dimensions noted above: those of utilitarian identification or pure indexation and symbolism. The former

2 Cultural meanings are partly related to the stereotypical images that a community holds towards names. Lieberson reports that in a study of popular English names in 1942, some names were found to generate certain stereotypical images: "a Mary would be 'quiet,' an Edward 'friendly,' a Richard 'good-looking,' a Joan 'young and good-looking,' a Barbara 'charming' and an Adrian 'artistic'" (1984: 78).

3 Because of this, names are judged to be an important topic for sociolinguistics and cognate areas: 'Proper names, as a sociolinguistic universal exhibiting variable cultural systematization, are an important topic for linguistic anthropology' (Bean 1980: 314). Lieberson considers the investigation of names in sociolinguistics to be a 'void': 'The social processes underpinning the naming of children are a "natural" topic for sociolinguistics which has yet to be studied systematically. It is a natural topic in that it combines linguistic phenomena with an underlying social phenomenon related to the sociology of knowledge' (1984: 77).

dimension signals the important but mundane functionality of names as indexical signs that may, additionally, serve as descriptive epithets by capturing in the name some significant feature or features of the named object. For example, referring to part of the topography of a Palestinian village as *'yūn* ('water springs') or *arḍ al-'ayn* ('land of the water spring')—which are real names in two villages, Sarra and Beit Surik, near Nablus and Jerusalem in Palestine, respectively—performs the twin task of naming that part of the topography of the village while, at the same time, describing this topography by signalling that it has or had had water springs. The image one pictures of such a topography is one of fertile land with cool water, mature fruit trees (perhaps fig, plum, grape, apricot, mulberry or olive trees) and shady canopies under which one can have respite from the heat of the sun or enjoy as a good place for a family picnic—in short, a land whose owners are proud to call theirs, as I have heard them sometimes talk. As identity markers, toponyms can serve symbolically as part of the ethnic or national lexicon that a group may use to construct its own narratives of, among other things, proud triumphs and fallen heroes, past glories and moments of pain and suffering, defining achievements and acts of resistance, independence and sovereignty. In the case of commercial and public signs, names can provide information on some of the important social and political undercurrents in society that touch on the sensitive subject of how a society conceptualises itself in relation to other societies, to modernity and to globalisation. This identity marking of toponyms and the symbolism they convey render them of great interest to social scientists.

Indexation and symbolism are also present in the names of temporal events, for example, the names given to natural phenomena such as hurricanes or the code names of military operations. At the point of inception, the names of hurricanes serve as indexical signs of individuation, with little or no sociocultural meanings. The name of Hurricane Dean, which struck the Caribbean and Mexico with such ferocity in August 2007, is an example of such a name, as is that of Hurricane Katrina, which devastated New Orleans and much of the Gulf Coast in August 2005. The code names used to label military operations or wars in modern times are also indexical; for example, *D-Day* originally signalled the day on which the Battle of Normandy began, June 6, 1944.[4] However, some code names are chosen because they carry rich layers of symbolism that speak in different ways to members of the in-group and the out-group, friends and foes; an example of this kind is the name '*Ghazwat New York*' which al-Qaeda used to refer to the 11 September attacks on New York in 2001, as will be discussed later.

4 The proper name of an event may be lexicalised into a common noun. An example of this is *D-Day*, which may be used to designate the day on which any large-scale military operation is scheduled to start. *D-Day* may also be used metaphorically to refer to the start of any task that is considered important to its participants. Used metaphorically, *D-Day* may function antiphrastically or in a mock-heroic style to dramatise the lack of importance of a particular undertaking. These two processes of lexicalisation and metaphorical extension show how proper names can develop symbolic sediments that enrich a language.

I aim to explore here the use of proper names to articulate individual and group identities in the Middle East, exile and the diaspora. This chapter will also explore how proper names are used in conflict situations to impose the hegemonic ideology or claims of one group against another or, indeed, how names can be used in resisting such hegemony by the weaker group. The chapter will further provide examples, narratives and self-reports of how names are experienced at the individual level and how they are bestowed to signal multiple identities in exilic or diasporic settings. The role of proper names in preserving personal and collective memories will also be explored. I will focus on the symbolic meanings of three subcategories of proper names: personal names, toponyms/place names and code names. My objective is not to provide comprehensive analyses of pools of data, although I will refer to such data, but to use data culled from a variety of sources, including anecdotal and self-reported material, to outline the ways in which proper names can be used to investigate symbolic meanings in relation to the Self, identity and conflict in sociolinguistics. The chapter, therefore, is exploratory and interdisciplinary in nature; it is intended to stimulate quantitative and qualitative research into aspects of names and naming in the Middle East that have hitherto not been fully investigated. Although the main focus will be on the Asian Arab Middle East (with little reference to North Africa), exile and the diaspora, reference will also be made to Turkey, Israel and Iran for contextual purposes, as well as to highlight aspects of name use that, to the best of my knowledge, have not been investigated vis-à-vis the Arabic-speaking world.

PERSONAL NAMES, SHARED VALUES AND SHARED IDENTITIES

Studies of the root/radical meanings of Arabic names (i.e., the meanings of the radical roots from which names are derived) in the Levant provide information on the social values that name givers, usually the parents, seem to hold. In a study of the root meanings exhibited in a pool of thirteen thousand personal/first names in Jordan, making up the student body at the University of Yarmouk in 1984–85 (Abd-el-Jawad 1986), the following values are said to have been dominant in the pool: beauty, blessing, generosity, glory, guidance and religiosity, happiness and joy, honesty, honour, justice, kindness, bravery, high status, luck and good omen, patience, peace and security, piety, sincerity, success, gratitude to God, victory, virtue and wisdom.[5] In another study of 2,550 male and female personal names in Jordan

5 Although in Arabic, names carry semantic import by virtue of their root meanings, it is, nevertheless, the case that not all name givers are aware of the full range of meanings of the names they bestow (for examples, see Schimmel 1995). Sometimes names are chosen because of their aesthetic qualities in euphonic terms, rather than because of their root meanings. Because of this, we should be wary of ascribing to the name givers naming intentions that are universally congruent with the root meanings of the names they bestow.

(Salih and Bader 1999), the authors found that more or less the same values dominate their pool.

What is interesting about the second study, however, is that it specifically targeted the names used by Arab Christians in Jordan.[6] The study makes the significant point in identity terms that, except in extreme situations,[7] Arab Christians in Jordan avoid only the most stereotypically Muslim of Muslim names, specifically the name Muhammad.[8] The study also points out that apart from a small category of specifically Arab Christian names—those designating biblical figures and saints—and a small set of foreign, mainly Western, names, the majority of the names in the pool could not be differentiated from the names used by Muslims.

To illustrate this, I will examine the names of the two authors of the study. The full name of the first author, Mahmud Hussein Salih, is identifiably Muslim; it contains two names that are stereotypically Muslim names: Mahmud and Hussein. The full name of the second author, Yousef Farhan Bader, contains no indication that its bearer, who is personally known to me, is a Christian Arab (of the Greek Orthodox faith). Yousef Bader could be a Muslim Arab name; in fact, I assumed that the bearer of this name was Muslim until I was told by a mutual friend that he is not. The fact that both Christian and Muslim Arab name givers in Jordan share a large pool of personal names, through which they express the same social values, is a strong indication that—in spite of their religious differences and the effect these may have on their name choices—Christian and Muslim Arabs in Jordan share a worldview that defines them in some respects as members of the same cultural community.[9] Salih and Bader consider this to be the most significant finding of their research: 'In sum, it can be said that the widespread use of Arabic names by Jordanian Christians is meant to preserve

6 The term *Arab* is used here to distinguish the majority of the Christians in Jordan from the Armenian Christians in the country who consider themselves to be ethnically non-Arab and who use Armenian personal names.

7 Salih and Bader explain this as follows: 'When a married couple have not been able to have children for a long period of time, they may make a pledge that if they have a male child, they will name him *Muhammad*. This is probably the only situation in which the Prophet's name *Muhammad* is bestowed upon a child by Christian parents' (1999: 36). Christian name givers hold less inhibition when it comes to the names of some of the Prophet's companions, for example, 'Umar, Khalid and Salman. One of the best-known examples of the use of the name Muhammad by an Arab Christian is the Lebanese Maronite writer Marun 'Abbud from the first half of the twentieth century, who called his firstborn son Muhammad to signal his strong pan-Arab identity, the assumption being that in addition to being the Prophet of Islam, Muhammad was the best-known Arab hero of all times.

8 In a recent study of the names of Lebanese male electors in 2004, nine out of the 80,644 people called Muhammad were of Christian background: five Maronites, three Greek Orthodox and one Roman Catholic. See http://www.aljazeera.net/News/archive/archive?ArchiveId=318403.

9 It is, of course, possible that different relative frequencies for shared first names in the common pool do exist between the two faith communities, signalling differences in the ordering of the social values held in the two communities, but we have no data of this kind to substantiate this judgement.

their Arab identity and ethnicity, to demonstrate loyalty and attachment to the Arab country of Jordan, and to show their solidarity with their Muslim compatriots, as the use of some purely Islamic names show. On the other hand, the use of purely Christian names is designed to underscore their Christian identity and to preserve their religious heritage. At a third level, the use of foreign, mostly Western names—which is actually a recent phenomenon—demonstrates in addition to religious association, a trend toward modernization and Westernization' (1999: 41–42).

However, the wording of this finding raises some very interesting questions. First, why is it judged that Jordanian Christians need 'to demonstrate'—a fairly loaded term—their loyalty and attachment to the 'Arab country of Jordan' through name bestowal? It may be that the use of the loaded verb 'to demonstrate' is a slip of the pen, which might have been replaced by a more neutral verb—for example, 'show' or 'display'—but as it stands, 'to demonstrate' seems to suggest that the attachment and loyalty of the Jordanian citizenry to Jordan, and particularly that of the Christians among them, are in need of display, assertion or public proof. But could it be that this display of attachment and proof of loyalty are specifically demanded of Christian, not Muslim, Jordanians as individuals and as a group? Witness the fact that replacing the term 'Jordanian Christian' with 'Jordanian Muslim' in the first sentence of the above quotation would, for most Jordanians, produce a more marked reading when juxtaposed with the need to demonstrate loyalty and attachment to the 'Arab country of Jordan.' In this connection, the fact that at no point in the paper do the authors refer to the Muslims in Jordan as 'Arab Muslims' is very telling: it signals that 'Arab Muslim' is the neutral or unmarked category in social and citizenship terms, making 'Arab Christian' a marked category.[10] As an unmarked category, 'Arab Muslims' further separates its referents from another marked category: the Circassian and Chechen Muslims in Jordan who, although they are full Jordanian citizens, refuse to be identified as Arab in spite of the fact that they have been culturally Arabised (see al-Wer 1999) as their personal name pools might/would reveal.[11]

Does this, therefore, mean that Jordanian Christians feel that their attachment and loyalty to their country may be 'suspect' or 'not taken on trust' or that others (the Muslim majority) feel it to be so and that the use of Arab names is, therefore, a strategy of countering this suspicion and of offering proof of belonging and loyalty? Also, can the conclusion that Jordanian Christians use Muslim names to 'show their solidarity with their Muslim compatriots' mean that the onus is on this subcategory of Jordanians, as the marked category, to display acts of loyalty to and identity with the majority Muslim population in Jordan (the unmarked category), which they do through having a shared name

10 See chapter 2 for a similar discussion of Middle Arabic and its varieties.

11 As an aside, this may imply that the citizenship norm in Jordan is captured by the two terms *Arab* and *Muslim*. Based on sociolinguistic evidence, I have suggested (Suleiman 2004b) that this norm includes 'East Jordanian' and excludes Jordanians of Palestinian origin. Thus, the 'ideal' or 'dominant' norm for Jordanian national identity may be described as Arab, East Jordanian and Muslim.

pool? And do 'to demonstrate' and 'show' in the above quotation imply that the attachment and loyalty of Jordanian Christians to Jordan and, therefore, their national identity as Jordanians are more complex than for Muslim Jordanians? In this context, can we interpret the conclusion that the use of Western names to 'demonstrate religious association' with the Christian West is a complicating factor in the identity construction of Christian Jordanians as full Jordanian citizens? In other words, does the above conclusion, thus deconstructed, justify making the claim that through name bestowal, Arab Christians in Jordan, in fact, put themselves in a liminal zone of group identity, as both insiders and outsiders, in the way they conceptualise themselves as a minority? Or can we conclude, following Borg and Kressel, that the adoption of 'an outwardly Arabic-sounding name [whatever that means] on the part of a non-Muslim [in a majority Muslim setting]' is a 'dissimulation' strategy intended to 'fend off discrimination and persecution' (2001: 35)?[12]

There is no doubt, as I will suggest later, that personal names are used for identity 'dissimulation' in situations where political volatility, conflict or disadvantage are judged to be salient features. This fact applies to Muslims and non-Muslims in the Arabic-speaking world, as it does to other countries in the Middle East, as we shall see later. The widespread use of noms de guerre (*asmā' ḥarakiyya*) by Palestinian guerrilla fighters and leaders after the June War of 1967, the most famous of which being Yasser Arafat, who also went by the teknonym Abu 'Ammar, is an example of onomastic dissimulation, although some of these names came to carry a high recognition value in the national struggle, which lost them much of their ability to dissimulate.[13] The recent

12 Following Wild (1982), Borg and Kressel claim that because of their 'delicate position' in an Islamic milieu, non-Muslims adopt Arabic-sounding names to fulfil two main 'societal objectives: (a) dissimulation (*taqiyya* . . .) [to fend off] discrimination or persecution; and (b) putting the lid on a private inner world by selecting patently Arabic-sounding names transmitting overtones of specific religious *Weltanschauung*. For a Christian Arab, [the name] *'Aṭṭiyya* 'gift of God' renders Gk. *Theodoros*, with its numerous European cognates: It. *Deodato*, Fr. *Diedonné*, etc.' (2001: 35). It is, however, not clear what Borg and Kressel mean by the expression 'Arabic-sounding names.' In this context, we may ask why it is that the name 'Aṭṭiyya, which is derived from an authentic Arabic root and is used by both Christians and Muslims, is regarded as an 'Arabic-sounding name' and not as an Arabic name pure and simple. And what does the term 'Arabic-sounding name' mean? Is an 'Arabic-sounding name' the same as an Arab name? Or is it a foreign name that phonetically sounds like an Arab name? Or is an 'Arabic-sounding name' an Arab name that is 'Arab' when bestowed on a Muslim Arab and 'Arabic-sounding' when it is bestowed on a non-Muslim Arab? My guess is the latter; if so, this raises serious questions about the 'dissimulation' claim made by Borg and Kressel.

13 A study of these noms de guerre would be very revealing in terms of what they could tell us about the political values prevalent in the Palestinian national movement in the second half of the twentieth century. In the Occupied Territories, such a study may provide insights into the values underlying national and factional politics among Palestinians. In this context, it would be especially interesting to investigate the inclination among Palestinian political activists to choose teknonyms as their noms de guerre, for example: Abu Jihad, Abu Iyad, Abu Nidal, Abu al-Hul, Abu Hakam, Abu Mazin, Abu al-Lutuf, Abu al-'Abbas, Abu al-Sa'id, Abu Mish'al, Abu-Layla. All of these names belong to members of the higher echelons of the Palestinian movements. Among ordinary members in the late 1960s and early 1970s, names referring to famous Arab heroes or international revolutionaries such as Ché Guevara and Fidel Castro could be found.

bloody history of Iraq, following the American-led occupation of 2003, provides examples of Sunni and Shi'a Iraqis opting for neutral, nondenominational/ sectarian-sounding names, either through formal name bestowals on newborn babies or through the adoption of such names by adults in volatile situations, the motivation for these practices being to avoid what has been termed 'death by identity card' in Baghdad and other dangerous (ethnic) hot spots in Iraq at large.[14] It is also possible that a similar strategy was used by both Muslims and Christians in Lebanon during the bloody Civil War of 1975–90, for exactly the same reasons. However, we should be careful not to turn what are no doubt features of aberrant situations into generalisations that are applied in a historically and socially decontextualised manner. With this in mind, let us examine the 'dissimulation' hypothesis by considering field-generated data that help shed further light on this issue.

Let us begin by considering a longitudinal study of names, covering the middle to late decades of the twentieth century, in a Christian (predominantly Greek Orthodox, similar to the Salih and Beder study in Jordan) Lebanese village near Tripoli ('Atiyya 1990).[15] This study investigated the frequency of three categories of personal names: names of saints and biblical figures, Arabic names and foreign names. According to the 'dissimulation' hypothesis, and in view of the worsening political situation in Lebanon during the period of the study, culminating with the start of the Civil War in 1975, we should expect a rise in the incidence of Arabic names in the village. In fact, the findings of the study run in the opposite direction, revealing a small decrease in the percentage of Arabic names. The percentage of this drop was higher for women's names as compared with men's names. The study also reveals that there was a significant increase in foreign names at the expense of the traditional names of saints and biblical figures for males, although this shift tended to be far less pronounced for the names of the guardian saints of the village, 'Ilyas (Elie) and Mikha'il (Michel, Michael), and for Miriam because of her special standing in Christianity. Some of the foreign names were Western equivalents of the traditional Christian names, such as Georges for Jirjis, Joseph for Yusuf, Jean for Hanna, Jacques for Ya'qub and Simon for Sam'an. The study also shows that the pool of Arabic names for both males and females contains new items that were not previously part of the name lexicon of the village, such as 'Isam, Ghassan and Wisam for males and Ranya and Samya for females.

14 See al-Samirra'i (1990: 74–89) for examples of different name-giving patterns between the Sunna and Shi'a in Iraq. Al-Samirra'i points out that the Shi'a rarely bestow the names Abu Bakr, 'Umar and 'Uthman or 'A'isha on their children, names that are used by the Sunni Muslims. However, following the custom of giving a child an animal or ugly name to ward off the evil eye or to enhance the child's chances of survival, the Shi'a may use the preceding names for this purpose. This derogatory use of the names shows the schism in naming between the two groups.

15 The village in this study is Markabta.

The reduction in Arab/ic names may, in fact, be higher than this study suggests, but this would require a modification in the classificatory schema that 'Atiyya adopts for his pool. I would argue that by treating the traditional names of biblical figures and saints as Arabic names, rather than as a separate category—and there is a strong case for treating them as such linguistically and culturally[16]—the drop in the percentage of the Arabic names thus interpreted would, in fact, be very significant. If we accept this interpretation, then we must accept the conclusion that instead of onomastic 'dissimulation,' per Borg and Kressel's (2001) claim, the name givers in 'Atiyya's study seem to be opting for onomastic dissimilation. Instead of blending in, they aim at visibility, in spite of the dangers of such a stance in what seems like a hostile environment. It is, of course, possible that when Christian Arabs are in the majority in their own localities, as is the case in the village under consideration here, they may be less inclined to opt for Arab names in the narrow interpretation of this term; in this case, the feeling of safety in numbers and the presumed Muslim associations of these names should act as two factors in this strategy of Arab name avoidance. Whatever the case may be, however, Borg and Kressel's statement about onomastic dissimulation among non-Muslims in Arab culture must be treated with extreme caution. In this connection, it is revealing to note that Borg and Kressel cite evidence from Egypt showing that the Copts do use a rich onomastic lexicon that publicly displays their 'confessional' identity, rather than submerging it in their Arab or Muslim milieu. According to Borg and Kressel: 'Confessionally marked personal names of Christians are particularly well attested among Egyptian Copts, who are able to fall back on a rich stock of ideological symbols and linguistic resources in their cultural heritage: the Bible, ancient Egyptian history, the Church Fathers, modern European (mostly French and English) names, confessionally neutral Arab names and Muslim names' (2001: 35).

There is no reason to believe that Christians in other parts of the Arabic-speaking world, such as the Levant, do not have 'a rich stock of ideological symbols and linguistic resources in their cultural heritage' on which they can draw, should they want to, in name bestowal, as do the Copts in Egypt, to convey 'confessional' specificity in their surroundings. Is it, therefore, possible that Christians in the Levant choose Arab names because they genuinely want to express their sense of belonging to their own culture, as well as to signify their identity as Arab Christians? Interpreting the use of Arab names by Christians as a case of dissimulation, rather than assimilation and belonging, may, in fact, rest on the subterranean assumption in some academic discourse on the Middle East that the Arabness of a Christian Arab is less complete, or more suspect and provisional, than the Arabness of an Arab

16 Some of the names of biblical figures and saints listed in 'Atiyya's study are, in fact, shared with Muslims: Ilyas, Ya'qub, Miriam, Musa, 'Isa, Ibrahim and Ishaq. Sam'an may have a predominantly Christian flavour, but it is not unattested among Muslims (I know at least one such person of Palestinian origin in Qatar). The fact that some names, such as Mikha'il, Niqula and Hanna, are used by Christians only does not make them non-Arab names. They are Christian Arab names in the same way that Muhammad is a Muslim Arab name.

Muslim, the implication being that Islam and Arabness are closely tied to each other and that, therefore, a non-Muslim Arab cannot be as Arab as a Muslim Arab.[17] Such a conclusion would be hugely problematic in view of the secular interpretations of Arabness in pan-Arabism, but this is a separate matter that, for reasons of space, I cannot pursue here (Suleiman 2003).

In fact, if we could go back more than a century ago and look at the names of native Jews in Damascus, we would discover that they were largely congruent with the names of Muslims in Nablus in Palestine for the same period, and many of the factors that went into acts of name bestowal in the two communities were more or less the same. If we were to accept Borg and Kressel's 'dissimulation' hypothesis, we would have to conclude that the Jewish community in Damascus at the beginning of the nineteenth century was engaged in a wholesale onomastic-invisibility drive covering not just the names bestowed by the community but also, more problematically, the application in naming of classificatory schemas that cut across the religious divide.

In a two-part study of names of Muslims (and, to a lesser extent, Christians) in Palestine and a cohort of three thousand names of native Damascene Jews at the close of the nineteenth century, MacAlister and Masterman (1904 and 1905) reveal that in spite of some faith-based differences in name bestowal between them, the two communities (Muslim and Christian Palestinians, on the one hand, and Damascene Jews, on the other) exhibit strong overlap and apply similar classificatory schemas. MacAlister and Masterman show this through the application of the same categories to classify the name cohorts for the two communities and by doing so without residue: (1) theophorous names (typically, compounds with *'abd*); (2) names denoting consecration to inferior beings or to religion; (3) names of angels, saints and heroes; (4) descriptive names; (5) territorial names; (6) titles, trades and occupations; (7) names derived from the circumstances of birth or from the sentiments provoked by the birth; (8) names derived from objects, including body parts, animals, plants, food, astronomical bodies, clothing and musical instruments. It is interesting to note here that many of the categories in this schema seem to apply to the name pools in Abd-el-Jawad's (1986) and Salih and Bader's (1999) studies in Jordan and, I would suspect, to 'Atiyya's (1990) study in Lebanon. In the Levantine context, one might expect this schema to have continued to apply among Muslims, Christians and Jews down to the present day, had it not been for the intervention of European Zionism, with its cataclysmic political and cultural consequences in the Arab Middle East.[18]

17 Anecdotal support exists for this among Israeli Jews, as reported to me by several Israeli Palestinians, Christians and Muslims. Yonatan Mendel (personal correspondence) has confirmed this. He related the following incident: 'I remember once in university when a Jewish girl said to her Jewish boyfriend, "Please meet my new friend Manar. She is an Arab, but don't worry, she is Christian."' In my experience, many Christian Palestinians resent this racist attitude, which condemns them ethnically while attempting to praise them: Christians are Arab (negative quality), but they are viewed less negatively (than Muslims) because they are Christians.

18 Variations on this schema exist in Arab countries outside the Levant, such as Saudi Arabia; see 'Asiri (2001).

There is no doubt that onomastic dissimulation takes place under certain conditions in Arab societies. I have mentioned some of these conditions above, which, interestingly, do obtain within the same faith community and not just between faith communities. I will have occasion to refer to other examples of onomastic dissimulation later. The point that I wish to stress here, however, is that the congruence over name pools among Muslims, Christians and, until recently, Jews in the Levant must be seen as the result of deep cultural synergies that, in some important identity sense, transcended the boundaries of religious belief. These synergies are expressed in naming conventions that articulate similar relationships to the deity, as well as to the natural and the social worlds of the communities concerned. Instead of declaring these synergies to be the result of some kind of 'conspiracy of onomastic dissimulation' on the part of the non-Muslim communities, of deliberate and calculated convergence of the minorities to the majority 'to fend off discrimination and persecution,' as Borg and Kressel would say (2001: 35), it is empirically and analytically more satisfactory, as it is also intellectually more honest and rational, to see these synergies as, on the whole, the result of an underlying cultural infrastructure that embodies similarities in worldview and signals overlapping identities. In this respect, research on names and naming in the past may, in fact, unearth commonalities of identity, which can act as a counterpoint to the fissures and cataclysmic ruptures of the present. As sediments from a past archaeology, archived names can act as reminders of a lost world in which communal and ethnic identities seem to have been less sharply demarcated than at present. Talk about intercommunal/ethnic onomastic differences needs, therefore, to be balanced against both intercommunal similarities and intracommunal differences. Moreover, to yield reliable information, these onomastic differences need to be contextualised in their historical settings.

Personal names are a useful tool in exploring value shifts in society, mainly in the direction of modernisation. The increasing percentage of foreign names in the Lebanese village discussed above signals a shift of attitudes in society from traditional to modern, Westernised values with a francophone accent. This is clear from the replacement of Hanna by the French Jean rather than the English John or the replacement of Mikha'il by the French Michel rather than the English Michael. These inflections in the choice of Western names signal allegiances that orient cultures differentially to each other. It says that not all modernisation as Westernisation is the same and that some connections are more salient than others interculturally, no doubt because of the different historical trajectories in existence between countries and societies.

Similar differences do exist at a more subtle level, as when Arabs, regardless of their religious background, transliterate their names in ways that suggest a choice between a francophone and an anglophone inflection, again for historical and cultural reasons. In this respect, it is telling whether the Arabic name Rashīd is transliterated as Rasheed or as Rachide, with or without a final *e* in the latter. The same applies to the transliteration of

Hishām as Hisham or Hicham or to the transliteration of Shākir as Shakir or Chakir. To this writer, the use of *ch* for the Arabic *shīn* in name transliteration signals a connection to francophone culture and, therefore, may be taken to indicate that the name bearer or the one who transcribes it is most probably of North African or Lebanese origin or one who lives in France or another French-dominated environment, as in Quebec.[19] By contrast, the use of *sh* for Arabic *shīn* in name transliteration signals an anglophone orientation. Either way, the transliteration of Arabic names into Latin script is not a neutral matter; it yields symbolic meanings about zones of cultural influence that are rooted in the colonial experience and its aftereffects.

PERSONAL NAMES, IDENTITY AND MODERNISATION

In the Lebanese study ('Atiyya 1990), modernisation has been observed in the Arabic name pool for both males and females, although the names for females exhibit greater shifts over time, and as a result, that pool is

19 In the wake of 11 September 2001 and the wars in Afghanistan and Iraq, the transliteration of Arabic names using Roman letters has become a security issue because of the variations that exist in transliterating even the most common of all Arab and Muslim male names: Muhammad. In an article on the subject under the title '*Al-Irhab wa-al-asma*' ('Terrorism and Names') in the leading newspaper *Al-Hayat* (21 August 2007), a Saudi academic ('Ali Bin Talal al-Jahni) calls on the Arab League and the General Secretariat of the Muslim States to institute a uniform system for transliterating Arabic and Muslim names to help track the terrorists internationally. The same issue is raised in the American context. In an online discussion of this topic on 6 August 2007, Courtney C. Rasdch, wrote:

> Three years ago a frustrated Congress passed a law requiring development of a standard way to transliterate Arabic names in travel documents and watch lists, but so far it is slow going. The inherent difficulty of transliterating Arabic names that include silent vowels and diacritical marks into English letters poses difficulties for creating effective terrorist watch lists and uniform travel documents. . . . Even the United States' government does not have one standardization rule, with each agency and department using their own transliteration standards, with variations within agencies as well. For example, spellings of Osama bin Laden include Usama bin Laden or Ladin by the CIA and the FBI. . . . Creating an international Romanization standard also poses difficulties because getting agreement on which . . . language should provide the standard could be difficult in the current political climate. Names sound different when pronounced in French or German or English, for example, and Arabic-speaking countries with significant French-speaking populations such as Lebanon and Morocco tend to have spellings that more closely adhere to French rules of pronunciation than English ones. . . . Thompson Yee . . . from the Library of Congress pointed out that when the United States switched from Wade Giles to Pin Yin Chinese took on 'political ramifications.' Turns out even names and the alphabet are political in this town. (http://www.arabisto.com/p_blogEntry.cfm?blogID=7&blogEntryID=716)

Three points are particularly interesting about this blog article: it highlights the political messages implicit in names, it notes the differences in name transliteration between the francophone and anglophone Arab countries, and it recognizes that even the most pressing security concerns may have to be subjected to Western national identity imperatives when it comes to transliterating Arabic names into the Roman script.

comparatively larger in size. For all of the names in this study, not just the Arabic names, 335 males shared 111 names, while the 186 females in the sample shared 134 names. Similarly, in the two Jordanian studies (Abd-el-Jawad 1986; Salih and Bader 1999) and the study of personal names in the Negev and Sinai (Borg and Kressel 2001), the female name pools are larger than the male name ones. This difference in name-pool size between the sexes seems to be a widespread phenomenon in many societies. It has, for example, been established for naming patterns in the United States and tentatively explained there as the result of the different role expectations of males and females in society, as well as the 'higher priority placed upon attractiveness for women than men' (Alford 1987: 155).[20] This emphasis on attractiveness is true of female name patterns in Arab societies. Name givers do take attractiveness into consideration very seriously when bestowing all names, encapsulating this in such expressions as '*ism ḥilu*' or '*ism kwayyis*' ('beautiful, good name'), but they seem to apply this principle with even greater care and aesthetic calculation when choosing female names than when bestowing male ones.[21] This may explain the greater incidence of foreign names for females than for males in Arab societies in recent years, regardless of religion, owing to the perception of 'modernity' that these names carry. The fact that these names lack some of the guttural or pharyngeal sounds in Arabic may be a factor in this assessment of their attractiveness, the idea being that names with these sounds are thought of as harsh. However, this judgement about name aesthetics would need further study.

Asecond aspect of modernisation in the female name pool in the Arabic-speaking countries is the occurrence of variable shifts away from some of

20 Alford writes: 'It may be that these sex differences in naming [in the United States] derive from the fact that American women are allowed greater expressive freedom than men. A perfect parallel can be drawn between fashions in clothing and naming. While for males there is a relatively narrow range of variation and a great deal of continuity over the years, for females there is a wide range of variation and considerable change in fashion over time. In fact, the use of fashionable names may be a manifestation of the higher priority placed upon attractiveness for women than men. While male names emphasize uniformity and continuity of the male role, female names may occasionally function as verbal jewellery, emphasizing attractiveness' (1987: 155). This is a problematic explanation intellectually and 'politically,' but I believe that it has a high degree of resonance for name givers in Arab societies.

21 Islam strongly enjoins its followers to bestow good/beautiful names on their children. Prophet Muhammad is reported to have said: 'On Doomsday you will be called by your names and the names of your fathers—so choose beautiful (or, graceful) names'. Islam also instructs its followers not to use demeaning nicknames to refer to others to counter the practise of using such names among the Arabs in pre-Islamic and early Islamic times. In fact, this practise was never eliminated. Commenting on this practise in the Middle East between the tenth and thirteenth centuries, Goitein writes: 'Jews and Arabs have had indeed an indomitable propensity for inventing offensive by-names. Therefore we find the religious literature of both peoples condemning this habit in the strongest terms' (1970: 520). This observation points to intercommunal cultural synergies in the Middle East, which became gradually extinct following the introduction of political Zionism in the Arab Middle East.

the traditional names of the past, for example, Fatima and Khadija.[22] This shift is not matched in male names; witness in this regard the high occurrence of the name Muhammad, its lexical cognates (e.g., Ahmad, Hamad and Mahmud) and other traditional male names in Arab societies. However, the shift from the traditional Muslim namesakes of the past to modern ones must not be considered a categorical or absolute shift away from Muslim names or values, as Gardner (1994: 119–20) explains in her study of naming patterns in the Sudan,[23] but as more of a shift away from traditional names.[24] This is supported by the rise in new names that express religious concepts such as 'faith, inspiration, supplication, submission and ascension.' The creation of new names that are culled directly from the text of the Qur'an[25]—for example, 'Āya ('sign'), 'Ālā' ('signs'), Tasnīm (name of a water fountain in heaven), Afnān ('a tree with many branches'), Firdaws ('paradise'), Malak ('angel'), Kawthar ('water') and Līnā ('palm tree')—lends support to the twin views that (a) the erosion in traditional Islamic names does not necessarily imply a move away from Islamic values and (b) onomastic modernisation/innovation is not exclusively tied to Westernisation, but it can be also rooted in Islamic values. These intergenerational shifts are viewed with suspicion by the older generation, as both Gardner (1994) and 'Atiyya (1990) point out for the Sudan and Lebanon, respectively. 'Atiyya relates how grandparents sometimes deliberately mispronounce the new names, particularly the foreign ones, or pretend not to remember them because of their difficulty, and he interprets these practises as passive resistance to the changes in name patterns in response to social modernisation. Most probably, it is not modernisation per se that the older generation is objecting to but the impact of modernisation on social structures in the naming sphere, as well as in other cultural domains that affect the traditional status of these individuals in society.

The reduction in the number of names with the final feminine marker *tā' marbūṭa* is a third facet of linguistic modernisation in the female name pool in the Levant and other Arabic-speaking countries. Although we do not have figures to substantiate this claim from the Levant, it is interesting to

22 The list of the fifty most popular female names in Abdel-Jawad (1986: 94) contains three traditional names only: Fatima, Khawla and Āmina, which are ranked 5, 18 and 38, respectively.

23 Gardner writes: 'The concern among some Sudanese was not so much that traditional names were decreasing in popularity, but that this might somehow be a sign of declining religiosity among people. While the traditional religious names are decreasing, the religious names that are increasing [suggest] that the value of religion is not being neglected in name-giving, but that it is being realized in a different form: changing from the names of women [strongly associated with Islam] to religious concepts such as faith, inspiration' (1994: 119–20).

24 This observation suggests that tradition and religion are not always tied together in expressing cultural authenticity.

25 See Schimmel for similar phenomena in name bestowal in Arab and non-Arab Muslim societies. She writes: 'Lately it has become fashionable in Egypt and probably in most Islamic countries to name their children after concepts taken from the Qur'an like *Rafraf* (Sūra 55/76), *Istabraq*, or *Sundus*, the 'brocade' mentioned in Sūra 76/21 and elsewhere' (1995: 26).

note that only twelve of the fifty most popular female names mentioned by Abdel-Jawad (1986) for Jordan end with the feminine marker. Support for this aspect of modernisation, however, is available for Sudan, as Gardner's four-generation longitudinal study of Sudanese name-giving patterns extending from the 1900s to the 1980s shows (1994: 123). At the start of the period of study in the 1900s, five out of the ten most popular female names end with the feminine marker. The number rises to seven for the 1920s, drops to six in the 1940s, drops to four in the 1960s and then drops further to two in the 1980s. Why this is the case is not clear, but it may be that the feminine marker in Arabic names has developed connotations of being old-fashioned, of not being attractive or cool, conjuring up old values and societal norms that are seen to be unsuitable to associate with today's modern Arab woman. If true, the perception of being old-fashioned may generate a carryover effect by feeding into judgements about onomastic attractiveness mentioned above.

In spite of this, some names with the feminine ending may be resistant to change. Of the top ten females names mentioned in Gardner's study, only two, Fatima and Āmina, may be regarded as traditional Muslim names. These two names appear for all the years of the Sudan study, which strongly suggests that some names with the feminine marker are more resilient than others in resisting name changes. The fact that Fatima is the Prophet Muhammad's daughter, as well as the wife of the Prophet's cousin and fourth Rightly Guided Caliph Ali ibn Abi Talib, may explain the continued popularity of this name. Furthermore, the fact that this name has a ready-made and positively viewed nickname, Fattum, which can replace it in everyday situations, may be another factor in its continued popularity. The resilience of the name Āmina is no doubt connected with the commanding status of its namesake, the Prophet's revered mother, Āmina bint Wahb.

Finally, the modernisation in female names seems to correlate with shifts in the social norms governing the mention of these names in the public sphere. In the past few decades, there has been a relaxation in some parts of the Arabic-speaking world of the old taboo of female-name avoidance in public. This is an impressionistic judgement on my part based on personal interactions with men in a number of Arab countries, although female-name avoidance may be sensitive to class, education, locality, religious commitment and social distance between interlocutors. However, in spite of the urbanisation and modernisation of Arab societies, it is still the case that for some (especially Muslims), mentioning female names in public is a taboo subject (*'aura*).[26] Thus, in talking to other males, Arab men sometimes use a variety of circumlocutions to suppress the mention of the names of their

26 Vom Bruck comments on this issue as follows: 'Women's names [in Yemen], like their bodies are conceived as *'aura* (that which is indecent to reveal). . . . The notion of women's personal names as *'aura* indicates that camouflaging the female body might involve more than the all-familiar veiling practices. Through veiling and naming the body cannot be sexualized by either the male gaze or the utterance' (2006: 228). For similar comments, see Bassiouney (2009: 148).

female relatives, especially wives and grown-up daughters. For these men, one's wife may be referred to as *al-'iyāl, umm al-'yāl* or *al-ahl* ('family'), or she may be referred to using a teknonym (*umm*, 'mother,' followed by the name of her first-born or her eldest son if she has one).

The relaxation of what may be called the name-avoidance rule (for females) under the impact of urbanisation and social modernisation in Arab culture seems to explain the shift from the invisibility of female names to their prominent visibility in Egyptian obituaries between 1938 and 1988. In a series of studies on the topic, Eid (1994a, 1994b, 2002b) has shown how female names gradually entered the public sphere of the obituary world and how this phenomenon varied for Egyptians at different times according to religion, social background and region, until in the end, the difference in name visibility shrank significantly between Christians and Muslims.[27] Here we have an example of how ethnic/religious identity correlates positively with name visibility/invisibility in its capacity as a measure of modernisation in society at a particular period in Egypt's history. However, the fact that, even when named, the deceased females are additionally identified through their male relatives in the obituary world tells us that there are social limits on this modernisation. Although for most obituary writers a deceased woman is now mentioned by name in the obituary, she still needs the names of her male relatives around her in the obituary world. These males, whether alive or dead, are normally mentioned with titles and occupations, acting in this regard as social props that signify the status and worth of the deceased woman.[28]

Modernisation has also affected male names in Arab societies, although shifts in these names are, as in other societies, including the United States, 'less subject to changes in fashion, and less likely to change from year to year, or from generation to generation, than are names for females' (Alford 1987: 150). Male onomastic modernisation is exhibited in the increase in the size of the male name pools in the Jordanian, Lebanese, Negev, Sinai and Sudan studies; this offers name givers more scope for individuation in name bestowal. The main reasons for this expansion in the male name pools seems to be a combination of urbanisation—for example, increased contact in the Negev study between Bedouins and urban centres in their vicinity through work, education and intermarriage with Gazan brides—and the reduction of the rate of recycling/reoccurrence of names through the agnatic chain. The second factor may, in fact, be considered an outcome of urbanisation, too. One of the known consequences of urbanisation is the loosening of the power of the extended family on social structures, thus allowing parents as name givers more freedom to choose names for their

27 The fact that Christians in Egypt display publicly their Christian names in the obituary world provides another argument against Borg and Kressel's (2001) dissimulation thesis, mentioned above.

28 As an aside, the female obituaries may, in fact, be more important as displays of the status of those who survived the dead woman than of the deceased herself.

male children without the pressure of naming the first-born male after his paternal grandfather.[29] 'Atiyya (1990) observed this in his Lebanese study, highlighting the fact that this trend knows no religious boundaries. It applies to Christians and Muslims; by so doing, this trend provides further evidence of the intercommunal cultural commonalities that exist in Arab societies across the religious divide, as well as how these commonalities underpin similarities of identity across space and even across time.

The modernisation hypothesis in male name patterns partly rests on the bestowal of new and foreign/Western names, the latter mainly by Christians. The use of names of these two types is related to a variety of factors, including the search for onomastic uniqueness, as I will suggest below, which name givers set out to express through name bestowal, although they tend to do so less for males than for females. Onomastic uniqueness has been studied empirically in the American context to determine what effect, if any, unusual names have on their bearers, whether they are a handicap or an advantage.[30] These studies revealed that on the whole, the effect of unique or unusual names is neutral for the whole population: while for some they can be a handicap,[31] a cross to bear, for others they can be an advantage. Similar studies do not exist for Arabic name pools. However, because of the availability of reflections on this matter and because of his status as one of the leading scholars of the second half of the twentieth century, I will consider this issue in relation to the late Edward Said, focusing in particular on the relationship between the name Edward and its bearer.

Said's autobiography, *Out of Place* (1999), is full of penetrating reflections on how he experienced his first name, Edward, especially in his childhood.[32] This subject of his name must have mattered a lot to Said for him to comment on it in the opening paragraph of *Out of Place* to signal his displacement spatioculturally at more than one level, as I have discussed in chapter 4.

29 Lieberson comments on this phenomenon as follows: 'A shift away from naming children after ancestors may represent a decline in the role of the extended family and the conception of maintaining historical continuity through the generations' (1984: 79). Borg and Kressel (2001) offer a similar interpretation for name pattern changes in the Negev and Sinai.

30 For a summary of findings from this research, see Alford (1987: 150–55).

31 Names can be a source of discomfort to their bearers if they stand out or appear to others to be out of step with the general politics or ideologies of the day. Leila Ahmed, who went by the name Lily at school (an anglicized version of Leila), relates the following story of a chance encounter she and her cousin had with President Nasser of Egypt at a showing of *Mutiny on the Bounty* in Cairo: 'As we shook hands [with Nasser], he asked us our names and my cousin readily replied 'Mona,' a perfectly good Egyptian Arab name. I, however, was rooted to the spot, unable to speak. I could not say 'Lily,' my name at school—not to this man, who I knew, hated the British. How could I, an Egyptian girl, have such a name? How could I confess to such a name?' (2000: 150).

32 In her autobiography *Teta, Mother and Me*, Jean Said Makdisi offers the following reflections on her name:

> My name is Jean, and in my name lies my history. I was named after my father's mother, Hanneh Shammas, but my name was anglicized. Naming me after his mother was, for my father, an act of devotion and affirmation. Anglicising her name,

In the full sweep of Said's autobiography, the name Edward acts a motif for his being 'out of place,' for an identity that defies complete closure and watertight classification and for a body that could not be hemmed in at any one place:

> [An] over-riding sensation I had was of always being out of place. Thus it took me about fifty years to become accustomed to, or more exactly, to feel less uncomfortable with, 'Edward,' a foolishly English name yoked forcibly to the unmistakably Arabic family name Said. True my mother told me that I had been named Edward after the Prince of Wales, who cut so fine a figure in 1935, the year of my birth, and Said was the name of various uncles and cousins. But the rationale of my name broke down both when I discovered no grandparents called Said and when I tried to connect my fancy English name with its Arabic partner. For years, and depending on the exact circumstances, I would rush past 'Edward' and emphasize 'Said'; at other times I would do the reverse, or connect these two to each other so quickly that neither would be clear. The one thing I could not tolerate, but very often would have to endure, was the disbelieving, and hence undermining reaction: Edward? Said? (1999: 3–4)

Said spent nearly five years working on his autobiography, and he is known to be a careful writer, so the wording of the above excerpt cannot be accidental. Occurring at the start of the autobiography, where writerly consciousness is often most conscious of itself and of the impact it wishes to create at its moment of inception and first encounter with the reader, the following chain of expressions, culled from the above excerpt, must be taken

---

> however, was an act of repudiation: like so many Arab men of his generation, my father saw the future as lying in Europe and America, to which he had emigrated in the early years of the twentieth century. He had returned to Jerusalem in the early 1920s to honour his mother's death wish, but never really forgave her for deflecting him from what he had seen as his destiny in the New World. In anglicising the name he bestowed on me, he showed his belief that my future lay, hidden, curled up, unborn in the English language. To him, Jerusalem and all its travails was tied up in the past. (2005: 27)

This quotation is very revealing for the following reasons: (1) Occurring as the opening statement in the first chapter of the autobiography, it suggests the importance of names in how the individual reads his onomastic script; Makdisi says that her history lies in her name. (2) The bestowal of the name Hanneh and its change to Jean suggest both the strength of naming traditions and their fragility in Palestine in the first half of the twentieth century. (3) The father inscribes himself in his onomastic choices as both conforming to and rebelling against his native traditions. (4) The change to Jean is tied up with the notions of modernity, opportunity and, therefore, identity marking. (5) The choice of Jean as a name is tied up with the belief that English is the language of modernity and opportunity, unlike Arabic (through the name Hanneh), which is the language of tradition and the 'travails [of] the past.' And (6) the name Jean therefore signals a new beginning for its bearer. I have no doubt that some of these consideration were at play in choosing Edward Said's first name. Leila Ahmed, who knew Edward and Jean Said from their Cairo days, reflects on this issue as follows: 'Our very names—Edward, Jean and my own school name, Lily, as an anglicized version of my given name—plainly suggest our parents' admiration of things European' (2000: 6).

as indicative of how Said experienced the socialising or desocialising impact of his name: 'become accustomed to,' 'feel less uncomfortable with,' 'foolishly English name,' 'yoked forcibly,' 'unmistakably Arabic family name,' 'rationale of my name broke down,' 'fancy English name,' 'rush past,' 'connect these two to each other so quickly that neither would be clear,' 'could not tolerate,' 'would have to endure,' 'disbelieving [reaction],' 'undermining reaction,' 'Edward [with a question mark/interrogative particle]' and 'Said [with a question mark/interrogative particle].' The thick accumulation of these expressions, making up most of the above excerpt, signals very strongly that Said was extremely dissatisfied with Edward—that Edward the name was too much of a cross to bear for Edward the person—instead of which he might have preferred a recognisably Arab name, just like those of his son Wadie (Wadī') and daughter Najla. For Said, Edward the name acted as a meeting point for feelings of 'out of place-ness' on his part, of the name not fitting the body, as if in contravention of the Arabic proverb *ismu 'alā jismu* (literally, 'his name fits his body').[33] The following excerpts from *Out of Place* make this point clearly:

> All around me [in Said's English school in Cairo] were Greenvilles, and Coopers and Pilleys: starchy little English boys and girls with *enviably authentic names*, blue eyes, and bright, *definitive accents*. (1999: 39; emphasis added)

And:

> I had no sustained contact with English children outside the school; an invisible cordon kept them hidden in another world that was closed to me. I was perfectly aware of how their names were just *right* [original emphasis] and their clothes and *accents* [added emphasis] and associations were totally different from my own. (42)

And when reflecting on his experience as a pupil at the Cairo School for American Children:

> I was struck by the fact that part of the American approach was to institute the teaching of Arabic, and having pretended that 'Sigheed' was an American name, I had some of my worst moments in Arabic class. Somehow I had to conceal my perfect command of what was my mother tongue in order to fit in better with the inane formulas given out to American youngsters for what passed for spoken (but was really kitchen) Arabic. There were provocations, however, like the pretty young teacher who, while describing her adventures at the just-opened amusement park in Gezira, placed particular emphasis on an airplane ride called 'Saida,' after the newly formed Egyptian airline company. In a tiny class of four people, she planted herself in front of me and proceeded

33 I am reminded here of the response when Alice, in *Alice in Wonderland*, asked Humpty Dumpty if her name must mean something: 'Of course it must,' Humpty Dumpty said with a short laugh: 'my name means the shape I am—and a good handsome shape it is, too. With a name like yours, you might be any shape, almost' (Carroll 2000: 239). Bodenhorn and vom Bruck sum this up by saying that names 'sometimes . . . are thought to reflect the true person-within-the-body' (2006: 25).

> to detail her excitement at 'Saida,' which she repeated again and again, as if emphasizing the lurking Arab quality in my name, which I had laboriously tried to scale down to the prevailing norms of American pronunciation. 'No, Edward,' she said emphatically, 'you couldn't have been on the best rides if you haven't tried Saida. Do you know how many times I rode Saida? At least four. Saida is the ride. Saida's just great.' In other words, stop pretending that you are Sigheed: You're Said, as in Saida. The connection was undeniable. (82–83)

I have dwelt on the case of Said at some length—in fact, not sufficient length—to highlight how names and identities are linked to how we conceptualise ourselves, interpret our life experiences, live our lives as social beings and think of how others see us or how we wish them to see us. For most people, this process may not be problematic, and it may not even be a matter worthy of reflection, but it can become acutely so when dissonance, tension or rupture occurs or is (deliberately) created between the originary provenance and connotations of a name and the way the name bearer imagines his or her own identity. The dilemma for Said was the lack of fit between what the name Edward signals and connotes symbolically and who he thought he was at different points in a life he lived in exile and diaspora. In his elegy to Said, parts of which were quoted in chapter 4, Palestinian poet Mahmoud Darwish comments perceptively on this dissonance in Said's name when he says on Said's behalf: 'I have two names which meet and part.' Relying on the wisdom and psychology embodied in the Arabic proverb *ismu 'alā jismu*, we can say that Edward the name did social, psychological and sociopsychological violence to Edward the person. Said captures this well when he refers to 'the lurking Arab quality' in his name, which he 'laboriously tried to scale down to the prevailing norms of American pronunciation' (83). The lack of fit between name, body and language, which Said inscribes in the references to 'accent' above, is another dimension of this violence.

Furthermore, as the above excerpts suggest, Edward the name alienated Edward the person from his surroundings on almost all fronts, none more so than in the way he was taunted by his Arabic-language teacher, who, no doubt, would not have sought and gained employment at the Cairo School for American Children (Said had American nationality through his father) had she lacked the appropriate pro-Western, pro-American sympathies. For a teacher of this background to taunt Said on account of his name shows how important names are in marking identities, in acting as a kind of border guard in society whose infringement as exemplified by the name Edward may be seen as a transgressive act.

Yet there is a huge onomastic irony in the life story of Edward Said. There is little doubt that the name Edward was given to him by his father, Wadie, a naturalised American of Palestinian origin with whom, it seems, Said had a tense relationship, as *Out of Place* suggests. The bestowal of the name Wadie on Said's only son is that irony. On the one hand, this bestowal may be interpreted as an act of revenge, of the son with the foreign name using his father's Arab name to name his own son. In this respect, the naming of Said's son Wadie is an act of rebellion against his father as a father figure.

On the other hand, this same name bestowal is an act of conformity: it enacts an established Arab name-giving practise of giving to the first-born male in a family the name of his paternal grandfather; by so doing, Said *conforms to rebel.* It is as though by naming his son Wadie, Said was trying to remind his father of the three-generation rule in the sociology of the American melting pot: the grandson will seek to remember what the grandfather wanted the son to forget. However, Said does this with an ironic twist: it is he who, by conforming to rebel, tries to make his son remember what his father, Wadie, wanted him (Edward) to forget.

PERSONAL NAMES, IDENTITY AND CONFLICT

The importance of names in the study of group identity is based on the premise that identity is subject to continuity and change, conformity and diversity, and that both conformity and diversity are themselves diverse. Thinking of change, mutations in name-giving patterns can occur as sudden shifts; this typically happens when name givers respond to the intense situations of their political and social environment. In the recent past, this happened through the bestowal of the name Saddam on male children in Jordan and, to some extent, Yemen during and after the first Gulf War (1991) following Iraq's occupation of Kuwait in August 1990. For some name givers, Saddam appeared to be the last Arab leader who 'had the guts' to challenge American imperialism and, indirectly, the Israeli occupation of Palestine behind which this imperialism is thought to stand. Naming their newly born sons Saddam was, therefore, for some name givers an act of publicly honouring this leader and the ideology for which he stood (whether or not they understood this ideology is a different matter), of demonstrating solidarity with and commitment to Iraq and its people and of sending a message of defiance to America, Israel and the West's 'corrupt' Arab allies in the region.

This sociopolitically impregnated onomastic gesture represented a flamboyant expression of identity, through which the name giver said, 'I am a proud Arab, and I am naming my nearest and dearest after Saddam, and I don't care if the whole world hates him or hates me!' In Jordan alone, 394 children were reported to have been given this name during this period. After the American-led occupation of Iraq and the fall of Saddam's regime in 2003, the Jordanian authorities, in an unprecedented move, gave parents the right to have these names changed automatically on application to the relevant authorities if they so wished[34]—instead of going through what is sometimes a fairly lengthy legal procedure—but it is not known how many

34 This was the subject of a cartoon by the Palestinian-Jordanian cartoonist 'Imad Hajjaj (2008: 189), in which the main character, Abu Mahjub, is seen trying to change his son's name from Saddam to the nonsensical but rhyming name 'Van Dam.' The irony is that the man who is helping him in the cartoon is referred to as Abu Udayy ('father of Udday'), Udayy being the name of Saddam Hussein's eldest son.

of them took up this offer.[35] In Israel, a Palestinian whose son was born on the day the Iraqi leader was executed (30 December 2006) named his newborn Saddam, an extremely daring and provocative act considering how hated Saddam was in Israel. When the authorities refused to register the name, the proud but angry father threatened the authorities with legal action. In Jordan, a father named his son Rabin after the Israeli leader Yitzhak Rabin, following the signing of the peace treaty with Jordan on 26 October 1994. The family, of East Jordanian origin, was hounded by neighbours, who put pressure on them to change the name; when the father refused and the threats against him and his family increased, the Israeli authorities offered the family refuge and work in Israel, which they accepted. This case signals in a sharp way the feeling of the Jordanian street towards the peace treaty with Israel; in fact, some Jordanians called this treaty a 'treaty of capitulation [*istislām*], not peace [*salām*],' playing on the contrastive meanings of the common root of these two words (*s-l-m*) to make the point.

These sudden changes, isolated though they may be, are significant: they represent onomastic grass-roots reactions to defining moments in the history of a group. In this respect, they provide telling and spontaneous expressions of identity—under conditions of conflict—that are at odds with, or even openly challenge, the official ideology of the state. Although I do not have empirical data to substantiate the following claim, there is no doubt that the establishment of self-rule in Iraqi Kurdistan before the invasion of Iraq in 2003 and the burgeoning sense of Kurdish national separateness since then have led to a rise in name-giving patterns away from Arabic to Kurdish names.[36] Names are a good indicator of the subterranean pulse of a group and its palpitations, politically and socially. They carry sensitive political information that should make them of interest to intelligence agencies in their effort to 'keep tabs' on what is going on in society, as I will suggest later with evidence from prerevolutionary Iran.

Sudden shifts of the type mentioned above are, however, the exception rather than the rule; nevertheless, they display in a pretty sharp way the connection between names and the politics of the day. In this vein, two naming practises that developed in the 1960s and 1970s among the Palestinians exhibit this connection. The first consisted of bestowing names that signified the politics of struggle or revolution in Palestinian life, such as Jihad ('struggle'), Kifah ('struggle'), Nidal ('struggle') and Tha'ir ('revolutionary'). The other practise consisted of taking up toponymic family names, in the form of relative nouns (*nisbas*) derived from village names in Palestine, to express their love for, belonging to and rootedness in the Palestinian homeland. Thus, if someone's family name in Jordan is al-Burini, it is a fair guess that he or she is of Palestinian descent and that his or her ancestors came from the village of Burin in the Nablus district; the same would be

35 See Suleiman (2006d).

36 This has been confirmed to me by Ronak Husni, an Iraqi Kurd, on the basis of names in her immediate family (personal communication).

true for someone with al-Disi as a family name; it is a fair guess that the person concerned would trace back his or her descent to the village of Abu Dis on the outskirts of Jerusalem. As acts of memorialisation that additionally express geographical nostalgia for a place denied, these names serve to tie together people who would have identified themselves differently had they not left their villages. As pointers to a map that a person carries, these toponymic names invite identification and the activation of social networks in public gatherings of ordinary normal interactions between strangers.

Furthermore, Palestinian children in the camps in Lebanon have been observed to use the name of the locality or village from which their ancestors originated in Palestine as part of their user names on the Web, although none of these children had ever set foot in that part of Palestine that they assert as theirs (see Khalili 2007: 80). Here we see how cyber-monikers can be used to signal spatially fine-tuned, down to the village, claims of national identity. It may be that, in the Palestinian context, none of the above practises on its own constitutes a major trend in name giving, but combined, they articulate a strong connection among names, identity, homeland and national politics.

In Israel, name changes are intimately linked with the nation-building project of the state. Hebrew name changes in Israel have traditionally been considered a strong expression of Israel's view of itself as a proud Jewish state that is ideologically the antithesis of the diaspora. Until the last wave of Russian immigrants of the 1990s of around a million people, immigration into Israel has been strongly associated with discarding the old names of the diaspora and adopting authentically Hebrew ones to signal a break with the past and the emergence of a new Hebrew-dominated identity with strong Zionist overtones.[37] In the Israeli context, these Hebrew name changes—in their capacity as linguistic material—are particularly effective as nation-building practises because of their association with the Hebrew-based nationalist ideology of the state, in which language plays a strong, if not the strongest, part. In this context, name changes can have a high-voltage emotional and ideological charge, because in most cases, the person concerned directly participates in choosing his name and in bestowing it on himself, no doubt with help from the immediate members of his family and his close friends. Whereas in normal situations a person inherits his or her name, here the name giver and the name receiver can be one and the same. The

37 The fact that the size of this minority (about one million) constitutes one-fifth of the Jewish population of Israel, that they were driven to immigrate to Israel more for economic rather than ideological (Zionist) reasons and that they hold a positive view of their preimmigration culture seem to be related to the reluctance of a sizeable proportion of this community, particularly the older generation, to change their names to Hebrew ones. Yonatan Mendel, one of my Israeli informants related that the Russian names in his class at high school included 'four Alexenders, one Pavel, one Anna, one Rita and one Sergey.' The situation is different for the Ethiopian immigrants. Their relatively small numbers, traditional religious backgrounds and marked ethnicity within the Israeli Jewish melting pot seem to have motivated a high rate of conversion to Israeli Hebrew names (Yonatan Mendel, personal communication).

person is agent and recipient, and in some cases the process of name bestowal constitutes a rite of passage in a conversion-like process in which the new identity is sanctioned, celebrated, publicly declared, circulated and accepted. The following excerpt from Tamar Katriel's book on *dugri* speech (straight talking) in Israeli *sabra* culture describes what, effectively, is a rite of passage that marks Katriel's entry into Israeli Hebrew culture: 'One of my earliest memories is of the day when, as a five-year-old newcomer to Israel, I was told to choose between two Hebrew-sounding names to replace the Yiddish name I had been given at birth in memory of a grandmother I would never know. I can clearly remember the scene: I was standing in the hall of my aunt's small apartment, my back pressed against the rough surface of her wardrobe, encircled by the adults in the family, who were glaring at me: 'What will it be, Tamar or Ruth?' I remember clumsily trying to roll the foreign sounds on my unaccustomed tongue, and, finally, exhausted by the piercing, expectant stares, I heard myself pronounce "Tamar"' (1986: 20).

As part of her socialisation into a new sociopolitical culture, Katriel had to symbolically give up her old ties, expressed through the sharing of her grandmother's name, in favour of new ones, those of the nation into which she was about to be onomastically baptised. In other words, Katriel had to be onomastically reborn to become a full Israeli. The passage from one name to another is symbolic of this transformation or transition; it represents a defining moment in Katriel's evolution as an Israeli Hebrew/Jewish person. This is why the details of this event, with its theatre-like quality, are indelibly etched in her memory. This process is very similar to the adoption of new names by converts to a new religion, a topic that is yet to be studied in the Arabo-Islamic context.[38]

In the Israeli context, a strong societal expectation with deep ideological and political underpinnings motivates the widespread Jewish name changes of the type Katriel describes.[39] Although this expectation pervades society, it does not, however, extend to the Palestinians in Israel, who have their own

38 To the best of my knowledge, there is hardly any systematic research on the topic. However, anecdotal data suggest that some new converts choose their own personal names, sometimes changing but most of the time keeping their family name. Those who join the Sufi *tariqas* are given names by their spiritual leaders or directors. Quite a few converts do not change their names at all, particularly if they are 'submarines,' that is to say, people who do not make their conversions public. I am grateful to Tim Winter for this information. The *Muslim Directory* for Great Britain routinely includes lists of names for males and females. The 2007–08 edition includes such a list on pages 587–98. This reflects the importance of names in Muslim culture. See Waugh (1995: 226) for some brief comments on the topic.

39 Debates over names in Israel have recently been widened to group names, particularly the names of the Jews from the Arab countries who have been referred to through a variety of names: 'Sephardim; non-Askenazi Jews; Jews of Islam; Arab Jews; Middle Eastern, west Asian, or north [*sic*] African Jews; Asian and African Jews; Jews of the Mediterranean; *Maghrebian* and *Mashreqian* (from western and eastern parts of the Arab world); Bnei Edot Ha Misrah (descendents of the Eastern communities); *yotzei artzot arav ve-ha-Islam* (those who left Arab and Muslim countries); Black; *Israel ha-Shniya* (Second Israel); Mizrahiyim or Mizrahim; or Iraqi Jews, Iranian Jews, Kurdish Jews, Palestinian Jews, Moroccan Jews, and so forth' (Shohat 2003: 52–53). This debate over names has strong political and ideological overtones.

name pools that are different from the Jewish Hebrew ones. However, there are cases when Israeli Palestinians deliberately adopt Hebrew-sounding names (this is how they are called in common parlance), these being seemingly equidistant in terms of sound and meaning from both Arabic and Hebrew.[40] In the very few cases of mixed Palestinian-Jewish marriages in Israel, the parents may choose names that can pass as both Arabic and Hebrew to respond to the dual identity of the child, such as Amir, Rani, Rami and Adam for boys and Amira, Yasmin and Layla for girls. It is, however, possible to argue that although such names as Amir, Rani and Adam are lexically Arabic, they are not part of the traditional Palestinian name pool as this is manifested among the Palestinians in the Occupied Territories or in the *shatat* (Palestinian diaspora), but they are chosen because of their similarity to Hebrew names; in fact, it is possible to argue that these are Hebrew names that are chosen because of their similarity to what could pass as Arabic names. Thus, instead of being equidistant from Arabic and Hebrew lexically, some of the so-called Hebrew-sounding names do, in fact, represent a convergence towards Hebrew onomastic norms rather than Palestinian Arab ones.

In other words, in their Arabic Palestinian forms, these names are tagged onto their Hebrew Jewish counterparts, rather than vice versa. The Arabic forms of these names are appendages, rather than equal partners of their Hebrew counterparts, a subordinate rather than a superordinate group of forms. Onomastic equality here is, therefore, more formal than real. In fact, instead of describing them as Hebrew-sounding Arabic names, Amir and Rani are better conceived of as Arabic-sounding Hebrew names. As forms of identity negotiation, names such as Amir and Rani masquerade as Arabic and Hebrew ones, but deeper analysis reveals that in the process of interethnic negotiation, these names operate with an accent that is more deeply embedded in or inflected towards Hebrew than Arabic culture. I will give further evidence in support of this conclusion later in this section.

The Druze, who among Israeli Palestinians (or non-Jewish Israelis, as some Druze would conceptualise themselves) have a strong connection with the state of Israel and its institutions, particularly the army and the security and intelligence services, seem to be the main users of the so-called Hebrew-sounding names. While mixed-marriage families involving a Muslim or a Christian Palestinian and an Israeli Jewish partner use these names for identity negotiation, the Druze seem to use them as an expression of their genuine desire to integrate into Israeli society. Thus, in addition to the so-called Hebrew-sounding male names Amir, Rani and Tamir, the 2005 census of births in Israel reveals that the Druze name pool contains typically Israeli Hebrew names, such as Daniel, Ayal and Ilan, the first of which has

40 I am grateful to Manar Makhoul and Yonatan Mendel for their help in providing valuable data for this part of the chapter.

been consistently ranked in the Israeli birth statistics as one of the most popular names in the past few years.[41] This same trend of using Israeli Jewish names extends to the adoption of female names by the Druze, such as A'nat, Dana, Maya, Ilanit and Osnat. The Druze choose these names not under duress or as acts of 'dissimulation,' as per Borg and Kressel's thesis (2001), but they do so actively and purposefully to express solidarity with the state of Israel, to show their allegiance to it and to signal sufficient distance from other Palestinians whose loyalty to the state is thought to be suspect.[42] In this context, one of my Jewish Israeli informants related the following story to illustrate the deep integration of the Druze community in the Israeli state:

> [I remember the following interesting example] concerning [the] Israeli military coordinator in the Occupied Territories, Yusuf Mashlab. He is Druze holding the rank of general in the Israeli army. When I worked for Physicians for Human Rights, we once [petitioned] the Supreme Court against the procedures of the military coordinating unit headed by Mashlab. [One day] I called his secretary for details about him, and I asked her if Mr. Yusuf Mashlab was around. She told me, 'No, he is not. And his name is [not Yusuf Mashlab but] Yosef [representing the Hebrew pronunciation of the name] Mishlav. Both Yosef and Mishlav are names in Hebrew. Even though he did not say it to me directly, I am sure his secretary said what he finds appropriate.

41 One factor behind the popularity of this name would seem to be its Western-sounding form. Names of this kind seem to be gaining popularity in Israel. I am grateful to Yonatan Mendel for this information.

42 The position of the Druze in Israel can be summed up as follows:

> [The Druze] serve in the Israeli army which, next to the *Ulpan* (Spolsky 1997), is one of the most important instruments for socio-political socialization through Hebrew in Israel. The Druze are linguistically Arab, but have a good competence in Hebrew, towards which they have strong integrative attitudes. They are not Israeli Jews, but they share with the Israeli Jews a deep sense of commitment to the state of Israel, in spite of the fact that, as an ethnic democracy, Israel does not accord them equal privileges with the Jews. While some Druze identify themselves as Arabs—mainly among the intellectual elite (e.g., the poet Samih Al-Qasim or the fiction writer Salman Natur)—others do not. This difference of opinion is reflected in scholarly discourse (Spolsky and Shohamy 1999: 107, 131). Lefkowitz captures this well when he refers to Druze identity as a blurred identity which 'forms a signifier intermediate between "Arab" and "Jew" in Israel, since it represents an Arab cultural identity that supports the Israeli state politically' (2004, 97). The Druze, therefore, ought to be an interesting topic of enquiry in national identity terms, but there are few studies that tackle the subject from the linguistic perspective. One study by Abu-Rabia (1996, 416), however, characterizes the Druze as a 'minority within a minority (presumably Arab) . . . which [i.e., the Druze minority] emphasizes its wish to be integrated into Israeli society more than its desire to be united with the rest of the macro Arab community in the Middle East.' Basing himself on a 1978 Master's dissertation on Druze identity in Israel (Al-Sheikh 1978), Abu-Rabia further adds that the Druze are 'Arab in terms of their language and culture, but not in terms of their emotions, principles or actions [and that they have] negative attitudes towards the establishment of a Palestinian state.' They, therefore, have a sense of 'shame regarding [their] language and culture' with which they 'do not emotionally sympathize.' (Suleiman 2006c: 134)

It is impossible to know from the above narrative whether the Druze general adopted this name or it was given to him. It is also impossible to know if this name bestowal was motivated by convenience considerations, was a result of the desire of its bearer to blend into his Jewish-dominated military work environment or, most probably, was an expression of his genuine loyalty to the state, or for all of these reasons together. It is also not possible to know whether 'Yosef Mishlav' is intended as a Hebrew-sounding name or as a Hebrew name proper. Whatever the case may be, there is no doubt that the Druze army general had exploited the phonetic proximity of his original and adopted names as a bridge to negotiate a new identity for himself that expressed his loyalty to the state and his desire to integrate, and not just onomastically, into Israeli society. Carrying inside it parts of its old Arabic phonetic archaeology, 'Yosef Mishlav' may be read as a symbol of an ambiguous identity and of a state of in-betweenness in which the sociopolitical inflection is more Israeli Jew than Israeli Arab. This interpretation of the name supports Lefkowitz's assessment of Druze identity in Israel as a blurred identity that 'forms a signifier intermediate between "Arab" and "Jew" in Israel, since it represents an Arab cultural identity that supports the Israeli state politically' (2004: 97).

In the above two cases of mixed marriages and the Druze, extended contact and reduced social and psychological distance between Israeli Jews and Israeli Palestinians seem to lead to some interethnic convergence on the part of the latter through the use of the so-called Hebrew-sounding names. In some cases, the convergence of Palestinians to Hebrew or Hebrew-sounding names occurs through contact in the labour market, as when a Palestinian works for an Israeli employer in a Jewish Hebrew environment. In this situation, Muhammad becomes Muhi or Miki, Ahmad is converted to Mudi, Suleiman changes to Shlomo, Dawud is transformed to Dudu (Jews use this name for David), Khadir turns into Kobi and 'Isam emerges as Itsik (the name used by Israeli Jews for Yitzhak). In some cases, the Israeli Palestinian may 'choose' the name, with active participation or through acquiescence, or he may have it bestowed on him. Whatever the case may be, however, the use of Hebrew names by Palestinians in Jewish work environments affords these Palestinians a degree of invisibility and reduces the perceptions of threat attributed to them by the dominant Jewish culture. As one of my Israeli Jewish informants related, a Jewish restaurant owner may prefer to call a Palestinian Musa who works for him Moshe, 'because the owner would feel better shouting Moshe to the kitchen than shouting Musa, [because the Arabic name] could intimidate the Jewish guests.'[43]

43 It is, in fact, an incident of this kind that triggered my interest in personal names among the Palestinians. In April 1995, I spent a day in Tiberias with my family. Tiberias is a special place for me, because my father spent the better part of his youth living and working in and out of the town. After a morning of sightseeing based on memories constructed out of family pictures and family stories, we went to have lunch in a restaurant that was built on the site of a partially demolished mosque. We spoke to the waiter in Arabic, and he told us, in what seemed like deliberately broken Arabic, that he came from a Palestinian village near Haifa. When I asked him for his name, he said it was Suleiman. But I was later surprised when I saw him respond to 'Shlomo' when he was spoken to in Hebrew.

The fact that the opposite—bestowing Arab names—hardly ever takes place for Israeli Jews in contact situations involving Palestinian Arabs indicates the asymmetrical power relations between the two groups and the hegemony that Israeli Jewish culture has over Palestinian Arab culture. This interpretation is further supported by the fact that while some Palestinians give their children Hebrew names to honour their Israeli Jewish friends, the opposite is almost nonexistent. Interethnically, the onomastic drift in Israel travels in one direction from Arabic to Hebrew names but hardly, if ever, vice versa.[44] This one-way drift, no matter how slight it may be, articulates the differential distribution of power between the Israeli Jews and the Palestinians in the Israeli-Palestinian conflict. This onomastic imbalance is part of a norm that applies to other cultural products in Israel, including language, as I have tried to suggest elsewhere (Suleiman 2004b; Suleiman 2006c).

However, acts of onomastic resistance against the imposition of Hebrew(-sounding) names on the Palestinians do occur. According to one of my Jewish informants, some Israeli Palestinians refuse to accept Hebrew name bestowals in the workplace. He supported this by the following story: 'I also heard the story of an Arab who was hired to work as a secretary in a clinic. [His boss] asked him to say, 'Good morning, this is Amir speaking!' when answering the telephone, rather than using his real name, Muhammad. When [Muhammad refused to accept the name Amir] he was fired.'[45] I have given this example here for two reasons: (1) it lends support to my interpretation that although Amir can pass as an Arabic name—presumably, the Jewish employer selected it to reduce the perceptual difference that Muhammad had to travel on the way to accepting the Hebrew-sounding Amir—it is, in fact, perceived by some Palestinians as a Hebrew name masquerading under an Arabic-sounding lexical guise; and (2) the fact that Muhammad was 'fired' when he refused to accept Amir as his workplace name carries connotations of onomastic resistance to the dominant culture for which he had to pay an economic price.

However, it is not clear whether this Israeli Palestinian would have resisted the imposition of the Hebrew-sounding name Amir on him had his name not been Muhammad, with all of the religious connotations this name carries in Arab Muslim culture. I say this because Israeli Palestinians seem to judge some name changes as more tolerable than others; for example, replacing Suleiman with Shlomo is judged to be not as offensive or unacceptable to Palestinians as replacing Muhammad

44 The following comment on the relations between Arabs and Jews in Israel explains why the onomastic traffic is in one direction: 'A subject's position vis-à-vis the dominant [group] is crucial [in Israel]. If a Jew desires to live up to the norms associated with Arabness, . . . that subject will be rejected by the dominant [group]' (Rottenberg 2008: 113).

45 This story made the news in Israel because of its 'racist' character. I am grateful to Yonatan Mendel for this information.

with Muhi or Miki because of the differential positions of Suleiman and Muhammad as Prophets in Islam.[46] It is this strong cultural resonance of Muhammad and its cognate names that makes them highly charged as symbols of otherness and conflict on the Israeli Jewish side. In this connection, one of my informants explained: 'As you can imagine, the names Ahmad, Muhammad and Mahmoud will be very 'unpopular' among Jews (who are afraid of the name, of the language, of the [Arabic] pronunciation and diction).' This is a revealing explanation, because it highlights the symbolic power of names as linguistic resources that have phonetic and lexical force in conflict situations.

The above examples suggest that the adoption of Hebrew or Hebrew-sounding names in Israel is a multilayered and ethnically variable phenomenon. When it occurs, this phenomenon may be driven by (1) instrumental considerations, such as securing material benefits in the workplace; (2) the desire to negotiate and create a middle space in which a mixed Arab-Jewish identity can be accommodated; and, in the case of the Druze, (3) to express loyalty to the state, solidarity with the Jewish people, to express the wish to integrate into mainstream Israeli life and to signal distance from the Muslim and Christian Arabs in Israel.

But there are other factors at play in the adoption of Hebrew or Hebrew-sounding names by Palestinians. For the Druze, these names seem to serve as a source of name modernisation, particularly for female names. By contrast, Christian Palestinians seem to opt for indigenous or foreign names (for example, Julian and George for males and Nicole, Karen and Carol for girls) in name modernisation, while Muslim Palestinians opt mainly for indigenous names in expanding and modernising their name pools.[47] Hebrew or Hebrew-sounding names may also represent an attempt at social 'upgrading' on the part of the Palestinians. When that happens, the immediate target of the 'upgrading' is not the Israeli Jews, although their social and political approval are ultimately aimed at, but the Israeli Palestinians. In this respect, the phenomenon of adopting Hebrew or Hebrew-sounding names is similar to the well-known phenomenon of code-switching to English or French in the Arabic-speaking world (see Suleiman 2004b). Palestinians who adopt these names are reported to declaim them with verbal swagger, using them to enhance their self-image and as an act of social one-upmanship.

It is, however, important to note that the adoption of Hebrew(-sounding) names among the Palestinians in Israel, with the exception of the Druze community, tends to affect males more than females; there are hardly any cases of onomastic switches to Hebrew female names among Christian and

46 The conventional nature of the Hebrew replacements for the name Muhammad may argue in the opposite direction. Conventionality implies acceptability and, therefore, the absence of active resistance.

47 This information is based on Israeli birth records for 2001 and 2005, for which I would like to thank Manar Makhoul.

Muslim Palestinian females. This is partly related to the fact that Palestinian women, whether Christian or Muslim, do not usually come into extended or sustained contact with Israeli Jews in situations where Hebrew cultural norms dominate. In addition, as attempts at 'ethnic-hopping,' the adoption of Hebrew(-sounding) names by female Palestinians is bound to the notion of female honour and the imperative of protecting this honour against external, onomastic penetration. The adoption of these names for Palestinian women would, therefore, carry strong moral and ethical connotations that border on what may be called, for lack of a better term, 'social adultery,' with all of its attendant consequences of disapproval, condemnation and symbolic ostracisation in society.

The Palestinians, mainly the Christians and the Muslims, in Israel exist in a complex world in identity terms. This complexity is captured by Israeli writer David Grossman in the metaphorical title of his book *Sleeping on a Wire* (1993), which aptly describes the liminal position of the Palestinians in Israel, their in-between-ness between the imperatives of their Israeli citizenship and the demands of their Palestinian national identity. Rottenberg sums this up well when she says that 'the place of the [Arab citizens of Israel] in the Jewish state has always been precarious: they are neither inside nor *totally* outside' (2008: 100; emphasis added).[48] This identity-linked complexity is a central theme of the Palestinian literature in Israel, whether penned in Arabic or Hebrew. Names are sometimes exploited in this literature as sites for expressing this complexity or the precarious position of the Palestinians as ill-fated insiders-outsiders in their native land. This is evident in Emile Habibi's masterpiece, *The Secret Life of Sa'id the Pessoptimist* (2002), where the name of the protagonist, Sa'id Abu al-Nahs al-Mutasha'il, combines the lexically recoverable notions of 'happiness, good omen' (from Sa'id), 'ill-fortune, bad omen' (from Abu al-Nahs) and the blend 'pessoptimist, opti-pessemist' (hence al-Mutasha'il), a neologism in Arabic created out of the two words *pessimist* and *optimist*.[49] In his novel *Dancing Arabs*, written originally in Hebrew, the young Israeli Palestinian writer Sayed

48 Azmi Bishara, the well-know Palestinian member of the Knesset now living in exile, takes issue with such descriptions of the Israeli Palestinians. Bishara describes the situation of the Palestinians in Israel as 'not on the seam between here and there, but simply not here and not there' (1992: 9), although this description may, in fact, be intended to describe Bishara's own position rather than that of the Palestinians as a collectivity. I am grateful to Yonatan Mendel for this quotation and the translation from Hebrew.

49 Muhawi discusses the complexities of being Palestinian in this novel. His comments on the name of the protagonist are relevant here: '[The protagonist's] name is Sa'id, which ordinarily means "happy," but which when coupled with *abu al-naḥs* alerts us to another meaning for this word: Sa'id also means one who is possessed of *sa'd* (good omen), which is the contradictory of *naḥs* (bad omen). So now we have a character who exists in a state of complete contradiction. . . . Further, the Arabic word . . . *al-mutashā'il* is a neologism that creatively combines parts of the two words, *mutafā'il* (optimistic) and *mutashā'im* (pessimistic). . . . There is no sense of a hyphen in the Arabic word; it does not sound as if it is composed of parts of two words, but as one word in which the states of pessimism and optimism are perfectly intertwined' (2006: 41).

Kashua inscribes the complexity of the Palestinian identity in Israel, with pathos and onomastic insight, through the tragicomic scene of name giving affecting the protagonist's first-born son:

> Nadia (named after the Romanian Nadia Cumanchi, and winner of five gold medals), wife of my brother Sam (named after the Egyptian missiles in Yom Kippur War)[50] gave birth to the first male grandchild in the family. My father doesn't want the baby to be named for him. He says it would be a bad omen, and the baby doesn't look like him at all. My older brother is searching for a meaningful name. They thought of calling him Beisan (known now as Beith Shean in Israel). And Izz-a-Din Al-Qassam.[51] And Ché Guevara, and Nelson Mandela, and Castro, and Nasser, and Sabra.[52] They thought of calling him *Watan* (homeland), which was what my father wanted to call me originally. They thought of *ard*[53] and of Ayyar[54] because my brother Sam had been born on May Day and Mother had received a gift from the maternity hospital.
>
> Eventually they opted for the name my younger brother Mahmoud suggested and called the baby Danny. Mahmoud said this name would save the kid lots of trouble. Maybe he would be laughed at in the school in Tira[55] but he'd have it much easier at the university and at work and on the bus and in Tel Aviv. Danny was better.[56] (2004: 225–26)

The above excerpt is a good example of the importance of names and naming practises for creative writers, setting out how they can be used to talk about the nation in an oblique way. Although the description above is a fictitious one, it is not far from the truth. In fact, it offers an intimate ethnological account of name-giving practises among the Palestinians, the only deviation from these being the bestowal of the Jewish Hebrew name Danny (short for Daniel) on the newborn baby. By doing this, the Palestinians in Israel signal their difference from their compatriots elsewhere who avoid Hebrew Jewish names completely. In what follows, I will analyse the above excerpt to highlight the ways in which names can be linked to issues of identity and conflict in the Middle East.

First, the name bestowal described above is a male-dominated group act from which the mother and other females in the family seem to be excluded; all of the voices we hear are male voices. This is the case for two reasons. On

50 The 1973 war between the Arabs and Israel.

51 Afamous Palestinian hero in the struggle for Palestinian independence from the British mandate and after whom the Palestinian Iz-adin Al-Qassam Brigades are called.

52 A Palestinian refugee camp in Lebanon where more than two thousand Palestinians were massacred by the Lebanese Phalange, with active acquiescence and support from the Israeli occupying forces, in Beirut in 1982.

53 'Land' in Arabic, conjuring up images of the annual Palestinian Land Day celebrations (30 March) to protest the Israeli confiscation of Palestinian land.

54 The month of May in Arabic.

55 An Arab village in Israel.

56 I am very grateful to Manar Makhoul, one of my informants, for directing me to Sayed Kashua and his novel *Dancing Arabs*.

the one hand, since the newborn is a male, it is traditional for close male relatives on the father's side to play the leading role in choosing the name for him. On the other hand, because the new child is the first grandson in the family, choosing a name for him is treated very seriously, and the task, therefore, is reserved for the men in the family. Second, the grandfather asserts his traditional privilege to name the child after him, but he forgoes this to save the newborn from bad omen, the assumption in Palestinian naming mythology being that the ill fortune associated with the namesake's name will be visited upon its recipient through the name that has been bestowed on the newborn. The irony here is that it is the fact of being Palestinian—a people whose land has been literally taken from under their feet by Israel—that is the biggest piece of ill fortune haunting the grandfather. By not allowing his name to be bestowed on his grandson, the grandfather wants to save the newborn from inheriting the life of discrimination and ill fortune that, in Israel, is his lot as a Palestinian. Against this background, the bestowal of the name Danny on the newborn boy is not just an instrumentally driven decision, as Mahmoud suggests, but an act of sympathetic magic, of attempting to break the cycle of ill fortune afflicting the grandfather's family, in the hope that Danny the Palestinian would inherit part of the good fortune of his Israeli namesake. Third, the names of the family members in the excerpt are chosen to express their aspirations and hopes for liberation from Israeli rule (Sam),[57] to signal their Islamic identity and their traditional outlook (Mahmoud) and to express hope for some success in a recognisable and proud way (Nadia). Fourth, the suggestion of Palestinian (Izz-a-Din Al-Qassam), Arab (Nasser) and international names (Ché Guevara, Nelson Mandela and Castro) of people known for their leadership of liberation movements or for the fight against colonialism signals the belief among the Palestinians that their struggle is not just a local and regional affair but that it is also international, as befits the justice of a cause that embodies in one go the fight against occupation, imperialism and apartheid. Fifth, the suggestion to name the child after the town of Beisan (in Palestine) and the Sabra refugee camp (in Lebanon) is a commemorative act of remembrance that reminds the reader of Palestinian geography, the loss of Palestine and its bloody history and the oneness of the Palestinian experience; the massacre of Sabra is as alive for an Israeli Palestinian as it is for a Palestinian in the camps of Lebanon. This naming practice further reminds us of the use of toponyms among Palestinians as family names or cyber-monikers, as noted previously. Sixth, the suggestion to name the newborn baby boy Ayyar, after the month of May, reenacts similar practise among Muslim Palestinians and Arabs of naming a child after the day—exclusively Khamis (Thursday) and Jum'a (Friday)—or the month in which

57 'Sam' also reminds us of 'Uncle Sam' and 'Sam' in Arabic as the common ancestor of the Semites (Jews and Arabs), but these meanings are eschewed in the origin of the name as interpreted in *Dancing Arabs*.

he was born. But there is a twist in this suggestion. The Arabs use the months of the Muslim calendar (Rajab, Sha'ban and Ramadan),[58] not the Gregorian ones, to enact this naming convention. In addition, Ayyar (May) is indelibly etched in the Palestinian memory as the month in which Palestine was dismembered and Israel was created by the Jewish occupation of Palestinian lands in 1948. Because of this, Ayyar functions as a site of national remembrance for the Palestinians, just as Beisan and Sabra do. The association of Ayyar with May Day carries further meaning when linked to the names of Nasser, Ché Guevara, Nelson Mandela and Castro: it signals that the politics of the family are those of the left, nationally and internationally. Finally, the two names *waṭan* ('homeland') and *arḍ* ('land') stand out from the rest. On the one hand, these are common words, not proper names. Using them to name a child would, therefore, break the onomastic conventions of Palestinian society and render the name a source of laughter. On the other hand, considering the importance of land for the Palestinians in Israel and their strong desire for a homeland to call their own, these putative names are somehow more apposite than the others to describe the Palestinian experience of dispossession and loss. The fact the name givers are willing to consider bestowing these common words as proper names reveals the depth of their loss and dispossession.

Finally, the point comes in the naming process when Mahmoud, whose name is a cognate of the Prophet's name, suggests that the newborn boy would be better off with an Israeli Jewish name. Living in Israel and dealing with the national prejudice that routinely exists among Israeli Jews towards the Palestinian Arabs, Mahmoud believes that the price in ridicule at the local Arab school in Tira is well worth paying considering all of the benefits the name will bring the child in the future. The name Danny is chosen not for any wish to make the baby boy integrate into the dominant Israeli Jewish culture when he grows up but to enhance his life chances instrumentally, to make him onomastically more visibly Israeli and/or less visibly Palestinian Arab.[59]

At every point in the above analysis, the issue of national identity is relentlessly present. In this respect, the above narrative of the naming process provides an insider's view of the importance of names as signs of identity for the Palestinians and of the complex juggling acts the Palestinian name givers in Israel have to perform, and the variety of factors they have to take into consideration, before deciding on their final choice. It is as though the name givers in the above excerpt are not naming for themselves only but are treating the body of the new baby boy as an open parchment on which to inscribe the Palestinian national narrative on behalf of the whole community. In the end, the new baby boy is called Danny but not before he acquires all of the other names that are mentioned, including the name

58 For the use of Ramadan as a personal name, see Hasluck (1925).

59 It is worth repeating here that Daniel is one of the top boy names in Israeli birth statistics.

waṭan ('homeland'), whose links with patriotism (*waṭaniyya* and national identity) are very clear, and, additionally, the name *arḍ* ('land'), which is strongly associated with the Palestinians' experience of the Israeli expropriation of their land. It is in these names, in fact, that the baby boy belongs, but it is through the name Danny that he will have to live his life in a society that discriminates against the Palestinians and will do so against him as one. There is an irony in this, however, because, in spite of his name, Danny will always be an Arab to the Jews, as the novel makes clear: 'Once an Arab, always an Arab. For [the Jews] you will always be an Arab.'[60] The divide between Arab and Jew is categorical and unbridgeable, no matter what stratagem or ruse a Palestinian may employ: 'An Arab subject may desire what Jews desire, but he or she is never allowed to identify as a Jew; there is no possibility of assimilation for Arab citizens, because the very intelligibility of the ethnic landscape in Contemporary Israel (and thus the 'Jewishness' of the state) depends on maintaining the Arab-Jew divide' (Rottenberg 2008: 102).

The decision not to give the newborn an Arab name is not imposed on the family by some coercive state legislation but is the result of careful instrumental calculation on behalf of the family. In some national contexts, name giving can be enshrined in the official ideology of the state in a way that does not tolerate any signs of ethnic or subnational difference. Turkey provides a good example of this state-interventionist approach to name giving. The drive to adopt Turkish names began among Ottoman Turkists in the nineteenth century as a cultural tool in the construction of an Ottoman Turkish identity that is culturally non-Arab and non-Persian.[61] This orientation gathered pace after the establishment of the Republic in 1923 and after the 1934 law[62] that stipulated that every citizen of the state had to adopt a surname in the European sense and that this surname had to be identifiably Turkish (i.e., non-Arabic and non-Persian).[63] There are differences in the literature about what was considered a Turkish name, the rate at which the 1934 law was implemented in the different regions of the republic and the agents of onomastic change—whether those be the

60 Quoted in Rottenberg (2008: 102). Miriam Shlesinger's translation of *Dancing Arabs* (Kashua 2004) does not give the second sentence in this quotation.

61 The intellectual father of modern Turkish nationalism, Ziya Gökalp (1876–1924), invented his surname, which 'combines the name of the earliest Turkic empire, Gök (Türk), and a heroic title, Alp, given to Oğuz warriors' (Başgöz 1983: 207). For his nationalist thought, see Gökalp (1968).

62 For further information on this law, see Türköz (2007). See also Mardin (2002) for a discussion of name changes in Turkey.

63 In this connection, Schimmel writes: 'The first to receive one of the new family names was *Mustafa Kemal* himself, who was acclaimed on November 1934 *Atatürk*, which was intended to mean 'Father of the Turks,' and his descendents were to bear the name *Atadan*, 'From the father.' Atatürk himself selected a number of family names for his close friends, sometimes changing them several times' (1995: 80).

military or government employers—but the general force behind this law was no doubt connected with Atatürk's nation-building project, which aimed at modernisation, secularisation and the suppression and the final elimination of all subnational state identities. As Başgöz observes in his study of Turkish names: 'The change in personal names was probably the most successful component of the complex process of modernization introduced by bureaucrat intellectuals. The movement secularized the names by eliminating more than half of the Muslim appellations, turkicized [*sic*] the names by replacing the Arabic and Turkish lexicology in this area, and personalized the name by ending many traditional practices concerning the selection of names' (1983: 217).

The Turkicisation of names was accomplished through a variety of measures in which construction and the invention of traditions were the favourite tools in the nation-building project. Schimmel (1995) comments on how this process invoked the ancient Turkish ideals of bravery, the names of Turkish heroes who hailed from Central Asia, the Turkish names for the fauna and flora of the Turkish lands and other ad hoc strategies to create a new name pool for both first names and surnames. This process was strongly linked to an onomastic-hygiene movement, which set out to eliminate Arabic and Persian names; in some cases, this was achieved by treating the lexical meaning of an Arabic or Persian name as synonymous with the meaning of its lexically equivalent Turkish word, for example, replacing the Arabic name Amin or its Turkicised form Emin with Inal or Inan, whose roots in the two languages mean 'to believe.'

As in Israel, the adoption of Turkish names was strongly associated with a strident linguistic nationalism, which, in Turkey, encroached on the cultural rights of the Kurdish and Arab populations in society. In Hatay (Syrian Alexandretta, or *al-Iskandarūn* in Arabic), Arabs were forced to adopt Turkish names after the annexation of the region by Turkey in 1938, names often given to them by the official authorities. Some of these names were nonsensical. In eastern Turkey, Kurds were subjected to strong onomastic culls that prohibited the use of Kurdish names as personal names or as toponyms. This is how one Kurdish journalist from Turkey described the effect of this policy: 'As a Kurd in Turkey you are born in a village or town the name of which is not valid, because [the] names of nearly all Kurdish villages and towns I know are today changed into Turkish. . . . If your parents wish to give you a Kurdish name, your name will not be registered by the authorities. It will be changed into Turkish. If your parents still insist to keep your Kurdish name, they will be prosecuted and forced by a court to change your name into a non-Kurdish name' (cited in Skutnabb-Kangas and Bucak 1994: 378).

The brutal suppression of Kurdish and other non-Turkish names in Turkey springs from the understanding that names are an important marker of ethnic and national identity that maintain and feed difference at the substate level. The onomastic campaign of the new Turkish republic was, therefore, conceptualised by the ruling and cultural elites as an important measure in building the state and in moulding its citizenry into one nation with little or no onomastic difference between them along ethnic lines. Operating at the level of symbolic meaning, the new names had to signal a return to a pristine, uncontaminated past free of Arab and Persian linguistic interference, as well as to point to a future that looks towards the new values of a secular modernity. However, when applied in a heavy-handed way, onomastic hygiene measures backfire because of the sense of grievance that they generate among those who are subjected to them, in addition to the feelings of solidarity that this can produce from transnational organizations and NGOs. This is more or less what happened in Bulgaria when the authorities instituted a series of repressive linguistic measures between 1984 and 1990, banning the use of Turkish in public and requiring all Bulgarians of Turkish ethnicity to replace their Turkish family names with Bulgarian ones. As Rudin and Eminov point out, these measures turned Turkish in Bulgaria into a symbol of 'political defiance' for the Turkish Bulgarians, highlighting in the process its importance in preserving their cultural identity (1990: 161).

The importance of names as expressions of identity and their role in tracking conflicts in society are not restricted to Arabic names or the Arabic-speaking world. Hebrew and Turkish names carry similar symbolic loads. As linguistic material, names are important for reading the pulse of a group, as well as the long-term political currents that run through the fabric of its culture and social life. Name giving that responds to the context of the moment, such as Saddam or Rabin, may not represent the pulse of the nation but does capture some of its palpitations. The parading of names in a name-giving situation provides a window on the values, fears, aspirations and politics not just of the restricted circle that is directly involved in the situation in question but also of the wider group from which this circle is drawn. The use of names for what may be called 'national engineering,' as in Turkey, may constitute an extreme case of state action, but this action was most probably consistent with the nationalist spirit of the day, which affected all aspects of language and cultural production. In this case, hegemony from the top may, in fact, be affirming some strong currents from the bottom, rather than being used coercively against the masses. In Israel, the transition from the frequent adoption of new Hebrew names by Jewish immigrants in the first few decades of the state to the relaxation of this norm in the last two decades may reflect significant changes in society. It could be read as a sign of national confidence, as a relaxation in the power of the group over the individual or as indicative of a transition from the politics of emergency to a state of normalcy in the politics of the nation. Names, like other aspects of language, provide a link to society that politics has tended to ignore, in spite of the fact that they are impregnated with political content.

PERSONAL NAMES, IDENTITY AND THE DIASPORA

The diaspora poses new challenges to the immigrant and to the exile. Some immigrants relish their new environments because of their liberating potential, which offers them the scope to 'reinvent' themselves, signalling this in the adoption of new names. Other immigrants find the diaspora a source of anxiety and a challenge to their old identity; immigrants with this outlook tend to refuse to change their names, and they view the adoption of new ones among the immigrants from their community, even within their immediate family, negatively. Using Bourdieu's notion of habitus—which refers to the 'subjective but not individual system of internalized structures, schemes of perception, conception and action common to all members of the same group or class' (1977: 86)—we can say that the diaspora challenges the immigrants' old habitus, leading some into habitus-maintaining practises and others into practises that break defining contours in the old habitus as a first step towards creating new diasporic ones. In both cases, issues of identity are paramount, in that both the adoption of new names and the maintenance of the old ones constitute what may be called a 'buffer zone' between the old and the new environments.[64] For the name maintainers, the onomastic buffer zone is erected to protect the old Self from some of the 'dangerous' or 'corrosive' effects of the new environment whose impact is to weaken and, finally, cancel the relation with the prediaspora world. In the Arab diasporic context, this may be coupled with the wearing of the *hijab*, in its variant forms, for Muslim women and the wearing of beards for Muslim men. For the name changers, the main function of the onomastic buffer zone or border guard is to limit the influence of the old habitus and allow the dynamic of the new one to function more freely. The differences in onomastic attitude between the two categories may be generation-related, but more research would be needed to confirm this observation.

The diaspora becomes a particularly testing and challenging environment when the old and new cultures come into conflict with each other politically. For Arab-Americans, this has become the case since 11 September 2001. In some parts of Europe, Arab diasporas have been increasingly seen as members of a fifth column that cannot be trusted because of presumed Islamic sympathies. But even before the events of 2001 and the invasion of Iraq in 2003, some Arabs in the diaspora have found it to their advantage instrumentally and, to a lesser extent, integratively to adopt foreign or foreign-sounding names or to use nicknames as labels for their public personas. Schimmel comments on a similar phenomenon in North Africa as follows: 'A problem arises today over the change of Arabic names into European ones, as in the case of Tunisians or Algerians who want to conform to French custom and therefore adopt names that are similar in sound to the original, like *Belli* for *Ben 'Alī*, *Raymond* for *Raḥmān*, or are approximate translations of the Arabic meanings as in the case of Lucien for *Munīr*, both from the root 'light,' *lux* and *nār* respectively. The tendency of Muslims in Anglophone countries to replace *ad-dīn* by *Dean* is part of this trend' (1995: 73).

It is clear that for Schimmel, the adoption of foreign(-sounding) names at home and the acquisition of new ones in the diaspora are part of a continuum. If we accept this, we may say that, in principle, the diaspora mind-frame has

64 See Kim (2007) for a slightly different application of the notion of 'buffer zone.'

no boundaries: it can start at home, in what some call internal colonialism, and extend to the new immigrant environment. Thus, we would expect those who are more accommodating of foreign names at home to be more ready to adopt new names in the diaspora. Research on the Koreans in Canada seems to confirm that this would be the case (Kim 2007).

There is a dearth of data on the adoption of new names by Arabs in the diaspora. I am, therefore, forced to rely on anecdotal data, which, I suggest, could provide the broad contours of what detailed empirical and statistical studies may reveal for larger name pools. Some of these data will be in the form of self-reports to shed light on naming as a process. Taking the United States as an example, it seems that some early Arab immigrants adopted new names but that the number of those who did so declined in the 1960s as a result of the rise of the civil rights movement, which, as a by-product, gave immigrants, whose numbers were on the rise, a pride in their ethnic backgrounds. The adoption of new names, however, has been traditionally strong among Arab Christian immigrants, particularly the Maronites of Lebanon, who chose American first names and/or Americanised their family names; some statistics put this historically at about 85 per cent for this community.[65] The difference in the extent of name adoption between these Christians and other Arabs, mainly Muslims, is a reflection of the differences between them in religious identity, but it also reflects the continuation of a trend that had started for some Christian Arabs back at home, along the lines suggested by Schimmel, as described above. However, regardless of religious background, Arabs adopted the new names voluntarily, citing as reasons for this the difficulty of pronouncing their original, prediaspora names by members of the host culture and the belief that their life chances of participating in the socioeconomic benefits of the host society would be improved if they adopted American or Americanised names.

Although these reasons have a strong instrumental dimension, there is no doubt that some immigrants from the Arabic-speaking world do change their names—for example, the Maronite Christians—because of the strong affinity they feel with the host culture into which they want to integrate more fully.[66] As

65 See Almubayei (2007).

66 The picture is more complex than this statement suggests. 'Most Maronites felt extreme pressure to assimilate during the pre-1960s era in order to survive, be successful and accepted in US society. As the political climate shifted, especially with the white ethnic revival in the 1970s, it became more acceptable to retain "foreign" names. Lebanese Maronites in the United States today . . . do not tend to alter names as readily as the early twentieth century waves of immigrants. Also, most of the Ottoman-era Maronites [were illiterate] and had their names changed by state officials who phonetically spelled them on naturalization documents, and/or changed them to English sounding equivalents [see Ashton 1999 for a similar phenomenon in Canada]. . . . The older Maronite diaspora members feel quite bitter in some respects about the acceptability of "ethnic culture" in terms of naming and language retention, amongst immigrants in the United States today; they lament they had no option to do this, that it was more severe in the first half of the 20th century and that it was unacceptable to remain different. [These members] feel stuck because they are often accused of being "ethnic deniers" today by recent Arab arrivals in the U.S.' Amy Rowe, personal communication.

acts of habitus reorganisation, the adoption of new names, even when done voluntarily, is not, however, free of cost to individuals; it may, in fact, have an impact on their identity, on who they think they are and how others perceive them. On the one hand, the adoption of new names is sometimes met with disapproval, even hostility, by members of the diaspora community. Adopting a new name may be seen as an act of cultural betrayal, of deserting the ethnic/community ship for morally dubious socioeconomic advantages. One of my informants, a cousin who lives in Chicago, has often felt a sense of shame and reacted very disapprovingly when her sons used their American or Americanised names in front of me, although she was aware of the instrumental value of these names at work or in education.[67] Perhaps I reminded her very strongly of her prediaspora culture, with its strict onomastic values that treat name changes of the kind applied by her children as a cultural sell-out. On the other hand, some immigrants who adopt new diaspora names may feel a sense of loss of identity, of somehow becoming less of the persons they had been before they shed their old names. In this case, the adoption of a new name is experienced as subtraction or amputation, and this may, in fact, be how others experience it. I know this is how I felt towards my now-deceased brother (who lived in Austria for more than fifty years) when I knew he had adopted a German name, Karl, partly because of its similarity to his old name, Khalil, which his Austrian friends pronounced 'Kalil' and spelt 'Calil,' and partly as an attempt to blend in and integrate in his host environment. In my own mind, I felt that my brother's adopted name signalled for me a loosening in the bonds I had with him and that extra work was required from me to propel the relationship back to where it used to be.

Continuing this line of reasoning, the following story from the *Boston Globe* gives an excellent illustration of the effect that the adoption of a new name may have on the person who undergoes onomastic transformation:

> Mary Elizabeth Gray, [a] 43-year-old social worker, who was born in Turkey, changed her first name, Muhubet, which is pronounced 'MOO-hoo-bet' [*sic*].
>
> 'Nobody could pronounce it,' said Gray, a resident of Randolph. 'And it was a disadvantage for me, in advancing my career, and everything else.'
>
> She said that since Sept. 11, 2001, her given name has held her up, especially at airports, and subjected her to unwanted scrutiny. She said she was often called upon to defend Islam, even though she is not practicing.
>
> 'It is very amazing,' she said. 'They see my name, and no matter what passport I have, they ask where I come from, do I know about the Shia and the

67 This is similar to the case of a Chinese student, Sze Lun Wong, at Bunker Hill Community College in the United States, who changed her Chinese name to April when she was naturalised in 2006. 'Wong said her parents were unhappy she would no longer be known as Sze Lun, which means 'family support.' . . . In China, your name has meaning, and they wish it will be good for you for your whole life.' A Vietnamese man who was naturalised at the same time as Sze Lun Wong said he would not change his name: 'I don't think we have to sacrifice anything to be American, not even my name. . . . I absolutely feel that would be a loss, culturally, identity-wise.' See http://pqasb.pqarchiver.com/boston/access/1210748881.html?FMT=ABS&date=Feb+4%2C+2007.

Sunni [*sic*]. It was really becoming uncomfortable for me. You felt like you're defending yourself every single day.'

But since she changed her name, Gray hasn't felt quite right: Perhaps she gave up too much to fit in more easily, she said.

'I do regret it,' she said, explaining that she chose Mary Elizabeth because it came closest to her old name. 'I feel like that's not really me. I really want to continue the name my grandmother gave me.' She is now considering changing her name back.

'I should deal with it in a different way; I should ignore people,' she said. 'I should not just give up who I am.'[68]

This story provides an insight into how immigrants may react to the pressure created by international conflicts, which, as a result, may cause them to opt for radical measures in what may be called 'onomastic self-engineering' or 'onomastic surgery.' More important is that it further shows how such acts of onomastic engineering or surgery can have a negative effect on the way a person imagines himself or herself. In particular, instead of offering an additional dimension to a person's identity or supplanting an unwanted one, onomastic surgery may, in fact, be experienced as an act of self-mutilation, of identity subtraction rather than identity enhancement. This is precisely what happened to Muhubet when she became Mary Elizabeth. Ridden with feelings of guilt for having cut herself off from her old Self and all of the meanings that Self had held for her, Mary Elizabeth plans to undertake corrective and restorative onomastic surgery, but she is unlikely to be able go back to the person she thought she was before she underwent the first surgery.

The loss of identity through onomastic change in the diaspora may be recorded in literature, as in the following poem, 'Dying with the Wrong Name,' by American poet of Muslim Arab descent H. S. (Sam) Hamod. Hamod dedicates the poem to 'all the immigrants who lost their names at Ellis Island':[69]

These men died with the wrong names,
Na'aim Jezeeny, from the beautiful valley
of Jezzine, died as Nephew Sam,
Sine Hussein died without relatives and
because they cut away his last name
at Ellis Island, there was no way to trace
him back even to Lebanon, Im'a Brahim
had no other name than mother of Brahim,
even my own father lost his, went from
Hussein Hamode Subh' to Sam Hamod.
There is something lost in the blood,
something lost down to the bone
in the small changes. Aman in a

68 See ibid.
69 The poem is dated 1978–79. Hamod was born in Gary, Indiana, in 1934.

> dark blue suit at Ellis Island says, with
> tiredness and authority, 'You only need two
> names in America' and suddenly—as cleanly
> as the air, you've lost your name.[70]   At first, it's hardly
> even noticeable—and it's easier, you move
> about as an American—but looking back the loss of your name
> cuts away some other part,
> something unspeakable is lost. (in Orfalea and Elmusa 2000: 169–70)

This poem spells out what the *Boston Globe* story says, as well as how I felt about my brother's new German name, but does so with greater insight and elegance. Dying with the adopted diaspora name is dying with the wrong name, a name that fails to tell the full story of roots, heritage and the connection to the home country. Hamod describes the official view of the adaptation of prediaspora names to suit the host environment as a 'small change' that enables the immigrant to 'move about as an American.' In America, two names are sufficient to identify a person, the implication being that an Arab immigrant would benefit from subjecting the long chain that traditionally makes up his name to heavy pruning. Onomastic pruning and adaptation are officially presented and diasporically accepted as inconsequential matters that are 'hardly noticeable,' but in implementing them, the immigrant undergoes fundamental changes, which affect his very blood and soul. Looking back, the immigrant comes to experience the adaptations to his name as a loss that cannot be put into words, as a kind of amputation that disfigures him for good on the inside.[71]

70 The extra space after 'name' is in the original. I think it signals the boundary set between the prediaspora and the diaspora worlds as this is symbolised in the adoption of new diaspora names or the adaptation of the prediaspora names to fit into the immigrant's new environment.

71 The following comment from one of my American informants makes a number of interesting points about name adaptations and new-name adoptions among Arabs in the United States that relate to different parts of the discussion in this section: 'I have found that those who adopt English names in place of their Arabic names tend to be from the older generation and/or those who are from abroad (i.e., immigrants who were not born and raised in the United States). Either these individuals will adopt new names or alter their names to remove the "stigma" associated with their names or in an effort to assimilate (Muhammad as Mo, Usama as Sam). In addition, I think that names are linked to issues of identity and assimilation, and in the case of the United States, one must consider the history of Arab and Muslim immigration to the United States, where earlier waves of immigrants may have attempted assimilation more than later waves. I have noticed also that first-generation Muslim Americans tend actually to choose Arabic names for their children, especially after 9/11, when there was an increased affirmation of their Muslim identity. This goes for males and females, except that there are male names that are probably avoided now that were used before, such as Usama and Jihad.' The last comment is quite interesting because its helps shed light on the popularity of the name Muhammad among Muslims in the United Kingdom, as I will discuss below. I am grateful to Reem Hilal for this information.

As the story of Muhubet above suggests, the events of 11 September 2001 had a great impact on the relationship of Muslim and Arab immigrants with the host culture in the United States. Newspapers carried reports of Arabs wanting to change their names and of how some 'shaved [their] moustaches and beards in hope of being able to pass as Latinos,' a status that may not be so much better in the white-dominated, ruling U.S. culture.[72] The fact that name changes and the removal of facial hair, as acts of disguise or veiling, are concatenated together in the same sentence in this report underlines the link between the physical and the abstract dimensions of identity. Aname is more than a label; it identifies and marks the name bearer at one and the same time. As an 'element of culture,' names serve as signifiers in a politics of identity that acts with discrimination and prejudice against immigrants in the United States.[73] The existence of a heightened sense of discrimination against people with Arabic names in the United States is part of this politics of identity that is further linked to the crude concept of 'clash of civilizations.' In some cases, this politics is played out through coercion in the workplace by bestowing on an employee a name he refuses to accept, forcing the employee to resort to the courts to remedy the situation. For example, a judgement given by the Ninth Circuit Court on 21 July 2005 found in favour of an employee called Mammoth (Mahmoud?) El-Hakem against the CEO of BJY Inc., his employer, for repeatedly forcing on him a Western-sounding name which he rejected.[74] The judgement is based on the principle that names are markers of identity and that the imposition of a name on a person against his will constitutes an infringement of the right that person has to his personal, ethnic or national identity.

Because of their ability to signify symbolically beyond their root meanings and utilitarian function of indexation or individuation, Arabic names can become a site of ideological contestation in the diaspora, both interculturally and intraculturally.[75] The capacity of names to act in this way rises in proportion to their sociocultural load in a community. On 6 June 2007, the London

72 See http://www.iht.com/articles/2001/10/15/rislam_ed3_.php.

73 See http://blog.lib.umn.edu/ihrc/immigration/2007/02/whats_in_a_name.html.

74 The following is a report of the judgement: 'Rejecting the idea that ethnic harassment must be based on distinguishing physical characteristics, the Ninth Circuit recently upheld a jury verdict against an employer for a hostile work environment based on the company CEO's repeated insistence on Westernizing an Arabic employee's name. Claiming customers might find employee Mammoth (most probably Mahmoud) El-Hakem's name difficult to pronounce, the CEO began referring to El-Hakem by the nickname, Manny in marketing meetings and e-mails. El-Hakem repeatedly objected to the nickname. Although no other direct evidence of race discrimination was provided, the court held that frequent misuse of the employee's proper name was (1) sufficient to create a hostile work environment and (2) indicative of a discriminatory intent by favouring a Western name over an Arabic given name.'

75 One of my informants, Mohammed Sawaie of the University of Virginia, comments on naming in the United States among Arabs as follows, highlighting a number of the issues dealt with in this section:

> One perhaps can categorise Arabic naming into two groups: those who shift to Western names and those who keep their ethnic heritage [witness the fact that he

Times published an article proclaiming that Muhammad was the number 2 boy's name in the United Kingdom in 2006. The article was based on an analysis of the top three thousand names provided by the Office of National Statistics (ONS) for boys born in 2006. The ONS name table, in fact, ranked the name in its most popular form, Mohammed, as number 23, but the authors of the article, Helen Nugent and Nadia Menuhin, trawled through the corpus of names and recalculated the figures differently by treating the different forms and spellings of the name Muhammad as tokens of the same name, thus generating the following distribution figures as the basis for their new calculation: Mohammed 2,833, Muhammad 1,422, Mohammad 920, Muhammed 358, Mohamed 354, Mohamad 29, Mahmmed 18, Mohammod 13, Mahamed 12, Muhammod 9, Muhamad 7, Mohmmed 6, Mohamud 5 and Mohammud 5. The article ascribed these differences in the spellings of the name to differences in the ethnic and linguistic backgrounds of the name givers and to personal preference. This methodology of recalculating the

considers those who keep their ethnic names as keeping their heritage.] This cuts across religion in general. However, there is a tendency among Christian Arabs to adopt Western names more readily than Muslims. Yet I know personally a Lebanese Maronite friend who gave his children Arabic names, despite the fact that the mother carries a Western name, given to her originally in Lebanon. . . . Muslim [Arabs] may have different experiences. It is true that many continue to give their children Arabic/Islamic names: Mohammed, Ahmad, Sami, Hasan, etc. Those names get Americanised, depending on the individual, of course: Mohammed becomes Mo or Michael, Mustapha becomes Steve, Rabee‘ becomes Rob, Badee‘ becomes Bud, Randa becomes Rhonda and so on. I have a colleague whose son's name is Waleed, but the parents call him Will or Willy. When asked why, the mother said that his high school [friends] advised him to adopt this American name because one of the terrorists in 9/11 carried the name Waleed. As you can see, there is pressure not to be identified as foreigner—a tendency to be accepted, to assimilation. On the other hand, I have a good friend from Lebanon whose girlfriend (now his wife of more than twenty years) gave him the name Ed for Adeeb when they were dating. Came a time when Adeeb stopped this practise and insisted on using his original name. I also have an Egyptian friend (Muslim) who gave his sons Western names yet Arabic-sounding as well: Alex (short for Alexandria), Neal (the River Nile in Arabic) and Dean (as in Alaa' al-Deen or the other 'Deen' names in Arabic). I recently asked him about his children's names, and he turned religious, and he told me that these names are Arabic-sounding and [that they] all have [authentic] Arabic names. . . . Muslim names were not well recognised until recently, when some started to be more easily recognised. As an example, I cite my name [Mohammed]. When I first arrived in the [United States] and whenever I mentioned my name, the usual response was 'Oh, like Muhammad Ali.' The boxer was still recognised then and had made a name for himself. Now the boxer's name is not at all mentioned, and my name gets recognised easily. Some even ask if I write it with one *m* [Mohamed] or two [Mohammed] or with an *o* [Mohammed] or a *u* [Muhammed], etc. [Arabs] who are U.S.-born but with foreign-sounding names are often asked about their names: 'What ethnic background is this name? Oh, but your English is very advanced.' The questioner forgets that the addressee is born and raised in the [United States]. A sign of bias in a way.' (personal communication)

I am grateful to Mohammed Sawaie for this information.

name's popularity was a legitimate one, because all of the variants of the name in English would receive the same spelling in Arabic; this put Muhammad at number 2, with 5,991 names, after Jack, with 6928 names, on the list of popular names in 2006.[76] This ranking of the name Muhammad was thought to be remarkable owing to the fact that Muslims in Britain make up only 3 per cent of the total population.[77]

On the same day, both Al Jazeera and Al Arabiya, the two leading TV satellite news networks in the Arab world, published on their Web sites the gist of the *Times* story in Arabic without any editorial comment. All three news providers set up comment sections for their readers to post their opinions on the story. My data, collected over a period of three days (6 to 8 June 2007), consist of 61 comments on the *Times* story, 132 comments on the Al Jazeera story and 238 comments on the Al Arabiya story. The comments were exclusively in English for the *Times* story and almost completely in Arabic for the stories on the Al Jazeera and Al Arabiya Web sites. Judging from their names and addresses, the comment writers were from a variety of backgrounds: Arabs and Muslims from the Arab world and the diaspora, Christian Arabs and, for the *Times* story, a high percentage of contributors from outside the United Kingdom, including 13 from the United States.[78]

Central to the comments on all three Web sites are the symbolic connotations of the name Muhammad, which the contributors situated in the present turbulent times of interfaith and intercultural strife between the Muslim and the Arab worlds, on the one hand, and the West, on the other. These connotations split into two opposing camps: most of those on the *Times* Web site were negative in nature, disapproving of the name and its symbolic meanings, although a few—as an exception—highlighted certain positive attributes that they associated with the name Muhammad through the Prophet's character, such as honour, love, compassion, peace and integrity. However, accusations of fascism, anti-Semitism, homophobia, terrorism, violence, paedophilia, Satanism and antiwomen and anti-Christian feelings are strongly represented in the comments. The most hate-filled comments came from contributors

76 The most popular names for baby boys in 2006 were: (1) Jack 6,928, (2) Muhammad (all spellings) 5,991, (3) Thomas 5,921, (4) Joshua 5,808, (5) Oliver 5,208, (6) Harry 5,006, (7) James 4,783, (8) William 4,327, (9) Samuel 4,320, (10) Daniel 4,303, (11) Charlie 4,178, (12) Benjamin 3,778, (13) Joseph 3,755, (14) Callum 3,517, (15) George 3,386, (16) Jake 3,353, (17) Alfie 3,194, (18) Luke 3,108, (19) Matthew 3,043, (20) Ethan 3,020. See http://www.timesonline.co.uk/tol/news/uk/article1890354.ece.

77 The article provides further contextualising information: 'Overall, Muslims account for 3 per cent of the British population, about 1.5 million people. However, the Muslim birth rate is roughly three times higher than the non-Muslim one. Statistics from the ONS show that Muslim households are larger than those headed by someone of another religion. In 2001, the average size of a Muslim household was 3.8 people while a third contained more than five people. Additionally a man named Muhammad is most likely to be aged between 25 and 34 and to have an average salary of £25,000. The leading name for girls born to Muslim parents in 2006 was Aisha in 110th place. Its meaning is "wife of the prophet"' or "life."' See ibid.

78 This information may not be completely reliable, as comment writers may not provide correct names, religious backgrounds and countries of origin.

with U.S. addresses, and one U.K.-based contributor strongly contested them. These and other comments accused the British of being soft on the Muslims in their midst, and they spoke of a Britain that would soon be overrun and dominated by Islam and Muslims. I will cite some of these comments as they appear on the *Times* Web site, without any changes to illustrate their flavours (I have deleted the commenters' names but include their locations):

1.

> It's hard to believe that ANYONE in the 21st Century want to be named Muhammad—(or any of its other spellings). Since this is a public forum [the Web site], I can't post further comments about how I feel about Islam—except to say that I'm proud to NOT be a Muslim! (Alpine, USA-TX)

2.

> In my OPINION Muhammad was no Profet . . . he was profiteer who murdered on a grand scale, a thief who encouraged his followers to rob conquered villages after the slaughtering of innocent men, women and children and a pedifile who took a pre-pubescent 14 year old as his 'wife.' So why name your child 'Mohammed' when 'Lucifer' is so much more unique, available and religiously synonymous. (NY/NY, USA)

3.

> *Londinistan* by Mealanie Phillips[79] should be required reading for all British school children. You are one or two generations away from losing your British identity and forced conversion to Islam. (Cleveland, OHIO)

4.

> Just more evidence England and Europe is screwed! Move to the US and defend yourselves. (US, DC, USA)

5.

> As an immigrant to the UK, longing for freedom (not politically, but simply to live my life the way I like), I am planning to leave it once the 'muhamed' generation grows up.
>
> There must be somewhere on the planet where islam won't penetrate? Or will we have to fight for a place where we can avoid Muslims who don't respect you in the future?
>
> God is great! (London)

79 See Phillips (2006).

6.

> OK . . . Mohammed is the number two name for newborn boys in the UK. Here in California it's probably Jose or Miguel, and most likely No. 1, as Caucasians make only 43% of the population here. (Cottonwood, CA, USA)

7.

> All these comments from contributors in the USAand not one Native American name amongst them—oh I forgot you've ethnically cleansed most of them!!
>
> By the way we Brits feel safer here than amongst trigger-happy Americans. (Leicester, UK)

These comments reveal some of the negative symbolic meanings that the name Muhammad has in the West and the strength of the antipathy towards it. It is not possible to establish the extent to which these negative connotations are representative of the Western attitudes to the name Muhammad, but there is little doubt that these connotations relate to some hostile and deeply rooted feelings and views in Western culture concerning Islam and Muslims. The name Muhammad may, therefore, be said to have acquired the status of a motif with strong negative stereotypes that are hardly far from the surface of Western culture when thinking about Arabs and Muslims. Against this background, it is not surprising that some Arabs and Muslims who have this name may seek to replace it with another name, such as Michael, Mike or Mo, to achieve onomastic invisibility in the diaspora. One of the comments from a British contributor to the *Times* Web site points out that 'the emergence of Mo as a moniker [for Muhammad] among children will be a handy barometer for social integration [of Muslims in British society].' This is a revealing comment; it signals that even some of those who seem to be tolerant of the presence of Muslims in the United Kingdom would still prefer the moniker Mo to its full-fledged version Muhammad, treating the widespread use of the nickname as an informal measure of the extent to which Muslims have integrated into British society. Finally, comment 6 above about the names José and Miguel in California being synonymous with the name Muhammad symbolically, shows that the issue with the name Muhammad is one of racism and prejudice, which appear under different names, in different guises and in different contexts. The notion that Muhammad in the United Kingdom is the equivalent of José in California suggests that racism and prejudice respect no colour or creed. This onomastic equivalence between the two names further suggests that the negative connotations of a name are context-dependent: for the Californian, the immediate danger seems to be located around Miguel, not Muhammad, highlighting Mexican immigration as the main danger for this person before terrorism.

In contrast, the comments on the Al Jazeera and Al Arabiya Web sites read into the popularity of the name Muhammad in the United Kingdom very positive meanings. Expressing joy and pride in the popularity of the name (*laqad athlaja hadhā al-khabar ṣadrī*; 'this news has quenched my scorching thirst'), some of the comments reiterate, but from the opposite perspective, the comments made on the *Times* Web site, to the effect that Islam will eventually triumph in the United Kingdom and Europe, turning them into Muslim dominions. If some of those who commented on the *Times* story most negatively could read the comments on the two Arabic sites, they might feel justified in expressing alarm at the spread of Islam in the West. Some comments talk about raising the banner of Islam in the West (*raf' rāyat al-islām*), say that Islam is coming (*al-islām qādim*) and say that the popularity of the name Muhammad is an immeasurable achievement for a group of people who make up only 3 per cent of the total population of the United Kingdom. Some predict that a rise of 12 per cent in the popularity of the name in 2007 would take it to the top of the names table in the United Kingdom.

However, some comments reject this triumphalist attitude and draw attention to the principle of quality over quantity in interpreting the popularity of the name Muhammad. A few writers put forward the view that what matters is not how many Muhammads there are in the United Kingdom or the world generally but whether these newborn Muhammads in the United Kingdom will grow up to embody the virtues found in their namesake. One writer says that no matter how many Muhammads there were in the world in the twenty-first century, they would be worth nothing (*ṣifr*), because Jack, the most popular name in the ONS statistics, will have the upper hand in the economic and political sphere over all of the Muhammads, as well as over all of the newborns named after the three Rightly Guided Caliphs 'Umar, Abu Bakr and 'Ali. Playing the numbers game is the argument of the weak and defeated, they continue. Another writer asks his readers and Web interlocutors to point to a single person named Muhammad who is among the leading scientists in the modern world (*hal hunāk ism wāḥad min al-muktashifīn aw al-mukhtari'īn bi-ism Muḥammad*?). In the same vein, one writer says that what matters is how many of the Muhammads on the ONS list will grow up to be leading scientists, doctors, engineers or just plain useful citizens in British society, the idea being that even the lowest level of achievement—that of being a useful British citizen—may, in fact, be beyond the capabilities of these Muhammads (*al-muhimm kam wāḥad minhum mukhtari' aw ṭabīb aw muhandis aw mufīd li-mujtama'ih al-birīṭānī*?).

Two doctors at a hospital in London write to express their feelings of shame because of the abominable actions carried out in the name of Islam in the West and to say that some of those called Muhammad might prefer different names to avoid the stigma associated with Islam. Another writer expresses his dismay at the ONS statistics, saying that he does not want to have any Arabs in London; without them, he 'feels relaxed because he will not have to deal with the Arab drama queens (!) who drive him to despair' (*hunā bi-dūnihim al-ḥayā ḥilwa wa-relāx wa-mā fihā drāmā qwīn wa-lā aḥtāj aspirīn*). One writer expresses the hope that in spite of the popularity of the name Muhammad, 'London and Paris will not become like Kabul; that the British or Dutch Queen will not be forced to wear the veil; that Mulla 'Umar [leader of the Taliban] will not become the governor (*walī*) of Belgium and Rome; that Stockholm will not become a stage for [the Shia] celebrations of '*Āshūrā*'; and that Copenhagen will not become a place where the birth of the Prophet is publicly celebrated [as a national day, I presume].' The writer goes on to demand that all of the Muslims in the United Kingdom be deported to Saudi Arabia and Afghanistan, where they belong.

And while some writers celebrate the popularity of the name Muhammad, they use the occasion to express their disgust at those Arabs who call their children Bush, Blair, Judi, Sally and Elizabeth. One writer tells the story of a man in an unnamed Arab village (most probably a made-up one) who immigrated to the United States, came back with a daughter, whom he named Elizabeth and sent to the fields to milk the cows. Commenting on the discrepancy between the name and what the girl does—the idea being that the name and the work are 'out of sync'—the writer aims at 'taking the mickey' when he suggests that Waḍḥa would have been a better-fitting name for a girl milking cows (Waḍḥa is a name with strong pastoral or Bedouin connotations: *amma fi qarya wa-tiḥlib al-baqar wa-ismhā Elizabeth, mā tirkab, al-mafrūḍ yghayyir ismhā Waḍḥa*).[80]

Some of the comments on the two Arab Web sites are interesting because they conflate Arab with Muslim. Other contributors are aware of the difference between Arab and Muslim. One, in particular, borders on racism. A writer with a Saudi address reminds those who posted comments on the Al Arabiya Web site that the rise in the popularity of the name Muhammad was a non-Arab phenomenon; because of this, the Arabs should not be very proud of this popularity. He then adds, in a twist, that because of their ethnic background (mainly Pakistani) these newly named Muhammads will not live up to the expectations that these names place on them. This comment brought the Saudi-based writer rebuke from another contributor, who reminded him of the spirit of equality that Islam detects among all Muslims, regardless of their colour or ethnic background.

The above analysis of the three sites reveals a variety of responses and a set of points that are worth reiterating here: (1) the importance of names as markers of internally and externally generated identity; (2) the potency of names as symbols with contradictory meanings in intercultural relations; (3) the historical depth of the symbolic meanings of some names and the

80 Some Arabic names have ecological or regional flavour. For example, the male name 'Ajlan has a strong ecological (desert/Bedouin) flavour. Similarly, the female names Hissa, Lulwa, Shaykha and al-'Anud have a strong Gulf flavour. See Schimmel (1995) and Borg and Kressel (2001) for similar suggestions about the regional and ecological flavours of names, respectively.

continuity of the negative stereotypes they evoke; and (4) the ability of names to serve as ideological battlegrounds and as proxies for extraonomastic/linguistic attitudes in society, both intra- and interculturally. The last point is particularly important, because it reveals that when it comes to names, communities do not speak with one voice. Thus, by no means are all of those who are critical of the name Muhammad non-Muslim and non-Arab. Some are non-Arab Muslims and some are Muslim Arabs, although their criticisms tend to be different in content and in terms of invectiveness from those offered by the non-Muslims and the non-Arabs.

The question arises, however, about what factors lie behind the popularity of the name Muhammad in the diaspora considering the hostility towards Islam, the Muslims and the Arabs in the West. It is difficult to answer this question with certainty, but the following considerations may (have) come into play in choosing this name. First, wishing to mark the newborn baby boy as Muslim in identity terms, a Muslim name giver could not, for obvious reasons, choose a better name to achieve this goal. Second, for the Arabs and the Muslims, names express the hope and the aspiration that the newborn will grow up to emulate his namesake in character and deeds. Naming a child Muhammad, therefore, acts as a trust and as a responsibility, which the name bearer must honour and live up to; this is why a person who fails this test may be told that he was not deserving of his name or that the name was wasted on him (often expressed as *khsāra hal ism fih* in Levantine Arabic). Third, names can tie the immigrant to his prediaspora society, and no more so than when the chosen name is popular in this society, as is the case with Muhammad. Fourth, in conflict situations similar to those that exist between the Muslim world and the West these days, a name such as Muhammad may be chosen for its strong symbolic meanings as an act of cultural defiance and community resistance against racism and discrimination in the diaspora society. The aim here is not invisibility but visibility, not dissimulation or assimilation but dissimilation as an act of identity protection and preservation. Names here are thought to act as a barrier that stops leakage from the inside to the outside and as a border guard that signals the limits between the in-group and the out-group.

However, the naming process in the diaspora is not beholden to the above considerations only. It can be more complex and more inclusive of the prediaspora and diaspora worlds. I will try to set this out by looking at my experience as a name giver in exile/diaspora—in this case, the occasion of naming our first son. I must, however, add that I am not doing this for any self-indulgent reasons but to offer a firsthand, albeit retrospective, report of the naming process as it unfolds in the diaspora. Also, I hope this foray into the personal and the subjective domain of the researcher, of turning the investigator into the subject of analysis, will encourage others in Middle Eastern studies to do the same, as I have set out in chapter 2. There is, therefore, a methodological dimension to the discussion below, which is part and parcel of my discussion of linguistic autoethnography in chapter 3.

Rejecting the social expectation of naming my first son Ibrahim, after his paternal grandfather, was not an easy decision, not least because I always looked up to my father. Also, my family back in the Middle East expected me to bestow this name on my first son, because my older brother Khalil, whom I mentioned above, never had children. The family must have reasoned that the name Ibrahim could not, therefore, be reserved for Khalil's use, and it would, if left that way, wither and die. I never told members of my family that my brother, who lived most of his adult life in Austria, adopted the name Karl, but had I done so, they would have thought that this was another proof of why Khalil was not onomastically trustworthy: he would have squandered a family heirloom as he had done with his name, the very name that Ibrahim gave him following an established Arab custom of calling a man named Ibrahim by the teknonym Abu Khalil in commemoration of the Prophet Abraham, called 'God's friend' in Arabic (Ibrahim al-Khalil). These were strong moral arguments; they are to do with continuity, with binding my son and myself through a recurring name to our common roots—in short, with identity. The family must have reasoned that this was very important because of the need to link us in the diaspora onomastically with them in our place of origin. After all, geographical distance, let alone cultural distance, can cause social drift. What the family wanted was as much maintenance of the onomastic habitus as possible. But these considerations had to be balanced against other considerations: my desire to give my son a fresh onomastic start, as I had done that myself twice through shifts between my two first names in the diaspora.

I have a compound first name (*ism murakkab*) consisting of two parts: Muhammad (and this has a long story behind it) and Yasir. Before coming to the United Kingdom to study in the 1970s, I was always known as Yasir to my family and friends. In fact, it was not until the fifth grade, back in Palestine, that I discovered that I had two first names. One of the first things I did when I arrived in Britain in the mid-1970s was to stop using the name Yasir and start introducing myself as Muhammad to fellow students, teachers and acquaintances, although it was not easy to get used to the new name. But I remember that I did this at the time to signal to myself onomastically that I was a new person and that I could be whoever I wanted to be, but I never thought of anglicising my name or choosing an English moniker. I wanted a change, but I wanted it to be limited and authentic. My pride in my roots and my home culture was and still is too strong and important for me to go that far. So Muhammad I became.

But Muhammad started to die in 1982, and, like a phoenix, Yasir rose out of the ashes the same year. This was the year when Israel invaded Lebanon, surrounded Beirut, bombarded it day and night and then aided and abetted the Lebanese Phalange in the massacre of thousands of innocent Palestinians at Sabra and Shatila. Although I denied it at the time, the fact that the second part of my first name was the same as that of Yasser Arafat—the PLO leader who, in fact, I never liked or admired, hence the difference in spelling between our names—must have been an important consideration in my decision to do an onomastic U-turn. Retreating from Muhammad and returning to Yasir was a return to an old identity site and an assertion of my Palestinian-ness, a symbolic act of resistance from afar in St. Andrews, a small university town on the east coast of Scotland. However, names, like running water, do not stand still; this is why the Muhubet to which Mary Elizabeth (of the *Boston Globe* article) may return will not be the same Muhubet that was shed. The Yasir I returned to was not the same as the Yasir I had left behind when I first came to the United Kingdom. The new Yasir was an amalgam, a kind of a portmanteau of the Yasir of old and the Muhammad that had ceased to exist.

Returning to the subject of our first son, my wife suggested calling him Ramsey (Arabic Ramzi), but I was not happy with this name. I was concerned that the spelling of the name would turn it into an English name rather than an English spelling of an Arabic name. I was obviously concerned about the identity implications of the English spelling for how my son may grow up to think of himself in identity terms. I hoped he would grow up with feelings of belonging towards our host culture but that he would also retain strong roots in our home culture. Ramsey, spelt this way, tipped the balance in favour of the host culture. The alternative spelling (Ramzi) would have been aberrant for a name with an established English spelling. This fact further militated against choosing this name.

We then thought of calling our first son Taym, after the name of an Arabian tribe. This name contained none of the guttural or pharyngeal sounds that make some Arabic names sound so glaringly foreign and difficult to pronounce. This was an important consideration for us in the diaspora. But on Scottish tongues, the name would sound like the Scottish pronunciation of the word *time*, thus opening up the possibility of onomastic ridicule, which could turn the name into too much of a cross to bear for our son. The search was on!

And so Tamir it was (with long *a* and short *i*). We chose this name for a variety of reasons. First, it lacked any of the Arabic sounds that would make it hard for a non-Arab to pronounce, although we later discovered that we did not pay enough attention to the difference in stress patterns between Arabic and English: in Arabic, the name is pronounced 'Tamir' (with a long *a*), whereas the English rendering of the name tends to be 'Tamir' (with a long *i*). Second, Tamir is not a popular or common name, giving it an element of uniqueness, this being an important attribute in Arab naming practices in recent times, as has been suggested earlier. It is more of an individuating than a deindividuating name. Like most parents, we thought of our son as unique and, therefore, deserving of a unique name. Third, the name has a meaning (to do with palm dates), but these meanings do not come through the name very strongly, giving it a broad range of signification and onomastic flexibility. Fourth, I, more than my wife, liked the name because it sounded both Arabic and Semitic; witness the existence of the name in Hebrew name pools.[81] In this connection, I reasoned that because

81 Tamir, pronounced 'Tameer,' means 'strong and tall' in Hebrew.

the name is Arabic and Semitic, it must, therefore, be pre-Islamic. This was an important consideration for me, because I did not want to give my son a recognisably Islamic name, not because of any reservations I had about Islam but because of my heated debates with the Islamists who, I thought (and still think), are doctrinally and socially blinkered, as well as extremely retrograde in their outlook on life. In this respect, I was treating my son as a parchment on which I wanted to record bits of my personal experience and some of my ideological orientations. Finally, and most important, as parents, we both liked the name because it allowed Tamir to negotiate his own identity. He could be the Palestinian Arab Tamir if he wanted to; but when the name was shortened to Tam, he could still be an Arab (through the meaning of 'perfection' associated with the Arabic word *tāmm*), but he could also be a Scottish Tam (I spent most of my adult life in my U.K. exile in Scotland). And the fact that I had the highest regard for the Scottish Westminster MP Tam Dalyel, who in his last stint as MP became the Father of the House of Commons, was a great fillip. The fact that Tam Dalyel was sympathetic to national liberation struggles, including the Palestinian cause, was no doubt a strong factor in thinking positively about our final name choice.

I started this section by talking about the opportunities and challenges of the diaspora and how these interact to create a dynamic of continuity and change in identity construction, in terms of either habitus maintenance or habitus redefinition. The story of my own name journey provides an example of how these impulses of continuity and change are subject to the contexts against which they unfold. My own personal journey from Yasir to Muhammad and back to Yasir is full of identity-linked meanings. These meanings had to do with where I wanted to locate myself in identity terms in respect to the two nodes that frame my person: the Palestinian or Arab node and the diasporic or exilic one. In particular, the issue for me was which accent I wanted to accentuate in my identity: the diasporic and exilic, which was linked with Muhammad, or the prediasporic and Palestinian, which I linked with Yasir. The words *accent* and *accentuate* in the preceding sentence are meant to suggest that the two dimensions of my identity do not exist in an either/or configuration but are constituents in a both/and amalgam. I have delved into these personal memories here to highlight the point that although identities have a strong group meaning, they are nevertheless experienced at the level of the individual. This explains my interest in the Self here.

My son's name provides another example of the interaction of the old and the new cultures in identity construction in the diaspora/exile. Tamir could not be Ibrahim, because he had to be himself and not a throwback to his paternal grandfather. Tamir could not be Ramsey, because Arabness had to be important to who he is. Tamir could not be Taym because of the need to eliminate the ridicule factor. So the boy who might have been Ibrahim, Ramsey or Taym in the end became Tamir, because his parents wanted him to be unique, and they wanted him to use the flexibility of his name to fit comfortably into the two cultures (the prediasporic and the diasporic) that they hoped would express his identity. It is not just the names we choose that are important in the naming process but also those we discount, as I have suggested above in my analysis of the naming scene in Sayed Kashua's *Dancing Arabs*. And at every onomastic turn in bestowing a name, issues of identity are always in the background. Choosing Tamir as Tamir's name was a matter of identity negotiation done by his parents on his behalf, so that Tamir would grow up with an onomastic platform from which he could make his own identity choices. A name is for life, not for the Eid or Christmas. It has to signify and symbolise, and it needs to do so in ways that can encompass a life's major identity currents. These considerations are always important in name bestowal, but they become particularly important in the diaspora and exile (see Heinze 2007: 192).

PERSONAL NAMES, IDENTITY AND SOCIOPOLITICAL HISTORY

In the Middle Eastern context, names can be a useful tool in the study of social and political history. Using first names as data, Richard Bulliet (1979), a social historian of the Middle East, was able to study conversion to Islam and the emergence of a Muslim society in Iran in the first four centuries of the Islamic era.[82] Using a corpus of 6,500 'patrician class' biographies for the two cities of Nishapur and Isfahan, culled from three biographical dictionaries, Bulliet establishes a number of naming trends in Iran and tries to correlate these with their sociopolitical contexts. While initially Arabic names were used by new Iranian converts to Islam to signal their status as *mawali* (non-Arab Muslims), this trend later gave way to the use of Qur'anic/Old Testament names—for example, Sulayman, Dawud, Yusuf, Ya'qub—which had the great value of ranging over a wide terrain of identity signification. These names did not pinpoint the exact religious background of the name bearer, allowing the person concerned greater scope for social and economic mobility in society. However, as Islam took root and was no longer in competition with Christianity and Judaism, the use of names with equivocal religious connotations started to fall out of favour. A trend, therefore, developed whereby Islamic names started to be adopted on a large scale, in particular Muhammad, Ahmad, 'Ali, al-Hasan and al-Husayn. However, the newfound confidence in Iranian culture in the eleventh century led to the emergence of traditional Persian names, such as Rustam and Isfandiyar, 'names that few Iranian Muslims had dared give their sons [earlier]' (Bulliet 1979: 47).

This case study shows how useful names can be in detecting the social and political movements in society, for although it is a matter of faith,

82 See Roff (2007) for the use of Muslim (Arab) names in the Malay Muslim World.

conversion to Islam is impregnated with sociopolitical meanings from which identity is never absent. In another study, this time from Turkey, Bulliet (1978) uses the first names of the members of Parliament in the Ottoman Empire and the Republic of Turkey between 1828 and 1967 to establish the political trends in society during this period. He does this by studying the popularity of the Arabo-Muslim names Mehmet (Arabic Muhammad), Ahmet (Arabic Ahmad) and Ali in the Parliament, identifying the following trends: (1) between 1828 and 1889, the popularity of the three names dropped from a peak of 33 per cent in 1840 to less than 10 per cent in 1889, owing to the modernising and secularising onslaught of the *tanzimat*; (2) between 1895 and 1899, these names recovered in popularity in a way that coincided with the brief Islamic revival movement spearheaded by Sultan Abdülhamit II; (3) between 1905 and 1909, the names reached their lowest popularity point, in line with the strident modernising tendencies of the Young Turks who were in political ascendance at the time; (4) between 1910 and 1924, the three names started to recover in popularity, in a way that coincided with the Balkan Wars, the outbreak of World War I and the war against Greece, particularly the last named, suggesting that these crises were felt as an attack against the Islamic character of the country; and (5) following the establishment of the Turkish republic as a secular state in 1924, the popularity of the three names started to drop, reaching a low point of 12 per cent in 1967. The downward trend in the popularity of the names Mehmet, Ahmet and Ali was accompanied by a meteoric rise in the popularity of indigenous Turkish names, which had risen from 8 per cent between 1910 and 1914 to 32 per cent between 1925 and 1929 and then to 65 per cent in the period between 1930 and 1941.

Statistical studies of the type conducted by Bulliet show the kinds of uses to which names can be put in tracking sociopolitical changes in society. Habibi (1992) follows this line of investigation in his study of names before and after the Islamic revolution in Iran in 1979. Studying personal names in the city of Hamadan, in midwestern Iran, between 1963 and 1988, Habibi correlates the rise in the popularity of Persian names—against Islamic and Arabic names—in the city to the secularising and modernising tendencies of the White Revolution, which the Shah regime launched in 1963. However, as this policy started to run out of steam and to meet with opposition from the landed class and other disaffected groups in the country, the city experienced a rise in Islamic female names between 1973 and 1979. This trend was later reversed in favour of Persian names between 1983 and 1985. Habibi correlates this with the Iran-Iraq war, when the Islamic names reached their lowest levels.

These fluctuations have great suggestive power when correlated with the sociopolitics of Iran in the period under study; they indicate that names are intimately linked with their sociopolitical contexts. The naming trends in Hamadan suggest that as a social phenomenon, names are sensitive to the changes in their political environment. They act, in this way, as barometers that read the sociopolitical 'mood' of a population. Read in this way, names may be conceptualised as early-warning sites that carry important sociopolitical meanings to those in power. Or, as has been said earlier, names provide a good indication of the sociopolitical pulse of a population and its palpitations. States that fail to read these signals do so at their peril, as the Shah of Iran seems to have done before he was overthrown by Khomeini in 1979.

TOPONYMS, IDENTITY AND CONFLICT

In *A War of Words: Language and Conflict in the Middle East* (Suleiman 2004b: 159–204), I dealt at length with the conflict over toponyms in historical Palestine between the Palestinians and the (Israeli) Jews before and after the establishment of the state of Israel. This conflict is linked to the larger conflict over the symbolic resources of the two communities, especially 'language,' in which names and naming are important features. In this section, I will outline the main contours of the conflict over toponyms in the Israeli-Palestinian dispute as discussed in *A War of Words*, adding new information and incorporating material from recent research on Egypt. Issues of identity, conflict and modernisation will be highlighted here to link the world of toponyms to similar issues in personal names, as these have been dealt with above.

Like personal names, toponyms serve the mundane function of marking the objects they refer to from others in the same class; but they also carry political meanings that come fully into play in situations of heightened conflict or at times of sociopolitical upheaval in society. In these situations, the instrumentality of toponyms gives way to their ability to carry ideological meanings by signalling the transition from one regime to another or the sudden shifts from one political order to another. As proxies, toponyms can be used to express opposition and resistance to the established political order in subtle yet unmistakable ways that can circumvent censorship and challenge in one way or another the coercive power of the state. This is particularly true in respect of commemorative toponyms regardless of their referents, whether they are streets, avenues, alleyways, public squares, buildings, cities, towns, bridges, universities, schools, public parks, forests, nature reserves and so on.

Examples of these practises abound in history. The change from St. Petersburg (1703) to Petrograd (1914) to Leningrad (1924) and back to St. Petersburg (1991) may be an extreme example, but each of these changes was first and foremost a form of political action intended to signal a change in the political order. Suggestions for name changes in autocratic or closed societies are sometimes used to test the political ground, as was the practise in the late Soviet Union (Murray 2000). In Iraq, the large Shia-dominated slums on the outskirts of Baghdad were brought under one name, Madinat al-Thawra, by the new republic in 1958. This name was changed to Madinat Saddam in the early 1980s to stamp the authority of the new Sunni-dominated regime on this part of the city. In 2003, following the American-led invasion of Iraq and the fall of Saddam, this quarter acquired the name Madinat al-Sadr to commemorate the memory of Ayatullah Muhammad Sadiq al-Sadr, who was assassinated by Saddam's Ba'thist regime in 1999.[83] Most of the changes in the names of countries in Africa in the twentieth century were occasioned by the end of colonialism and the emergence of the postcolonial nation-states, for example, Djibouti instead of French Somaliland or Ghana instead of Gold Coast. In 1935, Persia changed its name to Iran to forge a closer link with Europe through its claim of being the birthplace of the Aryan race.[84] The dismemberment of Palestine in 1948 resulted in the creation of three names to designate the territory: Israel, West Bank (annexed to Jordan) and Gaza Strip (under Egyptian control).

In Egypt, changes in place names after the 1952 revolution were politically driven, and they affected streets, squares, bridges and institutions, with the aim of constructing a new national narrative. These changes were intended to eliminate the memory of the monarchy from public spaces and to signal a new beginning with new republican values. In his study of central Cairo, Meital gives a list of place-name changes, the most significant of which was the replacement of *Maydan al-Isma'iliyya* (after the Khedive Isma'il who ordered the construction of modern Cairo) as the name of the main square in the city with *Maydan al-Tahrir* ('liberation') to signal the end of the monarchy and the European postcolonial influence on the life of Egypt (a phenomenon repeated in Iraq in 1958 to mark the replacement of the monarchy with the new republic under Qassim):

Pre-1952	*Post-1952*
Muhammad 'Ali	al-Qal'a
Ibrahim	al-Jumhuriyya
Jami'at Ibrahim	Jami'at 'Ain Shams
Sulayman Basha	Tal'at Harb
Maydan Sulayman Basha	Maydan Tal'at Harb
Tawfiq	Ahmad 'Urabi
Maydan al-Tawfiq	Maydan Ahmad 'Urabi

83 See Zeidel (2006: 208–9).

84 The Persianisation campaign in the 1930s in modern-day Iran aimed at purifying Persian of Arabic and Turkish words, imitating in this respect Mutafa Kemal Atatürk's campaign in the Turkish Republic. In 1934, a congress celebrating the millennial anniversary of Ferdowsi, the Iranian epic poet and author of *Shahnameh*, was planned. 'The preparations for the Congress of Ferdowsi took place at a time when Hitler, who had already become the German Chancellor in January 1933, proclaimed himself the Fuhrer following the death of President Hindenburg on 2 August 1934. Greatly affected by the events in Germany and the Nazi ideology which emphasized the superiority of the 'Aryan race,' the Iranian legation in Berlin suggested to the Persian foreign ministry in Tehran that since Iran was considered to be the birthplace and the original homeland of the Aryan race, the name of the country be changed from Persia to Iran. Reza Shah accepted the suggestion, and the Iranian government announced to the world community on the last day of 1934 that starting on 1 January 1935, the official name of the country would be changed from Persia to Iran (see Kia 1998: 21).

Isma'il	al-Tahrir
Maydan al-Isma'iliyya	Maydan al-Tahrir
Fu'ad	26 Yulyu
Jami'at Fu'ad	Jami'at al-Qahira
al-Malika Nazli	Ramsis
Faruq	al-Jaysh (Meital 2007: 869)

Returning to historical Palestine, toponymy was used by Israel as an arena for erasing from the territories that came under its control as many Arab names as possible.[85] This onomastic erasure followed hot on the heels of the depopulation of many cities and villages of their Arab residents, thus offering the new state a canvas on which to inscribe its own national identity as a Hebrew-speaking, Jewish-dominated country through the use of Hebrew toponyms. Within a decade or so of the establishment of the state, many Arab names disappeared off the map, the only exception being the names of the populated Arab villages[86] that remained within the borders of the new state.[87] But even here, some of these villages had their main streets named after Zionist leaders, some of whom are of the Arabophobic, far-right political spectrum.[88] Some of the Hebrew toponyms were chosen because they had a phonetic/semantic resemblance to these elided names, but others were selected to express the ideology of the new state. Thus, some toponyms were selected to express the rootedness of the new nation in the biblical past or its connection with the land, using in this regard the Hebrew names of the native flora and fauna to designate new towns and streets. Other toponyms were chosen to commemorate some of the leaders of the Zionist movement and its fallen heroes, as well as to acknowledge the

85 See Benvenisti (2000) for a fascinating discussion of this topic.

86 The names of some of these villages were Hebraised; for example, the Arab village (now town) of Shafa'amr in northern Israel has been rendered as Shfar'am. The same is true of villages beginning with the name Kafr, such as Kafr Qar' and Kafr Yasif, whose first name has been Hebraised as Kfar ('village' in Hebrew).

87 In Haifa, 50 per cent of Arab street names were replaced by Hebrew names in the first decade of the Israeli rule, but only six streets were given Arabic names since the establishment of Israel in 1948. Before this date, the city was petitioned by Arabs and Jews to allocate ethnic/national names to streets. Among the Arab population of the city there existed intraethnic rivalries among the notables of the city to have streets named after them. For more information on the battle of street names in Haifa, see Mansur (1999).

88 Zeidel gives two examples of this practice: 'The main street of Baqa al-Gharbiyya, an Arab town in the Triangle region in the Middle of Israel, is called "Hanasi Weitzman" (President Weitzman) after the first Jewish president of the state. The main street of Arab al-Hib, a Bedouin village in the north, is called Rehav'am Zeevi after a Jewish politician of the extreme right who advocated transferring [deporting] all the Arabs from Israel' (2006: 210). Zeevi exempted the Druze and the Bedouins from this plan because of their loyalty to the state.

role some non-Jews played in the creation of the state and in its continued survival.

In the summer of 2009, Yisrael Katz, the transport minister in the newly formed Likud-led government of Benjamin Netanyahu decided to replace existing road signs in Israel with new ones, 'so that all the names appearing on them in English and Arabic would be a direct transliteration of [their] Hebrew [names],' instead of being directly in English and Arabic.[89] Under this new policy initiative, the name of the city of Jerusalem would appear as Yerushalayim in English and Arabic, replacing the English and Arabic names Jerusalem and Al-Quds, respectively, in spite of the fact that Arab East Jerusalem is an occupied territory under international law. Nazareth (an Arab city in Israel), which appears under its English and Arabic names (*Nāṣira* in Arabic) on existing road signs, would under the new policy initiative be rendered as Natsrat in these two languages to reflect the Hebrew rendition of its name. The official reason for this initiative is said to be to eliminate the variations in place names, which are a 'problem for those speaking foreign languages, citizens and tourists alike,' in conformity with practise in many countries around the world.[90] The proposed name changes are further presented, albeit implicitly, as formal in nature, because they touch only on the shape of those names, their transliterations in Arabic and English, rather than on their substance. The proposal does not call for the elimination of Arabic and English from the linguistic landscape; it demands only that the Arabic and English letters on the road signs reflect the form of the names in Hebrew.

On the face of it, this policy initiative makes perfect sense on grounds of functionality: it creates uniformity in place of diversity, which is a legitimate policy objective for any government to pursue. Instead of having many different names for a place, each place will now receive the same name and will be rendered in three scripts: Hebrew, Arabic and English. This reading of the policy initiative is, however, undermined by its symbolic, ideology-impregnated meaning, which seeks to erase an aspect of the Palestinian memory of place and history. This is evident from the following gloss on the decision, offered by the transport minister: 'Almost all Israeli communities' names have previous names. Some Palestinian maps still refer to the Israeli cities by their pre-1948 names, since they see them as settlements. I will not allow that on our signs. This government, and certainly this minister, will not allow anyone to turn Jewish Jerusalem to Palestinian al-Quds. We will continue to serve the Arab public and have signs in Arabic. The names on the signs should reflect the reality of the local population, which is exactly why Israel signs must have Hebrew transliteration.'[91]

89 See http://www.ynetnews.com/articles/0,7340,L-3745563,00.html (accessed on 25 August 2009).

90 Ibid.

91 Ibid.

The above quotation reveals clearly that politics is a major factor behind this policy initiative. In fact, we could go further and say that politics is the *real* substance of this policy initiative. First, this is reflected in a statement by Barak Sari, Yisrael Kat's communication advisor, who considers those who oppose the initiative (Jews and Arabs) to 'represent a fringe minority which is willing to accept attempts by anti-Israeli and anti-Zionist elements to annul Israel's identity as a Jewish and democratic state. Anyone willing to refer to Jerusalem as al-Quds [its Arab name] on official State signs is collaborating with the Palestinian propaganda which does not recognize post-1948 Jewish communities and still demands they be called by their Arab names.'[92]

Second, the political nature of the new policy is also reflected in a subtle way in the response of the Israeli minister of minority affairs (which is synonymous with Arab/Palestinian affairs in Israel), Avishay Braverman, who criticised the decision by saying that 'road signs are not a political issue,' supporting his criticism with the statement that 'Arabic is an official language in the state of Israel.'[93] But even this criticism smacks of tokenism. It does not oppose the policy initiative outright; in fact, it seems to acquiesce to it. This is clear from what the minister of minority affairs says on this matter: 'I suggest that, instead of changing the road signs Katz should place street signs in the Arab villages. Even in 2009 most of these villages do not have such signs.'[94] In this statement, Braverman carries out a balancing act: he strikes out on behalf of the Arab/Palestinian minority in Israel, arguing (a) that they are in need of street signs in their communities and (b) that providing these street signs must take precedence over Katz's new policy but (c) significantly for our purposes, he does not reject Katz's policy outright. On the last issue, he remains silent, when, in fact, as we shall see below, the Arab reaction in Israel was for the rejection of this policy, not the provision of street signs in their communities.

In addition, Braverman's reference to the 'status of Arabic as an official language in Israel' reveals his awareness of the political implications of Katz's policy initiative. This status is a hotly debated issue in right-wing Israeli politics. Some want to revoke this status of the language on grounds that Israel is a Jewish state. In this context, Braverman's reference to the official status of Arabic may be read in two ways. On the one hand, it may be intended to assuage the concerns of the Arabs who fear that the intentions of the present government in this regard. On the other hand, it may be

92 Ibid.

93 Ibid.

94 The published version of this reads as follows: 'I would suggest that Minister Katz place much-needed street signs in Arab communities before he changes road signs.' I am grateful to Yoni Mendel for pointing out that this translation is not entirely accurate and for providing a translation of the original that better reflects Avishay Braverman's position. For the original story in Hebrew, see http://www.ynet.co.il/articles/1,7340,L-3745579,00.html (accessed 15 September 2009).

taken to signal that even if Katz's policy initiative were to be implemented, Arabic would not disappear off the new road signs simply because these signs would still carry the transliterated Hebrew names in Arabic characters, thus preserving the official status of the language. The second reading seems to negate the first. According to this second reading, any fears the Arabs may have about the status of Arabic as an official language in Israel (see below) would not be justified, because Arabic would still be part of the new road signs, albeit as a transliteration of Hebrew material. Either way, the political nature of Braverman's statement is very clear. Even when the minister of minority affairs tries to take politics out of the road signs, he cannot help but fall back on politics in articulating his views. He does this by invoking the politically charged issue of the status of Arabic as an official language in Israel.

Third, a contextual reading of Katz's policy initiative reveals its political nature. The new Israeli government has made the resumption of peace talks with the Palestinian National Authority conditional on its recognition of Israel as a Jewish state. In Israel, there is a strong move—which may be turned into a government policy in the future—to require every citizen, including its Palestinian minority, to swear allegiance to Israel as a Jewish state. This is coupled with strong demands to outlaw any acts of remembrance of the 1948 Palestinian *nakba*, treating these acts as a denial of the Jewishness of the state of Israel—in effect, as acts of treason punishable by the withdrawal of Israeli citizenship. These positions in Israeli politics are intended to counter the Palestinians' demand for the right of return. Katz's policy initiative and the various attempts to strip Arabic in Israel of its official status are part and parcel of the insistence on the exclusive Jewishness of Israel. The new road signs are, therefore, meant to enact this Jewishness in political terms in the public sphere. I would argue that it is the politics of the linguistic landscape, rather than its functionality, that is at stake in Katz's policy initiative.[95]

Fourth, the Palestinians in Israel and the Occupied Territories read Katz's policy initiative in political, not instrumental, terms. Ahmad Tibi, a member of the Knesset, highlighted this fact when he said: 'Minister Katz is mistaken if he thinks that changing a few words can erase the existence of the Arab people or their connection to Israel. This is a blatant attempt at harming the Arabic language and everything it represents.'[96] Another member of the Knesset, Jamal Zahalqa, said that this policy will not change the identity of the Arab cities and villages in Israel, that these villages will remain Arab because the Palestinians have their roots in the land, a land that will one day witness the return of the Palestinian refugees to their cities and villages, and that those in Israel who are against the Arab names in the linguistic landscape are, in fact, against the presence of the Arabs in this land.[97] In a similar

95 See Shohamy (2006) for a study of the linguistic landscape in Israel, which shows the power differential between Arabic and Hebrew.

96 Ibid.

97 These views were reported in the Jordanian newspaper *Al-Ra'y*, 14 July 2009, pp. 20, 24.

vein, Muhammad Baraka, another member of the Knesset, attacked the road-signs policy, accusing Katz of anti-Arab racism and of wishing to erase the Arab memory of the land. Baraka added that by taking this initiative, Katz has appointed himself the minister of history in Israel, but he warns that he will not succeed in his mission, because 'the land and its soil knows its [true] sons who, in turn, know it and know its names.'[98]

There is no doubt that politics, not instrumentality, is the major factor behind Katz's policy initiative. Instrumentality expressed as uniformity in the linguistic landscape is nothing but a 'fig leaf' for political action in an arena where claims and counterclaims over the right to own and to name the land are made and contested. The city of Acre in northern Israel provides an example that clearly displays this dynamic (see figures 5.1, 5.2 and 5.3). In June 2009, when the municipal authorities decided to name the city port after Ze'ev Frid, a 'leading figure of Israel's shipping industry and a founder of the Israeli navy,' the Arab inhabitants of the Old City responded by 'naming the port after 'Isa al-'Awam, one of the officers of Saladin, the 12th century Muslim general who fought and vanquished the Crusaders.'[99] These two port names, the official name and the unofficial name, were consecrated in two separate ceremonies and, at the time of writing, still exist in close proximity to each other. In justifying their position, the Arab residents of Acre point out that the 'city of Acre, and especially the old city [where the port is located], is an Arab city and every stone there is part of Arab history,'[100] hence the reference to Saladin, whose name is associated with the city and whose memory is inscribed in the minds of the Palestinians as a hero to be emulated in deciding the fate of their land. This politically impregnated battle over the linguistic landscape cannot be isolated from the larger issue of the Jewishness of Israel and the Palestinian response to it. The call by one of the Arab councillors of the city to name the 'road connecting the lighthouse in the old city to the port [after] the famous Palestinian poet Mahmoud Darwish'[101] is an integral part of this larger battle over the identity of the land. No decision has been taken at the time of writing. It is, however, likely that, based on past practise in Israeli cities,[102]

98 *Huwiyyat al-waṭan aqwā min 'unṣuriyyat Katz* ('The identity of the homeland is stronger than Katz's racism'), http://www1.wafa.ps/wafa/arabic/index.phb?action=detail&id=45922 (accessed on 25 August 2009.

99 See Jack Khoury, 'What's in a Name? Clashing Cultures in Acre's Port,' http://www.haaretz.com.hasen.spages/1106135.html (accessed 10 August 2009).

100 Ibid.

101 Ibid.

102 The opposition to using Arab names in the Israeli linguistic landscape may be exemplified by the following incident from Tel Aviv, the most liberal and cosmopolitan of all Israeli cities. When the family of two famous Jewish singers of Iraqi origin, Dawud and Salih al-Kuwaiti, succeeded in persuading the municipal authorities to name a small street after them, residents objected, thinking that the name was Arab. The objections subsided and then disappeared when the Jewish identity of the two brothers was known. See Khalid Khalifa, '*Tūrāth 'Irāqī yahūdī yatajaddad fī isrā'īl*', at http://www.bbc.co.uk/arabic/lg/artandculture/2009/08/090820_hh_israel_music_tc2.html (accessed 26 August 2009).

Figure 5.1. Acre Port (courtesy Ghussoun Bisharat).

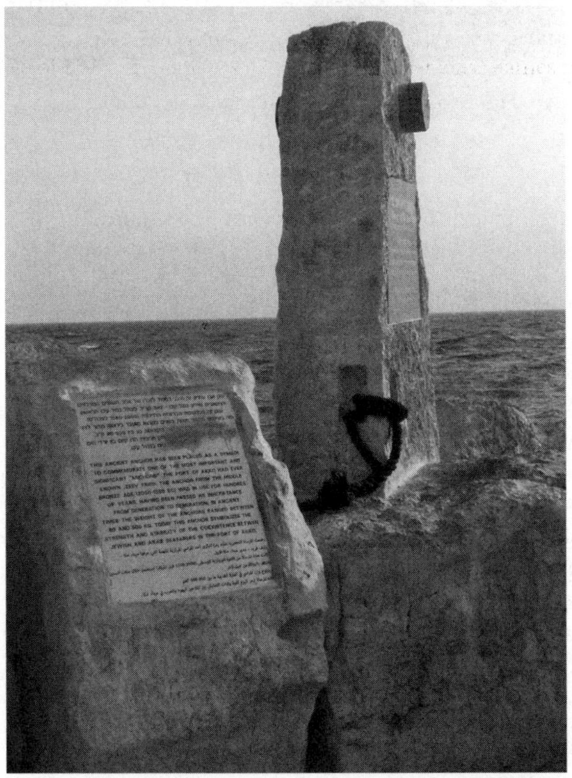

Figure 5.2. Acre Port (courtesy Ghussoun Bisharat).

Figure 5.3. Acre Port (courtesy Wael Abu Uksa)

the city authorities will reject this suggestion, no doubt on the grounds not just that Mahmoud Darwish is a Palestinian poet but that even in death, he is widely acknowledged as a Palestinian hero. It would be very surprising if the councillor who made this proposal thought differently, but that is beside the point, simply because the act of making the proposal is in itself an act of contestation and counterhegemony.

In the Occupied Territories, Israeli acts of onomastic commemoration express new meanings that take their semantic import from the ideology of the dominant party in government in Israel. Thus, Likud-dominated governments tended to emphasise continuity between the present and the past by giving biblical names to newly established Jewish settlements in these territories. In their naming practises, Labour-dominated governments tended to emphasise change in the political life of Israel; this was reflected in giving new settlements commemorative names from recent history.[103] Here

103 See Cohen and Kliot (1981).

we have an example of names reflecting differences in ideology between the dominant parties in the politics of the nation, rather than the ideologies expressed by different national movements. Moreover, academic discourse on the use of names for the settlements in the Occupied Territories is not immune from this injection of ideology. By censoring the word 'Occupied' in the name Occupied Territories, Israeli social science takes the occupation out of Occupation. And when this happens in publications in English-medium journals, as it does all too often, the impact is no longer localised.[104]

In Arab East Jerusalem, Hebrew names were superimposed onto existing Arabic and English street names from the Jordanian period,[105] as if to signify the Israeli claim that the city is part of the united and eternal capital of the state of Israel and the Jewish people.[106] In all of these practises, issues of identity, conflict and power are never absent.[107] However, this imposition does not go unchallenged on the Palestinian side. Plaques carrying street names are sometimes defaced or have the Hebrew names dug out from their positions in a wall.[108] In some cases, the imposition of a name in the city may lead to demonstrations and clashes with the authorities.[109] In other cases, Palestinians may choose commemorative names that evoke the glories of the Arab past to suggest the possibility of liberation from Israeli control.[110] These are low-key but daring attempts at civil resistance in a state that does not tolerate a whiff of Palestinian nationalism. What makes these attempts even more daring is the fact that most Palestinians have internalised the Israeli rules of the game in the toponymic sphere, two of which are 'no blatant ideological names, [and] no restoration of the pre-1948 names' (Zeidel 2006: 216). Another such daring attempt at resisting Israeli control and occupation by inscribing Palestinian history on the map occurred in the 1990s in Beit Hanina, a suburb on the outskirts of occupied East Jerusalem. When the city authorities asked the neighbourhood council to assist them with suggesting names for their neighbourhood streets, they did oblige but with a big nationalist twist. This is how Amir Cheshin, who worked in the Jerusalem municipality at the time, reports this attempt:

> It was several weeks before the list was sent to the city. As municipal officials reviewed the list, they slowly began to understand its significance. All the

104 See Cohen and Kliot (1992). In an article on the move from liberalism to fascism in national poetry in Europe (1815–1920), Aberbach (2008) refers to other contexts in which poetry played a part in national struggles. Instead of referring to Palestine under the British mandate by that name, the author describes it as 'pre-State Israel' (848). In this case, Palestine is written out of history in the same way that the Israeli occupation is written out of the occupation of the West Bank and Gaza.

105 See Suleiman (2004b: 192–93).

106 For a comparative perspective, see Demetriou (2006).

107 Maoz Azaryahu has been one of the leading scholars in the study of street names in Israel/Palestine; see Azaryahu (1992) and Azaryahu and Kook (2002).

108 See Suleiman (2004b: 193).

109 See Cheshin et al. (1999: 147) for an example.

110 See Azaryahu and Kook (2002).

> names were of Arab villages that had existed before 1948 but were destroyed by Israel during the [1948] war: Umm Rashrash, Banias, Majdal, Askalan, Yaffa, Pluga and others. The municipality contacted Darwish [head of the neighbourhood council], and he unabashedly explained the neighbourhood council's idea: 'We see the map of Beit Hanina as representing that of all Palestine,' Darwish said: 'In the north of Beit Hanina, we will give the street names of the villages that once stood in northern Palestine, in the west of the neighbourhood, the roads will have the names of the villages that once stood in the west of Palestine and so on.'
>
> Darwish was told to try again. The municipality would not accept such an expression of Palestinian nationalism on the streets of the city. 'You'd be better off choosing names of flowers and trees,' Darwish was told. 'You can also include great Arab figures, but stick to poets and writers, not conquerors. Do us a favour and include a short biography with each figure chosen. It would be good if you mentioned if he had any connection to Jerusalem.' The municipality had a Names Committee that had the final say on such matters as new street names. In those years [mid-1980s], committee members were known to be on the whole from right-wing parties that were suspicious about any Arab names and would want to know details about the candidate's relation to the Jews. Darwish got the picture of what he was up against. He followed the new orders to the letter, and the second list of flowers and trees and Arab poets he presented to city hall was approved by the Names Committee with hardly a peep. (Cheshin et al. 1999: 146–47)

This story describes the struggle of one Palestinian community to inscribe its own cartographic text, not just with a list of place names that memorialise the tragic history of Palestine but also with a palimpsest map of portions of Palestine that are woven, like a Palestinian embroidered dress, from the names of the Palestinian destroyed villages. As an attempt at making the absent present, of creating a record of a lost past, the proposed neighbourhood text of Beit Hanina is a creative construction whose aim is to resist Israeli occupation. There is no doubt that the Beit Hanina council knew the Israeli rules of the naming game well and was aware that it had no chance of succeeding, but that did not deter the council from entering into a duel with the Israeli-controlled municipality to contest its authority to organise its spatial sphere. In this duel, issues of identity, conflict and power are strongly involved on both sides of the national divide; it is these issues that power the naming practises.

The Beit Hanina example is the exception rather than the rule in onomastic resistance on the part of the Palestinians. Another, less flamboyant but no less significant attempt at laying claim to the land by Palestinians occurs as part of the celebrations that accompany Palestinian weddings. In a study of oral-duelling poetry in Palestine, Nadia Yaqub gives a thirty-nine-line excerpt from a poem in which more than twenty names of Palestinian localities are mentioned directly (2006: 18–19).[111] This density of place

111 See Yaqub (2007) for a more detailed study of names, including personal names, in Palestinian oral-duelling poetry.

names in the duelling poem raises the question of why Palestinian oral poets resort to this motif in weaving their constructions. Yaqub links this directly to the struggle over the land, who owns it and who has the right to continue to own it, as naming and ownership are interlinked: 'To utter the Palestinian names of Palestinian villages in the course of the *sahrah* [wedding-night celebrations] is to assert Palestinian presence in the areas in which wedding participants live and to lay claim to their right to reside there and make their mark on the landscape' (19). Yaqub contextualises her interpretation by referring to Israeli state policy over place names and how this is organically linked to the twin aims of promoting Jewish history and silencing the Palestinian narrative of past ownership, current dispossession and the yearning for returning in the future.

The discussion above revolved around how the Palestinians inside historical Palestine (Israel and the Occupied Territories) use names to lay claims to the land, to memorialise their own history and to resist Israeli hegemony and occupation. In this context, the question arises of how Palestinians in the diaspora/exile use place names to express their identity. In discussing personal names in this chapter, I mentioned two phenomena that exploit place names for personal-identity construction: the use of village names in their *nisba* form as surnames and their use as cyber-monikers. To this we may add the phenomenon of the memorial book in which Palestinians in the diaspora record information about, and personal memories of, their villages and cities as lived places 'to maintain a variety of connections to the past' (Davis 2007: 58).[112] The purpose of these books and others of a similar kind may be summed up by the main title of the monumental book *Kay lā nansā* (Lest We Forget), edited by Walid Khalidi (1997).[113]

This title explains the use of maps in the memorial books, some of which are etched on the page from memory (see figures 5.4 and 5.5). The fact that these maps are personal creations that lack the art of the professional mapmaker gives them an authenticity, intimacy and immediacy that characterise eyewitness accounts.[114] The Palestinian fear that the names and places of their homeland may be forgotten, especially by future generations, drives these efforts at cartographic representation and historical remembrance, as the author of a memorial book on Jaffa declares: 'These memories record what I have

112 The best-known projects of this kind are those of Bir Zeit University near Ramalla in the Occupied Territories (mainly of the destroyed villages) and the PLO project for the Palestinian cities inside Israel.

113 The full title of this book in Arabic is *Kay lā nansā: Qurā filasṭīn allatī dammarathā isrā'īil sanat 1948 wa-asmā' shuhadā'ihā* (Lest We Forget: The Palestinian Villages Destroyed by Israel in 1948 and the Names of Their Martyrs). The English version of the book appeared under the title *All That Remains: The Palestinian Villages Occupied and Depopulated by Israel in 1948* (Khalidi 1982). There are some audience-driven differences between these two books (see Suleiman 2004b: 180).

114 For similar images, see Davis (2007), Slyomovics (1998) and Twair (2008). Twair reports on the Jimzu map, which is a permanent exhibit at the Arab National Museum in Dearborn, Michigan.

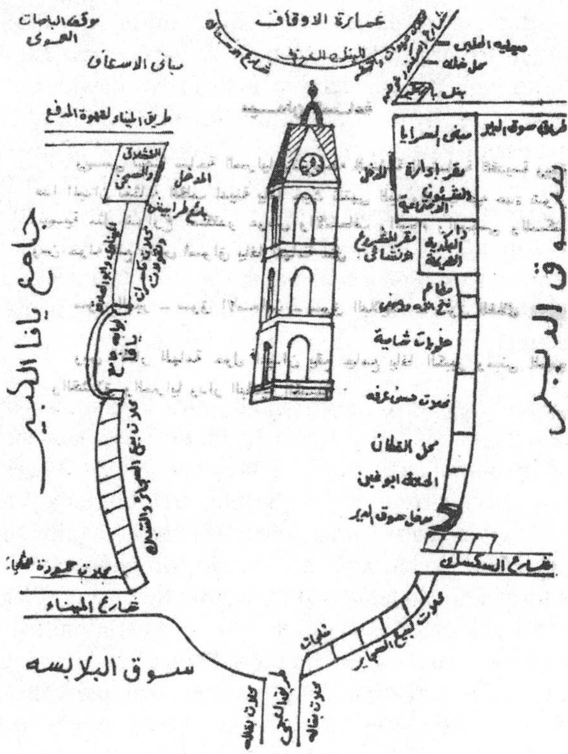

Figure 5.4. Maydan al-Sāʻa (Clock Square), Jaffa, Palestine (al-Dajani 1989: 41).

experienced and still remember. I am doing this to preserve these memories. The generation of Jaffans who experienced life in their pre-1948 city is dying out, leading to the disappearance of the social history of the city' (al-Dajani 1989: 13–14). Other writers in this genre make reference to this fear, which the authors typically encapsulate in the introductions to their books. The most impressive examples are the books by Salman Abu-Sitta (2004) and Shukri 'Arraf (2007).

The cover for Abu-Sitta's 240-page book (he calls it a guide) lists in both Arabic and English the material it incorporates, including '1500 Towns and Villages, 4000 Holy Sites, 4700 Land Features and Jewish Colonies'[115] before

115 The term *colonies* may strike us as odd, but this was the name used by the Zionist movement to designate the new Jewish 'settlements' in Palestine; see Cohen (1911, 142, 157, 165). Poole explains that the term *settlement* in English 'conjures an idea of a virgin, unpopulated territory: an image of building log cabins in the wilderness,' as well as carrying the 'secondary sense of agreement,' neither of which is true. Israeli settlements were built 'in heavily populated Palestinian areas' and have been declared illegal by the UN Security Council and the International Court of Justice. The Hebrew term for settlements is *hitnakhlut*, 'a word of biblical origin which means roughly settling on one's patrimony' (Poole 2006: 85). The Arabic term *mustawṭanāt*, from *istawṭana*, implies the act of an outsider to settle down in a location that does not originally belong to him or to which he is a stranger.

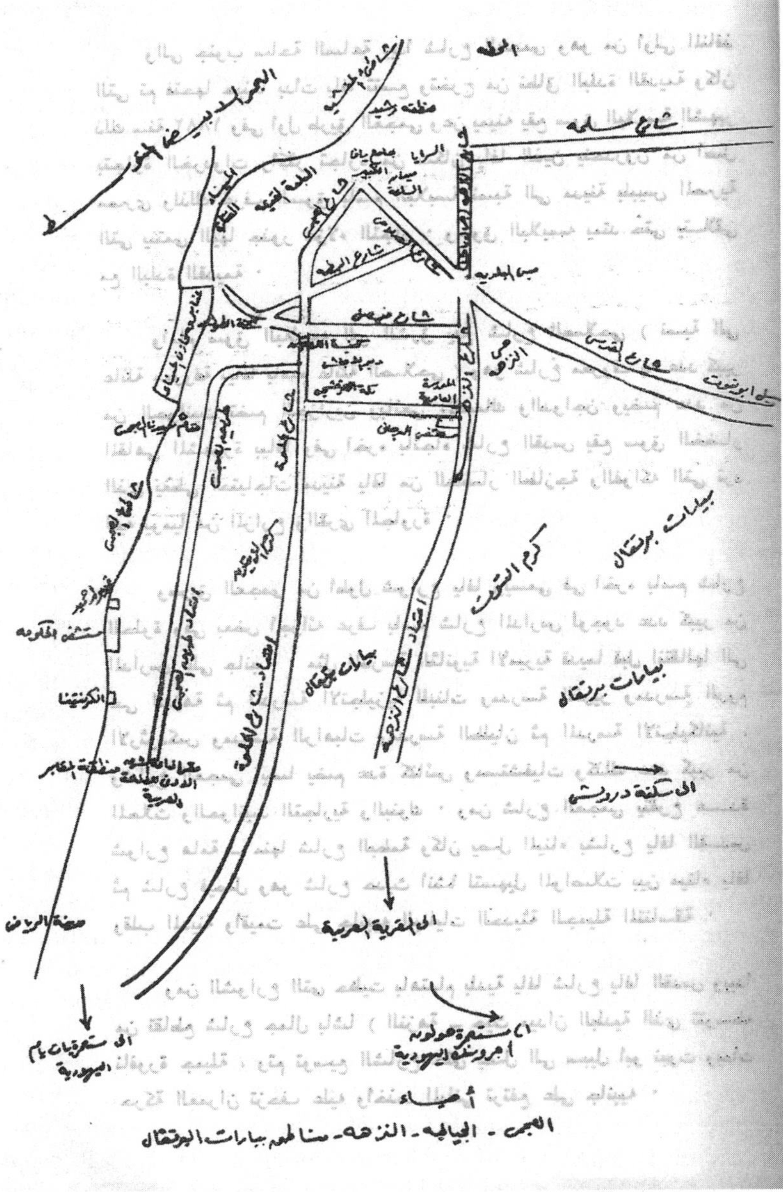

Figure 5.5. Residential areas and orange groves, Jaffa, Palestine (al-Dajānī 1989: 43).

and after 1948. Inside, the book contains two large indices: a localities index and an index of holy sites. On the maps, the names are listed vertically in Arabic, English and Hebrew, in that order. By making the absent present through mapping and listing the depopulated and destroyed villages inside Israel, Abu-Sitta intends to make visible the 'concealed geography of

Palestine' (2004: 243). The author further links his 'guide' to the right of return of the Palestinian people to their places of origin; hence the title of the book as *The Return Journey*.[116] Clearly, for Abu-Sitta, names, maps, ownership and return are the building blocks of a Palestinian national narrative pitted against the hegemonic Israeli narrative that claims the same land as its own.

'Arraf book is a monumental piece of work, 557 pages of list after list of names of places of various kinds, accompanied by notes on the listed names. Each entry gives the name in Arabic, then in English and then in its Hebrew form, with an Arabic transliteration of that form. The names are listed under the following headings: wells (*ābār*), towers (*abrāj*), gates (*abwāb*), inlets/bays (*akhwār*), Jordan River valleys (*aghwār*), Prophet's holy sites (*anbiyā'*), tunnels (*anqāb*), seasonal rivers and rivers (*awdiya wa-anhār*), seas and lakes (*biḥār wa-buḥayrāt*), pools (*birak*), animal enclosures in Bedouin-dominated areas (*bawāyik*), hills (*tilāl*), mountains (*jibāl*), islands (*juzur*), bridges (*jusūr*), pits/holes (*juwar*), neighbourhoods and suburbs (*ḥārāt wa-dawāḥī*), rocks (*ḥijāra*), inns (*khānāt*), ruins (*khirab*), outlets (*khushūm*), stone piles (*rujūm*), desolate/defaced old settlements (*rusūm*), hilltops (*ru'ūs*), squares (*sāḥāt*), salt marshes/swamps (*sabakhāt*), dwellings (*sakanāt*), plains (*suhūl wa-murūj*), mountain trails (*shi'āb*), streets (*shawāri'*), beaches (*shawāṭi'*), deserts (*ṣaḥārā/bawādi*), roads (*ṭuruq*), water springs (*'uyūn*), villages and cities (*qurā wa-mudun*), summits (*qurūn*), palaces (*quṣūr*), castles/fortresses (*qilā'*), lowlands (*qī'ān*), fruit orchards (*kurūm*), whirlpools (*makhāḍāt*), holy sites for saints and holy men (*mazārāt*), hospitals (*mustashfayāt*), flower mills (*maṭāḥin*), viewpoints (*muṭillāt*), caves (*maghāwir*), lookouts (*manāṭir*), ports (*mawāni'*), water cisterns (*harrābāt*), caverns/gorges (*huwwāt*), roadless/rugged terrain (*wu'ūr*), forests (*ghābāt*) and ravines (*wahdāt*). 'Arraf seems to have started from the indigenous toponyms that the Palestinians use to mark places and used these as the basis for his classification. I tested some of the more obscure names used in this system on old rural Palestinians and was struck by the degree of agreement among them on what each term means. Young Palestinians I have tested fared badly, as if to justify the Palestinians' rush to preserve their collective memory, including their onomasticon, in memory books and other books and media.

'Arraf is keenly aware that toponyms and the landscape they mark are part of the Palestinian narrative of land ownership, the homeland, dispossession, displacement and dispersion. In fact, he declares in the introduction that one of his aims is to preserve the Arabic names of the homeland for its people to remember. Furthermore, the link binding toponyms to memory to nation and to resistance is central to 'Arraf book, whose aim is ultimately political. While the act of listing the names, identifying their locations and providing information about them is the primary strategy for achieving this aim, the book employs two more subtle ones. On the one hand, by employing a Palestinian classification in listing the names, 'Arraf not only restores to and preserves for

116 See Kuzar (2008) for a discussion of the Palestinian concept of 'return,' in which he comments on Abu-Sitta's views on the matter.

Palestine those names that have been lost to it, or might be lost with the passage of time, but also records the extensive system of naming features of the landscape. This system evinces an intimate knowledge of this landscape, as if to assert that the Palestinian claim over the land resides not just in the names used to designate it but also in the abstract system that underlies this designation. By doing so, 'Arraf goes beyond the surface structure of the names to their deep structure, making the invisible visible.

On the other hand, 'Arraf makes a distinction between the terms *asmā'* and *tasmiyāt* in the subtitle of his book, using the former to designate the Arabic names (*al-asmā' al-'arabiyya*) and the latter to designate the Hebrew ones (*al-tasmiyāt al-'ibriyya*). In their ordinary senses, *asmā'* and *tasmiyāt* refer to names and to naming processes, respectively. However, *tasmiyāt* cannot mean 'naming processes' here, because the book contains no information about this; it only lists the Hebrew names for the Arabic ones. This calls for a different interpretation of the meaning of *tasmiyāt*, the closest, I suggest, being 'designations' or labels. In Arabic, a *tasmiya* (plural *tasmiyāt*) specifies persons or objects and marks them from others but without, technically speaking, naming them; hence the interpretation of this term as designation. Furthermore, unlike *asmā'*, *tasmiyāt* is hedged with some provisionality and semantic indeterminacy or vagueness. It is as if by using this term to refer to the Hebrew names, 'Arraf was questioning the Israeli claim over the landscape and, indirectly, implying its undurability. A*tasmiyya* stands to *ism* as a translation stands to the original text: each has its own reality, but the ultimate authority lies in the second member of each pair in this equation. The Palestinian *ism* is the rule, while the Hebrew *tasmiya* is the deviation. Or the Palestinian *ism* is the primary object, while the Hebrew *tasmiya* is the secondary one. This again reveals the subtlety and extensive nature of Palestinian onomastic resistance in the Israeli-Palestinian conflict. But it also reveals the rich potential of names as a site of cultural politics.

LINGUISTIC LANDSCAPE, IDENTITY AND MODERNITY

Landry and Bourhis define the linguistic landscape as the 'visibility and salience of languages on public and private signs in a given territory or region' (1997: 23). Serving instrumental/informational and symbolic purposes, the linguistic landscape acts as a 'marker of the relevant power and status of the linguistic communities inhabiting [a given] territory' (23).[117] In this section, I will restrict the discussion of the linguistic landscape to the use of foreign/Western names in commercial signs in a few Arab localities in the Arab Middle East. I will additionally deal with how this phenomenon

117 The linguistic landscape has been studied from a diversity of perspectives in recent years; see Backhaus (2005; 2007), Cenoze and Gorter (2006), Heubner (2006), Leeman and Modan (2009), Lou (2007), Shohamy and Gorter (2009) and Stroud and Mpendukana (2009).

has been interpreted in the literature on the subject. I am, therefore, interested not in the range of languages used in commercial signs but in the provenance of the names in those signs; in particular, I am interested in the use of foreign/Western names in commercial signs whether these are rendered in Arabic or Roman script. As used here, the category of foreign names excludes those that are wholly made up of words that have been borrowed by Arabic (*fuṣḥā* or colloquial dialects) and enjoy high recognition by ordinary language users. This category may include words such as 'centre,' 'supermarket,' 'boutique,' 'coffee shop' and 'mobile,' which have gained wide currency in the Arab Middle East, at least in the spoken varieties.[118] These restrictions imply a narrowing down of the scope of the linguistic landscape as defined by Landry and Bourhis above. We should also add to this that most of the countries of the Arab Middle East do not fall within the classic interpretation of the linguistic landscape as one that applies to bilingual or multilingual ethnic/national settings, for example, Belgium, Canada or Israel.[119] Although English or French may be used in linguistic landscape in the Arab Middle East, there are no sizeable communities that speak these languages as their own native tongues.

In one of the earliest studies on the subject, al-Zughul (1988) comments on the linguistic landscape in the city of Irbid (in the north of Jordan), saying that the widespread use of English in commercial signs may give the outsider the false impression that the city is a bilingual place. He then offers a sample of the foreign names that are used in Arabic-only signs, for example, *bestūrs li-l-siyāḥa wa-al-safar* ('Best Tours for Travel and Tourism'), *markiz sāyt 'ānd sāwnds* ('Sight and Sounds Centre') and *sharikat rīnbū li-l-siyāḥa wa-al-safar* ('Rainbow Travel and Tourism'). Western/foreign names are also found in commercial signs in both Arabic and Roman letters (mostly English, but some with a French inflection), with the Roman material serving as the primary target and Arabic as no more than a transliteration of this: *shūz jārdin* ('Shoes Garden'), *lūk 'ānd* ('Look and'), *yung shūz* ('Young Shoes'), *lākī stūrs* ('Lucky Stores'), *blū marīn stīm* ('Blue Marine Laundry'), and *swīt hūm stūrs* ('Sweet Home Stores'). These linguistic practises are further described in a study in Irbid by Salih and El-Yasin (1994), adding further confirmation concerning the spread of this phenomenon. The fact that Irbid in the 1980s and 1990s was (and still is) a small city reveals the depth of penetration of this phenomenon in Jordan.[120]

Another study from Jordan confirms this trend (Barhuma 2005). However, the value of this study lies in investigating the reasons behind the

118 Not all of the studies that I will use in this section agree on this, but this should not negatively affect the general direction of the discussion.

119 For Israel, see Ben-Rafael et al. (2004).

120 For further information on this phenomenon in Jordan, see Abdul-Fattah and Zoghoul (1996) and El-Yasin and Mahadin (1996); Bader and Minnis (n.d.) provide interesting information on the related phenomenon of brand names in Jordan.

spread of this phenomenon in a random sample of one hundred shopkeepers and consumers, covering subjects of both sexes and from a range of educational levels, from illiterate to university-educated. Differences were found between the two groups (shopkeepers and consumers), but these were minimal, allowing the researcher to generalise his findings to the entire population in the sample with minimal variation. Thus, the popularity of foreign/Western names is related to a number of factors in this study, including their commercial instrumentality, as well as their highly valued aesthetic properties, connotations of modernity, consumer impact, high quality of the merchandise and upward mobility in lifestyles.[121] These are some of the attitudes identified in Salih and El-Yasin's study, too (1994). By comparison, Arabic names are thought to be old-fashioned and outmoded and to carry connotations of low-quality goods.

Wafa' Fayid (n.d.) carried out three empirical studies on the use of foreign/Western names in commercial signs in Cairo, one of which covered the period 1972–83, while the other two were restricted to one year each, 1983 and 1993.[122] In an unpublished paper, Fayid (2005) returned to the topic, this time widening the scope of her study to include Jordan, Bahrain, Kuwait, Oman, Syria and Lebanon, in addition to Egypt. The research was based on a survey of the telephone directories of Jordan (1987), Egypt (1993), Damascus in Syria (1997), Oman (1999), Bahrain (1999–2000), Lebanon (2003–04) and Kuwait (2004–05). This survey calculated the percentage of foreign/Western names in each directory, as well as the breakdown of these percentages by profession or commercial sector. However, the survey did not distinguish names by foreign language, although we can be certain that

121 Barhuma (2005: 77–79) lists the attitudes according to their popularity in this descending order: (1) foreign names enjoy high currency; (2) foreign names are in tune with the customer base; (3) foreign names increase the curiosity of the shoppers and draw them inside the shop; (4) foreign names entice the shoppers and encourage them to purchase the goods; (5) foreign names are international trademarks; (6) foreign names are used in the West and some Arab countries; (7) foreign names are used for innovation; (8) foreign names draw Arab and foreign shoppers; (9) foreign names mean high class and fame (shopkeepers and shoppers); (10) foreign names are supported by the strength and widespread influence of Western civilisation; (11) foreign names have beautiful and effective meanings; (12) foreign names are in tune with the age of satellite TV and the world of the Internet; (13) foreign names suit the areas in which they are used; (14) foreign names are more distinctive than Arabic names; (15) foreign names are in tune with Western modernity; (16) foreign names imply foreign goods; (17) foreign names allow greater control over prices; (18) foreign names are easier to pronounce; (19) Arabic names imply local goods; (20) foreign (English) names are in tune with the popularity of the English language; (21) foreign names imply high prices; (22) foreign names imply aping the West; (23) foreign names imply pride in the goods and an opportunity for social one-upmanship; (24) foreign names are used because of weakness in Arabic; (25) foreign names are fit to (the commercial) purpose; (26) foreign names are used because Arabic lacks attractive names; (27) foreign names are used because Arabic names are old and out of fashion. The paper does not specify the locality or localities in which the research was conducted.

122 Judging from the preface, the book containing these studies was published in 2003. However, the individual papers were published separately in 1988, 1989 and 2001, respectively.

most of the names for Jordan, Oman, Bahrain and Kuwait were English, those for Lebanon French, with Damascus presenting a mixture.[123] The fact that the directories in the sample cover different years means that the data are uneven, a matter Fayid acknowledges. However, what matters for our purposes here is the overall percentage of foreign names for each country, which Fayid calculates as follows:

Jordan[124]	4.18%
Bahrain	23.89%
Kuwait	20.29%
Damascus	7.82%
Oman	16.26%
Lebanon[125]	56.7%
Egypt	9.66%

With the exception of Lebanon, these figures do not seem to justify the fear some Arabs have about the spread of foreign names.[126] However, fears are expressed, and no more so than by the scholars whose research forms the basis of this section; hence the conclusion of each of these papers[127] by a set of recommendations on how to combat the use of foreign/Western names in commercial signs, including the institution of laws that criminalise (*tujarrim*) the use of these names in the linguistic landscape (Fayid 2005: 45). Al-Zughul relates the use of foreign names in linguistic landscape to the question of cultural loyalty: 'The weaker the loyalty [to the indigenous culture and language is,] the greater the resort to foreign languages [in a community]' (1988: 33). In fact, al-Zughul goes further, implying that the use of foreign names in the linguistic landscape is an indication that a nation does not respect itself, for self-respect would demand giving primacy to Arabic in the linguistic landscape (34). A similar line is taken by Barhuma (2005), who ascribes the use of foreign names to the inferiority complex in Arab society towards the West, as well as to a false consciousness according to which adopting the linguistic accoutrements of Western culture is thought to enhance an Arab's status in society in relation to his peers. In framing his discussion, Barhuma employs such terms as *istislām*

123 In some of the Gulf countries, such as Qatar, Hindi and Urdu would be part of the linguistic landscape owing to the presence of members of these language communities in high numbers as expatriate workers.

124 The figures for Jordan are bound to be different now.

125 The figures for Lebanon reflect the long-standing contacts between this country and the West, especially France; in this sense, they may, in fact, be treated as naturalised/Arabised names rather than foreign/Western ones.

126 See al-Naqqash (2009: 126–29), who considers the use of English and other European languages in the linguistic landscape of Cairo an expression of contempt towards Arabic and a slur on the dignity of the Arab nation.

127 Salih and El-Yasin (1994) do not present any recommendations, perhaps because they were writing in English, where such practise is usually absent.

Figure 5.6. Cairo city centre: 'New Splendid Hotel.' The first word, *lukanda*, is an old-fashioned borrowing from Italian; the second, *Splendid*, is English; and the third, *Al-Jadīda*, is Arabic.

('surrender'), *wabāl* ('catastrophe'), *ghalaba* ('domination/hegemony'), *istīlā'* ('usurpation') and *thaqāfa hazīla* ('very weak culture').

Fayid adopts a similar attitude. She refers to the use of foreign names in commercial signs as a case of 'linguistic pollution' (*talawwuth lughawī*)[128] that threatens the very structure of the Arabic language through linguistic interference or leads to the injection of the colloquial dialects into what ought to be the domain of the *fuṣḥā* (see figures 5.6–5.10). She also quotes approvingly the titles of some of the articles that appeared in the Egyptian press over a number of years attacking this phenomenon: 'The Arabic Language in its Crisis' (*Lughatunā al-'arabiyya fi azamatihā*), 'The Defeat of a Nation, Not a Language Crisis' (*Inkisār umma la azmat lugha*), 'Woe to a Nation Whose Language Has Been Raped' (*Waylun li-umma maghṣūbat al-lisān*), 'They Are Deforming the Consciousness of Our Nation' (*Innahum yushawwihūn wa'ya ummatinā*), 'Before Arabizi Takes Over' (*Qabla an tashī'a al-'arablīziyya*) and 'Arabic in the Valley/Depth of Neglect' (*al-Lugha al-'arabiyya fi wadī al-ihmāl*) (2005: 1).

128 See Fayid (2005: 42).

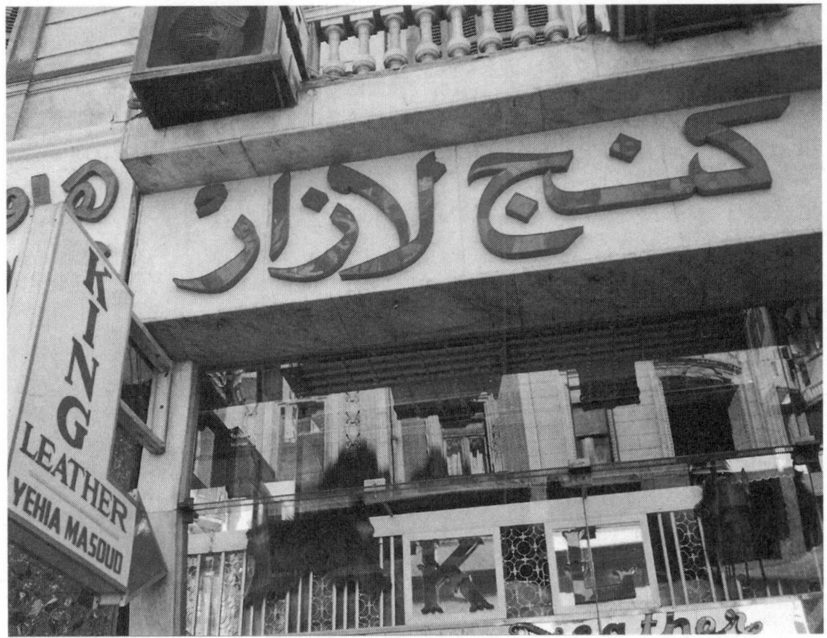

Figure 5.7. Cairo city centre: The [th] in *leather* is assimilated to Egyptian Arabic [z] and rendered by Arabic [z] instead of [dh], which would accurately reflect the corresponding English sound. Also, the [ea] in *leather* is rendered by long *alif* [ā]. As given in this shop sign, the English word *leather* is rendered as *lāzār*.

To give rhetorical and indigenously generated credence to their interpretations, al-Zughul (1988: 33) and Barhuma (2005: 85–86) refer to Ibn Khaldun (1332–1406), who ascribes cultural imitation to the defeat of one nation by another and the desire of the defeated to emulate the victorious party. Barhuma (2005: 86) uses the same excerpt, but he additionally supports it with another quotation from the Muslim thinker Ibn Hazm (994–1064), in which he links the cultural strength of a language to the political strength of its speakers. Fayid's interpretation of the use of foreign names falls within this framework, but she modulates her views by making specific reference to globalisation as the vehicle through which the use of foreign names spreads, aided by the widespread use of foreign language (English and French) through the education system and modern technologies. Within this overarching context, the use of names may be described as a carryover effect of deeper forces in society that sanction the extended use of foreign names into new domains that have so far been resistant to them.

The question arises of how representative the above views are of ordinary speakers' attitudes towards the use of foreign names in commercial signs. Is it possible that these interpretations of 'doom and gloom' are not

Figure 5.8. Cairo city centre: The [th] in *leather* is assimilated to Egyptian Arabic [z] and rendered by Arabic [z] instead of [dh], which would accurately reflect the corresponding English sound. Also, the [ea] in *leather* is rendered by long *yā'* [ī]. As given in this shop sign, the English word *leather* is rendered as *līzar* and might, in fact, be read as English *laser*.

shared by ordinary people? Or is it the case that ordinary speakers do view this phenomenon positively? Extensive fieldwork would be needed to answer these questions. However, Barhuma's (2005) research gives us some clues to the types of answers this fieldwork may generate. This research makes clear that the foreign names receive high ratings for their modernity, a fact corroborated by al-Zughul (1988), as well as Salih and El-Yasin (1994). This research further reveals that foreign names, even when used in Arabic-only signs, imply high quality, a refined aesthetic and an openness to the outside world. In comparison, Arabic names seem to be mundane and out of step with the spirit of the age when compared with their foreign counterparts, although this judgement is not expanded to refer to the use of the Arabic language in all domains. Could it be, therefore, that the anxiety about foreign names is an elite phenomenon, restricted to what may be called the culture guardians who use language as a proxy to protect the traditional values of society in the face of the forces of modernisation and globalisation? Or does this anxiety have a grass-roots dimension that makes its presence felt through commercial naming

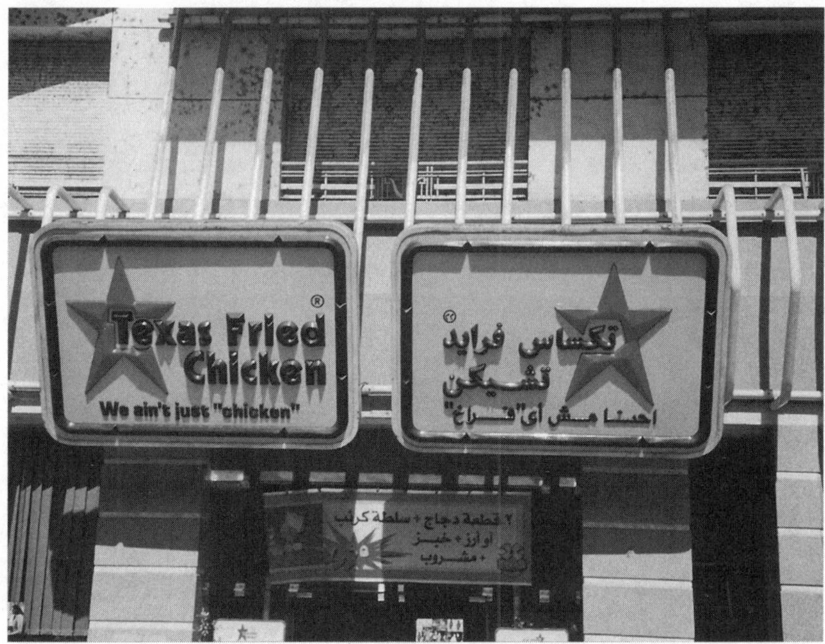

Figure 5.9. Cairo city centre: 'Texas Fried Chicken' is transliterated into Arabic; the slogan 'We ain't just "chicken"' is translated into Egyptian Arabic; and the menu below is in *fuṣḥā* Arabic.

Figure 5.10. Cairo city centre: 'Spanker.' Arabic transliteration uses a three-dotted [b] in Arabic to render English [p].

practices with a traditional inflection?[129] These are some of the questions that future research may answer for us. However, whatever the answer, the point remains that names constitute an important cultural site through which to access and track some of the most important debates about identity, conflict and modernity in society.[130]

CODE NAMES, IDENTITY AND CONFLICT

Code names, particularly those of military operations, have not traditionally been considered part of onomastics or objects of study in sociolinguistics. It is not my intention to deal with the reasons for this lacuna in sociolinguistics, but considering the centrality of identity and conflict in Middle Eastern politics and society, code names must constitute a prime domain for investigating how language may be used to shape public perceptions nationally and internationally. In this section, I will provide a brief discussion of code names insofar as they have been used in the Middle Eastern theatre of military operations over the past half-century. Reference will be made to English, Hebrew and Arabic code names to outline some of the considerations that determine the production and reception of these names.

From an early, albeit hesitant, start in World War II, the production of code names developed general orientations, country-specific conventions[131] and a high degree of media sophistication whose aim was to manage public relations at home and abroad. At times of war or in periods of extended conflict, shaping public opinion nationally and internationally may be enhanced or damaged by the code names used for military operations. For this reason, Winston Churchill had a keen interest in code names during World War II. He is reported to have objected to 'Soapsuds' as a code name for the American operation to bomb the Romanian oil fields in Ploetsi, on the grounds that this name was 'inappropriate for an operation in which so many brave Americans would risk their lives,' replacing it in the end with 'Tidal Wave' (Kimball 1984: 280; in Sieminski 1995: 3). Churchill is also said to have objected to 'Roundhammer' as a code name for the invasion of Normandy in 1944, choosing instead 'Overlord' because of its connotations of 'majesty, patriarchal vengeance and irresistible power' (Kahn 1967: 503; in Sieminski 1995: 3). This interest on Churchill's part led him to formulate some guidelines for use in coining code names—although he may have violated them in his choice of 'Overlord'—including avoiding boastfulness,

129 In a piece on the 2004 Cairo Book Fair published in *Al-Ahram Weekly*, the respected scholar and social critic Galal Amin (2004) mentions the names of some of the publishers and bookshops exhibiting at the fair: *Taqwa* ('Piety'), *Nur* ('Light'), *I'tisam* ('Sanctuary'), *Yaqin* ('Conviction'), *Wafa'* ('Loyalty'), *Fadila* ('Virtue') and *Iman* ('Faith'). These names embody religious values.

130 See al-Baḥrawi (1997) for an interesting example of this line of investigation.

131 See Arkin (2005) for a comprehensive list of the code names of American military operations.

overconfidence, creating an 'air of despondency' or choosing frivolous names that would make a widow or a mother very reluctant to say that her husband or son was killed in an operation called 'Bunnyhug' or 'Ballyhoo.'[132]

Churchill recognised the commemorative power of code names when he further suggested that these may include heroes of antiquity, as well as American and British war heroes as allies in World War II. This reference to the past was meant to extol and parade the pedigree of the nation, as well as to inspire the troops to fight in a way that is worthy of the heroes of the past. Inspiration, therefore, is an important aspect of code names, as is raising the morale of the troops and spreading the spirit of hope in situations of adversity. An example of the latter is the code name 'Operation Niagara,' which was used to refer to the round-the-clock air bombardment of the North Vietnamese force that surrounded a U.S. and South Vietnamese garrison in Khe Sanh in 1968. This name was chosen to 'invoke an image of cascading shells and bombs' to give hope and courage to the vastly outnumbered U.S. and South Vietnamese troops (Westmoreland 1976; in Sieminski 1995: 6). At the same time, this name was also designed to intimidate the enemy and to signal to them the use of overwhelming and unstoppable force.

Code names of this kind act as metaphors of nature. This use of nature as a trope in code names may be further exemplified in the first Gulf War following the invasion of Kuwait in 1990. The code name 'Peninsula Shield' was proposed by the Americans at the beginning of the conflict but was rejected because (1) it implied a policy objective involving the whole of the Arabian Peninsula rather than only a part of it (i.e., Kuwait), and (2) it gave the impression that the United States wanted to protect Saudi Arabia as a strategic oil producer, rather than liberate Kuwait, an impression the Saudi authorities wanted to avoid. 'Crescent Shield' was proposed as an alternative code name to appeal to Saudi, Arab and Muslim public opinion, but it was rejected because, it seems, of the double implication that could be read into it, to the effect that the Muslims were weak and that they needed the help of a Christian power to protect them. In the end, the code name 'Desert Shield' was chosen because of its semantic appropriateness (it describes the area) and its lack of geographical specificity. The term *shield* in this code name emphasised that the area was under attack and that the role of the American-led coalition was to protect it against the unsheathed sword of Saddam Hussein, thus gaining the high moral ground against the enemy.

At the start of the Gulf War in 1991, 'Desert Shield' was replaced by 'Desert Storm'; hence the connection with nature. The new term acted as a metaphor: it 'associated the [American-led] offensive [against Iraq] with the unleashing of overwhelming natural forces' (Sieminski 1995: 9). General Norman Schwarzkopf exploited the nature-bound connotations of this code name when he addressed his troops, telling them, 'You must be the thunder

132 See Sieminski (1995: 2–3). (All page numbers in this work refer to the electronic version.)

and lightning of the Desert Storm' (9). This code name proved to be a productive one, generating the code names 'Desert Sabre' to name the ground offensive, 'Desert Farewell' to refer to the redeployment of Coalition forces into Kuwait and 'Desert Share' to describe the distribution of surplus food provisions earmarked for the war to the U.S. poor. Sieminski describes this choice of code names well when he says that 'such careful and effective wordsmithing played well with domestic [U.S.] audiences and international observers, setting a context to garnering support for the operation' (9).

But not all attempts at coining code names can be as successful as the above. Sometimes code names may inadvertently create the wrong connotations from a public relations perspective. In 2003, the Americans used the code name 'Operation Iraqi Liberation' to designate their offensive against Iraq, but this code name was quickly replaced by 'Operation Iraqi Freedom' to avoid the implication carried by its acronym, OIL, that the United States was waging the war to gain control of the Iraqi oilfields. In 2001, 'Operation Infinite Justice,' which the Americans used as a code name for the invasion of Afghanistan, had to be changed to 'Operation Enduring Freedom' when it was pointed out that in Islam, Allah alone can dispense infinite justice. This, however, did not stop the media from commenting on the precariousness of the American aspiration to bring enduring freedom to Afghanistan, leaving some to comment on the ambiguity of this code name by suggesting that the 'freedom brought to Afghanistan by U.S. troops was something to be endured rather than enjoyed' (Poole 2006: 104). Interpreted in this way, 'Operation Enduring Freedom' would constitute an attack on Afghani culture by suggesting that a country ruled by despots and tribal chiefs cannot enjoy freedom.

In the Middle East, Israel has the richest lexicon of code names. In the 1948 War, Israel used about twenty-eight code names; the Arabs seem to have used none. In the 1956 Suez Crisis, Israel used five code names, while Egypt seems to have used none. In the wars against Lebanon, Israel used at least five code names, whereas Hezbollah used one. These and other discrepancies between Israel and the Arab countries may reflect differences of institutional practise, whereby the Arabs are less attuned to the use of code names than Israel. A more plausible explanation may be the difference in the volume of operations conducted by Israel and the Arab countries: the higher the number of operations carried out by one of the parties to the Arab-Israeli conflict, the greater the number of code names it has. For this to be valid, we must assume that the two parties have the same propensity when it comes to code-naming their military operations.

Some of the Israeli code names express the aspirations of the military planners, for example, 'Operation Peace for Galilee,' which ended with the bloody invasion of Lebanon in 1982 and the massacres of Sabra and Shatila. In 1996, Israel used the title of John Steinbeck's novel *The Grapes of Wrath*, evoking Revelation 14: 19–20, with its reference to divine justice and deliverance from oppression, as the code name for its bloody invasion of South Lebanon. This code name (*'Invei Za'am* in Hebrew) was aimed at the Israeli and international public who may be familiar with the novel—or at least its classic film version—and its intertextuality with the Bible. Its symbolic meanings were, therefore, lost on most Arabs, whose knowledge base does not incorporate these culture- and religion-bound references. However, on the Arab side, this became one of the most memorable of the Israeli code names,[133] gaining wide currency in its Arabic form (*'anāqīd al-ghaḍab*) because of the irony its surface structure contained: how could something that evokes something so sweet (grapes) cause so much destruction and bloodshed?

The Israeli bombardment of Gaza in the summer of 2006 to free the kidnapped Israeli soldier Gilad Shalit was code-named 'Summer Rains.' As a metaphor of nature, this code name is soaked in irony. On the one hand, although rain is always welcome in the Middle East, its occurrence in the summer would be an aberration of nature and might, in fact, lead some Arabs to consider it a punishment from God or, at least, a warning and an expression of his displeasure. On the other hand, based on this interpretation, this code name suggests not only that the Palestinians deserve the punishment meted out to them by the Israelis but also that they brought this punishment upon themselves. They have no one else but themselves to blame. 'Summer Rains' seems, therefore, to be aimed more at the enemy than at the home front. In 2006, Israel coined the code name 'Operation Just Reward' to refer to its massive bombardment of South Lebanon. Like the Palestinians, the Lebanese had to get their 'just reward' for harbouring Hezbollah and allowing it to operate from South Lebanon.[134] However, some of the Israeli code names are aimed at the home front, particularly the armed forces, such as 'Operation Focus' ('*Moked*' in Hebrew) for the devastating air strikes against Egypt, Jordan and Syria in 1967 or 'Operation Strongheart/Valiant' for the Israeli counterattack against Egypt in the 1973 War. Furthermore, Israeli code names display a strong sense of rootedness in Jewish culture and history, ancient and modern, but I will not deal with the themes they evoke here because of space limitations.

Arabic code names tend to aim at inspiration by borrowing the names of victories scored by the early Muslims/Arabs against their enemies. The early Islamic period is full of inspirational meanings for Arabs and Muslims; this is the time when a small number of men were able to triumph against huge adversity, leading to the establishment of Islam, and the Arabs through it, as a force to be reckoned with on the international stage. The names of battles from this period, therefore, carry a strong motivational

133 It was so popular, in fact, that some Lebanese remember this as the code name used by Hezbollah for its operations against the Israelis (Hibah George, personal communication).

134 Gavriely-Nuri comments that the use of the word *operation* in this code name, *mivtza* in Hebrew (short action in time and dimension), was intended to '[camouflage] the real dimensions of the IDF actions and [to present] the war as a small, local, almost trivial event' (2008: 7). By doing so, military planners wanted to 'annihilate' the war in the eyes of the Israeli public. The most famous example of this usage is 'Operation Peace for Galilee,' which led to the invasion of Lebanon and entry into Beirut in 1982.

and inspirational force for Arabs and Muslims. It is no wonder that the Egyptians and the Syrians gave their attack against the Israeli forces in Sinai and the Golan Heights in 1973 the code name 'Operation Badr.' Occurring in 624 during the month of Ramadan, this battle was the first major triumph of Prophet Muhammad and his followers against their enemies. Facing a much more powerful contingent, the Muslims stood their ground in spite of the fact that some were fasting Ramadan. Muslims, therefore, attribute the victory of Badr to divine intervention. The fact that the 1973 War did, in fact, take place during the month of Ramadan makes the use of the code name 'Operation Badr' in connection with this war highly appropriate from the Egyptian and Syrian viewpoint, the intention being to motivate and to inspire the soldiers on the front, as well as to rally the home, Arab and Muslim fronts behind them at the same time.

The same rationale underlies the use of the code name 'Qadisiyyat Saddam' by the Iraqi government (i.e., Saddam) to refer to the Iran-Iraq War (1980–88). This code name harks back to one of the greatest battles ever fought in early Islamic history. In this battle in 636, the Muslims scored a decisive victory against the Sassanian army, which ended in the death of Rostam, the commander-in-chief of the Persian forces, and ultimately led to the collapse of the empire he represented. By using this code name, which has strong anti-Persian overtones, Saddam aimed at (1) motivating his forces, (2) inspiring the home and Arab fronts and (3) projecting himself as the proud son of the early brave and victorious Arabs. This code name was commemorated in banknotes, stamps, medals and murals and on the dials of government gift watches embossed with an image of Saddam, the code name 'Qadisiyyat Saddam' and the inscription stating that the watch was made from the armour of the martyrs who fell in this war (see figures 5.11–5.13).

However, although the battle of Qadisiyya is presented in the historical sources as an Islamic victory over the Sassanians, and of the believers over the unbelievers, Saddam's Ba'thist regime filled it with Arab meanings that

Figure 5.11. Iraqi banknote, 25 dinar, Qadisiyya battle in the background.

Figure 5.12. Stamp showing 'Qadisiyyat Saddam,' with tank and missile.

Figure 5.13. The inscription on the dial reads, 'Made from the Weapons of the Martyrs of the Glorious Qadisiyyat Saddam.'

harked back to the ethnic strife between the Arabs and the Persians in the eighth to tenth centuries, called *shu'ubiyya* in the sources.[135] Thus, as a code name, 'Qadisiyyat Saddam' was not intended to evoke an Islamic past—after

135 See Agius (1980), Qaddura (1972) and Suleiman (2003: 55–63) for the original meaning of *shu'ubiyya*.

all, the Iranians are mostly Muslim—but a reconceptualised nationalist and secularist past that pits Arab against Iranian. This semantic reincarnation is consistent with the use of another secularist code name, '*Umm al-Ma'ārik*' ('The Mother of All Battles'), for the first Gulf War in 1991. As an inspirational code name, '*Umm al-Ma'ārik*' fell foul of one of Churchill's stipulations—it was boastful and overconfident—but it accurately reflected the secularist ideology of the ruling Ba'th Party in Iraq.

Sometimes an Arabic code name may not use the name of a battle from the early Islamic period but simply use the term *ghazwa* ('raid') to evoke the memory not just of one battle but of all of the battles that are classified under this term. This is precisely what Usama bin Laden did in code-naming the 2001 attacks on New York '*Ghazwat* New York.' The term *ghazwa* in Arabic carries multiple symbolic meanings, chief among which is the idea that the attack is morally justified, that it is carried out by a small party against a bigger and much stronger enemy, that God is on the side of the small party and that the success of the attacks will herald a new era in which Islam and the Muslims will triumph over their enemies. None of these meanings is available to the ordinary American, but this does not matter very much, because the code name is primarily aimed at the Muslim world, whose support it seeks to garner.

However, not all Arabic code names are cut to this Islamic mould. As mentioned earlier, 'Qadisiyyat Saddam' and '*Umm al-Ma'ārik*' follow a nationalist, even secular, path. In 1967, the Egyptians chose the code name '*Al-Fajr*' ('Dawn') to designate their aborted strike against Israel before the start of what the Arabs sometime call the June War and the Israelis call the Six Day War, a name intended to humiliate and to rub the Arab nose into its spectacular defeat. '*Al-Fajr*' may have been chosen because the strike was scheduled to take place at dawn; or it may have been chosen because, additionally, this term refers to the first prayer of the day (*ṣalāt al-fajr*), which coincides with the break of day, the dawn. It is, however, most likely that this code name was chosen because of its nationalist connotations. According to this interpretation, '*Al-Fajr*' here refers to the start of a new beginning of national revival, which the victory against Israel would herald in the Arab world. In this sense, this code name has an aspirational dimension more than an inspiring or motivational one. This interpretation is consistent with the dominant secularist politics in the Arab world at the time. Hence my interest in interdisciplinarity in this book (see chapter 2).

Like personal names and place names, code names are embedded in their sociopolitical contexts. They reflect the dominant ideologies in their societies at the time they are coined. As archived onomastic material that invokes the past, code names carry historically contingent meanings that cannot be divorced from questions of identity and conflict in society and between societies. The fact that most code names have a short shelf life does not compromise the validity of this observation. Code names offer us snapshots of symbolic meanings along a moving frame. However, by tracking the major breaks in this frame, we can identify the major sociopolitical ruptures in society.

CONCLUSION: NAMES, IDENTITY AND CONFLICT

A number of considerations underline the present study of names in the Arabic-speaking world. To begin with, Arabic personal names are considered linguistic material and, therefore, a legitimate target of study from a sociolinguistic perspective. Although personal names are not listed in Arabic lexica, the fact that most names in this category are reducible to roots that carry semantic import enables us to access the social values these meanings convey. The same principle does not apply to all toponyms, and less so to code names. Second, although the primary function of all names is to index the objects they refer to by marking them off from other objects in the same class or category, what makes names particularly rich data for sociolinguistic study is their ability to act as the carriers of symbolic meanings that touch on issues of Self, identity, conflict, modernity, modernisation, the diaspora and memory. In spite of the salience of these parameters, most studies of Arabic names from the sociolinguistic perspective have been restricted to the production of taxonomies or to identifying some of the major name-giving trends for a given name pool and how these might have evolved over time.[136] Studies that link names to the above parameters of analysis and interpretation hardly exist for Arabic. This may reflect the variationist and correlational bias of Arabic sociolinguistics in the second half of the twentieth century, or it may be the result of the difficulty of managing the multiplicity of perspectives that can feed into studying names, some of which have been mentioned at the beginning of this chapter.

This lacuna is not restricted to Arabic sociolinguistics but extends to the political study of the Arabic-speaking world and, it seems, to political science more generally. In a study of street names in Helsinki, Palonen, himself a political scientist, points to the fact that research on names is 'hardly ever conducted at all in political science departments, while traditional onomastics has been afraid of politics' (1993: 103). The first observation may be related to a dominant view that assigns names to the margins of politics in line with the discussion of what I have called the residual place of liminality in chapter 2. The second observation is acknowledged in a study of place names and politics in which the author sums up the traditional view of onomastics as a field of study that concerns itself with 'such matters as the spelling, pronunciation, morphology, grammar, meaning, content and usage of names in a descriptive, somewhat detached manner, deliberately setting aside emotive issues and anything that smacks of political controversy' (Nicolaisen 1990: 193–94). This is related to the issue of disciplinary boundaries I referred to in chapter 2. By holding to these positions, politics and onomastics do not pay sufficient attention to the idea that 'in times of linguistic controversy and cultural friction, names are apt to generate emotional . . . responses, and their symbolic force should never be

136 For example, Abd-el-Jawad (1986), Bean (1980), Gardner (1994), Yassin (1978), Yassin (1986).

underestimated, especially in the realm of politics' (195). In fact, the issue is more weighted in the direction of politics, in the sense that it is politics that leads to friction, controversy and conflict, which then tend to get reflected in the linguistic and onomastic domains in their capacity as a site of contestation in the public sphere. The present study is informed by this orientation of cause and effect between politics and onomastics. Names may signal and trigger conflict, but they hardly ever create it in the social world. They are symptoms rather than causes, but as symptoms, they direct our attention to the existence of underlying causes and help us track them.

Against this background, the present study locates identity at the core of names and naming. The political meanings of identity remain dormant or low-key in ordinary situations where conflict is not salient in society, but they erupt into action when ignited by cultural or political conflict. As the cause of many of the fault lines in the Middle East, political conflict fuels a corresponding onomastics of hegemony and counterhegemony, of coercion and resistance, of media manipulation and the deliberate shaping of public opinion, of assimilation, dissimulation and dissimilation both transethnically and transnationally. These onomastic currents apply to personal names and to place names on both the level of the Self and the group level of collective identity in various parts of the Middle East. Media manipulation is particularly pronounced in code names.

Furthermore, these same currents extend their influence to personal names in the diaspora, in which questions of belonging, loyalty and memory are accentuated against the background of competing allegiance to the host society or the imperatives of instrumentality. In the wake of 11 September 2001, Arabic names in the diaspora have become a more politicised phenomenon than before, leading to cyber-battles and to acts of self-imposed onomastic surgery that amount to amputation of some inner part of the Self. However, the response to this politicisation of names has not been uniform. Compliance to the norms of the host society leads some people to adopt neutral names or to adapt their names to suit the onomastic conventions of the diaspora. Noncompliance pulls in the opposite direction, leading some people to use stereotypically Arab and Muslim names, an example of which is the popularity of the name Muhammad in Britain; this practice may be interpreted as an act of defiance aimed at challenging the hegemony of the state and as a gesture of symbolic resistance against prejudice and racial discrimination in society.

Place names exhibit the scars of political conflict. The Israeli-Palestinian dispute provides ample data on the onomastic erasure of Arabic names and their replacement by Hebrew ones that promote a different narrative of national identity. The Hebrew onomasticon at times exhibits differences of ideology and national imagination between the ruling parties. Whether consciously or unconsciously, this onomasticon extends its influence to academic discourse, making science a(n) (un)witting agent of the state and its policies of land acquisition by force. In the case of the Palestinians in Israel and the Occupied Territories, acts of onomastic resistance in academic discourse are carried out, but they hardly succeed, because of the intensely coercive power of the state. The struggle over place names in historical Palestine is a struggle over the symbolic resources of representation and ownership.[137] This struggle lies at the heart of the graffiti skirmishes in Jerusalem between Jews and Palestinians whose mundane target is to deface the place names of the Other but whose ulterior motive is to contest symbolically any claim the other party may have over representation and ownership.[138] The conflict over place names extends to the names of countries. This has been particularly the case since the collapse of the Soviet Union and the Oslo Pact in the 1990s.[139]

If place names exhibit the scars of political conflict, military code names orbit close to the centre of political conflict. Code names of this type exist at the interface of conflict management, media manipulation and public relations campaigns. Most of these names are coined to convey symbolic meanings that are aimed at multiple audiences whose interests and worldviews may, in fact, be at odds with one another. Code names are sometimes used to motivate and inspire, but at other times, they are deployed to frighten and intimidate or to take the moral high ground to gain public support. Exploiting metaphors of nature, code names are used to mask the difference between the natural and the contrived, therefore justifying the actions they refer to by depicting them as part of human experience. In their exploitation of the past, code names circulate old meanings of adversity, steadfastness, justice, divine intervention and merited triumph. Unlike personal and, to a lesser extent, place names, code names operate at the cutting edge of symbolic functionality. Furthermore, because the creation of code names can be dated with accuracy, it is often possible to set them into their historical and

137 Bodenhorn and vom Bruck recognise this as an important part of naming: 'The political economy of place naming is not surprisingly ferociously fought when the stakes are conceived to underpin the formation of nation-states and when the peoples involved coexist in unequal positions' (2006: 12). The struggle over names in Palestine and Israel is a good example of this aspect of naming.

138 See Suleiman (2004b: 193, 202).

139 In 1990, a debate took place in Czechoslovakia concerning the new name of the country. In what was known as the 'great hyphen debate,' the Slovaks insisted on inserting a hyphen into the name of the newly reformed country, 'Czecho-Slovakia,' to give visibility to their national identity, which would be marked by an upper-case rather than a lower-case *S* in the proposed name. The proposal was rejected in the legislature in favour of a new name with two versions: 'Czechoslovak Federative Republic in Bohemia and Moravia' (the Czech-speaking part) and 'Czecho-Slovak Federative Republic in Slovakia' (see Coulmas 1994). The hyphen disappeared when the two parts of pre-1990 Czechoslovakia went their separate ways politically in January 1993. Greece provides another revealing example of the interest in names as signs of national identity. Coulmas reports that the Greek government was able to persuade other European Community members that the 'former Yugoslav republic of Macedonia would be granted EC recognition only on condition that it used another name' (1994: 39). Coulmas explains the reason behind this move as follows: 'Any association of [the republic of Macedonia] with the Macedonians of northern Greece, whose language enjoys no official status, had to be avoided. Greece considers the name "Macedonian" to be part of its heritage and fears it would imply territorial claims by the new state on the northern Greek province of Macedonia' (39). See Suleiman (2004b: 56–57) for further examples.

ideological contexts with some confidence. This fact aids the process of reading them symbolically.

Names are an important aspect of personal and collective remembrance in that they help to create mnemonic communities whose members identify with a common past and try to remember it, even though some of them may not have experienced it firsthand. In helping to perform this task, names invoke questions of identity and ownership. In some cases, place names are acquired as new surnames or cyber-monikers to keep the memory of places of origin and social networks alive. The memory-book genre among the Palestinians is partly aimed at preserving the national onomasticon and at protecting it against forgetfulness and oblivion. Gazetteers serve the same objectives, as do atlas guides. Going beyond the immediate aim of onomastic preservation, all of this effort is ultimately aimed at continuing to press the claim of ownership of the land. And this struggle over names is a continuation of the political struggle by other means. It serves notice to the other party that although the din of war has died out, the symbolic battle is still raging.

Names provide useful information on the shared values of a community that cut across its religious or ethnic divides. They can also provide insight into issues of modernity and modernisation. Whereas the dominant interpretation of modernisation tends to associate it with Westernisation (for the Druze, it is Israelisation), names can provide evidence to show that modernisation can be home-grown and tradition-bound. The culling of new personal names from the text of the Qur'an may be considered as much an aspect of modernisation as the application of foreign names is. Responses to these modes of onomastic modernisation can reveal generational differences that underline the cross-religious commonalities of a community. The fact that members of the older generation, Christian and Muslim, react negatively to the new names is an example of these commonalities.

In a more comprehensive study of names, Self, identity and conflict in the Middle East, one would have to tackle the use of ethnonyms and ethnolinguistic labels. I have referred to this in passing with respect to the names of Jews in Israel who originated in the Arabic-speaking world. In *A War of Words: Language and Conflict in the Middle East* (Suleiman 2004b: 114–24), I have discussed this issue in connection with the naming of the Jordanians of Palestinian origin in Jordan as *Beljikis* (Belgians) to signal their status as outsiders vis-à-vis the East Jordanians, correlating the inception of this ethnonym with the attempt by successive governments in the 1970s to establish Jordan as a nation-state for the East Jordanians first and foremost. In North Africa, the ethnonyms *Berber* and *Amazigh* are loaded terms sociopolitically; the transition from the former to the latter as the dominant name in recent years is correlated with the rise in ethnic, language-based politics in Algeria and Morocco. Similarly, the reference to North Africans in France as *Beur*, a syllable reversal of *Arabe*, was originally intended to exclude and stigmatise. The same is true of the term *Harkis* to refer to the 'descendents of Frenchmen of Algerian origin and Muslim faith who served in the French military' (Safran 2008: 447).

In this chapter, I have relied on different types of data. In some cases, I have used the name pools generated by other researchers but attempted to link them to issues of identity, conflict and modernisation, thus going beyond the taxonomic approach that tends to dominate the study of these pools. In doing this, I have aimed at interpretation and explanation, not description. In other cases, I have used data culled from a variety of nontraditional sources, for example, reader responses to news stories and newspaper reports. The reader-response sections on Web pages have opened up an important public space for people to post their views and for these readers to interact with one another in ways that have never been available in the print media in the past. The spontaneity and immediacy of these responses are reflected in their chatty style, copious spelling errors, glaring grammatical mistakes, use of colloquial dialects with heavy country-bound features and, most important of all, flouting of many of the internalised norms of self-censorship that many Arabs labour under in their home societies. This material contains pithy insights that help frame, in a contextualised manner, the main contours of the interaction between names and issues of Self, identity and conflict.

The third kind of data employed in this chapter are self-reports on name-giving practises. In these reports, the subject and the researcher share the same person, but they do so in different capacities. As I pointed out in chapter 2, the use of personal protocols as research data can lead to bias and to contamination in these data; however, these protocols can offer insights, and they present rich possibilities for fine-tuned analyses of empirically generated data. To capture these possibilities, while at the same time guarding against bias and contamination, the researcher needs to corroborate his analyses by calibrating them against one another or similar results that can be obtained through more orthodox research methods. In this connection, the *Boston Globe* story is calibrated with Sam Hamod's poem and with my self-reported reflections about my brother's name change. The same is true of my data concerning my son's name and the naming scene in *Dancing Arabs*. And, finally, to show the interdisciplinary potential of names, I have—for validation purposes—used literary material that, as with self-reported data, can be shown to accord with the results obtained from more traditional forms of knowledge production. Literary data of this kind are creative constructions of an anthropological kind. It is this fact that makes them particularly relevant in the study of names.

In dealing with these data, I have used two strategies. On the one hand, I provided macro-level analyses to outline in broad terms the interconnections involving names, Self and collective identity against the background of conflict in the Arab Middle East and in the diaspora. On the other hand, I augmented these by micro-level analyses of selected portions of data to point to some of the intricacies that exist in names and naming when pursued from the perspectives of the Self, collective identity and conflict. These twin approaches are intended to create a rich texture that can guide future empirical research and help in mining existing name pools to refine, or challenge, the analyses provided here.

Chapter 6

Conclusion

The study of the language-identity-conflict link in the Arabic-speaking world is a productive area of scholarship that straddles several disciplinary boundaries. I have tackled the language-group identity link and the language-conflict link in two previous studies (Suleiman 2003 and 2004b, respectively). In this book, I have tried to bring these two links together under one overarching theme to reflect the interdependence of identity and conflict insofar as they relate to language. Active political conflicts in the Arab Middle East are marked in language in its capacity as a symbolic resource in society and, in terms of instrumentality, as the means of communicating the content of these conflicts for action and counteraction. While this book continues the qualitative, interdisciplinary and symbolic trajectory of my earlier research, it, however, introduces a number of new elements that are at the heart of my research project on language and identity.

This book shifts the balance of my interest from group identity to the Self in studying the Arabic language in the social world while still recognising the importance of the former. It pursues this interest through an autoethnography that tracks the author's use of the *fuṣḥā* in a well-defined setting, reading into it a set of meanings to reveal the complexity of the Self, its positionality and the notion that the Self is not just a set of attributes or roles that the individual has and plays but also a resource that the individual uses to achieve instrumental objectives of various kinds, whether they are financial, professional or educational. I have pursued this interest in the Self and language further by investigating two autobiographies, those of Edward Said and Leila Ahmed, to set out how the language-Self link as a nexus of identity conceptualisation responds to political and social conflicts in society on the symbolic front. For Said, Arabic has been shown to be inextricably linked with his exilic life in various ways: as a sign of displacement, alienation, belonging, resistance and family pride as a father, as well as through its role in providing a link with an embargoed, archived, excavated and reconstituted past. Standing at the crossroads of all of these associations, Said views Arabic as that which links exile and the diaspora, on the one hand, with home, on the other, in a way that challenges their separateness while, at the same time, acknowledging their disjunctive impact on the Self. While Said declares himself to be 'living in Arabic' towards the end of his life, his earlier life was marked by a strong feeling of alienation from the language.

Ahmed constructs the language-Self link vis-à-vis Arabic differently. Her experience and her family's experience under Nasser's regime were riddled with conflict, alienation and the loss of privileges economically, educationally and socially. In articulating these themes in her autobiography, Ahmed constructs the *fuṣḥā* as a motif around which she expresses her personal anxieties and deep-seated anger, referring to the language as an instrument of internal colonialism in Egypt. Linking the Self to group identity, Ahmed attacks Nasser's regime for seeking to orient Egyptian identity in a pan-Arab direction—away from a purely Egypt-centred Egyptian nationalism—in which the *fuṣḥā*, rather than Egyptian Arabic, is promoted as a symbol of individual and group belonging. In addition to this presumed link with the hegemonic and coercive pan-Arab state ideology, the *fuṣḥā* is said to acquire its status as an instrument of internal colonialism via its deployment, according to Ahmed, as a tool of misogynist theology. As a male language, the *fuṣḥā* is said to be complicit in constructing discriminatory readings of the Islamic legal sources whose aim is to perpetuate female subjugation in Muslim societies.

The complexity of the language-Self link in the Arab context is further exhibited in the study of names. As linguistic material with transparent root meanings, Arabic personal names offer a rich arena in the Arab context for linking language to the Self and group identity, both at home and in the diaspora. Personal names index social and political values in society, and they track the contours of political and social conflicts over time. They can further reveal archaeologies of personal naming systems that point to greater past harmonies cross-communally where current conflicts reign supreme. Naming practises further reveal the structures of power and hegemony in society, but they also signal the rich scope for contestation that they offer. This is as true of personal names as it is of toponyms, ethnonyms and the code names of wars and military operations in the Middle East. In this context, the linguistic landscape and the map as a cartographic text emerge as an arena for ideological contestation through which claims of ownership, identity inscription and identity erasure can be pursued. The linguistic landscape can also be used as a public space for expressing the values of modernity in society, often linking them to outside (Western) sources of status and prestige. These acts of expression clash with the forces of tradition in the linguistic landscape in a way that enacts the tug of war between authenticity and change in society.

In the diaspora, naming practises may carry strong oppositional connotations that speak in different ways to the in-group and the out-group, signalling the desire for authenticity and continuity with the prediasporic culture, on the one hand, or indicating the desire to integrate in the host community, on the other. Either way, conflict is a motivating factor in these impulses. It is the engine that drives the forces of maintenance and change in society. However, name giving may aim at bridging the existing fault lines in the diaspora by offering the name giver and the named person possibilities for negotiation that keep identity maintenance and identity change in balance. Shedding an old name in favour of a new diaspora name may give the person instrumental and integrative advantages, but it could also lead to a feeling of estrangement from the old Self, onomastic self-mutilation or some identity loss.

Aprincipal underlying assumption in the study of the language-Self link in this book is the view of identity as a rhizomatic construct that embodies continuity and change. Although the Self is never fixed, it is, however, not fluid in a way that denies it any core or stability. We may point in this regard to Said's attitude towards Arabic, which underwent many changes in his life, while noting how his basic link with the language as a sign of belonging remained a constant in spite of the lure of English as an alternative site of Self conceptualisation. Ahmed's negative attitude towards the *fuṣḥā* has remained constant throughout her life, but it seems to have increased in intensity over time, owing to the new connotations it had acquired as the language of doctrinal misogyny in the Arabic intellectual tradition. In other words, whereas Ahmed conceptualised the *fuṣḥā* as the language of a pan-Arab internal colonialism in Egypt in her youth, the language later acquired new antifeminist connotations for her, no doubt in response to her professional identity as a scholar with interest in feminism in the Arab context. These new meanings of the language represent another form of internal colonialism (for her).

As I have pointed out above, social and political conflicts are at the heart of the language-identity-Self link in the Arabic-speaking world. This is reflected in names and name-giving practises at home and in the diaspora. The Arab-Israeli conflict, particularly for the Palestinians, and the events of 11 September 2001 (mainly for diaspora Arabs and Muslims of non-Arab background) have been shown to be motivating factors in the choice of names in these contexts. The use of toponyms, ethnonyms and (military) code names is linked in this regard to the violent conflicts of the Middle East. The dominance of the *fuṣḥā* is directly linked by Moustapha Safouan to the deep-rooted despotism of the Arab political order and its antidemocratic character, although this connection is very tenuous, to say the least. As far as this writer is concerned, only the resort to the vernaculars can change this situation. This call for vernacularisation is further linked to the much-needed cultural and socioeconomic modernisation in Arab societies in which the *fuṣḥā*, by virtue of its presumed sacredness, is said to be a huge stumbling block. Arabic is also linked to trauma in society. Globalisation has been depicted as a force that induces trauma-like anxieties that threaten the language-identity-Self link. The description of globalisation as a form of cultural penetration carries strong sexual connotations whose aim is to trade on the strong moral economies of Arab societies for task-orientation purposes. As a form of continued imperialism, the spread of English is often depicted as a direct attack on Arabic in the instrumental domain, as well as on the identities it symbolically marks in society. In this respect, globalisation is conceptualised as the continuation of colonialism against the Arabic-speaking peoples through nonviolent imperialist means.

Being forged under conditions of conflict, the language-identity-Self link is impregnated with ideology. The above readings of language and globalisation are ideological, not empirical. The treatment of the *fuṣḥā* as an obstacle to democracy and sociocultural modernisation is ideological, as are some of the responses to it. The connections I have made in my autoethnography in chapter 3 between the Self of the author and the *fuṣḥā* are linked to ideology. I am aware that 'ideology' calls forth impressions of intellectual fabrication and subjective bias in the social sciences. One response to this might be to dismiss ideology from the purview of the study of language in the social world altogether. But this would be a shortsighted response and one that is hardly feasible, considering the difficulty sometimes of sifting fact from fiction in social life. The elimination of the ideological would deprive the social sciences of some of the data that make language such a productive site for the study of identity. Furthermore, ideology is at the heart of whatever makes language a political phenomenon. Ideology will always be a mixture of fact and fiction, but when fictions take hold in a community over a long period of time, they can turn into founding myths that resonate with how the community comes to imagine itself, turning them into some kind of psychological 'truths.' The power of ideology lies in those acts of imagining that can serve as sources of motivation for action and counteraction in society. As one of the most important symbolic resources in society, language cannot avoid the intrusion of ideology, nor should it be protected against such an intrusion.

Any discussion of the language-identity-conflict link in the Arab context will inevitably invoke the concept of diglossia. Academic discussions have revealed the shortcomings of any binary treatment of diglossia into two oppositional categories: the *fuṣḥā* and the *'āmiyyas*. That intermediate forms of Arabic exist between the *fuṣḥā* and the *'āmiyyas* is not in dispute. This, however, does not deny the psychological validity of the *fuṣḥā*-versus-*'āmiyya* divide within the totality of the language in Arabic folk linguistics. Arabic speakers do conceptualise their language situation in more or less dichotomous way, ascribing different values to the *fuṣḥā* and the *'āmiyyas*. While Arabic sociolinguistics cannot ignore the descriptive facts of language behaviour, it must, however, strive to accommodate the above folk-linguistic reality in its treatment of the language. For this reason, I have tried to draw a distinction between the two concepts of 'mother tongue' and 'native language' in the Arabic-language situation by allocating the former to the *'āmiyyas* and the latter to the *fuṣḥā*. Involving ideology, this distinction takes account of the role of these two constellations of language forms in Arabic as sites of different feelings of belonging, which may sometimes sit comfortably with each other, while, at other times, they may compete against each other in irreconcilable ways. Said's relationship with Arabic accommodated both the *fuṣḥā* and the *'āmiyya*, but this is not the case for Ahmed, who conceives of the relationship between them as oppositional and antithetical in identity terms.

Intermediate forms of Arabic, such as Educated Spoken Arabic, do not evoke the same feelings of belonging as the *'āmiyyas* and the *fuṣḥā* do in

Arabic speakers, a fact that signals the low symbolic load of these forms as sites of identity in Arab cultural life. In fact, many Arabic speakers may not even be aware of the existence of these intermediate forms, such is the psychological pull of the two ends of the diglossic continuum. If true, this points to the need to work with the perceptual categories of Arabic speakers, in spite of the fact that these categories, as folk-linguistic constructs, clash with the descriptive accounts of the Arabic language as a variable system of communication. Ignoring these perceptual facts may reduce the interference of ideology in discussing the Arabic-language situation. But such a reduction can be achieved only at a price, this being the elimination of some of the deeply held attitudes and beliefs about Arabic that endow it with high symbolic value in the political domain.

The data in this book are varied. Some are autoethnographic. As self-reports, data of this type are introspective and retrospective. In these data, the researcher is the subject of research. Data of this kind are subject to memory limitations, memory attrition, subjective bias, deliberate manipulation and subtle mutations that can reduce the reliability of the research findings based on them. Although these problems characterise all research in the social sciences to varying degrees, it is believed that they are particularly acute in autoethnographic research because of the cognitive proximity of the researcher and the research subject. The problem here is how to ensure the validity of the research findings of autoethnographic research when value neutrality may be seriously compromised because of the distinct threat of subjective bias. Qualitative researchers dismiss such concerns as a throwback to a positivist model of enquiry in the social sciences that mistakenly believes in the supreme value of quantification and the unassailability of objectivity as the 'gold standard' in scientific enquiry. While radical positivism of this kind is not an option that can be supported in social science, an autoethnographic radicalism that gives free rein to unfettered introspection and subjectivity is not a viable alternative, either. Furthermore, while accepting that the boundary between the researcher and the researched is not hermetically sealed, it would be methodologically rash to say that there are no barriers between them. Extra measures will, therefore, have to be applied in autoethnographic research to make sure that the reliability of this research is enhanced. These measures may include (1) the use of fieldwork-style self-reports recorded at the time of the research to aid memory recall retrospectively; (2) the involvement of monitors wherever possible to authenticate the veracity of the behaviours being reported; (3) supporting the findings of autoethnographic research by showing them to be consistent with the findings drawn from similar empirical domains, and (4) aligning these results with established theoretical insights to give these results greater credibility.

Autoethnography is a form of autobiography. The difference between the two as research topics in this book, however, is that in autobiography, the researcher and the researched are different. This affords the researcher greater cognitive and emotional distance from the researched, reducing the threat of subjective bias that attends autoethnography. I have used two autobiographies in this work, those of Edward Said and Leila Ahmed. These autobiographies are interesting because of the significant role that language plays in the narratives of the Self that they offer. As has been pointed out earlier, both Said and Ahmed give prominence to language psychologically and symbolically as a motif in relation to which they express a multiplicity of feelings, including belonging and alienation, which directly relate to the identity-conflict nexus in society. This nexus is accessed through other data in this book, including the use of name pools, literary compositions and Internet materials about names in the diaspora. I am aware that this choice of materials may be unorthodox in the study of the language-identity-conflict link in society. However, this is not a barrier to using materials of this kind, owing to their empirical productivity in investigating what is a rhizomatic and, therefore, an interdisciplinary subject of enquiry. Casting the empirical net wide is not necessarily a challenge to rigor or a slide into subjectivity and bias but an enhancement of the database that can be brought to bear on our discussions of language as a cultural construct.

Researching the language-Self link raises the question of the generalisability of the results obtained through autoethnography, autobiography or individual self-reports to larger populations. Are these findings subject-specific? Or can they be generalised to other subjects or groups of subjects? The answer is not an either/or one. The point about linking language to the Self in articulating identity is precisely to generate material that operates on the level of the individual, albeit the fact that this is invariably set against, and is conducted in interaction with, considerations that pertain to group identity. In return, group identity itself is experienced at both the level of the individual—that is, the Self—and the group. It is, therefore, not possible to separate the Self from group identity, and vice versa, in the study of language in the social world. However, the question remains of how much of that which pertains to the Self is generalisable to the group in studying language in society. In other words, how much of my autoethnography can apply to other Arabic speakers?

This is not an easy question to answer because of the positionality and context-dependency of the Self that emerges in this autoethnography. However, it would be true to say that some Arabic speakers will share most, some, few or none of the attitudes I have towards the *fuṣḥā* and the interpretations they give to these. I have referred to this in this book as 'resonance.' The same is true of the ban on code-switching. The degree of cross-subject agreement will no doubt depend upon where and how other subjects locate themselves in their own social worlds. One thing, however, is certain: no matter where subjects locate themselves in the social world, language will continue to act as a linchpin of their identity, regardless of whether it is conceived as a repertoire of roles, a set of attributes or a resource with which to do things through language symbolism and language use.

Bibliography

Works in Arabic Cited in the Text

'Abd al-Salām, Aḥmad. 2001. Al-'awlama al-thaqāfiyya al-lughawiyya wa-tabi'ātuhā li-al-lugha al-'arabiyya. *Majallat majma' al-lugha al-'arabiyya al-urdunī* 60: 117–47. Amman: Majma' al-Lugha al-'Arabiyya al-Urdunī.

Abtaḥ, Sawsan al-. 2001. Al-Tabarruj al-lughawī: Al-ṭarīq al-asra' ilā al-hāwiya. *Asharq al-Awsat*, 13 August.

Abū Zayd, Bakr bin 'Abdallah. 1416, AH. *Taghrīb al-alqāb al-'ilmiyya*. Riyadh: Dār Al-'Āṣima.

'Alī, Nabīl, and Nadia Ḥijāzī. 2005. *Al-Fajwa al-raqamiyya: Ru'ya 'arabiyya li-mujtama' al-ma'rifa*. Kuwait: 'Ālam al-Ma'rifa.

Al-Waṭan. 2008. *Akādīmī su'ūdī yushabbih 'al-naḥwiyyīn al-'arab bi-al-muḥāfiẓ īn al-judud fī amrīkā* ('A Saudi academic likens the [modern] Arab grammarians to the neo-cons in America'). 5 January, issue 4507: 12.

'Arrāf, Shukrī. 2007. *Al-Mawāqi' al-jughrāfiyya fī filasṭīn: Al-asmā' al-'arabiyya wa-al-tasmiyāt al-'ibriyya*. Beirut: Mu'assassat al-Dirāsāt al-Filasṭīniyya.

'Asīrī, 'Abd al-Raḥmān bin Muḥammad. 2001. Al-'Awāmil al-ijtimā'iyya, wa-l-thaqāfiyya al-murtabiṭa bi-asmā' al-a'lām fī al-mujtam' al-su'ūdī. *Majallat al-'ulūm al-ijtimā'iyya* 29: 135–64.

'Aṭiyya, 'Āṭif. 1990. Al-Asmā' al-mutadāwala fī qarya lubnāniyya wa-l-taḥawwulāt al-latī ṭara'at 'alayhā. *Al-Fikr al-'Arabī* 62: 195–214.

Badawī, El-Sa'īd Muḥammad. 1973. *Mustawawayāt al-'arabiyya al-mu'āṣira fī miṣr*. Cairo: Dār al-Ma'ārif.

Baḥrāwī, Sayyid al-. 1997. Lughat al-salām shopping centre li-l-muḥajjabāt. In Maḥmūd Amīn al-'Ālim, ed., *Lughatunā al-'arabiyya*. Cairo: Silsilat Kitāb Qaḍāyā Mu'āṣira, pp. 135–38.

Bankī, Muḥammad Aḥmad al-. 2005. *Derrida 'arabiyyan: Qirā'at al-tafkīk fī al-fikr al-naqdī al-'arabī*. Beirut: Al-Mu'assasa al-'Arabiyya li-l-Dirāsāt wa-l-Nashr.

Barhūma, 'Īsā 'Ūda. 2005. Al-Lugha wa-l-tawāṣul al-i'lānī: Mathal min intishār al-asmā' al-ajnabiyya fī al-lāfitāt al-tijāriyya fī al-urdun. *Majallat majma' al-lugha al-'arabiyya al-urdunī*. Amman: Majma' al-Lugha al-'Arabiyya al-Urdunī.

Bāṭāhir, Bin 'Īsā. 2001. *Al-Dawr al-ḥaḍārī li-l-'arabiyya fī 'aṣr al-'awlama*. Sharjah, UAE: Jam'iyyat Ḥimāyat al-Lugha al-'Arabiyya.

Belqzīz, 'Abd al-Ilāh. 2002. *Al-'Awlama wa-al-mumāna'a: Dirāsāt fī al-mas'ala al-thaqāfiyya*. Lattakiyya: Dār al-Ḥiwār li-l-Nashr wa-l-Tawzī'.

Bin Salāma, al-Bashīr. 1974. *Al-Shakhṣiyya al-tūnusiyya: Khaṣā'iṣuhā wa-muqawwimātuhā*. Tunis: Mua'ssasat 'Abd al-'Azīz Bin 'Abdallah.

Bishr, Kamāl Muḥammad. 1995. *Khāṭirāt mu'talifāt fi al-lugha wa-l-thaqāfa*. Cairo: Dār Gharīb li-l-Ṭibā'a wa-l-Nashr wa-l-Tawzī'.

Dajānī, Aḥmad Zakī al-. 1989. *Madīnatunā yāfā wa-thawrat 1936*.

Dhuwadī, Maḥmūd al-. 1981. Judhūr al-franco-arab al-unthawiyya bi-l-maghrib al-'arabī. *Shu'ūn 'arabiyya* 22: 124–37.

———. 1983. Al-Takhalluf al-ākhar fī al-maghrib al-'arabī. *Al-Mustaqbal al-'arabī* 47: 20–41.

———. 1986. Al-Mazj al-lughawī ka-sulūk lughawī li-l-insān al-maghribī al maghlūb. *Al-Majalla al-'arabiyya li-l-'ulūm al-insāniyya* 6: 46–66.

———. 1988. Ba'ḍ al-jawānib al-ukhrā li-mafhūm al-takhalluf al-ākhar fī al-waṭan al-'arabī. *Al-Waḥda* 50: 79–94.

———. 1996. Al-Franco-arab al-unthawiyya al-maghāribiyya ka-sulūk iḥtijājī 'alā al-lāmusāwā ma' al-rajul wa-karamz li-kasb rihān al-ḥadātha. *Dirāsāt 'arabiyya* 3/4: 81–89.

Ḍubayb, Aḥmad bin Muḥammad al-. 2001. *Al-Lugha al-'arabiyya fi 'aṣr al-'awlama*. Rhiyad: Maktabat al-'Ubaykān.

Fāyid, Wafā' Kāmil. n.d. *Buḥūth fi al-'arabiyya al-mu'āṣira*. 'Ālam al-Kutub.

———. 2005. Ẓāhirat taghrīb al-asmā' al-tijāriyya fī ba'ḍ 'awāṣim al-mashriq al-'arabī. Paper presented at Fourth Conference of the Arabic Language Academy, Damascus, 14–17 November.

Ghalyūn, Burhān, and Smīr Amīn. 2002. *Thaqāfat al-'awlama wa-'awlamat al-thaqāfa*. Damascus: Dār al-Fikr.

Ḥajjāj, 'Imād. 2008. *Al-Maḥjūb 2*. Amman: Abu-Mahjoob Creative Productions.

Kawwāz, Muḥammad Karīm al-. 2006. *Al-Faṣāḥa fi al-'arabiyya: Al-mafāhīm wa-l-uṣūl*. Beirut: Dār al-Intishār al-'Arabī.

Khālidī, Ibrāhīm Ḥāmid al-. 2007. *Al-Mustaṭraf al-nabaṭī: Nawādir sākhira min al-shi'r al-nabaṭī*, vol. 2. Kuwait: Manshīt al-l-Di'āya wa-l-i'lān.

Khālidī, Walīd, ed. 1997. *Kay lā nansā: Qurā filasṭīn allatī dammarathā isrā'īl sanat 1948 wa-asmā' shuhadā'ihā*. Beirut: Institute of Palestine Studies.

Khalīfa, Ḥasan. 2008. *Shi'riyyat al-muṣṭalaḥ al-naḥwī wa-masā'iluh. Al-Bahrain Al-Thaqafia* 52: 71–81.

Khūrī, Yūsuf Qazmā. 1991. *Najāh al-umma al-'arabiyya fi lughatihā al-aṣliyya*. Beirut: Dār al-Ḥamrā'.

Kūsh, 'Umar. 2002. *Aqlamat al-mafāhīm: Taḥawwulāt al-mafhūm fi irtiḥālih*. Casablanca and Beirut: Al-Markaz al-Thaqāfī al-'Arabī.

Ma'lūf, Amīn. 1999. *Al-Huwiyyāt al-qātila: Qirā'a fi al-intimā' wa-l-'awlama*, trans. by Nabīl Muḥsin. Damascus: Dār Ward.

———. 2004. *Al-Huwiyyāt al-qātila*, trans. by Nahla Bayḍūn. Beirut: Dār al-Fārābī.

Manṣūr, Johnny (Jūnī). 1999. *Shawāri' ḥaifā al-'arabiyya*. Haifa: Jam'iyyat al-Taṭwīr al-Ijtimā'ī.

Ma'tūq, Aḥmad Muḥammad al-. 2005. *Naẓariyyat al-lugha al-thālitha: Dirāsa fi qaḍiyyat al-lugha al-'arabiyya al-wusṭā*. Casablanca: Al-Markaz al-Thaqāfī al-'Arabī.

Muqaddam, Yusrā. 2010. *Al-Ḥarīm al-lughawī*. Beirut: Sharikat al-MaṬbū'āt li-l-Tawzī' wa-l-Nashr.

Mūsā, Salāma. 1947. *Al-Balāgha al-'aṣriyya wa-l-lugha al-'arabiyya*. Salāma Mūsā li-l-Nashr wa-l-Tawzī' (first published 1945.)

Naqqāsh, Rajā'. 2009. *Hal tantaḥir al-lugha al-'arabiyya?* Cairo: Nahḍat Miṣr li-l-Ṭibā'a wa-l-Nashr.

Niāzī, Ṣalāḥ. 2008. *Law umtuḥina Imru'u al-Qays bi-mā saṭṭarahu al-naḥawiyyīn la-fashila fi al-imtiḥān. Al-Thaqāfiyya* 69: 68–70.

Qaddūra, Zāhiya. 1972. *Al-Shu'ūbiyya wa-atharuhā al-ijtimā'ī wa-al-siyāsī fī al-ḥayā al-islāmiyya fī al-'aṣr al-'abbāsī al-awwal*. Beirut: Dār al-Kitāb al-Lubnānī.

Ṣafwān, Muṣṭafā. 2001. *Al-Kitāba wa-l-sulṭa*. Manshūrāt Jam'iyyat 'Ilm al-Nafs al-Iklīnīkī.

Sa'īd, Naffūsa Zakariyyā. 1964. *Tārīkh al-da'wa ilā al-'āmiyya wa-athāruhā fī miṣr*. Cairo: Matba'at Dār Nashr al-Thaqāfa.

Sāmirrā'ī, Ibrāhīm al-. 1990. *Al-A'lām al-'arabiyya: Baḥth fī asmā' al-nās*. Beirut: Dār al-Ḥadātha.

Ṭarābīshī, George (Jūrj). 2005. *Al-Maraḍ bi-al-gharb: Al-taḥlīl al-nafsī li-'uṣāb jamā'ī 'arabī*. Damascus: Dār Petra li-l-Nashr wa-l-Tawzī'.

Zughūl, Muḥammad Rājī al-. 1988. *Al-Lāfitāt fī al-urdun: Dirāsa lughawiyya ijtimā'iyya li-ba'ḍ jawānib ghurbatinā al-ḥaḍāriyya. Nadwat al-izdiwājiyya fī al-lugha al-'arabiyya*, 25–36. Amman: Majma' al-Lugha al-'Arabiyya al-Urdunī.

Works in Other Languages Cited in the Text

Abd-el-Jawad, Hassan Rashid. 1981. Lexical and Phonological Variation in Spoken Arabic in Amman. Unpublished PhD thesis, University of Pennsylvania.

———. 1986. A Linguistic and Sociocultural Study of Personal Names in Jordan. *Anthropological Linguistics* 28: 80–94.

———. 1987. Cross-Dialectal Variation in Arabic: Competing Prestigious Forms. *Language in Society* 16: 359–68.

Abdul-Fattah, H., and M. Zoghoul. 1996. Business Signs in Jordan: A Sociolinguistic Perspective. *Al-Abḥāth* 24: 59–88.

Abed, Shukri B. 2007. *Arabic Language and Culture amid the Demands of Globalization*. Abu Dhabi: Emirates Centre for Strategic Studies and Research.

Aberbach, David. 2008. Byron to D'Annunzio: From Liberalism to Fascism in National Poetry, 1815–1920. *Nations and Nationalism* 14: 478–1920.

Abu-Absi, Samir. 1990. A Characterization of the Language of *Iftaḥ yā Simsim*: Sociolinguistic and Educational Implications for Arabic. *Language Planning and Language Problems* 14: 33–46.

———. 1991. The 'Simplified Arabic' of *Iftaḥ yā Simsim*: Pedagogical and Sociolinguistic Implications. *Al-'Arabiyya* 24: 111–21.

Abu-Odeh, Adnan. 1999. *Jordanians, Palestinians and the Hashemite Kingdom in the Middle East Peace Process*. Washington, D.C.: U.S. Institute of Peace Press.

Abu-Rabia, A. 1996. Druze Minority Students Learning Hebrew in Israel: The Relationship of Attitudes, Cultural Background and Interest of Material to Reading Comprehension in a Second Language. *Journal of Multilingual and Multicultural Development* 17: 415–26.

Abu-Sitta, Salman H. 2004. *The Return Journey: A Guide to the Depopulated and Present Palestinian Towns and Villages and the Holy Sites in English, Arabic and Hebrew*. London: Palestinian Land Society.

Agius, Dionisius A. 1980. The *Shu'ūbiyya* Movement and Its Literary Manifestation. *Islamic Quarterly* 24: 76–88.

Ahmed, Leila 2000. *A Border Passage: From Cairo to America—a Woman's Journey*. New York: Penguin (first published New York: Farrar, Straus and Giroux, 1999).

Alford, Richard D. 1987. *Naming and Identity: A Cross-Cultural Study of Personal Naming Practices*. New Haven, Conn.: Human Relations Area Files.

Almubayei, Dalal S. 2007. Language and the Shaping of the Arab American Identity. http://dspace.uta.edu/bitstream/handle/10106/1198/91-119-almubaye.pdf?sequence=1.

Alosh, Muhammad al-Mahdi. 1984. Implications of the Use of Modern Standard Arabic in the Arabic Adaptations of 'Sesame Street.' Unpublished MA thesis, Ohio State University.

Amara, Muhammad Hasan. 1995. Hebrew and English Lexical Reflexes of Socio-political Changes in Palestinian Arabic. *Journal of Multilingual and Multicultural Development* 15: 165–72.

———. 1999. *Politics and Sociolinguistic Reflexes: Border Palestinian Villages*. Amsterdam and Philadelphia: John Benjamins.

Amara, Muhammad Hasan, Bernard Spolsky and Hanna Tushyeh. 1999. Sociolinguistic Reflexes of Socio-political Patterns in Bethlehem: Preliminary Studies. In Yasir Suleiman, ed., *Language and Society in the Middle East and North Africa*. Richmond, Surrey, U.K.: Curzon, pp. 58–80.

Amin, Galal. 2004. The Middle Way. *Al-Ahram Weekly Online: 12–18 February*, Issue No. 677. See http://weekly.ahram.org.eg./2004/677/op8.htm (accessed 20 February 2004).

Arkin, William M. 2005. *Code Names: Deciphering U.S. Military Plans, Programs and Operations in the 9/11 World*. Hanover, N.H.: Steerforth.

Ashton, John. 1999. 'They Got the English Hashed Up a Bit': Names, Narratives and Assimilation in Newfoundland's Syrian/Lebanese Community. *Lore and Language* 2: 67–76.

Aytürk, İlker. 2004. Turkish Linguists against the West: The Origins of Linguistic Nationalism in Atatürk's Turkey. *Middle Eastern Studies* 40: 1–25.

Azaryahu, Maoz. 1992. The Purge of Bismarck and Saladin: The Renaming of Streets in East Berlin and Haifa: A Comparative Study in Culture-Planning. *Poetics Today* 13: 351–67.

Azaryahu, Maoz and Rebecca Kook 2002. Mapping the Nation: Street Names and Arab Palestinian Identity: Three Case Studies. *Nations and Nationalism* 8: 195–212.

Badawi, Elsaid, M. G. Carter and Adrian Gully. 2004. *Modern Written Arabic: A Comprehensive Grammar*. London and New York: Routledge.

Backhaus, Peter. 2005. Signs of Multilingualism in Tokyo: A Diachronic Look at the Linguistic Landscape. *International Journal of the Sociology of Language* 175–76, 103–21.

———. 2007 *Linguistic Landscapes: Comparative Study of Urban Multilingualism in Tokyo*. Clevedon, U.K.: Multilingual Matters.

Bader, Yousef, and Radwan Mahadin. 1996. Arabic Borrowings and Code-Switches in the Speech of English Native Speakers Living in Jordan. *Multilingual* 15: 35–53.

Bader, Yousef, and Denise Minnis. n.d. A Sociolinguistic Analysis of Brand Names in Jordan. Photocopy.

Başgöz, İlhan 1983. Meaning and Dimensions of Change of Personal Names in Turkey. *Turcica* 15: 201–18.

Bassiouney, Reem. 2009. *Arabic Sociolinguistics*. Edinburgh: Edinburgh University Press.

Batal, Mahmoud al-. 1994. The Lebanese Linguist Anis Frayha and His Contribution to Arabic Language Reform. In Raji M. Rammuni and Dilworth B. Parkinson, eds., *Investigating Arabic: Linguistic, Pedagogical and Literary Studies in Honour of Ernest N. McCarus*. Columbus, Ohio: Greyden, pp. 155–72.

Baugh, John. 2000. *Beyond Ebonics: Linguistic Pride and Racial Prejudice.* New York: Oxford University Press.

Bauman, Zygmunt. 2004. *Identity.* Cambridge, U.K.: Polity.

Bean, Susan. S. 1980. Ethnology and the Study of Proper Names. *Anthropological Linguistics* 22: 305–16.

Ben-Rafael, Eliezer. 2006. Review of Yasir Suleiman *A War of Words: Language and Conflict in the Middle East. International History Review* 28: 206–7.

Ben-Rafael, Eliezer, Elena Shohamy, Muhammad Hasan Amara and Nira Trumper-Hecht. 2004. *Linguistic Landscape and Multiculturalism: A Jewish Arab Comparative Study.* Tel Aviv: Tami Steinmetz Centre for Peace Research, Tel Aviv University.

Bentahila, Abdelali. 1983. *Language Attitudes among Arabic-French Bilinguals in Morocco.* Clevedon, U.K.: Multilingual Matters.

Benvenisti, Meron. 2000. *Sacred Landscape: The Buried History of the Holy Land since 1948,* trans. by Maxine Kaufman-Lacusta. Berkley: University of California Press.

Benwell, Bethan, and Elizabeth Stokoe. 2006. *Discourse and Identity.* Edinburgh: Edinburgh University Press.

Beynon, John, and David Dunkerley, eds. 2000. *Globalization: The Reader.* London: Athlone.

Bishara, Azmi. 1992. Bein Merkhav le-Makom. *Studio, Israel Journal of Art* 37: 6–9.

Blau, Joshua. 1959. The Status of Arabic as Used by Jews in the Middle Ages: Do Jewish Middle Arabic Texts Reflect a Distinctive Language? *Journal of Jewish Studies* 10: 15–23.

———. 1968. Judaeo-Arabic in Its Linguistic Setting. *Proceedings of the American Academy for Jewish Research* 36: 1–12.

———. 1987. Medieval Judaeo-Arabic. In Herbert Harry Paper, ed., *Jewish Languages: Themes and Variations.* Cambridge, Mass.: Harvard University Press, pp. 121–31.

———. 1988. *Studies in Middle Arabic and Its Judaeo-Arabic Variety.* Jerusalem: Magnes.

Blommaert, J. 2006. Language Policy and National Identity. In Thomas Ricento, ed., *An Introduction to Language Policy—Theory and Method.* Oxford: Blackwell, pp. 238–54.

Bodenhorn, Barbara, and Gabriele vom Bruck. 2006. 'Entangled in Histories': An Introduction to the Anthropology of Names and Naming. In Gabriele vom Bruck and Barbara Bodenhorn, eds., *The Anthropology of Names and Naming.* Cambridge, U.K.: Cambridge University Press, pp. 1–30.

Borg, Alexander, and Gideon M. Kressel. 2001. Personal Names in the Negev and Sinai. *Zeitschrift für Arabische Linguistik* 40: 32–70.

Bourdieu, Pierre. 1977. *Outline of a Theory of Practice,* trans. by R. Nice. Cambridge, Mass.: Harvard University Press.

Brewer, Dominic J., Catherine H. Augustine, Gail L. Zellman, Gery Ryan, Charles A. Goldman, Cathleen Stasz and Louay Constant. 2007. *Education for a New Era: Design and Implementation of K-12 Education Reform in Qatar.* Santa Monica, Calif.: RAND-Qatar Policy Institute.

Brogden, Lace Marie. 2008. art.I/f/act.ology: Curricular Artifacts in Autoethnographic Research. *Qualitative Inquiry* 14: 851–64.

Bulliet, Richard W. 1978. First Names and Political Change in Turkey. *International Journal of Middle Eastern Studies* 9: 489–95.

———. 1979. Conversion to Islam and the Emergence of a Muslim Society in Iran. In Nehemia Levtzion, ed., *Conversion to Islam*. New York and London: Holmes & Meier, pp. 30–51.

Cameron, Deborah. 1990. Demythologizing Sociolinguistics: Why Language Does Not Reflect Society. In John E. Joseph and Talbot J. Taylor, eds., *Ideologies of Language*. London and New York: Routledge, pp. 79–93.

———. 1992. 'Respect, Please!' Investigating Race, Power and Language. In Deborah Cameron et al. eds., *Researching Language: Issues of Power and Method*. London and New York: Routledge, pp. 113–30.

Cameron, Deborah, Elizabeth Frazer, Penelope Harvey, M. B. H. Rampton and Kay Richardson. 1992. *Researching Language: Issues of Power and Method*. London and New York: Routledge.

Carroll, John M. 1983. Toward a Functional Theory of Names and Naming. *Linguistics* 21: 341–71.

Carroll, Lewis. 2000. *The Annotated Alice*, ed. by Martin Gardner. London: Penguin.

Caruth, Cathy. 1996. *Unclaimed Experience: Trauma, Narrative and History*. Baltimore and London: John Hopkins University Press.

Cenoze, Jasone, and Durk Gorter. 2006. Linguistic Landscapes and Minority Languages. *International Journal of Multilingualism* 3: 67–80.

Chalmers, A. F. 1978. *What Is This Thing Called Science? An Assessment of the Nature and Status of Science and Its Methods*. Milton Keynes, U.K.: Open University Press.

Cheshin, Amir S., Bill Hutman and Avi Melamed. 1999. *Separate and Unequal: The Inside Story of Israeli Rule in East Jerusalem*. Cambridge, Mass.: Harvard University Press.

Cohen, Anthony P. 1994. *Self Consciousness: An Alternative Anthropology of Identity*. London and New York: Routledge.

Cohen, Israel. 1911. *Zionist Work in Palestine*. London and Leipzig: Jewish Chronicle and Jewish World.

Cohen, Saul B., and Nurit Kliot. 1981. Israel's Place Names as Reflections of Continuity and Change in Nation Building. *Names* 29: 227–48.

———. 1992. Place Names in Israel's Ideological Struggle over the Administered Territories. *Annals of the Association of American Geographers* 82: 653–80.

Cooper, Robert. 1989. *Language Planning and Social Change*. Cambridge, U.K.: Cambridge University Press.

Coulmas, Flourian. 1994. Language Policy and Language Planning: Political Perspectives. *Annual Review of Applied Linguistics* 14: 34–52.

Darwish, Mahmoud. 2004. Edward Said: A Contrapuntal Reading, trans. by Mona Anis. *Al-Ahram Weekly Online*, http://weekly.ahram.org.eg/2004/710/cu4.htm (accessed 1 January 2005).

Davies, Bronwyn, Jenny Browne, Susanne Gannon, Eileen Honan, Cath Laws, Babette Mueller-Rockstroh and Eva Bendix Petersen. 2004. The Ambivalent Practices of Reflexivity. *Qualitative Inquiry* 10, 360–89.

Davis, Rochelle. 2007. Mapping the Past, Re-creating the Homeland: Memories of Village Places in pre-1948 Palestine. In Ahmad H. Sa'di and Lila Abu-Lughod, eds., *Nakba: Palestine, 1948 and the Claims of Memory*. New York: Columbia University Press, pp. 53–75.

De Fina, Anna, Deborah Schiffrin and Michael Bamberg, eds. 2006. *Discourse and Identity*. Cambridge, U.K.: Cambridge University Press.

Demetriou, Olga. 2006. Streets not Names: Discursive Dead Ends and the Politics of Orientation in Intercommunal Spatial Relations in Northern Greece. *Cultural Anthropology* 21: 295–321.

Denzin, Norman K. 1997. *Interpretive Ethnography: Ethnographic Practices of the 21st Century*. Thousand Oaks, Calif., London and New Delhi: Sage.

———. 2003. *Performance Ethnography: Critical Pedagogy and the Politics of Culture.* Thousand Oaks, Calif., London and New Delhi: Sage.

Denzin, Norman K., and Yvonna S. Lincoln. 2000. The Discipline and Practice of Qualitative Research. In Norman K. Denzin and Yvonna S. Lincoln, eds., *Handbook of Qualitative Research,* 2nd ed. London: Sage, pp. 1–28.

Dhaouadi, Mahmoud al-. 2002. *Globalization of the Other Underdevelopment: Third World Cultural Identities.* Kuala Lumpur: Nerordeen.

Dimitriadis, Greg. 2008. Revisiting the Question of Evidence. *Cultural Studies—Critical Methodologies,* 8: 3–14.

Douglas, Mary. 2002 [1967]. *Purity and Danger: An Analysis of the Concept of Pollution and Taboo.* London and New York: Routledge.

Edwards, John. 1988. *Language, Society and Identity.* Oxford: Basil Blackwell.

Ehteshami, Anoushirvan. 2007. *Globalization and Geopolitics in the Middle East: Old Games, New Rules.* London and New York: Routledge.

Eid, Mushira. 1994a. Hidden Women: Gender Inequality in 1938 Egyptian Obituaries. In Raji M. Rammuny and Dilworth B. Parkinson, (eds.), *Investigating Arabic: Linguistic, Pedago gical and Literary Studies in Honour of Ernest N. McCarus.* Columbus, Ohio: Greydan, pp. 111–36.

———. 1994b. What's in a Name? Women in Egyptian Obituaries. In Yasir Suleiman, ed., *Arabic Sociolinguistics: Issues and Perspectives.* Richmond, Surrey, U.K.: Curzon, pp. 81–100.

———. 2002a. Language Is a Choice—Variations in Egyptian Women's Written Discourse. In Aleya Rouchdy, ed., *Language Contact and Language Conflict in Arabic: Variations on a Sociolinguistic Theme.* London: RoutledgeCurzon, pp. 203–32.

———. 2002b. *The World of Obituaries: Gender across Cultures and over Time.* Detroit: Wayne State University Press.

Elliott, Anthony. 2001. *The Concept of the Self.* Cambridge, U.K.: Polity.

Ellis, Carolyn. 2004. *The Ethnographic I: A Methodological Novel about Autoethnography.* Walnut Creek, Calif.: AltaMira.

Ellis, Carolyn, and Arthur P. Bochner. 2000. Autoethnography, Personal Narrative, Reflexivity: Researcher as Subject. In Norman K. Denzin and Yvonna S. Lincoln, eds., *Handbook of Qualitative Research,* 2nd ed. London: Sage, pp. 733–68.

El-Yasin, Mohammed K., and Radwan S. Mahadin. 1996. On the Pragmatics of Shop Signs in Jordan. *Journal of Pragmatics* 26: 407–16.

Ennaji, Moha. 2005. *Multilingualism, Cultural Identity and Education in Morocco.* New York: Springer.

Evans, Kevin D. 2007. Welcome to Ruth's World: An Autoethnography concerning and Interview of an Elderly Woman. *Qualitative Inquiry* 13: 282–91.

Fanon, Frantz. 1986. *Black Skin, White Masks.* London: Pluto.

Ferguson, Charles. 1959. Diglossia. *Word* 15: 325–40.

Fishman, Joshua A. 1984. Epistemology, Methodology and Ideology in the Sociolinguistic Enterprise. In Alexander Z. Guiora, ed., *An Epistemology for the Language Sciences. Language Learning* 33: 33–47.

Frazer, Elizabeth. 1992. Talking about Gender, Race and Class. In Deborah Cameron et al. eds., *Researching Language: Issues of Power and Method.* London and New York: Routledge, pp. 90–112.

Friedrich, Paul. 1989. Language, Ideology and Political Economy. *American Anthropologist* 91: 295–312.

Gannon, Susanne. 2006. The (Im)Possibilities of Writing the Self-Writing: French Poststructural Theory and Autoethnography. *Cultural Studies—Critical Methodologies* 6: 474–95.

Gardner, Sheena. 1994. Generations of Change in Name-giving. In Yasir Suleiman, ed., *Arabic Sociolinguistic: Issues and Perspectives*. Richmond, Surrey, U.K.: Curzon, pp. 101–25.

Gatson, Sarah N. 2003. On Being Amorphous: Autoethnography, Genealogy and a Multicultural Identity. *Qualitative Inquiry* 9: 20–48.

Gavriely-Nuri, Dalia. 2008. The 'Metaphorical Annihilation' of the Second Lebanon War (2006) from the Israeli Political Discourse. *Discourse and Society* 19: 5–20.

Genette, Gerard. 1997. *Paratexts: Thresholds of Interpretation*, trans. by Jane E. Lewin. Cambridge, U.K.: Cambridge University Press.

Goitein, S. D. 1970. Nicknames as Family Names. *Journal of the American Oriental Society* 90: 517–24.

Gökalp, Ziya. 1968. *The Principles of Turkism*, trans. and annot. by Robert Devereux. Leiden: Brill.

Gramsci, Antonio. 1985. *Selections from Cultural Writings*, trans. by W. Boelhower. London: Lawrence and Wishart.

Grand'Henry, Jacques. 2006. Christian Middle Arabic. In Kees Versteegh, ed., *Encyclopedia of Arabic Language and Linguistics* 1. Leiden and Boston: Brill, pp. 383–87.

Grossman, David. 1993. *Sleeping on a Wire: Conversations with Palestinians in Israel*, trans. by Haim Watzman. London: Jonathan Cape.

Habibi, Emile. 2002. *The Secret Life of Sa'id the Pessoptmist*, trans. by Salma Khadra Jayyusi and Trevor LeGassick. New York: Interlink.

Habibi, Nader. 1992. Popularity of Islamic and Persian Names in Iran before and after the Islamic Revolution. *International Journal of Middle Eastern Studies* 24: 253–60.

Haeri, Niloofar. 1996. *The Sociolinguistic Market of Cairo: Gender, Class and Education*. London and New York: Kegan Paul International.

———. 2003. *Sacred Language, Ordinary People: Dilemmas of Culture and Politics in Egypt*. New York: Palgrave Macmillan.

Hall, Stuart. 2000. Who Needs Identity? In Paul du Gay, Jessica Evans and Peter Redman, eds., *Identity: A Reader*. London: Sage, pp. 15–30.

Halliday, Fred. 2001. *Two Hours That Shook the World: September 11 2001, Causes and Consequence*. London: Saqi.

Hammersley, Martyn. 1995. *The Politics of Social Research*. London, Thousand Oaks, Calif., and New Delhi: Sage.

Hamod, (Sam) H. S. 2000. Dying with the Wrong Name. In Gregory Orfalea and Sharif Elmusa, eds., *Grape Leaves: A Century of Arab American Poetry*. New York: Interlink, pp. 169–70.

Hanna, Sameh. F. 2009. *Othello* in the Egyptian Vernacular: Negotiating the 'Doxic' in Drama Translation and Identity Formation. *The Translator* 15: 157–78.

Harry, Benjamin. 1995. Judaeo-Arabic in Its Sociolinguistic Setting. *Israel Oriental Studies* 15: 73–99.

———. 2003. Judaeo-Arabic: A Diachronic Re-examination. *International Journal of the Sociology of Language* 163: 61–75.

Harvey, Penelope. 1992. Bilingualism in the Peruvian Andes. In Deborah Cameron et al, eds., *Researching Language: Issues of Power and Method*. London and New York: Routledge, pp. 65–89.

Hasluck, Margaret. 1925. Ramadan as a Personal Name. *Folklore* 36: 280.

Heinze, Ruediger. 2007. A Diasporic Overcoat? Naming and Affection in Jhumpa Lahiri's *The Namesakes*. *Journal of Postcolonial Writing* 43: 191–202.

Herbolich, James. B. 1979. Attitudes of Egyptians toward Various Arabic Vernaculars. *Lingua* 47: 301–21.

Heubner, Thom. 2006. Globalization, the New Economy and the Commodification of Language and Identity. *International Journal of Multilingualism* 3: 31–51.

Hobsbawm, Eric. 1983. Inventing Traditions. In Eric Hobsbawm and Terrence Ranger, eds., *The Invention of Tradition*. Cambridge, U.K.: Cambridge University Press, pp. 1–14.

Holes, Clive. 1987. *Language Variation and Change in a Modernizing Arab State*. London: Keegan Paul International.

Householder, Fred. 1952. Review of *Methods in Structural Linguistics*, by Zellig Harris. *International Journal of American Linguistics* 18: 153–60.

Hussein, Riad Fayez Issa. 1980. The Case of Triglossia in Arabic with Special Emphasis on Jordan. Unpublished PhD thesis, State University of New York.

Hussein, Riad F., and Nasr El-Ali. 1988. Subjective Reactions towards Different Varieties of Arabic. *Al-Lisān al-ʻArbī* 30: 7–17.

Ibrahim, Muhammad H. 1986. Standard and Prestige Language: A Problem in Arabic Sociolinguistics. *Anthropological Linguistics* 26: 115–24.

Ivanič, Roz. 1997. *Writing and Identity: The Discoursal Construction of Identity in Academic Writing*. Amsterdam and Philadelphia: John Benjamins.

Jehani, Nasir Muhammad al-. 1985. Sociolinguistic Stratification of Arabic in Makkah. Unpublished PhD thesis, University of Michigan.

Joseph, John. 2004. *Language and Identity: National, Ethnic, Religious*. Houndsmill, U.K.: Palgrave Macmillan.

———. 2006. *Language and Politics*. Edinburgh: Edinburgh University Press.

Kahn, David. 1967. *The Codebreakers: The Story of Secret Writing*. New York: Macmillan.

Kamhawi, Dania L. W. 2000. Code-Switching: A Social Phenomenon in Jordanian Society. Unpublished MLitt thesis, Edinburgh University.

Kashua, Sayed. 2004. *Dancing Arabs*, trans. by Miriam Shlesinger. New York: Grove.

Katriel, Tamar. 1986. *Talking Straight: Dugri Speech in Israeli Sabra Culture*. Cambridge, U.K.: Cambridge University Press.

Kaufman, Jodi. 2005. Autotheory: An Autoethnographic Reading of Foucault. *Qualitative Inquiry* 11: 576–87.

Khalidi, Walid, ed. 1982. *All That Remains: The Palestinian Villages Occupied and Depopulated by Israel in 1948*. Washington, D.C.: Institute for Palestine Studies.

Khalili, Laleh. 2007. *Heroes and Martyrs of Palestine: The Politics of National Commemoration*. Cambridge, U.K.: Cambridge University Press.

Khan, Geoffrey. 2007. Judaeo-Arabic. In Kees Versteegh, ed., *Encyclopedia of Arabic Language and Linguistics* 2. Leiden and Boston: Brill, pp. 526–36.

Khatib, Mahmoud Abed Ahmad al-. 1988. Sociolinguistic Change in an Expanding Context: A Case Study of Irbid City, Jordan. Unpublished PhD thesis, University of Durham.

Kia, Mehrdad. 1998. Persian Nationalism and the Campaign for Language Purification. *Middle Eastern Studies* 34: 9–36.

Kim, Tae-Young,. 2007. The Dynamics of Ethnic Name Maintenance and Change: Cases of Korean ESL Immigrants in Toronto. *Journal of Multilingual and Multicultural Development* 28: 117–33.

Kimball, Warren F., ed. 1984. *Churchill and Roosevelt: The Complete Correspondence: Vol. I, Alliance Emerging, October 1933–November 1942.* Princeton, N.J.: Princeton University Press.

Kirova, Anna. 2007. Redefining My Professional Identity: A Journey as a New Canadian. In Alireza Asgharzadeh, Erica Lawson, Kayleen U. Oka and Amar Wahab, eds., *Diasporic Ruptures: Globality, Migrancy and Expressions of Identity*. Rotterdam and Taipei: Sense, pp. 53–67.

Köroğlu, Erol. 2007. *Ottoman Propaganda and Turkish Identity: Literature in Turkey during World War I.* London: I. B. Tauris.

Kuzar, Ron. 2008. The Term *Return* in the Palestinian Discourse on the *Right of Return. Discourse & Society* 19: 629–44.

Labov, William. 1966. *The Social Stratification of English in New York City*. Washington, D.C.: Center for Applied Linguistics.

———. 1972. *Language in the Inner City: Studies in the Black English Vernacular*. Philadelphia: University of Pennsylvania Press.

———. 1982. Objectivity and Commitment in Linguistic Science: The Case of the Black English Trial in Ann Arbor. *Language in Society* 11: 165–201.

Landry, Rodrigue, and Richard Y. Bourhis. 1997. Linguistic Landscape and Ethnolinguistic Vitality: An Empirical Study. *Journal of Language and Social Psychology* 16: 23–49.

LaRaviere, Troy Kamau. 2008. Chairman Fred Hampton Way: An Autoethnographic Inquiry into Politically Relevant Teaching. *Qualitative Inquiry* 14: 489–504.

Laroussi, Foued. 2003. Arabic and the New Technologies. In Jacques Maurais and Michael A. Morris, eds., *Languages in a Globalising World*. Cambridge, U.K.: Cambridge University Press, pp. 250–59.

Leeman, Jennifer, and Gabriella Modan. 2009. Commodified Language in Chinatown: A Contextualized Approach to Linguistic Landscape. *Journal of Sociolinguistics* 13: 332–62.

Lefkowitz, Daniel. 2004. *Words and Stones: The Politics of Language and Identity in Israel*. Oxford: Oxford University Press.

Lentin, Jérôme. 2008. Middle Arabic. In Kees Versteegh, ed., *Encyclopedia of Arabic Language and Linguistics* 3. Leiden and Boston: Brill, pp. 215–24.

Lewis, Geoffrey. 1999. *The Turkish Language Reform: A Catastrophic Success*. Oxford: Oxford University Press.

Lieberson, Stanley. 1984. What's in a Name? . . . Some Sociolinguistic Possibilities. *International Journal of Sociology of Language* 45: 77–87.

Lou, Jia. 2007. Revitalizing Chinatown into a Heterotopia: A Geosemiotic Analysis of Shop Signs in Washington, DC's Chinatown. *Space and Culture* 10: 170–94.

McDonough. Stephen. 1978. Introspection and Generalization. In *The Foreign Language Learning Process*. ETIC Occasional Paper, British Council. London: English Teaching Information Centre, pp. 133–48.

Maalouf, Amin. 1998. *Leo the African*, trans. by Peter Sluglett. London: Quartet.

———. 2000. *On Identity*, trans. by Barbara Bray. London: Harvill.

MacAlister, R. A. Stewart, and E. W. G. Masterman. 1904. Personal Names. *Palestine Exploration Fund: Quarterly Statement*: 150–61.

———. 1905. Personal Names. *Palestine Exploration Fund*: Quarterly Statement, pp. 48–61.

Machan, Tim William. 2009. *Language Anxiety: Conflict and Change in the History of English*. Oxford: Oxford University Press.

Magnet, Soshona. 2006. Protesting Privilege: An Autoethnographic Look at Whiteness. *Qualitative Inquiry* 12: 736–49.

Makdisi, Jean Said. 2005. *Teta, Mother and Me: An Arab Woman's Memoir*. London: Saqi.

Mardin, Şerif. 2002. Playing Games with Names. In Deniz Kandiyoti and Ayşe Saktanber, eds., *Fragments of Culture: The Everyday of Modern Turkey*. London: Tauris, pp. 115–27.

Massad, Joseph A. 2001. *Colonial Effects: The Making of National Identity in Jordan*. New York: Columbia University Press.

Meital, Yoram. 2007. Central Cairo: Street Naming and the Struggle over Historical Representation. *Middle Eastern Studies* 43: 857–78.

Mitchell, T. F. 1978. Educated Spoken Arabic in Egypt and the Levant, with Special Reference to Participle and Tense. *Journal of Linguistics* 14: 227–58.

———. 1986. What Is Educated Spoken Arabic? *International Journal of the Sociology of Language* 61: 7–32.

Muhawi, Ibrahim. 2006. Irony and the Poetics of Palestinian Exile. In Yasir Suleiman and Ibrahim Muhawi, eds., *Literature and Nation in the Middle East*. Edinburgh: Edinburgh University Press, pp. 31–47.

Mühlhäusler, Peter. 1996. *Linguistic Ecology: Language Change and Linguistic Imperialism in the Pacific Region*. London and New York: Routledge.

Murray, John. 2000. *Politics and Place-names: Changing Names in the Late Soviet Period*. Birmingham, U.K.: Birmingham Slavonic Monographs, University of Birmingham.

Myers-Scotton, Carol. 1993. *Social Motivations for Code-Switching: Evidence from Africa*. Oxford: Clarendon Press.

Nagel, Thomas. 1974. *The Structure of Science: Problems in the Logic of Scientific Investigation*. London: Routledge and Kegan Paul.

Nanes, Stefanie. 2008. Choice, Loyalty and the Melting Pot: Citizenship and National Identity in Jordan. *Nationalism and Ethnic Politics* 14: 85–116.

Nicolaisen, W. H. F. 1990. Place-names and Politics. *Names* 38: 193–207.

Niedzielski, Nancy A., and Dennis R. Preston. 2000. *Folk Linguistics*. Berlin and New York: Mouton de Gruyter.

Orfalea, Gregory, and Sharif Elmusa. 2000. *Grape Leaves: A Century of Arab-American Poetry*. New York: Interlink.

Palmer, Edward L. 1979. Linguistic Innovation in the Arabic Adaptation of 'Sesame Street.' In James E. Altais and G. Richard Tucker, eds., *Languages in Public Life: Georgetown University Roundtable on Languages and Linguistics 1979*. Washington, D.C.: Georgetown University Press, pp. 287–94.

Palonen, Karl. 1993. Reading Street Names Politically. In Karl Palonen and Tuija Parvikko, eds., *Reading the Political: Exploring the Margins of Politics*. Helsinki: Finnish Political Science Association, pp. 103–21.

Parkinson, Dilworth. 1991. Searching for Modern Fuṣḥā: Real Life Formal Arabic. *Al-'Arabiyya* 24: 31–64.

Pelias, Ronald J. 2003. The Academic Tourist: An Autoethnography. *Qualitative Inquiry* 9: 369–73.

Pennycook, Alistair. 1998. *English and the Discourses of Colonialism*. London and New York: Routledge.

Peteet, Julie. 2007. Problematizing a Palestinian Diaspora. *International Journal of Middle Eastern Studies* 39: 627–46.

Phillips, Melanie. 2006. *Londonistan*. London: Gibson Square.

Poole, Steven. 2006. *Unspeak: How Words Become Weapons, How Weapons Become a Message, and How That Message Becomes Reality*. New York: Grove.

Poplack, Shana. 1988. Contrasting Patterns of Code-Switching in Two Communities. In Monica Heller, ed., *Code-Switching: Anthropological and Sociolinguistic Perspectives*. Berlin: De Gruyter, pp. 215–44.

Popper, Karl. R. 1969. *Conjectures and Refutations*. London: Routledge and Keegan Paul.

———. 1975. *Objective Knowledge: An Evolutionary Approach*. Oxford: Clarendon Press.

———. 1976. *Unended Quest*. London: Fontana/Collins.

Rampton, M. B. H. 1992. Scope for Empowerment in Sociolinguistics? In Deborah Cameron et al., eds., *Researching Language: Issues of Power and Method*. London and New York: Routledge, pp. 29–64.

Roff, William R. 2007. Onomastics and Taxonomies of Belonging in the Malay Muslim World. *Journal of Islamic Studies* 18: 386–405.

Romaine, Suzanne. 1984. The Status of Sociological Models and Categories in Explaining Language Variation. *Linguistische Berichte* 90: 25–38.

Rottenberg, Catherine. 2008. *Dancing Arabs* and Spaces of Desire. *Topia: Canadian Journal of Cultural Studies* 19: 99–114.

Rudin, Catherina, and Ali Eminov. 1990. Bulgarian Turkish: The Linguistic Effects of Recent Nationality Policy. *Anthropological Linguistics* 32: 149–62.

Safouan, Moustapha. 2007. *Why Are the Arabs Not Free?—The Politics of Writing*. Oxford: Blackwell.

Safran, William. 2008. Names, Labels and Identities: Sociopolitical Contexts and the Question of Ethnic Categorization. *Identities: Global Studies in Culture and Power* 15: 437–61.

Said, Edward. 1978. *Orientalism*. London and Henley: Routledge s& Keegan Paul.

———. 1999. *Out of Place*. London: Granta.

———. 2000. *Reflections on Exile*. London: Granta.

———. 2004. Living in Arabic. *Al-Ahram Weekly* 677 (12–18 February 2004): http://weekly.ahram.org.eg/2004/677/cu15.htm (accessed 1 January 2005).

Salih, Mahmud, and Mohammed El-Yasin. 1994. The Spread of Foreign Business Names in Jordan: A Sociolinguistic Perspective. *Abhath Al-Yarmouk* 12: 37–50.

Salih, Mahmud Hussein, and Yousef F. Bader. 1999. Personal Names of Jordanian Arab Christians: A Sociocultural Study. *International Journal of the Sociology of Language* 140: 29–43.

Sallam, A. 1979. Concordial Relations within the Noun Phrase in ESA. *Archivum Linguisticum* 10: 20–56.

———. 1980. Phonological Variation in Educated Spoken Arabic: A Study of the Uvular and Related Plosive Types. *Bulletin of the School of Oriental and African Studies* 42: 77–110.

Sankoff, David. 1988. Sociolinguistic and Syntactic Variation. In Frederick J. Newmeyer, ed., *Language: The Socio-cultural Context*, vol. 4 in *Linguistics: The Cambridge Survey*. Cambridge, U.K.: Cambridge University Press, pp. 14–61.

Schimmel, Annemarie. 1995. *Islamic Names*. Edinburgh: Edinburgh University Press.

Schivelbusch, Wolfgang. 2004. *The Culture of Defeat: On National Trauma, Mourning, and Recovery*, trans. by Jefferson Chase. London: Granta.

Schmid, Carol L. 2001. *The Politics of Language: Conflict, Identity, and Cultural Pluralism in Comparative Perspective.* Oxford: Oxford University Press.

Seale, Clive. 1999. *The Quality of Qualitative Research.* London: Sage.

Sermijn, Jasmina, Patrick Devlieger and Gerrit Loots. 2008. The Narrative Construction of the Self: Selfhood as a Rhizomatic Story. *Qualitative Inquiry* 14: 632–50.

Shohamy, Elena. 2006. *Language Policy: Hidden Agendas and New Approaches.* London and New York: Routledge.

Shohamy, Elena, and Durk Gorter, eds., 2009. *Linguistic Landscape: Expanding the Scenery.* London: Routledge.

Shohat, Ella. 2003. Zionist Discourse and the Study of Arab Jews. *Social Texts* 21: 49–74.

Shorrab, Ghazi Abd-El-Jabbar. 1981. Models of Socially Significant Linguistic Variation: The Case of Palestinian Arabic. PhD thesis, State University of New York at Buffalo.

Sieminski, Gregory. 1995. The Art of Naming Operations. *Parameters: U.S. Army War College Quarterly* (Autumn): 81–98. See also http://www.carlisle.army.mil/usawc/Parameters/1995/sieminsk.htm (accessed 15 February 2007).

Silverstein, M. 1996. Encountering Language and Languages of Encounter in North American Ethnohistory. *Journal of Linguistic Anthropology* 6: 126–44.

———. 1998. Contemporary Transformations of Local Linguistic Communities. *Annual Review of Anthropology*: 401–26.

Skutnabb-Kangas, Tove, and Sertaç Bucak. 1994. Killing a Mother Tongue: How the Kurds Are Deprived of Linguistic Human Rights. In Tove Skutnabb-Kangas and Robert Phillipson, eds., *Linguistic Human Rights: Overcoming Linguistic Discrimination.* Berlin: Mouton de Gruyter, pp. 299–313.

Slyomovics, Susan. 1998. *The Object of Memory: Arab and Jew Narrate the Palestinian Village.* Philadelphia: University of Pennsylvania Press.

Spolsky, B. 1997. Ulpan. In Bernard Spolsky, ed., *Concise Encyclopedia of Educational Linguistics.* Oxford: Elsevier, pp. 677–78.

Spolsky, Bernard, and Robert Cooper. 1991. *The Languages of Jerusalem.* Oxford: Clarendon Press.

Spolsky, Bernard, and Elena Shohamy. 1999. *The Languages of Israel: Policy, Ideology and Practice.* Clevedon, U.K.: Multilingual Matters.

Stevenson, Patrick. 2002. *Language and German Disunity: A Sociolinguistic History of East and West in Germany, 1945–2000.* Oxford: Oxford University Press.

Stroud, Christopher, and Sibonile Mpendukana. 2009. Towards a Material Ethnography of Linguistic Landscape: Multilingualism and Space in a South African Township. *Journal of Sociolinguistics* 13: 363–86.

Suleiman, Yasir. 1992. On Being a Learner Again: An Experiment in Role Reversal. *Al-'Arabiyya* 25: 29–49.

———. 1993. The Language Situation in Jordan and Code-switching: A New Interpretation. *New Arabian Studies* 1: 1–20.

———. 1997. The Arabic Language in the Fray: A Sphere of Contested Identities. In Alan Jones, ed., *University Lectures in Islamic Studies.* London: Altajir World of Islam Trust, pp. 127–48.

———. 1999a. Language Educational Policies: Arabic Speaking Countries. In Bernard Spolsky, ed., *Concise Encyclopedia of Educational Linguistics.* Oxford: Elsevier/Pergamon, pp. 106–16.

———. 1999b. Language and Political Conflict in the Middle East: A Study in Symbolic Sociolinguistics. In Yasir Suleiman, ed., *Language and Society in the Middle East and North Africa: Studies in Variation and Identity*. Richmond, U.K.: Curzon, pp. 1–37.

———. 1999c. Under the Spell of Language: Arabic between Linguistic Determinism and Linguistic Relativity. In Ian Netton, ed., *Hunter of the East: Festschrift for Edmund Bosworth*. Leiden: Brill, pp. 109–33.

———. 2001. *Bayān* as a Principle of Taxonomy: Linguistic Elements in Jāḥiẓ's Thinking. In John F. Healy and Venetia Porter, eds., *Studies on Arabia in Honour of G. Rex Smith*, Supplement to *Journal of Semitic Studies*. Oxford: Oxford University Press, 2001, pp. 273–95.

———. 2003. *The Arabic Language and National Identity: A Study in Ideology*. Washington, D.C.: Georgetown University Press.

———. 2004a. Review of Niloofar Haeri (2003): *Sacred Language, Ordinary People: Dilemmas of Culture and Politics in Egypt*. *Journal of Sociolinguistics* 8: 162–66.

———. 2004b. *A War of Words: Language and Conflict in the Middle East*. Cambridge, U.K.: Cambridge University Press.

———. 2006a. Al-'arabiyya. In Kees Versteegh, ed., *Encyclopedia of Arabic Language and Linguistics* 1. Leiden: Brill, pp. 173–78.

———. 2006b. Arabic Language Reforms, Language Ideology and the Criminalization of Sībawayhi. In Lutz Edzard and Janet Watson, eds., *Grammar as a Window on Arabic Humanism: A Collection of Articles in Honour of Michael G. Carter*. Wiesbaden: Harrossowitz Verlag, pp. 66–83.

———. 2006c. Charting the Nation: Arabic and the Politics of Identity. *Annual Review of Applied Linguistics* 26: 125–48.

———. 2006d. Constructing Languages, Constructing National Identities. In Tope Omoniyi and Goodith White, eds., *The Sociolinguistics of Identity*. London: Continuum, pp. 51–71.

———. 2008. Egypt: From Egyptian to Pan-Arab Nationalism. In Andrew Simpson, ed., *Language and National Identity in Africa*. Oxford: Oxford University Press, pp. 26–43.

Suleiman, Yasir, and Alaa Elgibali. 2004. *Curriculum Standards for the State of Qatar: Arabic Grades K to 12*. Qatar: Education Institute, Supreme Education Council.

Suleiman, Yasir, and Ibrahim Muhawi. 2006. *Literature and Nation in the Middle East*. Edinburgh: Edinburgh University Press.

Suleiman, Yasir, Iman Aziz Soliman, Abeer Najjar and Gada Khalil. 2006. *Arabic Schemes of Work for the State of Qatar: Grades 1 to 12*. Qatar: Education Institute, Supreme Education Council.

Talib, Ismail. 2002. *The Language of Postcolonial Literature: An Introduction*. London and New York: Routledge.

Türköz, Meltem. 2007. Surname Narratives and the State-Society Boundary: Memories of Turkey's Family Name Law of 1934. *Middle Eastern Studies* 43: 893–908.

Twair, Pat McDonald. 2008. A Village Called Jimzu. *Middle East* 394: 62–63.

Versteegh, Kees. 1997. *The Arabic Language*. Edinburgh: Edinburgh University Press.

Vom Bruck, Gabriele. 2006. Names as Bodily Signs. In Gabriele vom Bruck and Barbara Bodenhorn, eds., *The Anthropology of Names and Naming*. Cambridge, U.K.: Cambridge University Press, pp. 226–50.

Warschauer, Mark, Ghada R. El-Said and Ayman Zohry. 2002. Language Choice Online: Globalization and Identity in Egypt. *Journal of Computer-Mediated Communication* 7:

1–14. http://jcmc.indiana.edu/vol7/issue4/warschauer.html (accessed 3 August 2005).

Waugh, Earle H. 1995. Names and Naming. In John L. Esposito, ed., *The Oxford Encyclopedia of the Modern Islamic World* 3. Oxford: Oxford University Press, pp. 224–26.

Waymer, Damion. 2008. A Man: An Autoethnographic Analysis of Black Male Identity Negotiation. *Qualitative Inquiry* 14: 968–89.

Wer, Enam al-. 1999. Language and Identity: The Chechens and the Circassians in Jordan. *Proceedings of the First International Conference on Arabic-English Contrastive and Comparative Studies, Dirasat* (special issue). Deanship of Academic Research, University of Jordan, pp. 253–68.

Westmoreland, C. William. 1976. *A Soldier Reports*. New York: Doubleday.

Widdicombe, Sue. 1998. Identity as an Analysts' and Participants' Resource. In Charles Antaki and Sue Widdicombe, eds., *Identities in Talk*. London: Sage, pp. 191–206.

Wild, Stefan. 1982. Arabisches Eigennamen. In Wolfdietrich Fischer, ed., *Grundriß der arabischen Philologie*. Wiesbaden: Ludwig Reichert Verlag, pp. 154–61.

Willcocks, William. 1926. Syria, Egypt, North Africa and Malta Speak Punic, Not Arabic. *Extrait du Bulletin de l'Institut d'Égypte* T. 8, session 1925–26.

Wodak, Ruth, Rudolf de Cillia, Martin Reisigl and Karin Liebhart. 1999. *The Discursive Construction of National Identity*, trans. by Angelika Hirsch and Richard Mitten. Edinburgh: Edinburgh University Press.

Woolard, Kathryn. 1998. Introduction: Language Ideology as a Field of Inquiry. In Bambi B. Schieffelin, Kathryn A. Woolard and Paul V. Kroskirty, eds., *Language Ideologies: Practice and Theory*. New York: Oxford University Press, pp. 3–47.

Yaqub, Nadia. 2006. The Production of Locality in the Oral Palestinian Poetry Duel. In Yasir Suleiman and Ibrahim Muhawi, eds., *Literature and Nation in the Middle East*. Edinburgh: Edinburgh University Press, pp. 16–30.

———. 2007. *Pens, Swords and the Springs of Art: The Oral Poetry Duelling of Palestinian Weddings in the Galilee*. Leiden and Boston: Brill.

Yassin, M. and F. Aziz 1978. Personal Names of Address in Kuwaiti Arabic. *Anthropological Linguistics* 20: 53–63.

———. 1986. The Arabian Way with Names: A Sociolinguistic Approach. *Linguist* 25: 77–85.

Zeidel, Ronen. 2006. Naming and Counternaming: The Struggle between Society and State as Reflected by Street Names in Iraq and the Arab Sector in Israel. *Orient* 47: 201–17.

Name Index

Subject Index